On Shoreless Sea

THE SUNY SERIES

HORIZONS OF CINEMA

MURRAY POMERANCE | EDITOR

RECENT TITLES

Dominic Lash, *Haunting the World*

Gohar Siddiqui, *Déjà-Viewed*

Stanley Cavell, *Cavell on Film*

Saverio Giovacchini, *The Celluloid Atlantic*

John Caps, *Overhearing Film Music*

Hannah Holtzman, *Through a Nuclear Lens*

Benedict Morrison, *Eccentric Laughter*

Matthew Cipa, *Is Harpo Free?*

Daniel Varndell, *Torturous Etiquettes*

Seth Barry Watter, *The Human Figure on Film*

Jonah Corne and Monika Vrečar, *Yiddish Cinema*

Jason Jacobs, *Reluctant Sleuths, True Detectives*

Lucy J. Miller, *Distancing Representations in Transgender Film*

Tomoyuki Sasaki, *Cinema of Discontent*

Mary Ann McDonald Carolan, *Orienting Italy*

Matthew Rukgaber, *Nietzsche in Hollywood*

Jason Sperb, *The Hard Sell of Paradise*

William Rothman, *The Holiday in His Eye*

David Venditto, *Whiteness at the End of the World*

Fareed Ben-Youssef, *No Jurisdiction*

A complete listing of books in this series can be found online at www.sunypress.edu.

On Shoreless Sea

The MS *St. Louis* Refugee Ship in History, Film, and Popular Memory

Roy Grundmann

Cover credit: The MS *St. Louis* at sea. Promotional postcard, HAPAG (Hamburg America Line), from the private collection of Michael Zell.

Published by State University of New York Press, Albany

© 2025 State University of New York

All rights reserved

Printed in the United States of America

No part of this book may be used or reproduced in any manner whatsoever without written permission. No part of this book may be stored in a retrieval system or transmitted in any form or by any means including electronic, electrostatic, magnetic tape, mechanical, photocopying, recording, or otherwise without the prior permission in writing of the publisher.

Links to third-party websites are provided as a convenience and for informational purposes only. They do not constitute an endorsement or an approval of any of the products, services, or opinions of the organization, companies, or individuals. SUNY Press bears no responsibility for the accuracy, legality, or content of a URL, the external website, or for that of subsequent websites.

EU GPSR Authorised Representative:
Logos Europe, 9 rue Nicolas Poussin, 17000, La Rochelle, France
contact@logoseurope.eu

For information, contact State University of New York Press, Albany, NY
www.sunypress.edu

Library of Congress Cataloging-in-Publication Data

Name: Grundmann, Roy, 1963– author
Title: On shoreless sea : the MS St. Louis refugee ship in history, film, and popular memory / Roy Grundmann.
Description: Albany : State University Press of New York, [2025]. | Series: SUNY series : Horizons of cinema | Includes bibliographical references and index.
Identifiers: LCCN 2025003043 | ISBN 9798855803754 (hardcover : alk. paper) | ISBN 9798855803778 (ebook) | ISBN 9798855803761 (pbk. : alk. paper)
Subjects: LCSH: St. Louis (Ship). | St. Louis (Ship)—In mass media. | Jews—Germany—History—1933–1945. | Jewish refugees—Cuba—History—20th century. | Jews—Migrations—History—20th century. | Antisemitism—History—20th century.
Classification: LCC DS134.255 .G78 2025 | DDC 940.53/18142—dc23/eng/20250527
LC record available at https://lccn.loc.gov/2025003043

To my Biene, Captain of my Ship

Contents

List of Illustrations — ix

Preface — xv

Acknowledgments — xvii

Introduction — 1

Part I

1 Jews During the Third Reich: Between Flight and Entrapment — 19

2 Neocolonialism, Biopolitics, and the Jewish Migrant Business: HAPAG and MS *St. Louis* — 49

3 Voyage 98: The Unfolding of a Fateful Odyssey — 79

4 The *St. Louis* Passengers and the Press Coverage of Voyage 98 — 103

5 On Shoreless Sea: The *St. Louis* Voyage, the State of Exception, and the Colonial Turn in Holocaust Studies — 125

Part II

6 The *St. Louis* Voyage in Popular Memory — 157

7	*Voyage of the Damned* on the Big Screen	183
8	Germany Revisits the *St. Louis* Voyage: *Die Ungewollten—Die Irrfahrt der St. Louis* (The Unwanted—The Voyage of the *St. Louis*)	217
9	The *St. Louis* Voyage and Grassroots Historical Revisionism: Robert M. Krakow's Independent Film *Complicit*	241
10	The *St. Louis* in Multidirectional Memory	261

Epilogue: "With Whose Blood Were My Eyes Crafted?" Philipp Scheffner and Merle Kröger's *Havarie* (2016), the Mediterranean Migrant Crisis, and the *St. Louis* Voyage — 289

Part III

Appendix 1: Introduction to Gustav Schröder and His Accounts of Voyage 98 — 319

Appendix 2: *Homeless on the High Seas* (1949) by Gustav Schröder, translated by Roy Grundmann — 325

Appendix 3: Captain's Log, Voyage 98, Part 1, translated by Roy Grundmann — 343

Appendix 4: Captain's Log, Voyage 98, Part 2, translated by Roy Grundmann — 347

Appendix 5: Addendum to the Captain's Log of Captain Gustav Schröder, MS *St. Louis*, on the 98th Voyage Home, translated by Roy Grundmann — 351

Notes — 353

Bibliography — 419

Index — 433

Illustrations

I.1	The MS *St. Louis* in the Port of Hamburg	2
1.1	Period postcard of Évian-les-Bains	25
1.2	Myron C. Taylor	37
1.3	Aliyah Bet refugee ship *Parita*	45
2.1	The MS *St. Louis* in Hamburg before the 1936 Olympic Games	51
2.2	Albert Ballin, the director of HAPAG	54
2.3	HAPAG travel brochure	60
2.4	HAPAG cruise brochure	61
2.5	HAPAG map of South America routes	62
2.6	The MS *St. Louis* cabin-class social hall	72
2.7	The MS *St. Louis* cabin-class social hall	73
2.8	The MS *St. Louis* cabin-class dining hall	73
2.9	The MS *St. Louis* cabin-class ladies' lounge	74
2.10	The MS *St. Louis* cabin-class smoking room	74
2.11	The MS *St. Louis* tourist-class/third-class social hall	75
2.12	The MS *St. Louis* tourist-class/third-class dining hall	75
2.13	HAPAG cruise brochure cover	76

3.1	HAPAG bulletin announcing the Cuba voyage	81
3.2	Members of the passenger committee of the MS *St. Louis*	85
3.3	Dinghies with relatives in Havana harbor	86
3.4	Newspaper coverage of dinghies ringing the MS *St. Louis* in Havana harbor	87
3.5	Announcement posted by Captain Schröder to passengers	89
3.6	*St. Louis* leaving Havana Harbor	90
3.7	Mr. and Mrs. Troper with passengers	99
3.8	The MS *St. Louis*'s arrival at Antwerp harbor	99
4.1	Members of the Dublon family pose on the deck of the MS *St. Louis*	105
4.2	The provisional pool on board the MS *St. Louis*	105
4.3	MS *St. Louis* cabin-class menu	106
4.4	The MS *St. Louis* cabin-class social hall ball	107
4.5	Passenger party at the MS *St. Louis*	108
4.6	German Jewish refugee Werner Lenneberg roller-skates on deck	108
4.7	View of Havana harbor	110
4.8	The MS *St. Louis* surrounded by dinghies with relatives of the passengers	111
4.9	A front-page article from *The New York Times*, June 3, 1939	117
4.10	A political cartoon in the *Daily Mirror*, June 6, 1939	118
5.1	Photograph of Havana harbor taken from aboard the MS *St. Louis*	126
5.2	Jewish children at Westerbork	138
5.3	Map of MS *St. Louis*'s Caribbean course	150

6.1	Retired Captain Gustav Schröder visiting the *St. Louis* in 1947	159
6.2	Retired Captain Gustav Schröder visiting the *St. Louis* in 1947	160
6.3	Retired Captain Gustav Schröder visiting the *St. Louis* in 1947	160
6.4	*Heimatlos auf hoher See* (*Homeless on the High Seas*), dust jacket	162
6.5	*Kein gelobtes Land* (No Promised Land), first edition, dust jacket	170
6.6	*Voyage of the Damned*, dust covers for hardcover edition and paperback edition	178
7.1	*Voyage of the Damned*: the MS *St. Louis* in Hamburg	182
7.2	*Voyage of the Damned*: passengers at a ball stop dancing	189
7.3	*Voyage of the Damned*: dissolve of multiple aerial shots of the ship	190
7.4	*Voyage of the Damned*: the tiny *St. Louis* on the open ocean	191
7.5	*Voyage of the Damned*: publicity poster	194
7.6	*Voyage of the Damned*: Denise forces Lili to look at herself in the mirror	203
7.7	*Voyage of the Damned*: Denise cradles a despairing Lili	203
7.8	*Voyage of the Damned*: Carl Rosen collides with Denise	204
7.9	*Voyage of the Damned*: Denise's blood-soiled dress	205
7.10	*Voyage of the Damned*: Carl Rosen storms on deck	214
7.11	*Voyage of the Damned*: Carl Rosen continues to slash his wrists on deck	215
8.1	*Die Ungewollten*: Captain Gustav Schröder (Ulrich Noethen) visiting the *St. Louis*	225
8.2	*Die Ungewollten*: Schröder overlooking the ship from its bow	226

8.3	*Die Ungewollten*: Schröder walking away from the ship at film's end	227
8.4	*Die Ungewollten*: MS *St. Louis* in Havana harbor	234
8.5	The SS *Bretagne*	236
8.6	The SS *Pennsylvania*	236
8.7	The MS *St. Louis* leaving Havana	237
8.8	The SS *Pennsylvania*	237
9.1	Canada's Prime Minister Justin Trudeau apologizing to the *St. Louis* passengers	244
9.2	Playbill for *Voyage of the SS St. Louis: The Trial of Franklin D. Roosevelt*	249
9.3	Actor playing prosecutor Supreme Court Justice Oliver Wendell Holmes	250
9.4	Actor playing council for the defense John F. Kennedy	250
9.5	The cast of *Voyage of the SS St. Louis: The Trial of Franklin D. Roosevelt* on stage	251
9.6	Actor playing Cordell Hull, Secretary of State, 1933–44	252
9.7	Actor playing Franklin D. Roosevelt	253
9.8	Hannah Rosenthal, Special Envoy to Monitor and Combat Antisemitism	254
9.9	Deputy Secretary of State William Burns apologizing to the MS *St. Louis* passengers	256
10.1	Leonardo Padura, *Heretics*; US Paperback edition	265
10.2	Leonardo Padura, *Heretics*; British Edition	266
10.3	Leonardo Padura, *Herejes*; Spanish-language edition	267
10.4	Daniel Libeskind, *The Wheel of Conscience*	280
10.5	Daniel Libeskind, *The Wheel of Conscience*	281
10.6	Daniel Libeskind, *The Wheel of Conscience*	282

E.1	*Havarie*	300
E.2	*Havarie*	301
E.3	*Havarie*	301
E.4	*Havarie*	302
E.5	*Havarie*	302
E.6	*Havarie*	303
E.7	*Havarie*	303
E.8	*Havarie*	304
E.9	*Havarie*	304
E.10	*Havarie*: ". . . to inform you of arrival in about 40 minutes."	308
E.11	*Havarie*: ". . . in the zone of deployment."	308
E.12	*Havarie*: "I will calculate this more precisely, but approximately 40 minutes to there."	309
E.13	Newspaper coverage of dinghies ringing the *St. Louis* in Havana harbor	312
A.1	Captain Gustav Schröder	318
A.2	Title page of *Heimatlos auf hoher See* by Gustav Schröder	324
A.3	Front page of captain's log, part 1, for Voyage 98	342
A.4	Front page of captain's log, part 2, for Voyage 98	346

Preface

This book was largely completed before October 7, 2023. But I soon realized that the historical episode I investigate in these pages—the dramatic voyage of the Jewish refugee ship MS *St. Louis* to Cuba and eventually back to Europe—stands in relation to the events of October 7 and their aftermath, even though it transpired on the eve of World War II. What links both events is colonialism. Jews have been settling in Palestine for over 150 years, a process that gradually took a more systematic form of colonization. But in the 1930s, other constellations of colonialism negatively impacted Jewish migration, particularly to Latin America. While antisemitism is responsible for the mass extermination called the "final solution," my assessment of the *St. Louis* voyage aims to show that colonialism and neocolonialism are important factors in why so few Jews were able to avoid that fate. Jews, in other words, have not only engaged in colonization but have also suffered from its historical effects.

This observation has theoretical and political implications. With regard to theory, it is poised to challenge Holocaust studies to expand its geopolitical and methodological purview from theorizing the "final solution" to studying the historical causes behind the fact that so many non-European countries, especially those located in the Caribbean and in South America, accepted far fewer Jewish refugees than they could have. Perhaps unsurprisingly, this line of inquiry aligns with recent efforts of resuming and redirecting Hannah Arendt's groundbreaking 1950s initiative of placing the Holocaust in relation to other genocides, some of which are also closely linked to colonialism.

The question of the extent to which one needs to factor in colonialism alongside antisemitism to deepen one's understanding of the Holocaust may seem primarily academic. But the negative responses to those who have argued for an inclusion of a postcolonial framework into Holocaust studies have revealed that there are considerable political stakes in upholding the epistemological status of antisemitism as the singular root cause of the death of over six million Jews. The events of October 7, 2023, and their aftermath have exponentially raised those stakes. The antisemitism charge with all its moral weight has become a crucial instrument to help preempt any criticism of the war in Gaza and of the advancing illegal settlements in the West Bank—indeed, to preempt any critique of Zionism.

I should not have to state that in no manner do I deny the historical role of antisemitism in the persecution of the Jews nor, for that matter, the increased threat of antisemitism that Jews face today. But if theorists and historians have for some time called for expanding the methodological toolkit with which to approach Jewish history and its less-discussed facets, such as the impact of colonialism on the diaspora and on the Holocaust, the present moment, in which we are witnessing the bloody culmination of decades of the colonization of Palestine, furnishes the most pressing incentive for us to perform such an expansion. I deem the reassessment of Jewish history through a consideration of colonialism and by consulting postcolonial studies to be of vital importance and it is my hope that this book can contribute to this project.

Acknowledgments

This book would not have been possible without the support of numerous individuals, who have read parts of the manuscript and have lent logistic support in many ways. And I would not have been able to include the pioneering primary research that is now a prominent part of it without the cooperation of several archives and their stellar teams, who enabled me to unearth numerous facts about the many facets of the *St. Louis* odyssey and its various contexts.

My greatest thanks go to Jürgen Glaevecke, grandnephew of Captain Gustav Schröder, who has given me permission to translate his great-uncle's book about the *St. Louis* voyage, *Heimatlos auf hoher See*, into English and republish it in full. I also want to thank Mr. Glaevecke for sharing with me Gustav Schröder's earlier, unpublished manuscript version of the book, which contains illuminating details about the Cuba voyage Schröder chose not to include for publication. My heartfelt thanks go to Mr. Glaevecke for taking the time to meet with me and to share his personal knowledge about Gustav Schröder. I further would like to thank Mr. Glaevecke for giving me permission to use some of Schröder's personal photographs as well as photographs about the fateful voyage of the *St. Louis*. Without Mr. Glaevecke's support, this would have turned out to be a very different book. I would further like to thank Gerrit Menzel, historian at the International Maritime Museum, Hamburg, for meeting with me and sharing access to Gustav Schröder's personal belongings related to the Cuba voyage.

My heartfelt thanks go to Ruth Schilling, Marlen von Bargen, Christian Ostersehlte, Dennis Niewerth, Bernd Darter, Petra Schütz, and Tobias Goebel at the Deutsches Schifffahrtsmuseum (German

Maritime Museum), Bremerhaven, who put one of the most extensive collections of maritime and naval history at my disposal and shared their considerable expertise on all matters related to the *St. Louis* and the contexts in which the ship's service history must be placed. My heartfelt thanks also go to Martina Fähnemann, Corporate Communications, Hapag-Lloyd AG, who gave me permission to access the files of the HAPAG archive at the Hamburger Staatsarchiv (Hamburg State Archive), as well as the Archive's wonderful staff of librarians, who assisted me with the holdings. I would like to thank the team at the Archive for logistically supporting my research of the history of HAPAG, its ships, its routes, its passenger data during the Third Reich and, especially, the *St. Louis* files. My thanks also go to Gabriele Giwan and Beatrix Haußmann at the Bundesarchiv—Abteilung Filmarchiv (Federal Archive, Film Division), Berlin, for giving me access to historical film material about the *St. Louis* and other ships of the period. I would further like to thank Marie Chapman, director of the Canadian Museum of Immigration at Pier 21, Halifax, and her team. My thanks here go to Colin Timm and to Nathaline Piedrahita-Budiman and especially to historian and archivist Steven Schwinghamer. I have benefited greatly from my visit to the museum and cherish my conversations with Marie and Steven on the *St. Louis* in the context of Canadian migration and on Daniel Libeskind's memorial *The Wheels of Conscience*, which is installed at the museum.

At the United States Holocaust Memorial Museum my thanks go to Diane Afoumado, who has authored an important book about the *St. Louis* and who kindly shared her expertise about the ship's historic voyage with me. I would further like to thank Misha Mitsel at the Archive of the American Jewish Joint Distribution Committee, who has made important materials related to the *St. Louis* trip to Cuba available to me. Every effort has been made to secure permission for the use of copyrighted material. If you have additional information, please notify the publisher so that appropriate credit acknowledgment can be included in any future editions.

Special thanks go to my two archival researchers. In Germany, Heide Pennigsdorf conducted a comprehensive survey of German media coverage of the *St. Louis* voyage on my behalf. Thanks to Ms. Pennigsdorf's penetrating archival research, we now have definitive archival information on how the press of the Third Reich covered the *St. Louis* voyage. In Boston, Megan Lu conducted valuable research on the US press coverage of the voyage. I would further like to thank Rhoda Bilansky at Boston University's Mugar Memorial Library for her invaluable assistance with obtaining the English-language version of the official proceedings of the Évian conference. Further thanks go to Jose Gatti for introducing me to *Heretics*, Leonardo Padura's historical novel about the *St. Louis*, to Xinkai Sun for his institutional research, to Birgit Opitz in Germany and Nathaniel Taylor, director of finance at Boston University's College of Communication, for their logistic support with obtaining research materials, and to Chris Spedaliere for helping me with image reproduction.

Several individuals have given me feedback on portions of the manuscript. My greatest thanks go to Christine N. Brinckmann, whose sharp eye and unfailing judgment has helped me improve on the contents and form of several chapters. A very special thanks goes to my Boston University colleague Michael Zell for reading my manuscript, which has greatly benefited from his expertise on ocean liners, and also for lending me images of the *St. Louis* from his private collection. I owe thanks to Paula J. Massood, Cindy Lucia, Kirsten Moana Thompson, Gary Crowdus, and Mark Hennessey for giving me valuable feedback on various parts of the manuscript, and I would like to thank Cindy also for her feedback on my English translation of Gustav Schröder's book. My heartfelt thanks also go to Betsy Walters for helping me with the formidable task of compiling the bibliography for this book.

I have presented research on the *St. Louis* and excerpts from my book at several conferences, including the 2019 conference Screening the Sea, hosted by the Christian-Albrecht university of Kiel, Germany; Visible Evidence XXVII, 2021, hosted by the Goethe University, Frankfurt, Germany; and the 2022 Society for Cinema and Media Studies Conference. My thanks go to the conference organizers and to the co-panelists of my panels and other conference interlocutors, including Hans-Jürgen Wulff, Kathrin Köppert, Dennis Niewerth, Gabriel N. Gee, Frances Guerin, Oksana Chefranova, Elizabeth Wijaya, and Rosalind Galt. An excerpt of chapter 5 has been published as the German-language article "Die Fahrt ins Uferlose: Das Flüchtlingsschiff St. Louis am Vorabend des Zweiten Weltkriegs," in *Das Schiff: Archiv für Mediengeschichte* 20. My thanks go to the editors Friedrich Balke, Bernhard Siegert, and Joseph Vogl for including my contribution and to managing and copy editor Mark Potocnik. A shorter version of chapter 7 is appearing as "The Quintessential Seventies Picture Show: *Voyage of the Damned* (1976) as Heritage Film Between Art Cinema and Disaster Flick" in *The Routledge Companion to American Film History*, edited by Pamela Robertson Wojcik and Paula J. Massood (2025). I would like to thank the editors for their helpful feedback on the essay. A version of chapter 8 has been published as "Germany Revisits the *St. Louis* Voyage: *Die Ungewollten*/The Unwanted—Die Irrfahrt der St. Louis," in *Germanic Review: Literature, Culture, Theory*, no. 4, 2024. I would like to thank Oliver Simons and my anonymous peer reviewers for their helpful feedback. A version of the epilogue has been published as "'With Whose Blood Were My Eyes Crafted?'[1] Critical Concepts of Seeing, Knowing, and Remembering in Philip Scheffner's and Merle Kröger's *Havarie* (2016)," in *Transit*. I would like to thank Nat Modlin, my anonymous peer reviewers, and Elizabeth Sun for their extremely helpful feedback on the essay.

Several individuals have had crucial roles in bringing this book into print. I would like to thank my editors James Peltz and Murray Pomerance at SUNY Press and also my copyeditor James Harbeck and my designers, Kirk Warren and Susan Morreale. My very special thanks go to Dean Mariette DiChristina-Gerosa at Boston University's College of Communication for generously supporting my research and the publication of this book.

My biggest thanks of all go to Mark Hennessey for his constant encouragements, his tireless logistical support, his nourishing meals, his patience, and his love for me.

Introduction

C AN A LUXURY LINER BE A concentration camp? This question may appear unseemly sensationalist and the comparison outlandish, but it is germane when the ship at issue is the MS *St. Louis*, a passenger liner sailing under the flag of Nazi Germany and widely remembered as "the ship of Jews."[1] On May 13, 1939, the *St. Louis* left Hamburg with 899 passengers and two days later added 38 more in Cherbourg, France. 930 of the 937 men, women, and children on board were Jewish. All were bound for Cuba, which had issued tourist landing permits to them. Most intended to stay there only temporarily to await permission to immigrate to the United States. Upon arrival in Havana on May 27, the migrants learned that their permits had been revoked and that Cuba was denying disembarkation. On June 2, after a week of unsuccessful negotiations, the *St. Louis* left Cuba in the hope of taking its passengers to the US. When the US declined asylum and Captain Gustav Schröder failed to land the passengers in Florida, the ship returned to Europe. The Jews on board feared they were heading back to Germany to be transferred to concentration camps. They had already lost their German citizenship in exchange for being allowed to emigrate. Not until June 13, when *St. Louis* was almost back in European waters, did Schröder receive confirmation that the Jewish refugee organization JDC (American Jewish Joint Distribution Committee) had negotiated asylum with the Netherlands, France, Belgium, and England. When the *St. Louis* docked in Antwerp on June 17, its infamous odyssey was over, but 254 of the passengers were caught by the SS after Germany invaded much of Western Europe in 1940. The fate of these people could not be more poignant: they had found themselves in Havana harbor and in viewing distance of Miami Beach before being deported to Auschwitz and Sobibor.

The longer the *St. Louis* was at sea, the more she turned into a ship of pariahs. What made the ship's voyage appear so doomed, even though more than 600 traveling on it would survive the war, is that the lives of all passengers hung in the balance until the very last minute—that is, until Captain Schöder received clearance to sail to Antwerp instead of Cuxhaven, Germany, where the Gestapo were already arranging to take the human freight into custody. The bizarre circumstances of the voyage, the drama of its unfolding, and the seemingly inescapable threat of annihilation that hovered over the lives on board drew the attention of the world's press in the late spring and early summer of 1939. It has since become the subject both of scholarly and popular historical accounts, including long-form journalism, TV reportages, feature films, fiction, poetry, cartoons, public memorials, and commemorative events. While this extensive cultural

Figure I.1. The MS *St. Louis* in the Port of Hamburg. *Source*: Courtesy of United States Holocaust Memorial Museum (USHMM), courtesy of Herbert and Vera Karliner.

engagement with the incident in history and popular memory has stemmed the effects of historical amnesia, it has obscured as much as it has illuminated the voyage's details and the underlying conditions that shaped it. Like any historical incident that has attracted attention from multiple political and cultural angles, the *St. Louis* voyage has been subject to historical misjudgment and revisionist interpretation.

The prevailing historical narrative about the *St. Louis* voyage is based on a set of long-standing misassumptions: (1) the main responsibility for its Jewish passengers becoming refugees is believed to lie with Cuba, because the country's rival politicians turned them into pawns in their feud; (2) while Cuba's declining of asylum was a shock to the world, Nazi Germany had known about Cuba's attitude all along—and, in fact, high-ranking NS officials had organized the voyage specifically to prove Hitler's claim that Jews are universally unwanted;[2] (3) the *St. Louis*'s owner, the Hamburg America Line (HAPAG), saw the trip as a sudden, unexpected opportunity to supplement its regular business operations and, hence, was unable to gauge the gravity of the danger into which the *St. Louis* passengers were sailing; (4) the democratic world's unwillingness to alleviate the Jewish refugee crisis created by Nazi Germany was due to nations' extremely limited capacity for taking in migrants, a vexing historical reality that affected all countries participating in the 1938 Évian conference on Jewish refugee aid; (5) US President Roosevelt's hands in rescuing the *St. Louis* migrants were completely tied due to stiff political resistance at home; (6) the bizarre and dramatic manner in which the events unfolded makes the *St. Louis* voyage a historical "freak occurrence," a concatenation of events that was as anomalous as it was tragic.

Above claims, as this book argues, beg fundamental correction or at least substantial qualification. To wit: (1) While Cuba's decision to decline asylum did, as scholars have argued, formally turn the *St. Louis* passengers into refugees, the arrangements that went awry due to political wrangling and intrigues over illegal fees and bribes were part of a larger mechanism of the illegal monetization of Jewish migration that originated not from within but outside of Cuba. As sources discussed in this book show, it transpired within the larger context of neocolonial trade relations between Cuba and other countries that involved European shipping lines and travel agencies selling passage to desperate Jews on dubious terms. (2) There is no hard evidence that the NS regime was behind the Cuba voyage or hoped it would fail—indeed, Berlin struggled to contain the fallout from the unexpected turn of the voyage. As my review of the daily press of Nazi Germany and Austria shows, newspapers hardly reported on the incident and even tried to falsify news of it so as to distance Nazi Germany from it. (3) HAPAG was hardly a novice to the economic context and political dynamics that led Cuba to reject the *St. Louis* passengers. My analysis of the company's history and business philosophy traces how HAPAG during the Third Reich parlayed emigration to the Americas, one of its traditional mainstays, into an operation increasingly focused on Jewish migrants. Neither was HAPAG's decision to use the *St. Louis* for this purpose as novel and sudden as it may seem. This helps account for the already known fact that HAPAG, which knew of Cuba's changed immigration policy before the voyage, kept the ship on course even when fears mounted that Cuba would make no exception for its passengers. (4) While most nations participating in the Évian conference gave similar reasons for their claimed inability to take in more refugees, negotiations revealed a geopolitical power differential in which European countries sought to impose a non-European solution to the crisis. Further, as a close reading of the proceedings shows, Latin American nations, if they were willing to accept Jewish migrants at all, did so mostly because their neocolonial governments wanted to whiten their countries' demographics as long as that did not jeopardize the effects of centuries of Christianization. My revisionist reading of Évian argues that it was not higher circumstances and insurmountable exigencies but concrete neocolonial and biopolitical considerations that prevented nations participating in the conference from accepting more migrants—an attitude that, among other things, calls into question the very term "refugee crisis." (5) As the country with the largest immigration quota and the initiator of the Évian conference, the US felt it had already done more than enough to help solve the problem. Hence, as a look at the correspondence between President Roosevelt and his negotiator and conference chair Myron C. Taylor shows, the US indirectly encouraged other countries to increase their immigration quotas. And though political pressure on Roosevelt to tightly control Jewish migration into the US was real, recent scholarship has found that the president's aloofness during the Caribbean segment of the *St. Louis* voyage at least in part owed to the fact that he was led to believe that his intervention would not be necessary. (6) As poignant as it is, the voyage was unusual only because of the size and intended purpose of its ship. In the late 1930s, Jewish migrant ships were common on the Atlantic, the Black Sea, and the Mediterranean. In contrast to the *St. Louis*, most were woefully unfit to carry passengers. While the *St. Louis* drama received the lion's share of attention from the press, my review of Jewish and left-wing publications shows that in the late 1930s there was a rich discourse with detailed information on the plight of Jewish migrant ships.

The following chapters lay out these corrective findings in detail with the help of recent scholarship on the voyage and supported by my primary research at the HAPAG archive in Hamburg and other maritime archives in Germany. The research helps us revise our knowledge about the *St. Louis*, its owner, HAPAG, HAPAG's Jewish migrant business to Latin America, and the ship's fateful voyage as viewed by its captain, its crew, its passengers, and the American and German press. Part I of this book devotes itself to discussing the history and pre-history of the trip and also debates its position vis-à-vis historical assessments of the Holocaust; the second part analyzes how the voyage has been remembered and how the texts and artifacts it has generated constitute a realm unto itself within Holocaust memory culture. That there is no clear-cut division between history and memory will not surprise anyone who has followed the relevant debates within historiography. This does not, however, absolve me from reckoning with the vicissitudes encountered by those of us, myself included, who nonetheless feel compelled to work with such a division, at least provisionally.

Part I: History

Part I does not simply "retell" history but reflects on it critically. One of the threats weaving through the first four chapters is migration and particularly the tension between voluntary and involuntary migration. The gray zone between both challenges us to understand under what circumstances German Jews left their home land during the Third Reich and why so many chose not to emigrate until it was too late. As was historically the case and is still the case today, the reasons people feel compelled to abandon their homes and home countries are manifold and complex, and, as the term "abandon" implies, invariably involve a measure of pain, in many cases full-blown trauma. Given this fact, it is baffling how frequently even the hardest-wrought decisions to leave behind all that one calls home are met with suspicion and sundry bad-faith responses. No group knew this better than Europe's Jews. While democracies readily acknowledged that Jews' efforts to escape from the Nazis were life-saving measures, few were prepared to accept those refugees into their own countries. Some nations viewed them as neither more nor less deserving of a new start than previous generations of emigrants and, thus, expected them to "get in line." Nazi Germany, for its part, did everything for much of the 1930s to coerce German Jews to leave. At the same time, the NS regime drew on preexisting laws that classified their emigration as an act of fiscal disloyalty warranting a special tax to reimburse the state for losses incurred. These are just some of the more polarizing examples of the plethora of connotations and legal implications that the concept of emigration carried for Jews. The gray zone between voluntary and involuntary migration is reflected in the wealth of terms used to denote the act of migrating, including "migration," "settlement," "resettlement," "relocation," "displacement," "expulsion," and "flight." Add to this the corresponding terms naming the subjects of those movements, which, in the case of the *St. Louis* passengers, included not only "settler," "migrant," "emigrant," "immigrant," and "refugee," but also the starkly oppositional sets of terms of "passenger," "tourist," and "traveler" on the one hand and "detainee," "prisoner," and "camp inmate" on the other hand.

The Nazis themselves operated in this conceptual and linguistic gray zone both willfully and inadvertently. This, as chapter 1 discusses, can be gleaned from their inconsistent attitude about Jewish expulsion. They compared Jews to vermin while claiming to ship them out on luxury liners; they created a number of fiscal and legal obstacles that made it hard for Jews to migrate while also enacting or envisioning intricate fiscal and logistic exchange mechanisms that enabled Jews to settle elsewhere (the Haavara Agreement, the Schacht plan). The NS regime was, of course, keenly aware of the intractable obstacles to large-scale Jewish resettlement that existed in the world. That these problems were primarily political and ideological and only secondarily logistic can be seen in the unspoken reasons behind the failure of the Évian conference on refugees. To identify these deeper causes, I reread the conference proceedings in terms of historically intertwined control mechanisms. One is biopolitics, the measures governments adopt to biologically manipulate the makeup of populations; the other is neocolonialism, the economic and sociocultural domination that colonial powers continue to assert on former colonies. The conference's outcome and the unwillingness of its participating nations to substantially revise their policies for both voluntary and involuntary migrants (frequently playing both concepts out against each other) even after the November 9, 1938, pogrom known as Kristallnacht dramatically worsened life for Germany's Jews. By the time the *St. Louis* was cruising through Caribbean waters in the hope of landing its passengers, Jewish refugees could be found on many oceans, and Jewish refugee ships were a prominent topic in certain newspapers and cultural circles in Europe and the US.

That the *St. Louis* and other refugee ships were adrift on the world's oceans in the late 1930s was the surest sign yet that the concept of human rights that was intended to endow every human on earth with irreducible dignity was woefully failing one group in need of precisely such protection. For protection, as Hannah Arendt chillingly observed, turned out to be not a right, but a privilege—the privilege of the citizen—and citizenship was exactly what the stateless lacked. The Nazis then seized on this conundrum by defining German citizenship in racial and, thus, racist terms. In fact, the plight of the *St. Louis* and other "ships of Jews" represented the convergence of two eras of forced migration—that which had already become a signature feature of the modern age in which various ethnic and religious groups suffered denationalization and displacement following World War I, and that which, beginning with Hitler's rise to power, marked Jews as destined for expulsion, encampment, and eventual extermination by the Nazis.[3]

The politics, economics, and logistics of voluntary and involuntary migration were driven by phenomena associated with modernity. These include the modern nation-state's desire to control its population biopolitically, an increase in migration to the US between the 1880s and 1920s, and a lesser, yet still significant, stream of migrants to Latin America as part of Europe's neocolonization of the subcontinent. Chapter 2 explores these developments through the example of one of the major logistic facilitators and economic motors of intercontinental migration—the Hamburg America Line (HAPAG). I trace HAPAG's rise from its mid-nineteenth-century beginnings to pre–World War I dominance, which entailed establishment of a large fleet and sprawling migrant processing facilities in Hamburg. Along with Ellis Island in New York and Pier 21 in Halifax, these formed a prominent part of the total apparatus facilitating migration between Europe and the Americas. I then investigate how HAPAG, after being forced to rebuild itself from scratch following the Versailles Treaty, developed the Jewish migrant business to Latin America as an organic part of its trade routes to the subcontinent and the West Indies, a move that paid off for the line during the Third Reich. Finally, I look into the service record of the *St. Louis* from its initial commission as a ship primarily for second-class and third-class passengers (many of whom were projected to be migrants) to the late 1930s, when plans emerged to repurpose it exclusively for Jewish migration. These investigations place Jewish migration into the intersecting contexts of antisemitic persecution, biopolitics, and neocolonialism—factors whose interconnections have yet to be explored in full depth and which impacted totalitarian and democratic states alike.

Nothing seemed to constitute stronger proof of the convergence of totalitarian and democratic states' views of migration, which political theorist Giorgio Agamben has provocatively characterized as the "inner solidarity between democracy and totalitarianism,"[4] than the voyage of the *St. Louis*. Chapters 3 and 4 detail the trip, recorded in HAPAG's annals as the ship's ninety-eighth voyage since entering service. Chapter 3 traces the prehistory and the various stages of Voyage 98. I analyze HAPAG's advertisement of the trip, the logistics of the ship's departure from Germany, its week-long anchorage in Havana, and its dramatic eastbound return to Europe. The JDC's efforts to broker asylum for the refugees and the political situation in Cuba and the US that made these efforts so challenging deserve special attention. Chapter 4 retraces the voyage from the perspective of the passengers and analyzes its coverage by US and German media. The voyage placed the passengers in the alternating and at times overlapping positions of tourist, migrant, refugee, and camp inmate. Passenger diaries and the logs and published reminiscences of *St. Louis*'s captain, Gustav Schröder, throw light on the passengers' confusing legal status. Exerting power over them from thousands of miles away, Nazi Germany turned them into exemplars of what Agamben has influentially defined as *"homo sacer"* or bare

Introduction

life: someone who "can save himself only in perpetual flight [to] a foreign land" and yet who is in "a continuous relationship with the power that banished him precisely insofar as he is at every instant exposed to an unconditional threat of death."[5]

But as my analysis of the US press coverage of Voyage 98 demonstrates, the *St. Louis* passengers refused to be victims. The actions they took to communicate their despair impacted the way the media reported the story and how the world perceived them. It is here that we first note how historical events cannot be separated from the way they are represented in the media. The passengers' strategic presentation of their own suffering as a signifier of moral virtue and the manner in which the media reported the unfolding rollercoaster drama of what, by then, had turned into a seaborne form of incarceration followed the playbook of melodrama. This cultural form, as chapter 3 discusses, shaped the way the *St. Louis* voyage made history.

Chapters 1 to 4 argue that the fate of the *St. Louis* passengers stands in unique relationship to the Holocaust and its traumatic center. Their story already contains the major elements pointing toward this center, the makings of historical trauma, including persecution, flight, incarceration and, for 254 of them, extermination. The *St. Louis* voyage occurred before the Holocaust's final phase at a point when the worst could still have been averted. By refusing to intervene, however, numerous democratic countries showed themselves complicit with the NS regime that had created the migrant crisis prior to launching "the final solution." As such, Voyage 98 possesses elements that almost made it an ordinary sea journey—until it no longer was. To put it the other way round, while hundreds of the passengers became victims of genocide, the waystations they traversed en route to their deaths were not specific to the Holocaust's final phase and neither were the broader geopolitical and economic reasons for their displacement and migration.

For us to relate the *St. Louis* voyage to the Holocaust's genocidal aspects demands methodological nuance. While the journey for 254 passengers ended in death, the *St. Louis* cannot be equated with a death camp. But by functioning as a vehicle that first took Jews away from ordinary concentration camps and then to internment camps, some of which later functioned as transit camps to Auschwitz, *St. Louis* certainly was part of what is termed the "concentrationary universe."[6] It is in the ship's assumption of this position that the biopolitical underpinnings that made the Holocaust an integral part of modernity reveal themselves most clearly. From its erstwhile historical role of transporting millions of migrants from Europe to the Americas in steerage and third class to becoming a key part of the concentrationary universe, the ocean liner as a ship type was crucial to the implementation of biopolitics.

Viewed from this vantage point, the *St. Louis* voyage prompts us to regard the Holocaust both as a unique event and as the result of certain historical and political contingencies. These, in turn, foreground the democratic world's involvement in the Holocaust. They make aspects of it comparable to other genocides without, however, giving any cause to question the horrifying specifics of industrial mass extermination that constitute the essence of the Shoah. Chapter 5 explores the political stakes of this insight for Holocaust studies. By comparing democratic nations' declining of asylum for the *St. Louis* Jews to the logic of what Carl Schmitt termed "the State of Exception" and through which he sought to legitimize the Nazi takeover of Germany and all it entailed, I foreground conceptual contiguities between democracy and totalitarianism. These contiguities, I argue, turned Schmitt's metaphor of the shoreless sea (meant to signify the irreversible decay of the Weimar state and its jurisdiction) into a bitter reality for Jewish refugee ships on the eve of World War II.[7] To further explore the implications of the concept of the shoreless sea, a term that figures centrally in the titles both of this book and of chapter 5, I engage in detail with Giorgio Agamben's thesis of the "inner solidarity" between democracy and totalitarianism, an argument that continues to provoke Holocaust historians.

A further challenge to the field of Holocaust studies is the need to explore possible correspondences between the Holocaust and other genocides. Hannah Arendt paved the way in the early 1950s by exploring analogies between the industrial mass murder of Jews by the Nazis and African populations' victimization by Imperial Germany and by the Boers. Assessing the *St. Louis* voyage, I argue, affords an opportunity to contribute to the field's so-called colonial turn[8] by building what is both a more nuanced and expansive diacritics of genocide. Understanding the neocolonial aspects that helped shape Voyage 98 can help us unlock the impasse Holocaust studies has come to by focusing too narrowly on a consideration of turn-of-the-century African colonial genocide.

In other areas of historical and cultural study, the *St. Louis* incident has generated extensive, if uneven, scholarly and popular discussion. While popular accounts of the voyage appeared already in the late 1940s, it was not until the 1960s that historians began to engage with the subject, particularly as part of a new wave of interest in America's role in World War II and the Roosevelt administration's complicated relationship to Jewish migration.[9] Much *St. Louis* scholarship from the 1960s, '70s, and '80s is superficial or apocryphal (which is why the present study reassesses a key early account, Gordon Thomas and Max Morgan-Witts's *Voyage of the Damned*, as popular culture rather than as a scholarly work). Several more recent studies featuring materials from various international archives have shown greater rigor.[10] An increasing number of studies now center on specific aspects of Voyage 98, such as the role of the JDC,[11] Canada's domestic politics that caused the country to decline asylum,[12] and the fate of the passengers after completion of the trip.[13]

My book is indebted to many of these studies. At the same time, I eschew an intrinsic distinction between history as pre-narrated and narrated or, to use a concept by Hayden White, as "emplotted"—in other words, between "hard" facts and their interpretation.[14] Part I already includes several texts that do not merely report on the Jewish migrant crisis but instead offer critical reflection, while others deal with it artistically. Indeed, as we see in chapter 4, the responses by the *St. Louis* passengers to their seaborne detention and their uncertain fate show that for them these events were already inflected with narrative meaning.[15] The way they dramatize their isolation on the ocean and their choice of metaphors expressing imprisonment display a phenomenon pinpointed by Martin Jay, namely that witness testimony tends to be filtered through established historical topoi.[16] And as my analysis of the press coverage of the *St. Louis* voyage demonstrates, there was a fluid and dynamic relationship between the events that transpired and the way the press reported them, and it is this dialectic that ultimately shaped the voyage's perception by the American public.

One group of sources this book discusses comprises internal HAPAG analytics and memos as well as private correspondence between politicians, administrators, and business agents. Many other texts were authored for a broader public. This goes without saying for post-1948 mass-market *St. Louis* memory culture but also includes 1930s journalistic and literary texts that responded to the crisis as it was unfolding. All texts aimed at a public require us to pay particular attention to modes of authorship and dissemination and to historical and cultural contexts. At issue are generic conventions that shape not only a given text, but also the expectations of its recipients, which, to a certain extent, are inscribed within that text.

Part II: Memory

The second half of this book concerns itself with how Voyage 98 has been remembered through different periods, across shifting cultural contexts, and in media ranging from literature and theater to film, television, and public memorials and in such diverse genres as popular history, autobiography, mystery novels, melodramas, cartoons, and experimental nonfiction and essay films. These texts' hindsight perspectives raise the question as to what shapes historical memory. Postwar West German culture was marked by historical trauma and amnesia, whereas works produced in reunified Germany reflect long-established practices of Holocaust remembrance. But discussing US books and films also requires attention to shifting cultural contexts. At issue are, for instance, America's changing perception of Jews and the government's assuming of the role of custodian of Holocaust history. Holocaust memory, as any memory, flows in complex ways that manifest both directly and obliquely, and it turns mass-distributed texts and artifacts into palimpsests as much as motors. At issue is as much how a given artifact enables mnemonic activity as how it makes specific memories legible.

Chapter 6 analyzes the first two phases of *St. Louis* memory culture in their respective German and US contexts. The first instance of industrially disseminated memory about the *St. Louis* voyage emerged in the newly founded Federal Republic of Germany. It came from the ship's captain, Gustav Schröder, who in 1949 published a short book about the voyage titled *Heimatlos auf hoher See*, which is republished in English translation as *Homeless on the High Seas* in the appendix of this book. While its self-published format suggests that the book had little impact on the 1950s West German public, it formed part of a mosaic of memory culture that also included plays inspired by the *St. Louis* voyage and articles about Schröder. His relative visibility in the media until his death in 1959 ensured that Voyage 98 did not fall into oblivion. I approach Schröder's book as both a historical record of the voyage and a document of the quiet heroism of this remarkable man. But I also explore its complex and contradictory functions in the larger context of postwar memory culture, which was characterized by West Germans' proclivity to initially see themselves more as victims than as perpetrators of the horrors of the Third Reich. The second example of postwar West German memory culture is Hans Herlin's account *Kein Gelobtes Land: Die Irrfahrt der St. Louis* (No Promised Land: The *St. Louis* voyage), published both in book form and as an article series in *Stern*, a widely read illustrated magazine. Whereas Schröder's account operated within the context of postwar trauma, Herlin's reflects the shifts that a decade later marked the country's efforts of coming to terms with its past. Those efforts were catalyzed by West German media's coverage of the Adolf Eichmann trial in Jerusalem and the world premiere in West Berlin of the Hollywood film *Judgment at Nuremberg*, which, like Eichmann's trial, confronted the West German public head-on with the Nazi period and its legacy.

Schröder's and Herlin's accounts have existed in complete obscurity in the Anglo-American sphere and Herlin's book, despite its 1970 republication, is largely forgotten also in Germany. The same can hardly be said for two mass-market American books that in the late 1960s and early '70s brought the *St. Louis* voyage to the attention of a large readership—Robert D. Morse's *While Six Million Died: A Chronicle of American Apathy*, first published in 1967, and Gordon Thomas and Max Morgan-Witts's *Voyage of the Damned*, first published in 1974. While Morse only devotes one chapter to the *St. Louis* voyage, Thomas and Morgan-Witts place it at the center of their fast-paced, partly fictionalized account. I discuss each text in relation to changing perceptions of Jews in American culture. These included a shift of the Holocaust survivor from victim to victim-hero and a broadening of the status of the Holocaust as a signifier for evils not limited to the Nazi regime (such as the Vietnam War). In particular, Thomas and Morgan-Witts create a dramatis personae from the list of passengers that aligns with 1960s and '70s cultural perceptions of Jewish Americans.

Thomas and Morgan-Witts's treatment has rightfully raised objections by historians proper. That said, their book's fluid, if undocumented, featuring of oral history evinces a certain affinity to the many aspects of the voyage that to this day remain the subject of speculation. If the authors' use of popular storytelling techniques ultimately trivializes the subject matter, the book's 1976 film adaptation of the same title deploys generic conventions to interesting effect. Chapter 7 seeks to counter the charge that *Voyage of the Damned* is ultimately mere "Holocaust kitsch." Of interest is how the film's use of stars and of genres such as the melodrama and the horror film yield productive commentary on Jewish myth and culture. Of interest is also the film's depiction of certain savior figures, which says more about the role the US had assigned to Zionism in the context of cold war politics than about those figure's historical roles.

1970s Holocaust remembrance culture in Europe saw the state emerge as custodian and sponsor of historical memory. In West Germany, the Holocaust had become the subject of public ceremonies and a moral referent for local, regional, and national administrations. It was also becoming a regular topic on West German television, which, until the mid-1980s, was exclusively state sponsored. In 1979, West German TV aired the US-produced miniseries *Holocaust*, a momentous event that catalyzed intense, widespread discussion among the public. The US government, too, emerged as an official sponsor of Holocaust remembrance. In 1978, President Jimmy Carter assembled a presidential commission for the establishment of the United States Holocaust Memorial Museum (USHMM), which, after being in development for many years, opened in 1993. By then, local and state administrations in the US had already for decades worked with private interest groups to establish Holocaust memorials and museums in various parts of the country.[17]

Since the 1990s, the growing infrastructure of state-sponsored museums and archives has steadily advanced awareness of the Holocaust's manifold aspects, including the *St. Louis* voyage. Chapters 8 and 9 discuss two recent films, which, each in its own way, reflect the influence of the state as official custodian of Holocaust history and as author and sponsor of memory culture. Chapter 8 focuses on *Die Ungewollten* (The unwanted), a 2019 feature-length retelling of the *St. Louis* voyage commissioned by state-sponsored German television. The film uses Voyage 98 to indirectly invite solidarity with current migrants from the Global South trying to reach Europe or the US, but it is constrained by Germany's compromised political position regarding Europe's role in the Mediterranean migrant crisis, which has disproportionately affected Arabs. Chapter 9 analyzes *Complicit*, an American independent film produced between 2012 and 2014 by the Florida-based Holocaust memorial organization The SS *St. Louis* Legacy Project. I place *Complicit* in the tradition of subversive grassroots movements' efforts to offer a counter-narrative to official state-sponsored versions of historical events and I discuss the film's complex relationship to the US government. *Complicit* critiques President Roosevelt and the State Department for denying asylum to the *St. Louis* Jews, but the film's centerpiece is a theater production hosted by the State Department under Secretary of State Hillary Clinton, which thus indirectly functioned as a co-sponsor of the completed film.

Chapter 10 examines three further examples of *St. Louis* memory culture as instances of memory's tendency to flow in multiple directions via mechanisms of displacement and substitution. Drawing on the concept of "multidirectional memory" pioneered by Michael Rothberg, discussion first centers on the novel *Heretics* by Cuban author Leonardo Padura, which weaves the voyage of the *St. Louis* to Cuba into a multigenerational mystery story of Jewish migration. *Heretics* represents an instance of multidirectional memory that originates neither in Europe nor in the US. It yields insight into the intersection of the Holocaust and neocolonialism in a manner that established Holocaust studies have thus far left unexplored. The next object of interest is Art Spiegelman's cartoon "The *St. Louis* Refugee Ship Blues," published in 2009 in the *Washington Post* and featuring his well-known Maus avatar. Spiegelman seizes on political cartoonists' treatment of the *St. Louis* voyage for his biting critique of the state of political cartoons in America. The chapter ends with a discussion of Daniel Libeskind's memorial of the *St. Louis* voyage, *The Wheel of Conscience*, which is located in the lobby of the Canadian Museum of Immigration at Pier 21 in Halifax, one of the *St. Louis*'s regular ports of call as an immigrant ship and transatlantic liner. Spiegelman and Libeskind mobilize multidirectional memory to prompt their publics to explore the first world's role in current migrant crises.

The epilogue returns discussion of the Holocaust to the context of colonialism. I place media comparisons between the *St. Louis* voyage and the Mediterranean migrant crisis in relation to the 2016 German experimental film *Havarie*. The film is based on a cell-phone video made by a European passenger on a cruise ship in the Mediterranean and showing a dinghy with African migrants headed for the coast of Spain. I read *Havarie* as a kind of memory portal to the *St. Louis* voyage to further illuminate the impact of colonialism and neocolonialism on different historical instances of forced migration.

The appendix to this book consists of several primary sources related to Voyage 98. At the center is my annotated English translation of Gustav Schröder's account of the trip, preceded by a biographical sketch of Schröder's life. The appendix also includes translations of the logs that Schröder filed with HAPAG for all segments of the trip. Hopefully, these primary sources will give readers an impression of the challenges faced by the ship, its captain and crew, and especially its passengers.

Part I

1

Jews During the Third Reich

Between Flight and Entrapment

IN 1932, WEIMAR GERMANY held two federal elections. Neither produced a clear winner, but in each the National Socialists emerged as the strongest party. The results emboldened Adolf Hitler to pressure Paul von Hindenburg, President of the Reich, to appoint him chancellor on January 30, 1933. When the March 1933 election extended the political stalemate, Hitler requested that the German parliament, the Reichstag, be dissolved, so he could rule the country without parliamentary consent. The legislative act performed for this purpose was the so-called Enabling Act, a type of martial law that empowered Hitler to rule by decree. Together with the Reichstag Fire Decree, a law suspending all civil liberties in the wake of the Reichstag fire of February 1933, the Enabling Act turned Hitler into a de facto dictator. Hitler blamed communists for setting the Reichstag on fire, but it was Germany's Jews who, in the years to come, would become the most prominent target of Nazi persecution. In September 1935, the regime passed the Nuremberg Laws. Billed as a decree to protect racial purity, the laws legalized anti-Jewish discrimination on racial grounds. They prohibited Jews from having sexual intercourse with and marrying "citizens of German or cognate blood." They also deprived German Jews of citizenship, classifying them as National Subjects Without Political Rights.[1]

Legal discrimination against Jews went hand in hand with other forms of antisemitism. Nazi ideology racialized Jews by contrasting them to "Aryans." Lacking any grounding in science, "Aryanism" nonetheless became a legal category and the term entered street parlance. The Nazis used the Aryan/non-Aryan distinction to label Jews unclean, uncivilized, and subhuman. Sports clubs and social organizations excluded Jews. Educational institutions and the media reinforced preexisting stereotypes of Jews as conspiratorial and greedy. Non-Jewish Germans were encouraged to scorn and shun their Jewish fellow citizens and were given license to commit acts of violence against them. During the "Kristallnacht" pogrom of November 9 to 10, 1938, Jewish businesses, social institutions, and synagogues were destroyed on a massive scale. The regime arrested thousands of Jewish men and temporarily interned them in concentration camps. Yet all this was only a prelude to the large-scale industrial murder of Germany's and Europe's Jews, decided upon by Nazi leaders at a secret meeting in January 1942, the so-called Wannsee Conference. In its wake, the regime had camps built outside of Germany specifically for mass extermination.

Given that Hitler's 1925 book *Mein Kampf* already centrally relied on antisemitic rhetoric, and in light of the Nazis' swift adoption of antisemitic legislation, the question seems legitimate why Jews did not flee Germany sooner and in greater numbers. There are three factors to consider: (1) Hitler came to power through a democratic election that denied the NSDAP the absolute majority and forced it to form a coalition with another party—the threat initially seemed containable; (2) related to that, while Hindenburg's appointment of Hitler was a decisive step in setting the Nazi takeover in motion, many expected him to moderate against the NSDAP; (3) while the antisemitic measures that followed violated international law, the regime shrewdly adopted them as amendments of—and thus in close reference to—numerous laws already established during the Wilhelminian Empire or the Weimar Republic.[2] These facts contradict the belief that Nazism entered the Weimar Republic from without as a quasi-alien force. As a mass movement, it clearly had emerged from within German society. Nazi leaders seized on the flaws of Germany's first democracy and overthrew it from within its vulnerable political structure. By pretending to frame its antisemitic laws with this structure, NS legislature created the impression of their reversibility and respectability. A further form of respectability motivated Berlin's hosting of the international community for the 1936 Olympic Games. Ahead of them, the Nazis temporarily removed the most blatant signifiers of antisemitism from the public sphere. The assimilated status of German Jews aided the impression of normalcy. Many led secular lives and regarded themselves primarily as Germans and only secondarily as Jews. Their services as lawyers, doctors, and business people were in high demand among the population. These factors help account for the fact that between 1933 and 1936, fewer than 100,000 Jews left Germany. In 1935, over 1.5 million "non-Aryans" still called Germany their home, of which 800,000 were categorized as fully Jewish and over 700,000 were categorized as racial hybrids (with at least one grandparent being Jewish).[3]

Jews were an important part of the German economy, and the government did not want to jeopardize its growth. The NS State rationalized its decision to initially permit Jews to engage in commercial trade by labeling them with the hypocritical euphemism "guest people" (*Gastvolk*). Jews thus inhabited the double status of same and other. The NSDAP strenuously disavowed Jews' assimilability. But by presenting "the Jewish question"[4] as a quasi-existential referendum on national belonging, NS propaganda created a dilemma for NS politics: how to rid Germany of part of its own public that, for all intents and purposes, was German? Eager to turn antisemitism into a grassroots sentiment, the NS regime decided upon an invidious strategy of racial othering intended to justify and reinforce the government's gradual denationalizing of Jews. In 1938 a set of new laws made life even harder for Jews in Germany but also, paradoxically, created more obstacles for them to emigrate. The Law on the Registration of Jewish Assets forced Jews to disclose all belongings surpassing 5000 Reichsmark, thus acting as an instrument for the eventual expropriation of Jewish funds and property. Next came a law titled Executive Ordinance on Jewish Atonement, which cynically billed Jews for the damages and destruction incurred during the November pogrom. By year's end, all Jews had to divest themselves of 20 percent of their assets.[5] The so-called *Reichsfluchtsteuer*—a capital control tax ordering Jewish and non-Jewish migrants to leave most of their assets in Germany—left many Jews lacking the funds most countries required as assurance against migrants becoming public charges.[6] If the majority of German Jews during the first half of the decade were still unwilling or hesitant to leave Germany, toward the end of the decade, when they were desperate to leave, many had lost the ability to do so.[7]

Between Flight and Entrapment

On November 20, 1938, less than two weeks after the pogrom, the German Jewish newspaper *Der Neue Vorwärts* published an article titled "Die Schmach" (The shame) whose uncredited author made the sobering and prescient observation that Nazi leaders had decided to exterminate the Jews still living in Germany.[8] The article regards the law forcing Jews to declare their assets as a harbinger of worse things to come, but it also links it to the much older, medieval practice of "Judengeleit"—a term that is translated as "safe-conduct" and refers both to a kind of protection toll for traveling Jewish merchants and a means of monitoring their income. The author keenly understands the law as a tool for the destruction of Jews' economic livelihood. But, as the article goes on to say, German Jews did not dare to think their fate through to the end, because they wanted to live rather than die ("weil sie nicht sterben, sondern leben wollen").[9] At this late point, some Jews appeared to be stricken by a kind of lethal paralysis (*Totenstarre*) that kept them from taking any action at all.

Germany's contradictory move of simultaneously encouraging and foiling Jewish emigration was motivated by two concerns equally central to antisemitism: ridding Germany of Jews while trying to prevent the formation of a Jewish state elsewhere in the world.[10] This second goal was to be accomplished by suppressing bulk emigration and by raising the level of antisemitism around the world to increase other countries' resistance to accepting Jewish migrants.[11] The main geopolitical referent for the Nazi's double agenda was, of course, Palestine. Germany had initially sponsored Jewish emigration to Palestine by signing an agreement with Jewish leadership, the 1933 Haavara Agreement. It facilitated the transfer of Jewish assets to Palestine by converting these into German-manufactured goods exported to Palestine by the Haavara company. Haavara sold the goods and transferred the proceeds to the migrants so they could, upon arrival, obtain housing and land.[12] As the treaty, which lasted until the beginning of World War II, enabled the migration of some 60,000 Jews and the transfer of assets in excess of 40 million US dollars, it is understandable that, in January 1939, Emil Schumburg, who held the position of "Judenreferent" (specialist for Jewish affairs), condemned it for its key role both in advancing the establishment of a Jewish state and in draining Germany of Jewish assets. His 1939 circular includes an urgent warning that Germany cannot afford to lose even a fraction of Jewish money. As that money, so he argues, really belongs to Germany, it is a sum receivable rather than payable in return for Germany allowing its Jewish population to leave.[13]

That Schumburg's reasoning is purely ideological becomes clear with his contradictory claims, made in one and the same document only paragraphs apart, that (1) most Jews had originally come to Germany as poor immigrants from the east and then quickly enriched themselves by using Germany's resources, and (2) that the Haavara Agreement had failed because it had only catered to the Jewish money elite, which was small in comparison to the large number of impecunious Jews still residing in Germany. Notwithstanding this contradiction, Schumburg's comments are remarkable for their unselfconscious equation of human lives with money and property. His circular has a chillingly pragmatic character regarding how to manage the transnational flow of people as a form of national capital that can be used to shape a country's body politic.

The willful shaping of whole populations, which may entail furthering the increase of some parts and reducing or fully eliminating other parts, was first theorized by Michel Foucault through the concepts of "biopower" and "biopolitics."[14] The terminology references the modern state's historical function as central disciplinary agent not only of individuals, but of sizable demographics. The state performs regulatory acts, such as manipulating the ratio of births to deaths, the rate of reproduction, and the fertility of a population.[15] The state thus exercises its traditional sovereign powers directly "at the level of life, the species, the race, and the large-scale phenomena of population."[16] In this function the state also extended its regulatory activities to extermination, as evidenced in European colonial powers' treatment of native populations in Africa, Latin America, and parts of Asia. Colonizers have invariably rationalized such biopolitics with racist ideologies.[17]

According to Foucault, "racism is bound up with the workings of a State that is obliged to use race, the elimination of races and the purification of the race, to exercise its sovereign power."[18] For

Foucault, Nazism was the pinnacle of the practice of biopolitics. It unleashed its murderous and sovereign power throughout the entire social body—which, as he notes, also included Germany's non-Jewish population, which the NS regime conscripted into a sacred war until death.[19] This suicidal aspect of biopolitics is, of course, what distinguishes Nazism from the biopolitics implemented by Europe's colonial powers. If Nazism was thus the most extreme and consequential—or, to use Foucault's wording, paroxysmal—form of biopolitics, its handling of Jewish migration shared practices with other European countries. While the policies of asylum varied from country to country, Germany's creation of a tidal wave of Jewish refugees would inexorably weave most of those policies into a dialectic of international rejection. For example, when Switzerland saw itself confronted with large numbers of Jewish refugees from Austria in the wake of Austria's annexation by Germany, it mandated visas for all Austrians and requested that Germany mark the passports of German and Austrian Jews with a "J."[20] Traditionally a document of rights and privileges, the passport now connoted the opposite. Used simultaneously for inclusion and exclusion, it exemplified what Foucault describes as the state's bureaucratic subjectivization of the individual for biopolitical purposes.

Historical evidence is inconclusive as to whether the marking of Jewish passports owed to a unilaterally Swiss initiative or had bilateral roots. But as Schumburg's Foreign Office circular shows, Nazi leaders were keenly aware of the larger geopolitical context in which they were preparing measures of expulsion. Assuring his readers that Germany is far from alone in adopting an anti-Jewish position, Schumburg mentions that Poland, Italy, Romania, annexed Austria, and invaded Czechoslovakia had begun to turn against their Jewish populations. And he does not fail to note the rising tide of antisemitism in North and South America, France, Holland, Greece, and Scandinavia. This groundswell of documented antisemitism served the NS regime to gloatingly reiterate its "no one wants them!" claim. It was the Nazi press, specifically the *Völkischer Beobachter*, which used those very words to headline its July 13, 1938, report on the resounding failure of the Conference of the Intergovernmental Committee at the French spa of Évian-les-Bains, where from July 6 to July 15 thirty-two Western countries unsuccessfully tried to secure asylum for Europe's Jews (see fig. 1.1). The July 13 article in the *Völkischer Beobachter* dovetailed with an earlier article in the same publication from July 8, as well as with an op-ed of the same date by its deputy editor-in-chief, Alfred Rosenberg, the head ideologue of Nazi antisemitism and chief architect of Germany's "final solution." Translatable as "What to do with the Jews? Thoughts on the World Conference of Évian," Rosenberg's article seizes on the tenor of some of the participating countries' opening statements to conclude that the nations of the world are unable to accommodate the Jews of Europe.[21] Predictably, Rosenberg gloats over the fact that key attendees—including France, the host country, and the US, which had initiated the conference—had already signaled little willingness to expand their refugee intake. It soon became clear that this position would be shared by nearly all countries represented at Évian.

The world community's unwillingness to suspend domestic concerns in the face of the Jewish populations' threatened status has led to the view that Évian was primarily a moral failure. Yet Rosenberg's remarks compel us to revise this assessment. As a leading ideologue of Nazi antisemitism, he is quick to recognize the role of

Figure 1.1. Period postcard of Évian-les-Bains, the site of the Intergovernmental Conference on Refugees. *Source:* Courtesy of United States Holocaust Memorial Museum.

race in shaping the biopolitical makeup of a country's population and correctly identifies racial biopolitics as a prevalent concern at the conference. This concern clearly shaped the positions of participating nations, though many concealed their racial motivations by invoking economic factors and "higher circumstances." This mentality as well as Britain's shutting off its mandate Palestine to Jewish migrants for fear of exacerbating tensions between Arabs and Jews lead Rosenberg to conclude that Jews are not assimilable—they must be kept unto themselves and placed in territories not yet settled by Europeans. Arguing that, prior to the emergence of Palestine as a candidate for resettlement, "representatives of the anti-Jewish fight" had considered Uganda and Madagascar as options, he urges that a search for a "large African territory" be resumed.[22] None of these ideas would materialize. Berlin's approach vacillated between trying to reach an agreement with Great Britain for the large-scale resettlement of German Jews (the "Schacht plan")[23] and making vague threats about developing its own ways of handling the Jews in case such an agreement could not be reached. Nonetheless, Rosenberg's comments foreground the racial logic of Western democracies' biopolitics of immigration and the link between racism and colonialism. That NS commentators would read the failure of Évian as vindication of Germany's politics is not surprising. But that Germany's press could effectively interpret Western democracies' positions on the resettlement of Europe's Jews as a mirror image of the NS State's own racist and colonialist logic prompts us to revisit Évian in greater detail.

Rereading Évian

Nearly all countries present at Évian claimed that their domestic infrastructures were unable to absorb substantial numbers of migrants. The problem was cast as one of "higher circumstances." In fact, it was racially driven biopolitics and colonialism that caused Évian's failure. Different nations' reasoning reflects different facets of colonialism. Most European countries advocated resettlement outside the continent. France's representative argued that Britain's dominions and the Americas ought to shoulder the lion's share of migrants. He added that, having owed their expansion to the influx of emigrants, refugees, and exiles from Europe for centuries, these "new worlds" should absorb the new wave of refugees by virtue of what, in his words, functioned according to "the logic of world history, by a kind of reversion of the century-old trend."[24] Belgium, Sweden, Denmark, and Holland made similar claims, with Belgium alluding to "certain overseas territories,"[25] Sweden suggesting that Jewish emigration be directed to "countries outside of Europe," and Denmark appealing to "the help of other continents."[26] Holland argued that the tropical location of its overseas territories left "migration of white people for settlement [with] little hope of success."[27] Belgium's representative made no mention of his country's overseas territories Belgian Congo and Ruanda-Urundi as possibile settlements. Lord Winterton, the representative of Britain, after listing many caveats to Britain's ability to make its colonies available for resettlement, announced that his government was exploring the feasibility of limited settlement in certain East African territories.[28] Several representatives found Winterton's remarks encouraging. Ireland suggested that the ability to facilitate a large-scale resettlement lay entirely with Europe's colonial powers.[29]

Winterton's comments offer insights not only into the logic of colonialism proper, but also into how this logic shaped Europe's highly ambivalent and historically contradictory relationship to its Jews. He does not posit the colony as a place of complete otherness. In fact, he deems it to be consistent with the "motherland" regarding the socioeconomic obstacles to Jewish settlement, only that these "are further complicated by considerations of climate, of race and of political development. Many overseas territories are already overcrowded, others are wholly or partially unsuitable for European settlement, while in others again local and political conditions hinder or prevent any considerable immigration."[30] For Europe's Jews to settle in sub-Saharan Africa would have required adjustment, though none so stark as to have presented a categorical deterrence.[31] Winterton's caveat is disingenuous. With regard to the overcrowding of or adverse political conditions in overseas territories, however, Winterton speaks from experience. For the native populations of Europe's colonies to witness non-consensual settlement of Europeans within their own territories would present but further evidence of their own disenfranchisement by the colonizer. The main precedent in this regard is the 1917 Balfour Declaration by which Britain officially declared its support for the establishment of a Jewish state in Palestine, then a region of the Ottoman Empire (with which Britain was at war) and home to a small Jewish population. In discussing the Declaration, the British cabinet had not invited input from Palestinians. Although the Declaration pledged to protect "the civil and religious rights of non-Jewish communities in Palestine," it was overwhelmingly opposed by Palestine's Christians and Muslims. Edward Said has characterized the Balfour Declaration as having been made: "(a) by a European power, (b) about a non-European territory, (c) in a flat disregard of both the presence and the wishes of the native majority resident in that territory, and (d) [having assumed] the form of a promise about this same territory to another foreign group, so that this foreign group might, quite literally, *make* this territory a national home of the Jewish people."[32]

Winterton's caveats reveal the cageyness and the protective mentality of Europe's colonial powers toward their colonies, protectorates, and mandates. During World War I, Britain laid the groundwork for large-scale Jewish resettlement in Palestine. Now, it sought to contain the fallout from this policy for the sake of keeping peace in the region. In doing so, Britain assumed the same colonialist attitude over its mandate as over its African colonies. Just as the 1917 Balfour Declaration "take[s] for granted the higher right of a colonial power to dispose of a territory as it saw fit,"[33] Winterton's comments at Évian show that he views the colony as a replica of the colonizer, a sort of backyard that merits the same shielding from outsiders as does the "motherland." The same colonialist logic that moved Britian in the 1910s to create a home for Europe's Jews in Palestine now made it disinclined to address the mortal danger in which Europe's Jews found themselves. Whereas climate, race, and politics had posed no deterrent for the English to colonize half the world in the nineteenth century, when it came to Jewish resettlement, those factors suddenly compelled the Empire to consider the peace of its colonized populations and the health and well-being of the prospective Jewish settlers (for whom most standards of safety in Germany were rapidly eroding). To Jews, the logic of Winterton's reasoning, if read against the groundswell of racial antisemitism in Europe, presented itself as follows: In the eyes of the European nations present at Évian, Europe's Jews were neither white enough nor European enough to stay in Europe, but neither were they black enough to resettle in Africa.

Winterton fails to acknowledge another well-known problem: migration between England and its dominions Australia and New Zealand had been negatively affected by demographic changes. Those were reported in a document to which Winterton would have been privy, a report by Britain's Oversea Settlement Board, which was published in May 1938 and presented by the Secretary of State for Dominion Affairs to the British Parliament the following month, directly ahead of the Évian conference. Its statistics show reverse migration from the dominions to the UK triggered by Britain's post-Depression recovery and improvement of social benefits and services. But while reverse migration was leaving Australia and New Zealand underpopulated and overaged, it was, as the report finds, not significant enough to counter the more dramatic aging of the British.[34] The report, in other words, shows that both Britain and its dominions were in need of fresh migrants.

While acknowledging that the dominions' agricultural infrastructure struggled to absorb migrants, the report emphasizes that with the help of their secondary industries the dominions could—and should—support a population substantially larger than at present, not the least to strengthen their defenses during war.[35] Acknowledging that new migrants "from the countries from which their stocks have been drawn," may be hard to come by,[36] the report recommends to supplement "the growth of British stock in the Dominions . . . by a carefully regulated flow of other immigrants of assimilable types."[37] The report remains silent on the criteria for assimilability. Western culture had long stereotyped Jews as feigning assimilability for opportunistic reasons. At Évian, opinions about what constitutes assimilability varied. The proceedings show that many, though not all, nations invoked racial criteria only indirectly, asking instead whether merchants, doctors, and teachers could be turned into farmers. One exception was Australia. Using racist-colonialist logic and blithely disavowing Australia's treatment of its Aborigines, its representative, Lt. Col. T. C. White, stated that "as we have no real racial problem, we are not desirous of importing one by encouraging any scheme of large-scale foreign migration."[38]

Speaking directly after White, Canada's representative, Hume Wrong, took advantage of White's speech, stating he had "nothing much to add to what has already been said."[39] Canada's immigration policy in the 1930s was far more restrictive than that of the US, but was motivated by similar factors, including fear among the public that refugees would create an economic liability and slow the country's recovery from the Great Depression. Seeking to differentiate Canada's policies from those of the US, Wrong added that Canada has no immigration quotas and that exceptions had been made only for "certain classes of agriculturalists and near relatives of those already in Canada, exceptions which do not include many political refugees."[40] Family-based immigration is also recommended by the Oversea Settlement Board, which notably terms the practice "Settlement by 'Infiltration.'"[41] The notion of a stealth accrual of immigrants based on kinship clearly shows that Australia and Canada sought to control immigration for the purpose of maintaining racial purity. Further, Canada's Prime Minister Mackenzie King shared US President Roosevelt's personal fear that accepting Jewish refugees would jeopardize the odds of getting reelected. Quebec posed a particular problem for King. The province was rife with anxiety that Jewish settlers would bring it under the influence of monetary and cultural internationalism—specifically, that Jews would speak English rather than French.[42] There was considerable anti-Jewish sentiment among the population and the government. Frederick Blair, the director of Canada's immigration branch, was a known antisemite.[43]

Although statistics indicated underpopulated territories' need for migrants, Europe's colonial powers and their dominions were largely unwilling to grant Jewish resettlement within those spaces. But what about the other large group of nations present at Évian, the seventeen Latin American nations—Brazil, Chile, Argentina, Uruguay, Paraguay, Peru, Venezuela, Colombia, Mexico, Ecuador, Nicaragua, Honduras, Costa Rica, Panama, Haiti, Cuba, and the Dominican Republic? Most made migration contingent on migrants' qualifications and training and their ability to bring monetary assets with them. Beyond these factors, representatives argued that their nations' fragile infrastructures and vulnerable economies as well as the mandate not to disturb given socio-demographic makeups placed tight limits on migration. As we'll see below, such claims are only partially valid and, at the very least, beg wider contextualization.

Acknowledgment of Latin America's history of colonial and neocolonial exploitation has spared the subcontinent from the same degree of negative historical judgment leveled at Europe for not doing more to save Europe's Jews. The impression persists that Latin American nations, euphemistically labeled "young countries" by the Chilean representative at Évian, had legitimate reasons to stem an influx of migrants. But the root cause for their economic fragility—their dependency on Europe and the US—was something neither they nor other nations at Évian were willing to acknowledge. In contrast to Europe's colonial territories in Africa and Asia, many Latin American countries had gained independence, while others had never been officially colonized. Their colonization was economic, consisting of a circle of exchange in which Europe and the US exploited Latin America's natural resources without reinvesting into national infrastructures. As a result, these remained just as underdeveloped as the populations they were meant to serve. Revenue was immediately siphoned off by local and regional oligarchs, who ruled over their natural and labor resources remotely, spending most of their time and money in Europe and the US. As Eduardo Galeano axiomatically put it, "Latin America is the region of open veins. Everything, from the discovery until our times, has always been transmuted into European—or later United States—capital, and as such has accumulated in distant centers of power. . . . The well-being of our dominating classes—dominating inwardly, dominated from outside—is the curse of our multitudes condemned to exist as beasts of burden."[44] Thus, it is not the populations of Argentina, Mexico, or Brazil that deserve historical judgment, but rather their neocolonial ruling elites, whose positions closely aligned with those of the US and Europe.

At Évian, neocolonialism informed the positions of Latin American representatives in two ways. First, many were flattered that First World powers had called them to the negotiating table. They perceived the invitation as a gain in national prestige rather than as Roosevelt's and Europe's attempt to foist the bulk of the migrants onto them.[45] The representatives of Costa Rica, Honduras, Nicaragua, and Panama even termed their conference invitation an accreditation.[46] Second, when hailed to the table of world politics, Latin American diplomats tended to depoliticize the migrant crisis. They narrowly focused on its humanitarian rather than its biopolitical dimension and downplayed or disavowed the fact that their countries' perceived economic obstacles to accepting migrants owed to Europe's and the US's neocolonial stranglehold over them. For instance, Colombian representative J. M. Yepes prides himself on Colombia being the oldest constitutional nation in Latin America but does not mention the exploitative role of the country's plantation and mining oligarchy. Yepes applauds Roosevelt's "humanitarian and Christian feelings" without saying a word about the history of US domination over Colombia, such as when the US took control of Colombia's Panama Canal zone without the consent of Colombia's congress.[47] Argentina's delegate, Tomas A. Le Breton, states that the country has little need for labor, as its livestock agriculture is not labor intensive and its industry is of a moderate scale. Unsurprisingly, he skips over the reason for this—the parasitical role of domestic oligarchies of European origin, dynasties which President Juan Perón failed to challenge and which deliberately kept the country in a state of placid backwardness that suited their personal economic needs.[48]

In his speech, Le Breton cites Argentina's past acceptance of Jewish migrants as evidence of his country's lack of prejudices but openly admits to biopolitical factors shaping Argentina's new migration policy. He identifies underpopulation as a factor in accepting immigrants ("to govern is to populate"), but adds that his government prefers agricultural workers. He does not explicitly exclude Jewish migrants but emphasizes that, for Argentina, resettlement comes down to a migrant's willingness to assimilate.[49] Uruguay, Brazil, and Venezuela used a similar logic at Évian, while seeking to dispel any suspicion that their motivations were rooted in racial antisemitism. Brazil's representative, Hélio Lobo, voices concerns that immigration from Eastern Europe and Asia has been surpassing Latin immigration. Subtly reinforcing his bias against Eastern European Jews, he states that before World War I, Germans had the fourth highest contingent of immigrants to Brazil "with the happiest of results for the country."[50] This reference to Germans hints at Brazil's desire to counter-balance the racial legacy of having been the biggest market of African slaves in the Americas. Lobo mentions Brazil's efforts to stabilize its fluctuating labor market but does not say that the problem is rooted in the vulnerability of the country's large coffee and cotton monocultures (established by or on behalf of European and US importers) to the vagaries of the European and US commodities markets.

Brazil was not alone in voicing concerns that immigration may impact a country's racial mix and undermine its government's biopolitical shaping of its population—although few countries admitted that such a position constituted a racial othering of the Jews. (Not even Australia acknowledged that such racial othering was fueled by and in turn supported Nazi ideology and politics.) Venezuela's delegate, Carlos Aristimuño Coll, states that his country is looking for agricultural laborers but is operating under the mandate to "maintain the demographic equilibrium essential to racial diversity."[51] While Aristimuño Coll is clear that Venezuela wants to biopolitically control its populace, he is less clear about how to accomplish that and where, for that matter, one would have to place Jews on the racial spectrum. At Évian, the criteria for what constitutes race, ethnicity, and cultural heritage were neither clearly defined nor did the participating nations seem to use one and the same definition of race.

The views expressed by Peru's representative, Francisco García Calderón Rey, further illustrate this. He suggest that racial diversity is desirable as long as it exists under the umbrella of Hispanic racial hegemony: "The great Spanish race, whose chivalry and heroism you all know, mingled with the Indians in an unprecedented fashion which has produced an extraordinary mixture of races . . . and constitutes the original and dramatic feature of our history."[52] García Calderón's wording reflects how economic interests of Latin America's oligarchies were shaped by racism and neocolonialism even when their approaches included certain progressive elements. He announces several initiatives to improve Peru's infrastructure, including the "incorporation of the Indian into the national civilisation, the formation of a middle class, [and] the creation of small landowners who, as in France, will furnish a firm basis for democracy if we arrest the excessive growth of capital."[53] At the same time, he adamantly advocates for his country's seeking to maintain "the Spanish nucleus which is the essential factor in our social and political formation and which is Catholic and Latin."[54] Typical of neocolonial governments, the agenda of national economic uplift, anticolonial on one level, is still shaped by a Eurocentric racism that reproduces colonialism's very mentality and practices.

The same holds for the Dominican Republic, except that the latter regarded Jews as white and thus similar to how Brazil regarded non-Jewish Germans—that is, as an instrument of racial biopolitics. Its delegate, Virgilio Trujillo Molina, states that his government is prepared to grant "special advantageous concessions to Austrian and German exiles."[55] His country would provide "for colonisation purposes . . . large areas of fertile, well-irrigated land, excellent roads and a police force which preserves absolute order." In addition to the Department of Agriculture giving colonists seed and technical advice, the government would also "grant special conditions to professional men immigrating who, as recognized scientists, would be able through their teaching to render valuable service to their Dominican colleagues." When speaking before Évian's Technical Sub-Committee, Trujillo Molina states he would admit 10,000 migrants.[56] The only nation willing to accept such a large number of migrants (and to name a concrete figure), the Dominican Republic did so in the hope of shifting its racial balance from black to white.[57] Thus, while some Latin American nations deemed Jews insufficiently white, others seized on their Caucasian origins to "whiten" their population.

Stipulating that Jews bring their own assets caused some delegates to allude at least indirectly to the effects of neocolonialism on their countries. Mexico's representative, Primo Villa Michel, explains that, while Mexico had welcomed political refugees, immigrants were now seen as an obstacle to the country's economic and social reforms. Part of the Mexican Revolution, these reforms included the redistribution of land to the rural population who was "formerly in a state of serfdom." His government, Villa Michel explains, "is endeavouring, within the limited framework of our embryo industrial system, to raise to a level worthy of being called civilized our workers' standard of life."[58] Cuba's representative, Juan Antiga Escobar, characterizes Cuba as "an essentially agricultural nation, dependent almost exclusively on one single product—sugar."[59] He explains that, as the world price of sugar has dropped so low that it barely covers the cost of production, Cuba has curtailed production and laid off 50,000 foreign workers, who remain in Cuba at government expense.[60] Cuba did not give a public declaration at Évian. Antiga Escobar made his comments before the Technical Sub-Committee, whose records were not included in the published proceedings, because the US hoped that confidentiality would encourage nations to unofficially increase their resources for resettlement.[61] Mexican land reform and Cuban monoculture are signs of neocolonialism. Yet both countries' delegates gloss over neocolonialism's root cause, foreign domination. The dominators, as it were, all sat at the table at Évian.

Whether posing an actual problem or functioning as an alibi for protecting other interests, Latin America's polarized socio-demographic structures—composed of landowners and peasants, of mine owners and miners, and, more generally, of a tiny social elite and the disenfranchised masses—was the main obstacle to middle-European Jews emigrating to the subcontinent. Its nations were ambivalent toward Jewish professionals and intellectuals. Peru's delegate states that, having received German professors, scientists, and intellectuals in the past, Peru knows that "Jewish influence, like leaven or ferment, is of value to all nations."[62] Though intended as compliments on one level, words like "leaven" and "ferment" also invoke the perceived role of Jews as political subversives. Technical experts and agriculturists, in the delegate's view, are acceptable, but traders and workmen might disturb the economic system and doctors and lawyers might even generate an intellectual proletariat. For Peru and other Latin American countries, any change to national demographics harbored threats to the quasi-feudalist order that was colonialism's legacy and in which many governments remained invested.

Attempts at classifying Jews incurred a blurring of bio-racial, ethnic, religious, and cultural features—categories that, even if they could be disentangled, always tended to produce the most unwanted legal and political category of a minority in need of protection. Colombia, in a confidential statement to the Technical Sub-Committee, emphasized that any acceptance of Jewish refugees could proceed strictly on humanitarian grounds: "[The government rejects the] impossibility of introducing into American law the idea of racial minorities. . . . It would refuse to accept anything which might be taken as establishing a precedent favourable to the introduction into America of the minorities system which is and must remain the exclusive property of the Old Continent."[63]

Évian did indeed constitute a moral and political disaster by failing to save Europe's Jews from the Nazis. Yet the positions of both the so-called first-world nations and the developing countries reveal that this failure owed less to timidity, complacency, ignorance, or callousness than to shrewd biopolitical calculations. Many nations at Évian cited the world economic crisis as a major reason for their restrictions on migration. Historians have failed to identify this reasoning for what it was—a cover for racial biopolitics. As we have seen, racism and colonialism shaped both the logic of antisemitic expulsion and of asylum withheld, and it did so in three ways: (1) Colonialism, among other factors, informed Nazi Germany's racialization of Jews in order to denationalize them as an inferior tribe, which, after having been released from Germany for a fee, had to be relocated to a non-European territory deemed compatible with Jewish life in its perceived "primitivism"; (2) but colonialist thinking also shaped the reasoning that Jewish resettlement must not negatively impact Europe's own colonies—at Évian, Europe's colonial powers showed more concern for the socio-demographic equilibrium and well-being of their colonial populations than when they first colonized those territories; (3) colonialism and neocolonialism shaped the attitudes of the Latin American states at Évian. Politically sovereign yet economically dependent on Europe and the US, they regarded the conference as a world stage. They eagerly presented themselves on a par with the global north by claiming, in a falsely universalizing move, that their restriction on immigration owed to similar exigencies as those plaguing Europe and North America. Even when admitting that their countries were less industrialized than Europe and the US, delegates refused to acknowledge that they were run by quasi-feudalist elites, whose reign Jewish migrants could threaten by disturbing demographic and political structures.

The impact of colonialism, racism, and racially driven biopolitics does not change the fact that Évian was also a profoundly moral failure. Nor does hindsight consideration of those factors in any way relativize the Holocaust or occlude the specificity of its barbarism. At the same time, antisemitic persecution must be reassessed in its intersection with other historical phenomena. These include the colonization of numerous territories and countries and the enslavement and exploitation of whole peoples. The task of comparing different genocides is complex and delicate. Yet such comparisons do not have to amount to establishing a ranking, something that should be avoided at all cost. Nothing could be further from the intention of the present study. If the legacy of the Holocaust obliges us to refine our analyses of racial, religious, and political persecution, we must concurrently hone our understanding of the complex interplay of seemingly unconnected world historical and geopolitical pogroms. Ignorance of this interplay has not only bred fallacious hindsight assessments of the Holocaust and its causes. It was already in evidence at Évian in 1938. As the failed negotiations between the thirty-two conference participants showed, the unwillingness of nations to look beyond their own domains and the inability to view the migrant crisis in broader economic and geopolitical contexts bred the lamentable conviction that saving the lives of a whole people should first and foremost be the work of others.

On Friday, July 15, 1938, the chairman of the Intergovernmental Committee on Refugees, Myron C. Taylor, closed the conference with remarks that struck a decidedly positive tone (see fig. 1.2). He notes that the conference has more than fulfilled its agenda of exploring initial steps to facilitate the settlement of political refugees from Germany and Austria and of setting up an administrative machinery for that purpose: "We have done more. We have heard from the Governments of refuge and settlement confidential statements which hold out prospects for an increased reception of refugees within the framework of existing immigration laws and practices."[64] That none of those confidential statements, with the exception of that from the Dominican Republic, offered specific acceptance figures or a concrete plan of action for the rescue of Germany's and Austria's Jews did not dim Taylor's outlook. It did not take the Nazi press's cynical coverage

Figure 1.2. Myron C. Taylor addresses the International Conference on Refugees at Évian-les-Bains. *Source:* Courtesy of United States Holocaust Memorial Museum.

of the conference to make clear that Taylor's statement embellished what in reality was an extremely dire situation for those who were the conference's subject. If anything, Évian furnished the Nazis with official proof for their claim that no one wanted the Jews.

Nonetheless, in a letter he sent to Taylor in November, 1938, four months after the conference and mere weeks after the November pogrom, President Roosevelt displayed the same optimism with which Taylor had closed the conference. Roosevelt took Nazi Germany's stepped-up persecution of its Jewish population and its lack of cooperation with Western democracies as a signal that "the work of the committee must not only be continued but must be intensified to solve the problem without such cooperation."[65] Maintaining Taylor's optimism, Roosevelt notes that "there are many parts of the world which could accept substantial numbers of these people without injury to their economic or demographic organisms."[66] Roosevelt also believed, however, that the US should not be counted among those nations:

> This Government is already accepting involuntary emigrants to the fullest extent permitted by law. I do not believe it either desirable or practicable to recommend any change in the quota provisions of our immigration laws. You are authorized to make a public statement that this Government can, under its existing laws, accept annually 27,370 persons from Germany. . . . While this Government is thus apparently doing as much, if not more, toward a solution of the problem than any other Government, you may add that it is nevertheless continuing to study actively any other possible means by which it might be able to contribute further toward a solution.[67]

Roosevelt believed that maintaining its annual quota of 27,370 immigrants from Germany and Austria entitled the US to sit back and observe how other nations at Évian might follow suit. Having initiated the meeting as the nation with the largest annual acceptance rate of migrants was sufficient proof, in Roosevelt's eyes, that the US had fulfilled its responsibilities. But for the president to use his country's quota as proof that the US was, as his letter put it, "already accepting involuntary emigrants to the fullest extent permitted by law"[68] rested on a de facto suspension of the categories "voluntary/involuntary." The quota Roosevelt cites had been established for traditional types of immigrants, people who had not been exiled from their home country and who, in most cases, had carried a passport or some comparable travel document. All the US intended to do to address the refugee crisis was to take its existing quota and redesignate it for refugees—in other words, the State Department allowed the quota to be filled by whoever from Germany and Austria had their immigration number come due, no matter whether this was a political refugee or someone intending to leave Germany for non-political reasons. The US had no intention of creating a separate visa for those in need of asylum—which was precisely the process most other nations at Évian were faced with establishing if they, as non-immigrant countries, wanted to accept and nationalize foreigners. In this sense, the US certainly did not go "the extra mile" it expected other countries to go. By subsuming the category of involuntary migrant under the traditional one of voluntary migrant, the US did two things: It cemented its leading status among all nations willing to accept migrants from Germany and Austria; at the same time, it suspended any effort to do domestically what Roosevelt instructed Taylor to do to engage the international community, namely to "create the proper spirit in the countries of potential settlement." It was precisely this spirit that, as Roosevelt knew all too well, was lacking in the US. He was keenly aware that the country's abiding economic problems and a group of conservative, nativist politicians in Washington made it politically risky for him to increase immigration quotas or create new ones for refugees.

In urging Taylor to make other countries understand that the issue of settlement "is humanitarian in its urgency but from which they can draw ultimate practical benefit,"[69] Roosevelt signaled that for him any distinction between voluntary and involuntary migration had little meaning. His view was far from exceptional. The blurring of the voluntary and the involuntary, of refugee and traditional migrant (the latter also including the related category of tourist), was what defined Jewish migration in the late 1930s. This conceptual fluidity and its juridical and bureaucratic implications owed to the fact that the expulsion of Jews from Germany had been a gradual process. Marking Jews with the Star of David and a "J" in their passports were steps toward escalating the "final solution." That moment had been preceded by a decade-long process during which, as mentioned, the NS State gradually radicalized existing legislature, which it then implemented through an established bureaucracy and which it executed through existing infrastructures, logistics, and practices of incarceration and deportation. When a majority of Jews nonetheless decided not to emigrate voluntarily despite Nazi persecution, NS leadership, by 1937, began to consider schemes of mass deportation to other countries and continents.

The Repercussions of Évian and the Emergence of the "Death Ships"

During the late 1930s, the NS State began recruiting shipping lines such as HAPAG to assist in broader, if tentative and ultimately incoherent, schemes of expulsion, which, especially after the November 1938 pogrom, increasingly turned Jews into involuntary migrants. But before the war, the NS government, with a few notable exceptions, did not round up Jews in large numbers and dump them outside of Germany's borders.[70] Jews were coerced to leave the country on their own through existing means of travel. Many purchased train tickets and booked passage on ships or gave shipping lines deposits for future travel. Many hoped to find temporary respite in transit countries. As is well known, a large number of German Jews had immigration numbers for the US, which, however, did not come due (that is, they would not translate into permission to immigrate) until it was too late. Possession of those numbers gave their holders the prospect of future statehood and raised their hopes of winning temporary stay in transit countries. But acceptance of that status was far from certain. The outcome was existential, for it turned stateless travelers into either migrants or outcasts. Some were expelled even after having been admitted to a transit country.

While Germany's Jews shared one fate—the loss of citizens' rights—their prospects of finding a new host country greatly varied. Many had left Germany on passenger ships of various sizes that traveled on regular routes to the Americas. Often, those ships also carried numerous other passengers who, in contrast to the Jewish migrants, were free citizens. Refugees and free citizens traveling side by side compounded the confusion between voluntary and involuntary migration. The occluding effect of the umbrella term "emigrant" did not escape intellectuals. In 1937, Bertold Brecht, whose mother was

Protestant and whose father Catholic and whose books were burned after he left Nazi Germany in February 1933, wrote the poem "On the Term Emigrants," which criticizes the obfuscation of the distinction between emigration and exile. The poem starts by proclaiming that its author always thought the term "emigrants" was a misnomer. His kind did not freely choose a different country, nor did they ever intend the country that accepted them to be their final destination. It was only an exile. The truth, Brecht concludes, is that they were forced to flee: "We are expellees, banished."[71]

Whether and on what terms foreign countries would grant entry to Jewish migrants was contingent on rapidly shifting asylum and immigration laws. There were several kinds of entry permits—immigration visa, tourist visa, or transit visa—and they could be canceled any step of the way: In December 1938, migrants about to leave Germany on the liner *Campana* had their visas canceled by their country of destination, Paraguay, immediately *before* departure.[72] In June 1939, the passengers of the *St. Louis* learned of their rejection by Cuba *after* their arrival in Havana. The news of Cuba's rejection of the *St. Louis* changed the fates of the 200 passengers on the HAPAG ship *Orinoco* during their trip. Likewise en route to Cuba, *Orinoco* got called back from Antwerp to Germany after it became clear that Cuba no longer accepted German Jews carrying tourist visas.[73]

Other migrants never had any prospect of legal entry. They usually left Germany in the dead of night and found themselves crossing borders illegally on foot or traveling on small, decrepit cargo ships toward some coast, often that of Palestine, where they would be set into life boats, hoping to reach shore undetected by border patrol. But no matter the scenario, all migrants shared in one and the same overarching reality: After Germany had imposed its home-made refugee crisis onto Western democracies, the latter sought to shield their borders and those of their colonies, protectorates, and mandates from what international organizations termed the "uncontrolled dumping of migrants." This period, which lasted approximately from 1938 to 1941, was the period of the "death ships," the refugee ships that sailed international waters with a cargo of outcasts.

On June 30, 1939, the American journalist H. R. Knickerbocker published an article in the (at that time) left-wing French newspaper *L'Oeuvre*, titled "The Wandering Jews." In it he speaks of "ten thousand helpless, abandoned Jews, ten thousand human beings worth nothing, ten thousand wandering Jews without visa and money" who were "driven away like animals onto a no man's land, a no man's sea."[74] Some camped out in a no man's land between Germany and its neighboring countries. Knickerbocker characterizes them as "black slaves." Others were hoarded onto "Levantine freighters that cruise off the coast of Palestine without being able to discharge their desperate cargo on the shores of the Promised Land."[75] The article goes on to describe refugees living half-starved and clad in rags on deserted islands and in secluded bays in the Aegean. "In the ports of the Black Sea they wait in fear in the hope that a ship may take them aboard. From Cuba to Brazil, from Hamburg to Shanghai they search the globe for a place where they may come ashore. Endlessly, the ships with Jewish passengers are crisscrossing the world's oceans. There is no country they did not approach for asylum. One thousand of them even spent a full three months aboard a ship."[76] Readers learn that, according to an investigation, in the two months prior to Knickerbocker's writing, eighteen transatlantic ships with 5,627 Jewish refugees were forced to return home after failing to find a port of disembarkation.[77] The article explains that the label "illegal," which the refugees carry, simply means that they are poor. "If they had money, they could have obtained valid papers. They *used to* have money. But they were bulldozed by the Nazis and have nothing left."[78] Many refugees, Knickerbocker goes on to say, were being robbed a second time—that is, by the captains and crew of the ships on which they found themselves traveling. He references Britain's Colonial Secretary Malcolm MacDonald, who had bitterly complained about the greedy shipping agents and captains plundering the refugees they had on board and charging "first class transatlantic fares for a place on deck of their Mediterranean freighters." Other reports spoke of passengers who could obtain food and drinking water from their captain only by giving him their jewelry and all their money, which made them arrive at their destination penniless.[79]

Between April and June, 1939, the New York–based German Jewish newspaper *Aufbau* devoted a series of articles to refugee ships. The first was titled "Die Totenschiffe Fahren" (The death ships are sailing).[80] It mentions that German newsreels had recently shown Jewish refugees disembarking in Shanghai and, after receiving food in emergency barracks, being carted off on trucks to an unknown destination. But, so the article continues, "at least these Jews were on dry land. At least they did not share the darkness that shrouds the refugee ships that nowadays cross the oceans, ghost ships, death ships, Flying Dutchmen of 1939."[81] The article mentions the steamer *Königstein*, which reached Venezuela with 780 refugees after a long voyage, during which it was turned away by Trinidad and British Guyana. It also mentions two other ships, the glamorous Italian Liner *Conte Grande*, which went to South America carrying among its passengers Jewish refugees who were blocked from disembarking in Argentina and finally allowed to land in Uruguay, and a Greek freighter, which had left the Baltic port of Danzig (Gdansk) with over 500 refugees who lacked travel documents.[82] Knickerbocker, too, writes about this ship. He reports that its name was *Agios Nicolaos* and that its captain had led his passengers to believe that he would organize immigration visas for them for Palestine. After being turned away from Palestinian shores by the coast guard, who shot one passenger dead, the freighter went on a four-week-long voyage through the Aegean and then on to Romania, where it was also turned away.[83]

Knickerbocker devotes a separate section in his article to the plight of Greek cargo ships with refugees.[84] Among them was the *Astir*, which on April 6 sailed to Palestine with 641 "Illegals" and, having been rejected there, was forced to anchor off the coast, its passengers languishing without provisions. Another Greek ship, the *Marmora*, left a Romanian Black Sea port with over 500 refugees for Palestine and had not been seen at the time of Knickerbocker's reporting. The tiny freighter *Assimi* carried 320 passengers in its cargo holds and successfully reached Palestine, but after its passengers had landed, they were detected and forced back onto the ship. Something similar happened to the 182 passengers of the Greek freighter *Panagiya Correstrio* who were found by British authorities near Tel Aviv. After being forced back onto the ship, they thought of a way to obtain internment on land by making a British patrol witness them throwing all their provisions overboard. The Romanian steamer *Sandu* left the Black Sea port of Constanța with 269 refugees for Palestine. After being rejected there, it returned its passengers to their port of departure, only to learn that Romania now also prohibited disembarkation.

The ships that traveled from Europe to South America tended to be larger than the Mediterranean and Black Sea freighters.[85] Many were prominent ocean liners or sizable passenger-cargo ships and, as such, were well maintained and equipped for transporting passengers.

Yet the situation of the refugees they carried—mostly as part of a larger passenger load, though in a few notable cases by way of exclusive charter—was no less dire. The Canadian newspaper *Globe and Mail* reported the story of the *Monte Olivia*, a liner owned by the Hamburg-South America Steamship Company (Hamburg Süd) that, since the mid-1920s, had serviced the regular Hamburg–South America route. In May 1939, the ship carried among its passengers seventy-eight Jewish refugees who were refused entry into Chile, Paraguay, and Argentina.[86] Knickerbocker's article for *L'Oeuvre* mentions similar refugee dramas on the liners *Cap Norte*, *General St. Martin*, *General Artigas*, and *Flandre*, which unsuccessfully tried to land refugees at Buenos Aires, Montevideo, and other South American ports.

The most comprehensive report on refugee ships came from the Social Democratic Party of Germany in their Germany Report for July 1939. While it corroborates and amends much of the data reported by Knickerbocker and *Aufbau*, its circulation was limited by the fact that it was published in exile in Paris.[87] The report included the year's most high-profile cases of refugee ships. In addition to the *St. Louis*, the report mentions two ships whose fates intersected with that of the *St. Louis*. One was the already mentioned *Orinoco*, which, upon leaving Antwerp with 200 Jews, was ordered to return to Germany after news of Cuba's rejection of the *St. Louis* went public;[88] the other was the French liner *Flandre*, which, carrying 104 migrants, tried to beat the *St. Louis* to Havana to increase its odds of disembarking its passengers. The report fails to mention a third ship, the British liner *Orduña*, which, like *Flandre*, reached Cuba shortly after the *St. Louis* and, like the *St. Louis*, was allowed to disembark a small number of migrants with landing permits before being turned away with seventy-eight migrants remaining on board.[89] SOPADE's account leaves out the ships of Aliyah Bet, the clandestine Jewish immigration movement that ran numerous ships, such as the *Parita* (see fig. 1.3) between the Black Sea and the coasts of Palestine, Syria, and Lebanon.[90] Refugee ships continued to sail into the early years of the war.[91]

The *St. Louis* was but one among many ships carrying Jewish migrants on harrowing voyages across the world's oceans. While the international press reported on several of these cases, the *St. Louis* received the most attention. Chapter 4 discusses this aspect in detail. For now, we need to understand how the *St. Louis* is both typical and atypical of Jewish seaborne migration prior to World War II. On one

Figure 1.3. Aliyah Bet refugee ship *Parita* attempting to disembark "illegal" refugees. *Source:* Stiftung Preußischer Kulturbesitz/Art Resource. Used with permission.

level, the ship's voyage is exemplary of the treatment of most Jewish seaborne refugees by the NS State, the operators of the ships they traveled on, the ships' countries of destination, and the international community. On another level, the size of the *St. Louis*, her prominence and popularity in the international cruise market, and the fact that her refugee load was the largest on record—large enough to merit an exclusive charter—made her an exception. The publicized drama of the *St. Louis* passengers eclipsed the stories of many other refugee ships or made them pale in comparison.

In attributing their last-minute asylum in Europe to the visibility of the *St. Louis* and the worldwide attention her passengers garnered with their suicide threats, Knickerbocker foregrounds the humanitarian dimension of their story.[92] But *Aufbau*, which published several articles specifically related to the *St. Louis* as part of their broader coverage of the Jewish refugee crisis, hones in on a different aspect. In the paper's June 15 edition, the prominent lyricist and director of stage and film, Berthold Viertel, published a poem titled "Das Schiff von Cuba" (The Cuban ship). Its first stanza frames the *St. Louis* case as one fully determined by biopolitics. He writes of a ship laden with human cargo, which it peddles to the coasts like a panhandler offering his wares. Who covets those refugees?, he asks. Where is the land that buys, rents, or trades humans? Where will a port open up, the second stanza asks, to receive the one thousand exiles who, coming from the world of merchants and minions, have boarded and now huddle in the cabins?[93]

Aufbau had already compared seabound refugees to cargo in two articles prior to the *St. Louis* incident. One article, titled "Dr. Paul Kl.: Refugees," compares the status of Jewish exiles to that of medieval scoundrels, who, after having been chased from their home country, received the status of "vogelfrei"—a term which literally means "free as a bird" but with the negative connotation that anyone is free to kill it with impunity.[94] The already mentioned article "Die Totenschiffe Fahren" (The death ships are sailing), which compares Jewish refugee ships to ghost ships, mentions that the Jewish death ships have a historical precedent, the Spanish Inquisition, except that in those days, as the article explains, some coasts, especially those of Holland and Turkey, were more welcoming.[95] The *St. Louis*'s arrival in Antwerp occasioned several more articles in *Aufbau* that characterize migrants as a subhuman, tradable biomass that gets stored in warehouse-like internment facilities. One article reminds readers that, while the passengers of the "ship of misery" have been spared a return to Germany, the facts remain unchanged: The Jewish human merchandise, wanted nowhere, has been deposited in European camps. This was not where the passengers wanted to go and neither do they know how to leave again from there.[96] The most comprehensive framing in these terms can be found in a lengthy article titled "Vergässe ich Deiner Je, St. Louis . . ." (If I ever forget you, *St. Louis* . . .). It labels the ship a death ship, a ship of exiles, a cradle of despair, and an object of blackmail and barter.[97]

The media's coverage of Jewish migration indicates that refugee ships were widely discussed by the German-language Jewish press and, to a lesser extent, by the international press even before the *St. Louis* incident. The term "death ships" seems to have resonated with a transnational readership. In this light, the *St. Louis* voyage may not have been quite such big news. To most Jews, but also to many non-Jews, it represented the culmination of the refugee ship phenomenon. Another *Aufbau* article calls for turning the tables on Nazi Germany. Titled "Nehmt 900 Nazis!" (Take 900 Nazis!), its author calls for seizing 900 Nazis living in other countries, dispossessing them of everything they own, removing them from their habitat with no consideration for family, friends, work, and home, and loading them onto a ship without passport and visa to dump them onto German shores.[98]

While most diplomats at Évian did not miss the opportunity to decry the humanitarian nature of the refugee crisis and to make vague and vacuous promises how to help solve it, Jewish intellectuals and political leaders knew perfectly well that this crisis was rooted in biopolitics. Above-referenced articles may not have mentioned colonialism as the main factor impacting Évian, but their comparisons of refugee ships with slave ships indicated at least an intuitive grasp of the role of racism and colonialism. And Jewish resettlement organizations such as the Freeland League for Jewish Territorial Colonisation drafted their own proposals with regard to Jewish resettlement in Africa showing a keen awareness of the biopolitical logic behind the flow of people and goods. Jewish organizations realized that the most promising, indeed the only possible, areas of Jewish resettlement lay in colonial territories, which, underpopulated as they may have been by European standards, had been connected to Europe by the shipping lines of Europe's colonial powers.[99] It is this context that forms the backdrop for the next chapter of our investigation of the *St. Louis*'s role as a refugee ship: a consideration of the history and role of HAPAG, the shipping line that owned the *St. Louis*, and the service history of the ship itself. Far from being the unexpected instruments of Nazi Germany's expulsion efforts, the ship and its owner were central, organic components in the historical picture of the Jewish refugee crisis on the eve of World War II. The traffic in humans NS Germany instigated, however incoherently, as a prelude to the "final solution" relied on infrastructures of colonial maritime trade that had evolved over decades.

2

Neocolonialism, Biopolitics, and the Jewish Migrant Business

HAPAG and MS *St. Louis*

IN A SPEECH GIVEN IN THE East Prussian city of Königsberg on March 25, 1938, which, among other things, sought to justify the recent annexation of Austria, Adolf Hitler articulated his rhetoric of blood and soil, underscoring the imperative for Germany to rid itself of undesirable elements. While not explicitly referencing Jews, Hitler describes Germany's enemies as "incorrigible opponents," stating that "part of them, in any case, will go where all the European 'honorable men' of that kind have gathered in recent years,"[1] and leaving no doubt as to whom he means. He goes on to say, "I can only hope and expect that the other world, which has such deep sympathy for these criminals, will at least be generous enough to convert this sympathy into practical aid. We, on our part, are ready to put all these criminals at the disposal of these countries, for all I care, even on luxury ships."[2] Hitler's suggestion to use luxury liners for the transportation of what his regime considered its worst enemy at first glance seems odd, even counterintuitive. Ocean liners were symbols of national prestige. For Hitler and his government, their visibility was especially important for restoring Germany's image as a proud seafaring nation after the defeat of World War I and the humiliation of the Versailles Treaty.

How Berlin felt about ocean liners became clear in an incident in New York on July 27, 1935, that made front page news in the US and abroad. Around two thousand communists staged an anti-fascist demonstration at the West Side passenger ship terminals in front of the liner *Bremen*, Germany's largest and most prominent ocean liner, which was being readied for its departure for Europe.[3] During the melee, demonstrators snuck aboard, tore the swastika flag off the staff of the *Bremen*'s bow, and threw it into the Hudson River, where it had to be retrieved by the ship's crew.[4] For Berlin, the provocation was twofold: Not only had a German ship been attacked by American communists, but the attack had defiled the Nazis' main political symbol. What made things worse for the NS regime was that, since the swastika had not yet been made the official German flag, those who had abused it could not be prosecuted for flag desecration.[5] As a result, Germany sent a strongly worded protest note to Washington and Goebbels announced that the failure to convict the perpetrators showed that the swastika deserved additional protection and would thus be declared exclusive national flag of Germany.[6]

For the NS regime, Germany's superliners, but also lower-profile ships such as the *St. Louis*, were prestige objects (see fig. 2.1). But Hitler's willingness to use ocean liners to transport what Nazi ideology deemed an "inferior race" was not as inconsistent as it appears. Berlin aspired to launch a large-scale overseas resettlement of Jews, and ocean liners regularly carried thousands of passengers to far-away places. Whether Hitler had any particular shipping lines or any specific ships in mind is not known—he may simply have wanted to reassure the public that for Nazi Germany to expel its Jews no effort would be too big and no price too high. For Germany's shipping lines, Jewish emigrants had long been an important clientele. By late 1938, a new set of antisemitic laws and the terror of the November pogrom led to a notable increase in bookings.

Archival documents show that HAPAG saw considerable potential for revenue in the migrant business—and this even after the onset of the war had grounded its fleet. In a letter directed at the Ministry of the Interior, dated January 13, 1940, HAPAG's director of passage, Claus-Gottfried Holthusen, emphasizes that in the years leading up to the war, HAPAG had already heavily invested in the infrastructure for the transportation of "non-Aryan emigrants" and, by mid-1939,

Figure 2.1. *St. Louis* in Hamburg before the 1936 Olympic Games hosted by Germany. While not quite ranking with *Bremen* and *Europa*, the *St. Louis*, too, was used to project NS might and glamour. *Source:* Courtesy of United States Holocaust Memorial Museum.

had succeeded in preventing foreign shipping lines from garnering the lion's share of this business. Requesting strict confidence, the letter adds a remarkable detail: At the time of Holthusen's writing, HAPAG was in possession of 3.5 million Reichsmark in deposits from Jews planning on leaving Germany on HAPAG's ships. But the onset of the war, so the letter continues, was presenting a serious problem for the company. Not only was said infrastructure now lying fallow, but many of the migrants were asking that their deposits be returned to them so they could book passage with foreign lines.[7]

To alleviate the loss of revenue and to deter Jewish customers from demanding the refund, Holthusen requested that HAPAG be allowed to charge a "processing fee" of 15% per booking.[8] In a response dated March 4, 1940, the Ministry gave HAPAG permission to do so. Interestingly, the response acknowledges that levying such a fee implicitly violates Germany's still active 1897 emigration laws, which directed the state to exercise "care" and "guidance" in its administration of emigrant affairs. But this approach, so the missive continues, does not apply to Jewish migrants, given that the highest goal of the country's "Judenpolitik" (policy toward Jews) was to effect "the most timely and most comprehensive emigration of Jews from Germany."[9] And since the war was keeping HAPAG from using its fleet, the Ministry, as further correspondence reveals, also granted HAPAG at Holthusen's request permission to act as a booking agent that arranges passage for Jewish migrants on foreign lines. Unsurprisingly, this service also carried a fee and became a source of revenue that, as Holthusen writes in a note to his overseas staff, grew in importance for HAPAG as the war went on.[10] The war was imperiling HAPAG's livelihood, but Holthusen held a long view on the migrant business. In a July 1940 presentation to the Board of Directors, he states that "recent events have shown us that, after the redistribution of the peoples' Lebensraum at war's end, considerable resettlements must be expected that won't be limited to the European continent."[11]

HAPAG's correspondence with the Ministry of the Interior reveals several aspects about this phase of antisemitic persecution. The Ministry's response constitutes yet more evidence of the inconsistent nature of the regime's politics toward Jews. Berlin created ever more financial and bureaucratic obstacles for Jews to leave. At the same time, the administration supported shipping lines' efforts to facilitate the expulsion of as many Jews as possible. Expulsion was, in Zhava Litvac Glaser's words, the "Nazi *modus operandi*" until October 18, 1941, when Heinrich Himmler decided to close Germany's borders to Jewish emigration.[12] The staggering size of Jewish deposits and the large number of refund requests indicate just how many Jews planned to leave their home country in the late 1930s and early 1940s. Holthusen's comments show how hard HAPAG worked to secure the Jewish migrant business for itself into the early stages of the war, and how fiercely protective the company was of the government's concessions that allowed it to book Jewish migrants on its own ships and, when that was no longer possible, on those of foreign lines. To better understand HAPAG's deep investment in the migrant business, we must consider the company's business philosophy and history.

"Mein Feld ist die Welt"—My Field Is the World

HAPAG was founded in the city of Hamburg in 1847. The formation of the German Empire was twenty-four years away and steam ships had barely made their presence felt on the Atlantic. By the beginning of World War I, HAPAG had become the world's largest shipping line. Its slogan "Mein Feld ist die Welt" (My field is the world) proudly proclaimed its hegemony. Like its main rival, Norddeutscher Lloyd (North German Lloyd, or NDL), which was founded ten years later in the city of Bremen, HAPAG was the brainchild of merchants aiming to establish regular trade between Germany's Hanseatic centers and North America's east coast. HAPAG stands for Hamburg-Amerikanische Packetfahrt-Actien-Gesellschaft, and while the company went by the catchier, more cosmopolitan name Hamburg-Amerika Linie, the term "Packetfahrt" has significance, as it identifies the transportation of packages to be the company's livelihood. Most packages HAPAG transported were filled with mail—parcels, pouches, and letters—and key to establishing North America trade was a concession from an official governing body to carry mail. Winning a concession required a carrier to operate a line between two ports—that is, regular service with standard arrival and departure times.[13] Mail service carried prestige, as it constituted a bestowal of trust.[14] HAPAG's rise, like that of other shipping lines, was thus bound up with the standardization of mail services and of shipping in general as well as with the normativization of time and the increasingly complex relationship between government and the private sector—all of which were epiphenomena of the Industrial Revolution and of the high period of nationalism and colonialism.

In addition to carrying packages to the New World, HAPAG, from the very first moment, carried passengers. When its first ship, the sailing ship *Deutschland*, departed for New York in October 1848, it carried twenty cabin passengers and 200 migrants in steerage.[15] In the aftermath of the 1848 Revolution, it was mostly Germans who emigrated to America; in the 1870s, when the economic boom of the founders' period improved the domestic labor market, the migrant profile shifted to Austrians, Hungarians, and especially Russians. A significant portion of those were Jews, who had been subject to increasing hostilities and pogroms under the Czar. The migrant business was crucial for both HAPAG and NDL, and even after the US restricted immigration in the early 1920s to curb the influx of Eastern European Jews (among other groups), for both companies passenger service remained an operational mainstay. But their approaches differed. For NDL, its cargo business, though not negligible, was less important than its ability to compete in the top segment of the transatlantic passenger market that was driven by size and especially by speed. HAPAG, by contrast, prioritized freight service. In the 1920s and '30s, its biggest liners, the so called "Hamburg class," were half the size of NDL's superliners *Bremen* and *Europa*, but their staid appearance, which owed to large freight compartments, belied their considerable comfort, a feature that HAPAG placed at a premium.[16]

When it was losing ground to NDL in the 1880s, HAPAG hired Albert Ballin, who, within ten years, turned the line into a global player (see fig. 2.2). After the fall of the German Empire, Ballin saw his life's work destroyed and he committed suicide, but his legacy shaped HAPAG for decades to come. Among his many

Figure 2.2. HAPAG Director Albert Ballin. *Source:* Public domain.

achievements, six stand out: (1) Ballin succeeded in gaining the attention of ship-loving Kaiser Wilhelm II, whose personal interest in HAPAG elevated the company's profile and economic clout.[17] It also paved the way for what cultural historian Mark A. Russell has termed "steamship nationalism"—the cultivation of ocean liners as objects of national prestige and economic and, indirectly, military might.[18] (2) Ballin's biography is bound up with the migrant business. He was born the thirteenth child of a Jewish travel agent in Hamburg who booked emigrants onto HAPAG liners and other ships. After taking over his father's agency and growing it through partnerships, Ballin eventually persuaded HAPAG to join forces with them and hire him. Eventually, HAPAG made him their director.[19] His business acumen helped Ballin enter the shipping business "from left field," via the adjacent booking business. Once at HAPAG, he expanded that business by establishing a pan-German network of sales offices for HAPAG. As Holthusen's request to secure concessions for booking Jewish migrants onto foreign lines shows, sales remained a key source of revenue for HAPAG after the onset of the war.[20] (3) Ballin's migrant business background helped him revolutionize its logistics. In the 1890s, HAPAG's new third class attracted migrants because it was only slightly more expensive than the primitive steerage category that dominated that market. But instead of discontinuing steerage, Ballin made it more comfortable by moving passengers out of large halls into cabins sleeping six.[21] Most importantly, Ballin built a complete village for emigrants in Hamburg with its own train station, shops, congregation halls, and quarters separating different confessions and religions. Five thousand people at once could be processed, medically examined, disinfected, showered, and quarantined, before boarding barges to the ships. Jewish migrants from Russia in particular were forced to use these facilities.[22] The focus on mass processing indicates that HAPAG understood the biopolitical dimension of migration. (4) Ballin did not neglect HAPAG's focus on cargo, a part of overseas trade not affected by the state of public health and immigration regulations.[23] He built a fleet of midsize cargo/passenger "combi" ships that accorded people and goods equal importance. Their comfortable cabin-class and third-class quarters attracted middle-class tourists and kept ocean travel affordable for migrants of the post-steerage era, which included Europe's and Germany's Jews in the 1920s and '30s. (5) As early as the 1890s, Ballin explored the viability of cruise tourism and turned it into a business model.²⁴ Cruises would become important revenue generators for HAPAG during the Third Reich and also impacted the service history of the *St. Louis*. (6) Just as Ballin had bent HAPAG to his will by coercing the company to fuse with others, merging with and acquiring other companies remained a key strategy for HAPAG to rise to the top by World War I and rise again from its ashes.²⁵ It is particularly instructive to look at Ballin's expansion of HAPAG's routes to the West Indies and to Middle and South America, because it is here that the company's approach to the Jewish migrant business reveals itself most clearly.²⁶

HAPAG's Latin America Routes and Jewish Migrant Traffic

Latin America has been shaped by neocolonialism, a form of political and economic dominance through which Europe and the US have coerced the political leaders and socioeconomic elites of Latin American nations to exploit their countries' natural and labor resources for European and North American markets without reinvesting into domestic infrastructure and improving living standards. Germany was a big importer of raw materials from Latin America. Working in close conjunction with German and European merchant houses, HAPAG and other shipping lines played a central role in this development.²⁷ Archival data shows that HAPAG's presence in the Caribbean and the Gulf of Mexico was strong.²⁸ The line started to send its ships into the region as early as 1870. By 1890, it had established four routes from Hamburg to several ports in the West Indies. In 1906, it commissioned larger ships specifically for a Hamburg-Bilbao-Havana service to take advantage of the increased traffic of migrants and seasonal workers between Spain and Cuba. On the eve of World War I, HAPAG regularly serviced Venezuela, Colombia, Mexico, Cuba, Jamaica, St. Thomas, Trinidad, Haiti, La Plata, and Northern Brazil on the east coast of South America and the Caribbean and Chile and Peru on the west coast.²⁹ After the war, HAPAG resumed service to these destinations with chartered ships before rebuilding its own fleet. By the mid-1930s, HAPAG operated several new cargo/passenger combi ships to service numerous destinations in Latin America.³⁰

Before World War I, HAPAG also ran a regular passenger service between New York and Havana, made possible through the acquisition of a US company, the Atlas Line.[31] This foothold on the US market ended after the war, when the powerful American United Fruit Company sought control over New York–based trade routes to Latin America. But while HAPAG was no longer allowed to use US ports for regular liner service to Latin America, the company in the 1930s reclaimed New York as a base for its cruise business to Bermuda and the Caribbean, for which it used the *St. Louis*, among other ships. These self-contained cruises signaled the increasing role of tourism within the neocolonial economy. As is customary with cruises, most of those operated by HAPAG tended to have only one class. However, on its regular freight and passenger lines to the West Indies, the Gulf, and the west coast of South America, HAPAG offered accommodations in more than one class, which enabled the company to target business travelers, tourists, and migrants.

Touting the flexibility of HAPAG's combi ships, Holthusen, in a speech given to the Board in mid-1937, explains the company's philosophy of making its fleet prioritize comfort over size and speed.[32] HAPAG liners *Cordillera*, *Caribia*, and *Orinoco* had large cargo holds and relatively limited passenger capacity, but they were popular for their comfort and service. Holthusen reports that, while business to Latin America was thriving, it varied according to booking category. He adds, "One might say that in the less expensive classes only those travel who '*must*' travel, whereas in the higher classes apart from those who '*must*' travel one can also find passengers who '*can*' travel."[33] Holthusen's reference to more privileged passengers—those who "*can* travel"—will be discussed further below. Of interest at the moment is his allusion to passengers who "*must*" travel, by which he means third-class passengers.[34] Between 1937 and 1938 outgoing traffic increased by 61.6% for the third-class market share, which includes both HAPAG and its direct competitors, the Pacific Steam Navigation Company and the Italia Line.[35] This jump in bookings must be related to the fact that life for Jews in Germany was becoming ever more difficult and dangerous.

Another statistic found in the HAPAG archive, termed "Unsere Juden-Beförderung ab Hamburg" (Our Transportation of Jews from Hamburg), shows just how central the Jewish migrant business was to HAPAG's balance sheet in the late 1930s. Between January and August, 1939, 40 percent of all passengers traveling on HAPAG liners from Hamburg to the Caribbean and the Gulf region were Jewish (1068 in total), while 35.8 percent of HAPAG's passengers traveling to South America's west coast were Jewish (558 in total). Of HAPAG's passengers traveling to Cuba and Mexico during this period, 41.3 percent (1099 in total) were Jewish.[36] Listed as a separate item are the 930 Jewish passengers who had booked passage to Cuba on the *St. Louis*.[37] In light of the visions of large-scale Jewish resettlement that, albeit never realized, were circulating in the Nazi press and among the regime's leaders at that time, these figures seem modest. But as Holthusen's confidential comments about the large amount of Jewish deposits indicate, it was clear that HAPAG expected numbers to skyrocket after the war.

Just as important to note is that, while HAPAG's third-class bookings went up in 1938, the increase was smaller than at competing lines. In fact, compared to its competitors, HAPAG's third-class market share declined from 21.7 percent in 1937 to 16.9 percent in 1938.[38] Some of the reasons were structural. Competitors such as the Pacific Steam Navigation Company and the Italia Line were using larger ships with greater passenger capacity on migrant routes. But the decline also owed to politics. German shipping lines were feeling the impact of anti-fascist sentiments, particularly in the US, where most German Jews hoped to resettle and where a portion of their travel money came from in the form of funds provided by family and friends living there. Notwithstanding the large sum of Jewish deposits HAPAG held in 1940, Jewish migrants increasingly preferred to travel on foreign ships.

HAPAG addressed this problem by bolstering its non-Jewish passenger volume to Latin America. In fact, the main focus of Holthusen's speech to the Board is HAPAG's thriving second-class business—which, as statistics for the years 1937 and 1938 confirm, actually showed a sharper rise in bookings than did third class.[39] While archival documents show that even at this late point, some Jewish passengers were able to travel second class, we must assume that the clientele that accounts for most of the increase were non-Jewish tourists—referred to by Holthusen as those who "*can*" travel. Albert Ballin had single-handedly invented ocean tourism in the form of the cruise and HAPAG over the years had continually refined those offerings. In the 1930s, the firm launched a new product, so called study tours ("Studienreisen"). Conceived for the Latin America and East Asia routes, study tours, as HAPAG's travel brochures point out, combined the pleasures of ocean travel with the benefits of education. In contrast to cruises offered through the "Strength Through Joy" (Kraft durch Freude, or KdF) organization that were reserved for NSDAP members and functioned as ideological training programs, HAPAG's study tours billed themselves simply as forms of cultural tourism. They were integrated into HAPAG's regular freight and passenger liner service, which gave them the appearance of adventurous, open-minded globetrotting—a mode of traveling that HAPAG had promoted for decades through an ever-expanding apparatus of media, including promotional posters and brochures and, since the early 1920s, filmed travelogues.[40] As we shall see, however, HAPAG's promotion of globetrotting concealed more subtle ways of indoctrination.

Analyzing the wealth of archival materials about HAPAG's study tours exceeds the parameters of this book. What merits consideration is how HAPAG's liner service to Latin America, even as it followed the seemingly neutral, utilitarian dictates of international shipping, operated within the intersecting parameters of nationalism and National Socialism. And even this segment of HAPAG's activities, which did not primarily target Jewish travelers, yields insights into the logic behind HAPAG's Jewish migrant business. In HAPAG's study tour brochures and in the company's deliberations about new ship commissions two things reveal themselves: (1) HAPAG's Latin American business, like that of its competitors, was part of the neocolonial infrastructure linking Europe and the Americas; (2) in contrast to competing shipping lines from democratic countries, however, HAPAG (whether voluntarily or through coercion) put its infrastructure at the disposal of a fascist state apparatus to support the latter's logistic needs and ideological goals—and those goals also came to inform HAPAG's role and self-image as an exporter of people, of goods, and of people as goods.

In HAPAG's travel brochures, Latin America's native populations, which in Nazi Germany were considered "non-Aryan" or "racially inferior" similar to the Sinti and the Roma, suddenly acquire exotic appeal, as becomes clear in the image of three peasant women, who are depicted carrying market wares and walking piglets on leashes (see fig. 2.3). HAPAG promises its prospective customers a polyglot, multicultural experience that affords encounter with the "colorful ways

Figure 2.3. HAPAG travel brochure. *Source:* Archiv Deutsches Schifffahrtsmuseum (DSM) Bremerhaven/German Maritime Museum Archives. Used with permission.

in which the local population carries on."⁴¹ Another brochure praises "the full wealth of colonial cultures, the industrial fight for valuable natural resources, and a mixture of peoples and races of unrivaled colorfulness"—including visits to "picturesque negro villages" and encounters with "Indio and negro types."⁴² These descriptions praise colonization as a historically inevitable and, indeed, necessary project in which the Spanish (whose fascist leader Franco was enjoying Germany's support) figure as the colonizing master race. Indeed, the ad copy seeks to distinguish between good colonizers and bad ones. The latter, unsurprisingly, are identified as British and US American. One brochure identifies the port city of Cartagena as the congregation point for the "famous Spanish silver fleets," but also points out that even though "Francis Drake conquered the city and Henry Morgan and other known leaders of the Filibuster stormed and robbed it, its inhabitants always succeeded in rebuilding what had been destroyed."⁴³ HAPAG's marketing materials harnessed Latin America's colonial history to reinforce ideological positions about Nazi Germany's friends and foes.

The neocolonialist mentality finds its most overt expression in the graphic design of several maps advertising HAPAG's routes to Latin America. One is a centerfold display of HAPAG's fleet servicing North America, the Caribbean, and the Gulf region (see fig. 2.4). The map arrays the ships like an armada laying siege to the Americas and displays countries and cultures through icons of cultural stereotypes. Another drawing shows a fleet of ships servicing South America's west coast, the contour of which is, in fact, all that remains visible of the continent, the rest being literally erased by the towering presence of HAPAG's fleet (see fig. 2.5). It is hard to imagine a blunter vision of

Figure 2.4. HAPAG cruise brochure. Map of Latin American travel routes. *Source:* Archiv Deutsches Schifffahrtsmuseum (DSM) Bremerhaven/German Maritime Museum Archives. Used with permission.

Figure 2.5. HAPAG Map of South America routes and fleet. *Source:* Archiv Deutsches Schifffahrtsmuseum (DSM) Bremerhaven/German Maritime Museum Archives. Used with permission.

a company's consummate ambition to economically colonize a whole subcontinent. But the map also holds a compensatory function for HAPAG. The company had long had a foothold on west-coast trade routes, but market fluctuations had necessitated that it join operations with its competitors. The map speaks to HAPAG's unrealized ambition to gain hegemony in the region. To increase its market share, HAPAG in the mid-1930s commissioned a new ship, the SS *Patria*. News of the project triggered enthusiastic responses by Nazi Party offices in South America. The NDSAP Deputy Office of the Führer sent a letter to HAPAG relaying the contents of two telegrams from Nazi Party officials in Peru. One of them, the Regional Group Leader of the Peru office of the NSDAP and Chair of the German Colony Committee (Vorsitzender des deutschen Kolonieausschusses), praises HAPAG for raising the esteem of German shipping in the region; the other, carrying the title of Head of the Economic Office of the NSDAP Regional Group, asks the Deputy Office to relay the good wishes of the "German Colony, Peru."[44] The senders' status illustrates the presence of Nazi organizations in South America and shows how closely an eye the NSDAP kept on German business initiatives abroad, including the establishment and maintenance of shipping routes by lines such as HAPAG.

While at times feeling ambivalent about being under the sway of the NS State, HAPAG appreciated the party apparatus providing support in regions beyond Germany's direct reach of power.[45] This becomes clear in a 1938 presentation given by HAPAG's director of operations, Dr. Walter Hoffmann, about his journey to South America.[46] He claims that HAPAG's activities on the subcontinent contribute to Germany's economic and national interests and demonstrate the importance of the political project and cultural values of National Socialism. Noting that the region's elite is keenly aware that Germany had never harbored any imperialist designs on the subcontinent, Hoffmann claims that Latin Americans appreciate Germany's positive economic and cultural influence. They know, he goes on to say, that Germans did not come to South America to unilaterally reap profit, but that they have "given back" by furthering their guest countries' economic and cultural infrastructures. Hoffmann's presentation reveals the logic by which Germany's business elite superficially condemned colonization-by-conquest only to redefine colonization through cultural and settler colonialism—a non-military, neocolonial way of advancing National Socialist world hegemony. In this vein, Hoffmann praises what he calls the "pioneering spirit" (*Pioniergeist*) of German merchants and "colonists" (*Kolonisten*) and claims that they have created a positive impression of "Germanness" (*Deutschtum*) in Latin America, not least supported by the "pioneering" work of shipping lines like HAPAG. He continues that any "misunderstandings" and "misjudgments" about the new Germany that are caused by the "democratic-parliamentary face" of Latin American countries are offset by grassroots admiration for National Socialist Germany and its Führer. Hoffmann reinforces his claims with a statement by former Colombian minister in Berlin, Rafael Obregon, who had praised Hitler as a genius for having restored autonomy to Germany, including all the rights of which the Versailles Treaty had "robbed" the country. Apparently, Obregon had characterized Germany as "democratic in the deepest sense," as its people are "identical" with its leader. (For the Colombian diplomat, "the essence of democracy" meant "having respect for one's government and for the thinking of others.") Hoffmann's gleeful referencing of Obregon's points reflects a deep affinity between NS ideology's belief that a people must be identical with their leader (see chapter 5) and the autocratic mentality of certain Latin American countries, notwithstanding their official parliamentary systems.

In light of these affinities, it is not surprising that for Germany's and Latin America's political and business elites the HAPAG liners were a place to convene and rejoice in shared worldviews. VIP passenger information HAPAG shared with the NSDAP between 1937 and 1939 includes the following individuals: General Francisco Aguiler, minister of Mexico, and Ibrahim Urquiaga, minister of Cuba to Denmark, traveling in September 1937 on Hamburg-bound liner *Orinoco*; Patricio Aldunate, director of the Chilean Customs and Tariffs Division, traveling in December 1937 on liner *Rakhotis* to Hamburg as an official envoy of his government, accompanied by his sister, Judith, likewise officially appointed by the Chilean government to study music in Europe; Dr. Voelckers, the German envoy in Havana, traveling in May 1938 to Hamburg on liner *Orinoco*; Augusto Carballo, official representative of Costa Rica, appointed to study European coffee markets, traveling in April 1938 to Hamburg on liner *Cordillera*; Swedish minister Carl Gotthard Anderberg, traveling in May 1938 to Hamburg on liner *Orinoco*; Emilio Bello Codesido, Chilean minister of defense, traveling in August 1938 on liner *Patria* to Valparaiso after having vacationed in the South of France; Friedrich Adolf Koch, deputy regional group leader of NSDAP Colombia, traveling in November 1938 on liner *Caribia* to Hamburg; Dr. Villalaz, envoy of Panama to Berlin, Gil Guardia Jaen, chancellor of the Legation of Panama, Antonio Isaza, general consul of Panama in Hamburg, and Werner Esperstedt, local leader of the NSDAP Bogotá, all traveling in January 1939 on liner *Caribia* to Hamburg; José Llach, attaché of the Colombian Legation in Berlin, and legation council Dr. Erich Kordt, traveling in February 1939 on liner *Cordillera* to Hamburg; and Dr. Alberto Zérega-Fombona, minister of Venezuela in Germany, Fritz Woelfert (and family), deputy regional group leader for the NSDAP Colombia, Albrecht Krauss, local group leader, NSDAP Bogotá, and Erich Müller, administrator of the NSDAP Bogotá office, all traveling on liner *Caribia* to Hamburg in June, 1939. Information sometimes includes further details. One letter from HAPAG to the NSDAP, dated August 17, 1939, states that on August 19, Dr. Claudio Cortés, trade attaché of the Costa Rica Legation in Paris and appointed by the Foreign Ministry of Costa Rica, will arrive on motor ship *Caribia* in Hamburg. Cortés, the note adds, is a brother of Costa Rica's current president and is accompanied by his wife. The note adds that Dr. Edmond Jacobsen, local group leader of the NSDAP, Curaçao, is traveling on the same ship and is accompanied by his family.[47]

Ocean liners provided social elites with a place to meet and mingle. Yet the elites that traveled on HAPAG's ships were not only movie stars or athletes. They represented the intersecting contexts of neocolonialism and National Socialism. At the very least, such encounters functioned as informal feedback loops about policies born from higher-level negotiations. Diplomats cherished such exchanges for their informal and undocumented nature. VIP passenger lists are historical documents. They identify HAPAG's ocean liners as sites of cultural and ideological exchange on which all aspects of Nazi Germany's political and trade relations to Latin America intersected in comprehensive manner. These relations also included questions of Jewish migration—in other words, the affairs of the people who traveled in third class on the very same ships and possibly on the same voyages as did the elites that decided over their fates.[48]

Hoffmann's flowery comments about Latin America's gratitude for the "pioneering spirit" of German merchants and "colonists" and his rose-tinted impressions about the advancement of "Germanness," supported by the "pioneering" work of lines like HAPAG, seem ironic, to say the least, in light of the fact that HAPAG's ships regularly landed dozens of Jewish migrants on Latin American shores. It is hard to imagine that this irony escaped Latin American leaders like Obregon. But those leaders played their own complex role in the economic and political dynamics of neocolonial exchange. While they understood that Jews flocked to Latin America because as "non-Aryans" they could not be "identical" with the Führer, they knew perfectly well that their countries would have few problems assimilating Jewish migrants. HAPAG's Jewish passenger statistics and other figures released by the United States Holocaust Memorial Museum indicate that the Jewish migrant business was an organic component, not an anomaly, of neocolonial politics.[49] But if most Latin American nations had made it clear at Evian that they were not prepared to veer from their narrow immigration laws to accept Europe's Jews, how exactly did HAPAG succeed in landing considerable numbers of Jewish migrants on Latin American shores?

One factor, which revealed itself in Cuba's handling of the *St. Louis*, was the efforts of individual politicians and administrators to personally enrich themselves. Yet it would be reductive and, indeed, Eurocentric to identify Latin America as the center of unethical financial practices; their origins clearly lay in Europe. Latin American nations' de facto approaches to Jewish migration were far from unified and they displayed a notable pragmatism. The exchange between Franklin D. Roosevelt and his representative at Evian, Myron C. Taylor, about the need to create unofficial channels of communication suggests that Roosevelt understood that many Latin American countries had greater use for Jewish migrants than they were prepared to admit in the presence of the press.

Consider the case of Bolivia, whose mining magnate, Mauricio (Moritz) Hochschild, a German Jew, controlled one-third of Bolivia's mineral production and had ties to the Bolivian president. Economic reasons and his Jewish heritage motivated Hochschild to lobby his government to admit 20,000 Jewish refugees between 1938 and 1941. From Bolivia, many would go on to other South American countries, such as Argentina, where in addition to the 24,000 Jewish refugees that country admitted officially between 1933 and 1943, another estimated 20,000 arrived illegally.[50] Beyond the role played by individual Latin American leaders, an important factor enabling and facilitating a "slow leak" of Jewish migrants into Latin American countries was Jewish refugee organizations. The American Jewish Joint Distribution Committee (JDC), for instance, supported the efforts of Hochschild in Bolivia and Saldivar in Mexico[51] and sponsored countless cases across the Americas before and during World War II. The JDC did so through its own offices or by sending its agents to work with regional or local immigration agencies in several countries. The JDC preferred advocating on behalf of individuals and small groups of refugees because of the inconspicuous nature of such cases.⁵² A further party inclined to act on behalf of Jewish refugees was the shipping lines bringing them to their ports of destination. Sometimes, lines such as HAPAG required a return deposit as part of the fare (also in the case of the *St. Louis* trip) to defray the cost of transporting rejected Jewish passengers back to Germany. But this was not a consistent practice, and even when such fees were being levied, the line, to dodge red tape abroad and bad press at home, was highly motivated to land its migrant passengers at their destination. While more research is needed about this phenomenon, I find it probable that the relationships HAPAG cultivated with Latin American diplomats and business leaders who traveled on its ships increased HAPAG's options of intervening on behalf of its migrants by, say, using back channels to mobilize negotiations or by being instrumental in hiring immigration lawyers. Unfortunately, in the case of the *St. Louis* passengers, HAPAG agents failed to intervene with officials. But the reasons for Cuba's rejection of the *St. Louis* Jews were manifold. And if one such reason was Cuba's President Federico Laredo Brú's disruption of the relationship between HAPAG and Cuba's immigration minister, Manuel Benítez y González, the fact that this arrangement between a private-sector company and a government official had existed in the first place and could impact matters of immigration is worth noting.⁵³

HAPAG and Cuba

While the *St. Louis* case constitutes an instance in which Jewish migration to Latin America infamously failed, it contrasted sharply with Cuba's previous record of being a haven for Jews, who had been coming there since the 1880s. Only in the 1930s did Cuba officially reduce its immigration rate as part of economic reforms. Yet it was common knowledge in Cuba that most Jews sought to stay there only until US immigration would clear their path for becoming American citizens. It took relentless agitating from nativists and antisemites to make the country (and its press) more skeptical of immigration. Their efforts compelled Cuba to officially take a restrictive position at Évian. These facts, however, are only half the story. Manuel Benítez, the head of Cuba's immigration authority and the protégé of Colonel Fulgencio Batista y Zaldívar, the powerful head of Cuba's military, had been bypassing Cuba's immigration laws for personal gain. He had been selling Jewish migrants affordable tourist visas and personally pocketed the profits. It is widely assumed, though not proven, that some of the proceeds went to Batista. In the wake of the November 1938 pogrom in Germany, Batista approached the JDC with the news that Cuba would increase the number of Jews it would admit.[54] Before its discovery and suspension by President Laredo Brú in the spring 1939, Benítez's arrangement had facilitated entry into Cuba for thousands of Jews. By early 1939, between five thousand and six thousand Jews were living on the island.[55]

While the full extent of HAPAG's involvement in Benítez's scheme is unknown, it is clear that the company greatly benefited from it. The November 1938 pogrom prompted the shipping line to organize a voyage whose sole purpose was the transportation of a large number of Jews out of Germany. Archival data suggests that HAPAG had intended to use the *St. Louis* as early as November 1938 for a special trip "from Hamburg to Trinidad and back for the execution of a Jewish transport" (von Hamburg nach Trinidad und zurück zur Ausführung eines Judentransportes) but was forced to cancel this voyage "due to the problems that have arisen on the Jewish side" (infolge der auf jüdischer Seite eingetretenen Schwierigkeiten).[56] The wording likely alludes to the mass incarcerations of Jews in the wake of the pogrom of November 9 to 10, which deprived HAPAG specifically of its male passengers, who would remain in concentration camps for weeks or months. The canceled voyage of November 1938 was thus a direct precursor to the voyage to Cuba that the *St. Louis* undertook in May 1939.

On January 6, 1939, the National Coordinating Committee of Refugees in New York contacted Morris Troper at the JDC in Paris with a request for assisting with recruiting 500 Jewish emigrants, as there was the possibility of a special voyage to Cuba and Trinidad.[57] Troper, who months later brokered asylum for the *St. Louis* passengers with England, France, Belgium, and the Netherlands, forwarded the telegram from the National Coordinating Committee to HICEM (a cluster of three Jewish emigration organizations), which, in turn, cautioned the JDC regarding, among other things, the fact that boatloads of refugees would adversely affect migration, as they risked blindsiding officials in the countries of destination. It would also be much harder for Jewish refugee organizations to produce the funds for hundreds of refugees all at once.[58] In Cuba this became once again a reality after President Laredo Brú discovered Benítez's scheme and reinstated the regular immigration laws. On May 6, 1939, the Cuban government issued what became known as Decree 937, a law that announced the official reversal of its immigration policy (that 937 was the number of passengers on the *St. Louis* was purely coincidental). HAPAG was immediately informed about it. In addition, on May 8, five days before the departure date of the *St. Louis*, Viscount Duncannon, the high commissioner of refugees, urged HAPAG by telegram not to let the *St. Louis* sail, as the Cuban government would likely cause problems.[59] HAPAG nonetheless let the *St. Louis* sail because Benítez assured HAPAG that the passengers were exempt from Decree 937, or rather, that they could consider themselves grandfathered in, as they had purchased their passage to Cuba before the new law was issued. HAPAG was satisfied.[60] A news bulletin issued April 15, 1939, which advertised the special voyage to Cuba, merely included a brief statement that only those passengers whose travel papers were "completely in order" were allowed to book passage.[61] When, on May 23, HAPAG received confirmation that Duncannon had been right about Cuba's resolve to close its borders, the *St. Louis* was already so close to Havana that HAPAG balked at recalling the ship.

The question of HAPAG's historical responsibility in the fate of the *St. Louis* Jews will be discussed in detail in the following chapters from various angles, but this much can be said: as this chapter has tried to argue, it was not humanitarianism that drove HAPAG's Jewish migrant business. The shipping line transported Jewish refugees for profit and facilitated transportation as part of its servicing the neocolonial trade infrastructure between Germany and Latin America. And by helping to implement the NS state's "Judenpolitik" of coerced migration, HAPAG became a crucial site of the intersection of neocolonialism and the Nazis' strenuous efforts to expel Germany's Jews. HAPAG's decision to risk letting the *St. Louis* Jews run afoul of Cuban immigration thus reflected the hope to be able to complete a business transaction for which it had already received payment. But for us to understand every aspect of HAPAG's migrant business and to appreciate how the special voyage to Cuba came about finally requires a consideration of the ship that was at the center of it all.

MS *St. Louis*

That HAPAG chose the *St. Louis* for the special migrant voyage to Cuba was not a coincidence. The ship's deployment history shows that its position within the HAPAG fleet was unique. HAPAG commissioned the *St. Louis* in 1927 as a ship for middle-class business travelers, tourists, and relatively prosperous migrants and put her into service in 1929.[62] Since the US had restricted immigration in a series of laws in the early 1920s, emigrants represented a much smaller category of travelers. In the fall of 1929, six months after the ship's maiden voyage, the Wall Street crash ushered in the Great Depression. While the US during the early 1930s did not significantly change its immigration quotas for countries like Germany, President Herbert Hoover directed US consulates abroad "to interpret existing public charge statutes to exclude non-wealthy immigrants."[63] This is what HAPAG board member Victor Neumann presumably alluded to when he claimed in a July 26, 1939, presentation to the board that a "sharp restriction in US immigration, which set in as early as 1930," sent the westward passenger traffic on all lines into steep decline.[64] According to Neumann, HAPAG's westward passenger transportation decreased from 48,272 in 1929 to 25,288 in 1931 (a 47.8 percent drop) and then modestly increased again to 29,374 in 1937.[65]

While the global economic recession and the changes in US immigration affected all of HAPAG's transatlantic ships, the *St. Louis* and her sister ship *Milwaukee* (launched the same year) were particularly impacted. Both ships were smaller and slower than the premium liners of HAPAG's so called "Hamburg" class, *Hamburg*, *Deutschland*, *New York*, and *Hansa*.[66] HAPAG had not equipped them with first-class accommodations, but with the more affordable cabin class, followed by tourist class and third class.[67] This gave them an initial total passenger capacity of between 1,000 and 1,100.[68] With their technical specifications putting them at a disadvantage to larger and faster ships in transatlantic service and with the migrant business remaining at a low ebb for much of the 1930s, both ships became difficult to deploy. In the early 1930s, HAPAG converted the *Milwaukee* to a full-time cruise ship, a move that proved successful. The *St. Louis*, however, remained a financial liability for the rest of the decade. HAPAG decided to keep the ship in transatlantic service for part of the year while otherwise using it for cruises.

In his presentation, Neumann makes a case for HAPAG to keep the *St. Louis*. In transatlantic service, so he argues, the ship was small enough to merit deployment on the route that included Galway and Cobh in Ireland as well as Halifax, Nova Scotia—ports for which HAPAG could not afford to use its larger, more competitive liners.[69] In addition, when those ships had to suspend their transatlantic service due to technical problems or when HAPAG used them on profitable cruises to the West Indies, the *St. Louis*, so Neumann argued, could temporarily replace them. This was especially important to avoid a disruption of the cargo business, which for HAPAG represented a large source of revenue.[70] In addition, the *St. Louis* also operated cruises, both for HAPAG and on charter to the NS organization KdF. Statistics show that the ship was popular with cruise passengers. In 1935, it carried an average of 1,066 passengers on eleven cruises and in 1936 an average of 1,038 on seven cruises.[71] As additional data shows, however, the days on which the *St. Louis* was idling in port were far too many for the ship to operate in the black. To make things worse, in 1937 to 1938, KdF, HAPAG's main charter client for the *St. Louis*, within a period of twelve months launched two large cruise ships of its own.[72]

Neumann thus admitted that, even under the best of circumstances, profitable deployment of the *St. Louis* remained doubtful. It does not surprise, then, that HAPAG eventually considered repurposing the ship specifically for its Jewish migrant business. Neumann concludes his speech as follows:

> If all the signs are to be believed, we must expect a rather strong non-Aryan emigration for the next few years. But considerateness for our other customers compels us to limit the number of non-Aryan passengers in tourist class and third class of the ships of our "Hamburg" class. It is impossible to transport a larger percentage of non-Aryan persons in these classes without incurring a gradual churn of Aryan customers from our ships to those of the competition. The *St. Louis* would be especially suitable for the purpose of transporting non-Aryans.[73]

In 1938, HAPAG announced that it would reconfigure *St. Louis*'s passenger categories and refurbish its facilities by combining tourist class with third class. HAPAG had publicity post cards printed that feature the ship's comely cabin-class spaces, such as the social hall (see fig. 2.6 and fig. 2.7), the cabin-class restaurant (fig. 2.8), the cabin-class ladies' lounge (fig. 2.9), and the cabin-class smoking room (fig 2.10), as well as the recently combined and updated tourist-class/third-class spaces, which included a social hall (fig. 2.11) and a dining room (fig. 2.12). These images were also widely publicized in a cruise brochure HAPAG released to travel agencies in the late 1930s (see fig 2.13).[74] Whether HAPAG performed these changes on the *St. Louis* specifically with an eye to migrant travel cannot be said with certainty. They were likely completed prior to the November 1938 date of the letter that advised the JDC of the cancellation of the voyage to Trinidad. It appears that HAPAG intended to continue to use the ship for the purpose of cruising and perhaps even transatlantic travel. One reason the 1939 Cuba voyage became a problem for HAPAG was that it jeopardized the ship's summer 1939 cruise schedule out of New York to the Caribbean.

Figure 2.6. Postcard of the MS *St. Louis* cabin-class social hall. *Source:* Private collection of Michael Zell. Used with permission.

Figure 2.7. Postcard of the MS *St. Louis* cabin-class social hall. *Source:* Private collection of Michael Zell. Used with permission.

Figure 2.8. Postcard of the MS *St. Louis* cabin-class dining hall. *Source:* Private collection of Michael Zell. Used with permission.

Figure 2.9. Postcard of the MS *St. Louis* cabin-class ladies' lounge. *Source:* Private collection of Michael Zell. Used with permission.

Figure 2.10. Postcard of the MS *St. Louis* cabin-class smoking room. *Source:* Private collection of Michael Zell. Used with permission.

Figure 2.11. Postcard of the MS *St. Louis* updated and combined tourist-class/third-class social hall. *Source:* Private collection of Michael Zell. Used with permission.

Figure 2.12. Postcard of the MS *St. Louis* combined and updated tourist-class/cabin-class dining hall. *Source:* Private collection of Michael Zell. Used with permission.

Figure 2.13. Cover of HAPAG cruise brochure for MS *St. Louis*. Source: Deutsches Schifffahrtsmuseum Bremerhaven. Used with permission.

If anything, the renovations performed on the *St. Louis* in 1938 reflect HAPAG's long-standing intention of operating a fleet of ships that could be used for every branch and aspect of the company's business. *St. Louis*, in many ways, was the ultimate HAPAG liner. The ship combined in itself the largest number of qualities with which the company traditionally endowed its fleet. It was built for carrying large amounts of cargo and migrants—the two cornerstones on which HAPAG was founded in 1848. It was big enough to serve on the

North Atlantic, yet the fact that it prioritized versatility and comfort over size and speed placed it squarely within HAPAG's traditional fleet philosophy. Indeed, the fact that HAPAG launched the *St. Louis* after migration to the US had peaked and that its Cuba voyage still stood in this tradition shows that HAPAG continued to value the migrant business even after competitors began to pay less attention to it. Finally, *St. Louis*'s suitability for cruises aligned the ship with HAPAG's cruise portfolio developed by Ballin decades earlier.

Paradoxically, however, being the quintessential HAPAG ship made the *St. Louis*'s cost-efficient deployment more difficult in a rapidly changing political and economic climate. The ship's late-1930s renovation and partial repurposing was borne out of crisis and opportunity. The decision to reduce the classes to two (cabin and third) reflected a shift away from carrying Jewish and non-Jewish passengers on one and the same ship and toward exclusively carrying either Jewish migrants or non-Jewish tourists on pleasure cruises. It seems appropriate to characterize this mode as "bulk" transportation, and given the state of modern mass tourism, it would not be jejune to apply the term also to modern cruises, notwithstanding the obvious differences between cruising and antisemitic mass expulsion.

To sum up, the Cuba voyage of the *St. Louis* stood in complex relationship to HAPAG's business philosophy and history. In many ways the ultimate HAPAG liner, the *St. Louis* was also an outlier in HAPAG's transatlantic fleet. While the ship remained unprofitable for most of its existence, HAPAG neither sold it nor used it in its regular Latin America freight and passenger liner service the way it used, say, the *Orinoco* or the *Patria*. Latin America figured into the ship's operations only through cruises to the Caribbean. The Cuba trip, too, is marked by a duality. As a special migrant transport, it distinguished itself from HAPAG's Latin America service and had little precedent in the annals of the Jewish migrant business on the Atlantic. But it revealed the importance for a shipping line such as HAPAG to maintain close ties to Latin America's political elite. Benítez's selling of tourist visas to Jewish migrants only fueled HAPAG's projections of Jewish migration. Although HAPAG may not have refurbished the *St. Louis* expressly with future migrant trips in mind, the reduction to two classes still suggests that the company sought to make the ship more compatible with the "bulk" passage model. As Victor Neumann's speech shows, the *St. Louis*, despite being a handsome and comfortable ship, was increasingly being thought of as a means for transporting people as a form of cargo.

These tensions, as the next two chapters discuss, inform all aspects of the Cuba voyage. While modest compared to the era's superliners, the *St. Louis* was big enough to invoke the glamour of ocean liner travel—it was noticed everywhere it went, which at least in part accounts for why the Cuba voyage became a media spectacle. And while the ship made its Jewish passengers feel different from the countless migrants crisscrossing the Mediterranean and the Black Sea on dilapidated freighters, the atmosphere of glamour, comfort, and freedom otherwise enjoyed only by non-Jewish passengers was fragile. Upon arrival in Havana, it was shattered in the most painful ways.

3

Voyage 98

The Unfolding of a Fateful Odyssey

HAPAG, LIKE OTHER shipping lines, fastidiously documented the voyages of its ships. The trip to Cuba and back to Antwerp was the ninety-eighth that the *St. Louis* undertook. Gustav Schröder chronicled the journey in his official captain's log and his travelogue, *Heimatlos auf hoher See* (*Homeless on the High Seas*). So did several passengers. Their diaries have been excerpted in popular history books and on the website of the United States Holocaust Memorial Museum.[1] Once Cuba denied entry to the Jewish migrants, reporters rushed to Havana to cover the unfolding crisis for the US and international press. These primary and secondary sources have produced a wealth of archival information about Voyage 98, though not always with full accuracy. The present chapter has two goals: while not giving an all-inclusive account of the voyage, I aim to correct long-standing errors and misassumptions about it; and I explore how the gray zone between voluntary and involuntary migration—caused by the NS State's exploitation of the paradoxes of international law and compounded by the effects of neocolonialism—placed the *St. Louis* Jews within overlapping frameworks of tourism, migration, and flight, with the latter holding the opposite prospects of rescue and death. While these conditions to varying degrees impacted all Jewish migrant ships in the late 1930s, they converged paradigmatically on the *St. Louis*.

The murky, multi-faceted conditions of Jewish migration during the NS period, discussed in chapter 1, registered in the way HAPAG advertised the trip. Jewish migrants had become an important part of HAPAG's revenue base. Still, prior to the company's aborted plans to organize a special migrant trip to Trinidad in late 1938, HAPAG's plans to use any of its ships exclusively for migrant traffic to Latin America had never materialized. Travel there had proceeded as part of the line's regular passenger and cargo service and by virtue of HAPAG's New York–based cruises. In 1939, the *St. Louis* was still locked into a tight schedule of cruises and transatlantic crossings. As plans to use the ship more systematically for transporting Jewish migrants remained tentative, HAPAG treated the Cuba voyage as an out-of-schedule trip and downplayed its actual purpose.

This is evident in a bulletin announcing the trip in mid-April, 1939 (see fig. 3.1). Its wording is notable for a kind of doublespeak that reflects Jews' double status of being included and excluded—a form of distancing that the Nazis implanted into all areas of German culture, down to the mundane use of language, so as to erode any impression of likeness between Jewish and non-Jewish Germans.[2] Without referencing the actual circumstances behind the trip, the pamphlet directs itself to "all those interested in Cuba" and announces the *St. Louis* trip as a special charter (*Sonderfahrt*).[3] HAPAG charged 800 Reichsmark for first-class tickets, 500 Reichsmark for tourist-class tickets, and a collateral (*Rückreise Depot*) for costs incurred in case the line had to return passengers to Germany. None of this needed to be explained to the clientele the bulletin targeted. In its pretense of normality, the language reveals how HAPAG participated in the NS regime's othering and expulsion of Jews.

Jewish refugee organizations had learned about HAPAG planning a special migrant transport already in late 1938 and, following its cancellation, HAPAG in early 1939 informed Morris Troper at the Paris office of the American Jewish Joint Distribution Committee (JDC) about a new trip, for which the date of May 13 was set.[4] According to one historical source, HAPAG's director of passage service, Claus-Gottfried Holthusen, spoke of "refugees" and "foreigners" when briefing Captain Schröder on his upcoming assignment and his charges. Only when Schröder pressed him about what kind of refugees were

Figure. 3.1. HAPAG bulletin announcing the Cuba voyage. *Source:* Public domain, from www.blechner.com/german/ssstlouis.htm.

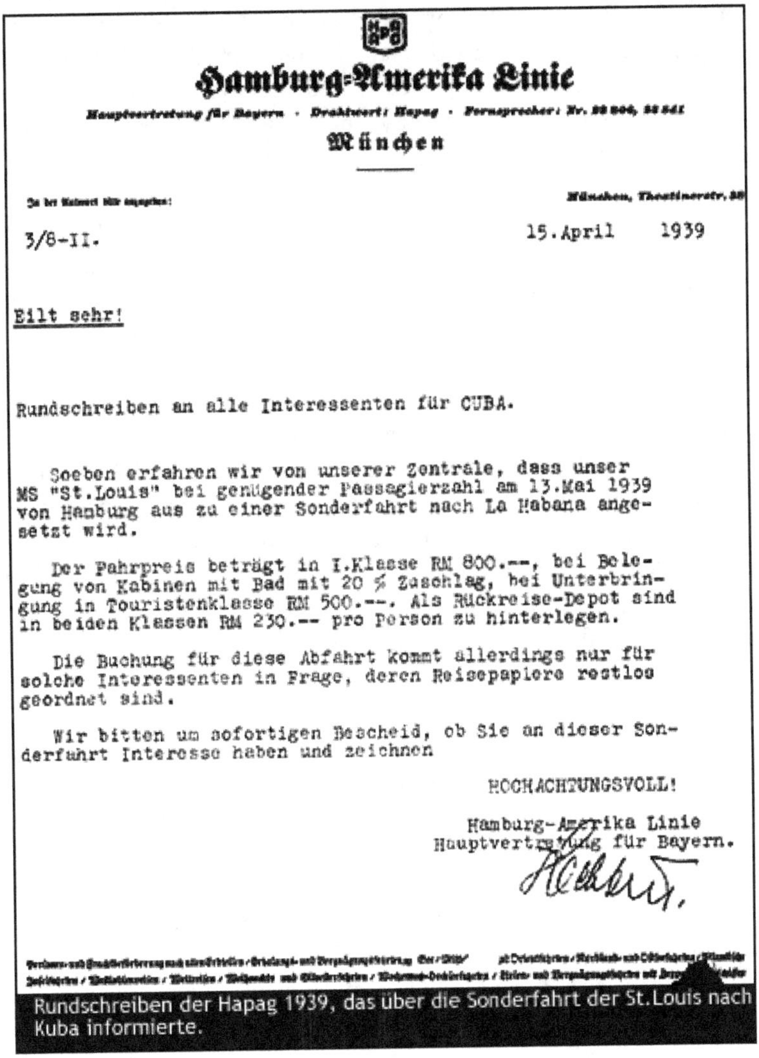

> **Hamburg-Amerika Linie**
> *Hauptvertretung für Bayern · Drahtwort: Hapag · Fernsprecher: Nr. 28 806, 28 541*
>
> **München**
>
> In der Antwort bitte angeben:
> 3/8-II.
>
> München, Theatinerstr. 38
> 15. April 1939
>
> Eilt sehr!
>
> Rundschreiben an alle Interessenten für CUBA.
>
> Soeben erfahren wir von unserer Zentrale, dass unser MS "St.Louis" bei genügender Passagierzahl am 13.Mai 1939 von Hamburg aus zu einer Sonderfahrt nach La Habana angesetzt wird.
>
> Der Fahrpreis beträgt in I.Klasse RM 800.--, bei Belegung von Kabinen mit Bad mit 20 % Zuschlag, bei Unterbringung in Touristenklasse RM 500.--. Als Rückreise-Depot sind in beiden Klassen RM 230.-- pro Person zu hinterlegen.
>
> Die Buchung für diese Abfahrt kommt allerdings nur für solche Interessenten in Frage, deren Reisepapiere restlos geordnet sind.
>
> Wir bitten um sofortigen Bescheid, ob Sie an dieser Sonderfahrt Interesse haben und zeichnen
>
> HOCHACHTUNGSVOLL!
>
> Hamburg-Amerika Linie
> Hauptvertretung für Bayern.
>
> Rundschreiben der Hapag 1939, das über die Sonderfahrt der St.Louis nach Kuba informierte.

at issue did Holthusen acknowledge that they were Jews, describing them as "plain folk who want to leave the country."[5] Placing Jewish migrants on the same ships as non-Jewish passengers (although these often protested), HAPAG passed them off as ordinary travelers, whereby Germany's quiet but steady dumping of its migrants onto

Latin American shores appeared like a normal facet of global traffic. In this sense, Hitler's eyebrow-raising proclamation to requisition luxury ships for the deportation of Germany's Jews (see chapter 2) had long been a reality. In the late 1930s, Berlin oscillated between making noisy threats to expel Jews and seeking pragmatic solutions to advance their resettlement by engaging in discreet negotiations with Britain and by supporting the existing infrastructure for Jewish migration. HAPAG was a prominent part of this infrastructure.

To the *St. Louis* passengers, the double designation of Voyage 98 as a migrant transport and a tourist cruise that, as it were, harbored the opportunity to leave Germany for an indefinite length revealed its cynical nature in the authoritarian execution of its logistics. Having been dispossessed of most of their property (including real estate, stock, and art objects) and forced to pay a tax on fleeing the Reich, Jewish migrants were allowed to take 20 Reichsmark in cash on board, as well as personal belongings worth 1000 Reichsmark.[6] First-hand accounts also report the nerve-racking ordeal prior to and during embarkation—the hazards of traveling to Hamburg and finding accommodation in hotels (where Jews were no longer allowed), the constant threat of random arrests and body searches, and the threat that passage could be denied at the last moment.[7]

Though dispossessed of their belongings, passengers were told they could bring up to ten pieces of luggage onto the ship. Many in fact carried the remainders of their belongings in a single valise, which did not deter longshoremen from offering their service. Thus, unless one knew the reasons for this trip and what motivated the tears shed when the ship departed, there was little that outwardly distinguished the boarding procedures from those of any other departure. By 6 p.m. on May 13, all passengers were on board. At 8 p.m., tug boats towed the *St. Louis* away from its berth at HAPAG's Quay 71 in Hamburg harbor.[8] There was little that distinguished the boarding procedures from those of any other departure, including the orchestra playing "Muß i' denn, muß i' denn zum Städtele hinaus," a nineteenth-century folk-style song traditionally played at passenger ship sailings from German ports.[9] Once aboard, the expelled Jews found themselves being treated as tourists enjoying all the amenities available to regular cruise passengers, including use of the spacious cabins, the elegant social rooms, the swimming pool (set up after departure in a loading hatch) and, most surprisingly to them, the professional and courteous shipboard service performed by the non-Jewish crew. Another source of amazement was the high quality of the food and the kitchen crew's efforts to approximate kosher dining. Captain Gustav Schröder ordered that the portrait of Hitler be removed from the dining hall during religious services.[10] He imparted on his crew to treat the Jewish migrants with the hospitality and respect HAPAG extended to all its passengers. The crew also learned that these passengers had been denationalized and could not be forced to observe German holidays or salute Hitler.

Westbound and Cuba

The *St. Louis* departed Hamburg on May 13 with 899 passengers and added 38 passengers in Cherbourg, France, on May 15 before sailing to Cuba. Of the total of 937 passengers, 930 were Jewish. Of the 937, 409 were men, 350 women, and 148 children. On the westbound crossing, one passenger, Moritz Weiler, died from a heart condition and received a sea burial, leaving 936 to arrive in Havana on May 27; of those, 29 remained there—28 by legal disembarkation (22 had the means to upgrade their visas to meet Cuba's tightened regulation, 4 were citizens of Spain, 2 were Cuban) and one, Max Loewe, by jumping into Havana harbor and requiring stationary medical treatment.[11] For its eastbound journey *St. Louis* departed Havana on June 2 with 907 passengers, of which one, Istvan Winkler, was not a refugee and eventually returned to his native country, Hungary, after the ship docked in Antwerp on June 17.

Their dramatic journey and their status as refugees made the passengers enter the annals of history as "the *St. Louis* Jews." This term belies the considerable diversity between them regarding national, economic, and cultural background as well as visa status and personal history with the NS regime. Of the 899 passengers leaving Hamburg, 388 were booked in first class and 511 in second class;[12] 872 of the passengers came from Germany, and while all had forfeited their citizenship, many at least culturally still identified as German. A portion of the passengers came from Poland, Hungary, and Czechoslovakia.[13] Numerous male passengers had been incarcerated in concentration camps after Kristallnacht, a factor that drove the threats of mass suicide on the return journey. Another criterion of differentiation was the passengers' transit status: Nearly 80 percent of the passengers (734) possessed quota numbers for US immigration; the prospects and intentions of the other passengers are not fully clear. Quite a few, but certainly not all, had relatives waiting for them in Cuba.

When it departed Hamburg, the ship's status and that of those traveling on it could not have been more ambiguous. The *St. Louis* officially operated as a cruise ship on a special charter, but the fact that passengers traveled in different classes rather than in one class, as is customary on cruises, likened the trip to regular transatlantic crossings, as did the scheduled stop in Cherbourg, a regular port of call on the transatlantic route for most shipping lines. All passengers enjoyed the amenities of middle-class tourists. But since that demographic entails citizenship, it no longer included Jews, nor did the tourist label reflect the passengers' intention to leave Germany for good (as discussed below, it was precisely the passengers' lack of a return address that foiled their entry into the US Virgin Islands). In that regard, they were migrants. But because the ship served Germany's agenda to expel Jews, most of them migrated involuntarily. They had been formally denationalized and Cuba's refusal to accept them would officially turn them into refugees. The *St. Louis* was about to become a floating camp of stateless rejects under order to return its passengers into the hands of the Gestapo. Yet their status as refugees was also ill-defined. Their possession of US quota numbers made many of them at least prospective immigrants[14]—a circumstance that Germany generally welcomed for the sake of advancing Jewish resettlement.

On May 5, 1939, one week before the *St. Louis* left Hamburg, Cuba's President Federico Laredo Brú overruled the validity of tourist visas by reinstating Cuba's old immigration laws. The decision became formalized as Decree 937. Manuel Benítez González, the immigration minister, assured HAPAG's Havana representative Luis Clasing that those who had booked passage prior to the issuing of this law (which included all *St. Louis* passengers) were grandfathered in. This arrangement was a last-minute face-saving device by Laredo Brú, who had been caught off guard by Benítez allowing passengers from another HAPAG liner, the *Iberia*, to disembark in Havana.[15] It was the last time Benítez got his way. He resigned from his post the week of May 14 (effective June 1) and went on leave.[16] His successor proceeded to strictly enforce Decree 937 and the immigration offices in Havana were all but closed for months.[17] HAPAG, for their part, did not share the news about Decree 937 with Captain Schröder and the passengers. On May 13, the *St. Louis* left Hamburg and, after calling in Cherbourg on May 15, made its way across the Atlantic toward Cuba. While en route to Cherbourg, HAPAG informed Schröder that two other ships carrying Jewish migrants, the French liner *Flandre* and the British liner *Orduña*, were also on their way to Havana. Fearful that an influx of Jewish migrants into Cuba could hamper the *St. Louis*'s ability to land its passengers, HAPAG advised Schröder to reach Cuba before the other two ships. On May 23, the Jewish Relief Committee (JRC) in Cuba wrote to the National Coordinating Committee for Aid for Refugees (NCC) that Cuban immigration authorities had just informed shipping lines that all ships that had left for Cuba twenty-four hours after the issuing of Decree 937 would no longer be allowed to unload their passengers.[18] HAPAG shared the news with Schröder, but since the *St. Louis* was already in the vicinity of Bermuda, Schröder was ordered to steam ahead rather than turn back. As news of possible problems leaked to the passengers, Schröder assembled a passenger committee (a.k.a. "board committee") (see fig. 3.2). Initially, their main task was to monitor the mood on

Figure 3.2. Members of the passenger committee of the MS *St. Louis* pose on the deck of the ship. Pictured from left to right are Sally Guttman, Max Weiss, Herbert Manasse, Max Zellner, Josef Joseph, Arthur Hausdorff, and Ernst Vendig. *Source:* Courtesy of United States Holocaust Memorial Museum.

board, but their responsibilities would considerably expand in the course of the trip (see chapter 4 and appendix).

The *St. Louis* arrived in Havana shortly after 4 a.m. on Sunday, May 27, ahead of *Flandre* and *Orduña*, and docked at the pier. Gustav Schröder immediately started disembarkation in the hope that President Laredo Brú's authorities would not detect the ship right away under the shelter of darkness. But Laredo Brú had instructed port officials to block disembarkation.[19] Armed guards boarded the *St. Louis*, forced those who were in the process of leaving the ship back on board, and blocked the gangway. Several hours after its arrival, the *St. Louis* was ordered to move away from the pier and to anchor in the outer harbor area. Police guarded the ship, which was illuminated with spotlights like a prison complex. A flotilla of dinghies with relatives of the passengers hoping to make contact with their loved ones surrounded the liner (see figs. 3.3 and 3.4).

Soon thereafter, Cuba officially declared the tourist visas of the *St. Louis* passengers invalid.[20] During the week the *St. Louis* was in Havana harbor, anxiety among the passengers steadily increased. On

Figure 3.3. Photo of dinghies with relatives in Havana harbor, taken by *St. Louis* passenger Hella Roubicek (née Loevinsohn). *Source:* Courtesy of United States Holocaust Memorial Museum.

Figure 3.4. Newspaper coverage of dinghies ringing the *St. Louis* in Havana harbor. The article gives delayed coverage of the ship's June 2 departure from Havana. The caption's last sentence falsely claims that the ship anchored twelve miles outside Havana harbor. The image shows the ship isolated mid-harbor before its expulsion from Cuba. *Source:* Central Press. Public Domain.

WATCH THEIR KIN SAIL BACK TO GERMANY

(Central Press Phonephoto)

Small boats crowded with tearful relatives mass about the German liner, St. Louis, as that vessel sailed from Havana with 907 Jewish refugees on board. Cuba denied them entry because they lacked legal permits. The ship anchored 12 miles out of the harbor.

Tuesday, May 30, one of the passengers, Max Loewe, slit his wrists and jumped ship (a crew member jumped after him and pulled him out of the water; according to Schröder, he received first aid on the *St. Louis* before being taken to a Havana hospital, where he remained behind).[21] Another passenger attempted to poison himself in his cabin but was rescued. When other passengers threatened similar actions, Schröder consulted with the committee, which organized suicide watches and acted as an official liaison authorized to convey news from the captain to the passengers. Everyone on the ship witnessed the *Orduña* leaving Havana harbor after discharging some, though not all, of its Jewish passengers.[22] Another ship, the *Iller*, arrived from Germany and was also told that its twelve Jewish migrants would not be allowed into Cuba. The *Flandre*, which had arrived shortly after the *St. Louis*, was also barred from disembarking any of its passengers.

On May 31, the American ambassador, J. Butler Wright, and the consul general, Coert du Bois, learned from Juan J. Ramos, Cuba's Secretary of State, that Laredo Brú's cabinet had voted against giving asylum to the *St. Louis* passengers.[23] According to Ramos, Laredo Brú had stated that, by ignoring the country's immigration laws, HAPAG had "deliberately slapped the President of the Republic in the face" and while he pitied the passengers, forcing the *St. Louis* to return to Germany was "the lesser of two evils."[24] Aboard the *St. Louis*, a group of female passengers sent a telegram to Laredo Brú's wife with a plea to grant them asylum, describing themselves as "389 unhappy, homeless women and 105 children."[25] On June 1, another group of female passengers tried to overwhelm police stationed aboard the ship and push down the gangway before being fought back.[26] By then, Captain Schröder had already made several unsuccessful attempts to visit the offices of Cuban immigration officials and politicians, but on June 1, he felt compelled to go on land again to seek a personal meeting with the president. Laredo Brú refused to see him and, instead, served him with the formal order for the *St. Louis* to leave or be prepared to be removed by force by the Cuban navy.[27] He immediately had a message posted to the passengers that Cuba was forcing the ship to leave by 10 a.m. Friday, June 2, but that negotiations would continue (see fig. 3.5).

Crisscrossing the Caribbean

On Friday, June 2, at 11 a.m., the *St. Louis* slowly pulled out of Havana harbor (see fig. 3.6). Privately chartered dinghies were told to steer clear of the ship, but they still followed the liner as far as they could. The diplomatic negotiations that unfolded between the JDC and Cuba after the *St. Louis*'s departure have been amply documented and do not need to be reiterated in full.[28] However, to understand Cuba's position better, it is worth considering what motivated Laredo Brú's denial of asylum. Several historical accounts mention the

Figure 3.5. Captain Schröder's message informing the passengers that Cuba was forcing the ship to leave within twenty-four hours. The posting emphasizes that the ship's departure was what enabled the JDC's Lawrence Berenson's intervention. The announcement further states that the ship's operator continued to work with refugee organizations to secure a landing outside of Germany and the ship would remain close to the US coast. *Source:* Courtesy of United States Holocaust Memorial Museum.

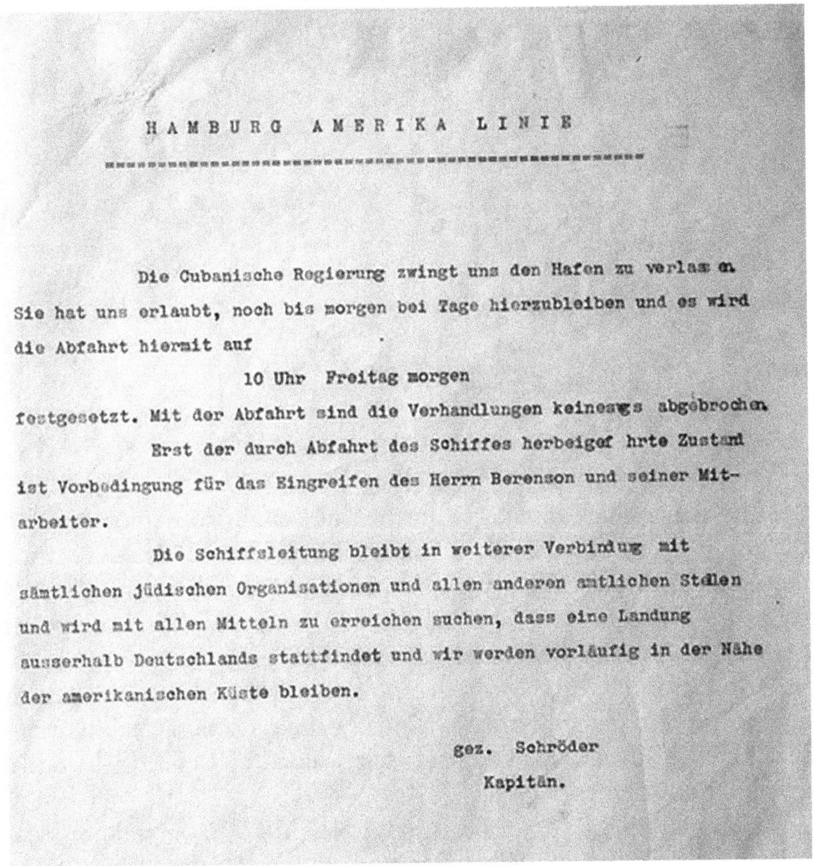

HAMBURG AMERIKA LINIE

Die Cubanische Regierung zwingt uns den Hafen zu verlassen. Sie hat uns erlaubt, noch bis morgen bei Tage hierzubleiben und es wird die Abfahrt hiermit auf

10 Uhr Freitag morgen

festgesetzt. Mit der Abfahrt sind die Verhandlungen keineswegs abgebrochen.

Erst der durch Abfahrt des Schiffes herbeigeführte Zustand ist Vorbedingung für das Eingreifen des Herrn Berenson und seiner Mitarbeiter.

Die Schiffsleitung bleibt in weiterer Verbindung mit sämtlichen jüdischen Organisationen und allen anderen amtlichen Stellen und wird mit allen Mitteln zu erreichen suchen, dass eine Landung ausserhalb Deutschlands stattfindet und wir werden vorläufig in der Nähe der amerikanischen Küste bleiben.

gez. Schröder
Kapitän.

groundswell of anti-immigrant sentiments in Cuba, stoked by right-wing newspaper tycoon José Ignacio Rivero and by Nazi agents who sought to spread antisemitism among the population.[29] Laredo Brú likely felt pressured by these developments, yet there were also other reasons for his decision. He intended to punish Benítez for his visa scheme and both HAPAG and the JDC for making arrangements with

Figure 3.6. The *St. Louis* leaving Havana harbor on the morning of Friday, June 2, 1939. *Source:* Chalmers Library, Kenyon College Digital Collection, Bulmash Family Holocaust Collection.

Benítez rather than with him. Further, he sought to demonstrate to the world that Cuba did not tolerate bribery. He was also concerned that any perceived inactivity on his part could jeopardize his chances to secure his reelection, in which he would have to compete against Manuel Batista, the powerful head of Cuba's armed forces and Benítez's protector. Hence, he was determined to show the public he was able to protect Cuba's borders.[30] Finally, unverifiable accounts claim that he and other Cuban officials felt jealous of Benítez's lucrative immigration business.

On May 29, Lawrence Berenson, a New York lawyer and president of the Cuban-American Chamber of Commerce, arrived in Havana to lead negotiations for the JDC on behalf of the *St. Louis* refugees. Berenson's role is also well documented and will be rehearsed here only in its essentials.[31] It was Berenson to whom Batista in the wake of Kristallnacht had directed the offer to increase Cuba's intake of Jewish refugees. When Laredo Brú refused to honor Benítez's promise to HAPAG that the *St. Louis* passengers would be grandfathered in to Decree 937, Batista chose not to challenge Laredo Brú's decision so as not to appear to have acted against Cuba's national interest. Combined with the country's anti-immigrant and antisemitic climate, Batista's unavailability as a mediator between the JDC and Laredo Brú made Berenson's effort to broker a solution in Havana an uphill battle.[32] Laredo Brú held Berenson responsible for the *St. Louis* crisis. In the president's eyes, Berenson had deliberately ignored Cuba's official position on accepting refugees and, instead, had gone along with Benítez's scheme and HAPAG's practice of bringing ever more Jews to Cuba.[33] When Berenson met with Laredo Brú on June 1, Berenson learned that Benítez had resigned.[34] In the meeting, Laredo Brú accused HAPAG of human trafficking and ordered the *St. Louis* to leave Cuba. But he told Berenson that, once the ship was outside Cuban waters, he would entertain rescue scenarios contingent on financial guarantees that would prevent the *St. Louis* Jews from becoming a burden to his country.[35]

When learning that Laredo Brú was not categorically against granting asylum, Berenson proposed to settle the passengers on the Isle of Pines (*Isla de Pinos*), an island off the southern coast of Cuba. Laredo Brú neither accepted nor rejected the proposal.[36] On June 3—the day after the *St. Louis* had departed—Berenson made a financial offer that included a $50,000 surety bond, guarantees that the passengers would not become public charges for six years, and assurance that male passengers over twenty-one years of age who had no occupation would leave Cuba within three years. In exchange, the passengers would be allowed to disembark in Havana. The same evening, Laredo Brú stipulated modifications to that offer. He demanded $150,000 as a surety bond, an increase to nine years of the period in which the Jewish passengers would not become public charges, and a guarantee that all males would leave the country as soon as possible. In addition, the passengers were to land at a location sixty miles away from the capital. While JDC staff were discussing the new terms the following day, they learned from Berenson that Laredo Brú had yet again raised his terms steeply, now demanding a $450,000 cash bond in addition to the surety bond that Laredo Brú had already raised to $150,000.[37] The JDC felt they were being blackmailed. The Isle of Pines proposal went nowhere, nor did Berenson act on the advice of the State Department to entertain an offer from the Dominican Republic, initially made at Évian and now renewed, to accept the refugees for a $500 per person bond. The reason why Berenson declined to negotiate for this option remains unclear.[38] As C. Paul Vincent has found, by June 5 it became clear to the JDC that Berenson had lost all negotiating power and refused to divulge whether he had ever spoken to the consul of the Dominican Republic. According to Berenson, the JDC's acceptance notice of the terms quoted by Laredo Brú had been sent to Laredo Brú's office on June 5, but the president, half an hour earlier, had irreversibly shut down negotiations because his conditions had not been met.[39] On June 7, the JDC made a last-ditch attempt to sway Laredo Brú by executing a transfer of the funds Laredo Brú had demanded to Chase National Bank, Havana. At this point, US President Roosevelt got involved by personally backing US financial support to keep the refugees in Cuba. In Vincent's assessment, the reason Roosevelt had not involved himself any sooner was that Berenson, having misjudged his leverage as a negotiator, had given neither the JDC nor the US government any reason to believe the crisis needed Roosevelt's personal engagement. Berenson's role as a negotiator ultimately looked rather diminished even in the eyes of his own organization.[40]

Once the *St. Louis* took course toward Florida on June 2, Schröder received encouraging telegrams from HAPAG's New York office that the JDC was continuing to negotiate with Cuba. He harbored hopes of obtaining permission to land his passengers in Florida, but the lack of any positive signs from US politicians or immigration officials increased his feeling of despair. It has been impossible to clarify what exactly transpired between the *St. Louis* and naval authorities near Florida. The prevailing narrative has been that Schröder forged a plan to release a large number of passengers into lifeboats close to Florida but that the US Coast Guard learned of the plan and intercepted the liner, ordering Schröder to keep moving.[41] The captain's report of the journey to HAPAG contains no information on the exact spot of the interception. *The New York Times* on June 5 reported that the *St. Louis* encountered the US Coast Guard cutter CG 244, based in Fort Lauderdale, just off the coast, but on the open ocean.[42] This information is at variance with Schröder's version of events. In his travelogue *Heimatlos auf hoher See* he writes,

> And so, one fine morning, we entered one of the small ports, just to test whether or not this move was being anticipated and whether measures to address it were under

way. . . . When we reached our place of anchorage, planes and Coast Guard cutters approached us to prevent us from landing. So, I steered the ship back out of port. Staying close to the coast to keep the passengers calm and distracted, I took a southwest course toward Havana.[43]

Historians have long repeated a combination of the differing accounts by Schröder and by *The New York Times*, starting with Hans Herlin's 1961 book *No Promised Land* and continuing with Arthur D. Morse's 1967 book, *While Six Million Died: A Chronicle of American Apathy*. Recently, the United States Coast Guard presented its version of the story. In a detailed entry on its "Frequently Asked Questions" website, the Coast Guard not only dismisses Herlin's and Morse's accounts as unsubstantiated and false, but also questions Schröder's.[44] The statement explains that the size and draft of the *St. Louis* would have severely limited the captain's options of approaching the shore. The shallowness of Florida's coast even at high tide (36 feet) would have presented a considerable hazard for the ship. The article does not deny the presence of CG244 at the scene, though it claims that there is no information on where exactly this encounter may have taken place. It asserts that neither US Coast Guard records nor US State Department records nor US Treasury Department records "substantiate any claim that CG-244 or any other Coast Guard vessels had standing orders to interdict St. Louis should she attempt to make a run toward the Florida coast in an attempt to disembark her passengers."[45]

The Coast Guard does, however, assert that the *St. Louis* was "of considerable concern" to Secretary of the Treasury Henry Morgenthau, Jr., and the statement cites two conversations between Morgenthau and Secretary of State Cordell Hull. In the first, on June 5, Hull infamously decided on the unfeasibility of issuing US tourist visas to the *St. Louis* refugees because they had no addresses to return to. Further, Hull imparted to Morgenthau that the issue was between Cuba and the passengers and that the US had no role in it. In the second conversation, on June 6, Morgenthau said that the exact location of the *St. Louis* was currently unknown and asked whether it was "proper to have the Coast Guard look for it." Hull's response was affirmative but he cautioned Morgenthau against sharing the search for the ship with the press, in response to which Morgenthau assured Hull, "Oh no. No, no. They would just—oh, they might send a plane to do patrol work . . . There would be nothing in the papers."[46] After receiving Hull's consent, Morgenthau instructed Coast Guard Headquarters in Washington, DC, to search for the ship discreetly and to notify him when they located it.

The Coast Guard's online statement vigorously refutes the charge that it prevented the *St. Louis* passengers from landing in Florida. The statement concludes that "given [Morgenthau and Hull's] conversations it becomes quite apparent that there were no orders to interdict the ship and the US Coast Guard units were dispatched out of concern for those on board, not as is supposed by Morse, Schroeder, and Herlin, to interdict the refugees and prevent them from landing."[47] Given its official source, the defensiveness of the Coast Guard statement surprises. For instance, the unnamed author, who was commissioned to write the piece, finds it appropriate to speculate as to why Schröder crafted his version of the story and claims that one possible reason was that "the fates of many of his passengers in the Holocaust would have been known and it may very well have influenced his retelling." The fact that this article, which is not issued by a historical archive or museum, but by a US organ of defense and border security, ventures such speculations gives one pause, as does the fact that the Coast Guard, in sharp disregard of standards of maritime accuracy, leaves the author's misidentification of the *St. Louis* as a steam ship ("SS") uncorrected. This would never have passed muster in descriptions of its own or the navy's vessels. The writer comes across as a hired amateur, who is strongly motivated (or advised) to clear the Coast Guard of any charges of callous conduct toward the *St. Louis* passengers.

The reasons for the rejection of the *St. Louis* passengers by the United States are well known. Like Cuba, the US was still suffering from the effects of the Great Depression. This made Roosevelt prioritize domestic political interests over helping refugees. While one shipload of them hardly presented a challenge for the US economy, Roosevelt was vulnerable to pressure from nativists and antisemites who regarded refugees, and Jews in particular, as politically and economically undesirable.[48] Further, Roosevelt felt he needed to appease isolationist hardliners in Congress, so as to garner support for his longer-term anti-fascist course in the event of a war, and thus was reluctant to test their goodwill on a relatively limited political issue. Vincent writes that the failure of the Wagner-Rogers bill (which proposed granting asylum to 20,000 Jewish refugee children outside the set immigration quota) to make its way to the floor of the Senate the very week the *St. Louis* was idling off the coast of Florida may have further discouraged Roosevelt from intervening.[49]

As the conversation between Morgenthau and Hull indicates, even after Cuba had expelled the *St. Louis* from its waters the US kept the focus on a Cuba-centered solution. The State Department did not object to the Jewish migrants on the *St. Louis* landing in their own backyard—as long as it was not US territory. A proposal to have the passengers temporarily settle on the US Virgin Islands was practical and easy to implement and may not have alarmed Washington, DC, nativists. But as Hull's petty rationale about the unfeasibility of issuing tourist visas shows, so intent was the State Department on preventing the proposal that it hid behind a litany of bureaucratic catch-22s.[50] Its "you first" attitude toward Cuba and its anxious protectionism over its portion of the Virgin Islands makes the State Department's position comparable to those voiced by Europe's colonial powers at Evian.

On June 4, the State Department met the many pleas for asylum from passengers, relatives, friends, and prominent allies, such as actor Edward G. Robinson, with an official response—that entry into the United States is regulated by established immigration laws and that "the German refugees must await their turn before they may be admissible to the United States."[51] It is possible that Washington, if it had realized how rapidly the situation was deteriorating for the refugees due to Berenson's mishandling of the negotiations, might have intervened sooner to help solve the crisis. Be that as it may, on June 7, Roosevelt instructed officials to facilitate a final meeting between Berenson, Cuba's President Laredo Brú, and Chase National Bank Havana. But when the passengers sent another telegram imploring Roosevelt to help, since 400 of the over 900 passengers on board were women and children, the US did not respond.[52] Cuba, for its part, mimicked the State Department's petty bureaucratic reasoning. On June 6, *The Washington Post* reported Laredo Brú's blunt explanation for the change in Cuba's asylum politics: "The president said that under the Evian Conference agreement Cuba had had a 'moral duty' to accept the landing of 3,000 German Jewish refugees. He added, however, that since the agreement, more than 7,000 had landed, so the obligation was ended."[53]

In contrast to the US, Canada never received an asylum request directly from the *St. Louis*. Following the Canadian press's coverage of the crisis, prominent Jewish and non-Jewish Canadians petitioned Prime Minister Mackenzie King to allow the migrants to come to Canada. The petition, however, was not sent to King until June 7, the day the *St. Louis* went on her return trip to Europe, and did not receive an official response from the government until June 19, two days after the ship's arrival in Antwerp.[54] Reiterating his country's position at Évian, Oscar Shelton, Canada's undersecretary of foreign affairs, argued that granting asylum to the *St. Louis* Jews was not in compliance with Canadian immigration law and policy. Canada, he explained, sought only permanent immigrants with agricultural skills, technical and scientific expertise, or investment capital. Shelton took pains to cite numerous technicalities that supposedly prevented Canada from granting asylum to the *St. Louis* Jews. He argued that the passengers' selection of Cuba rather than Canada as a transit country to the US proved their keen awareness that Canada does not grant temporary asylum. Shelton also pointed the finger at HAPAG, noting that the company had ignored Cuba's cancellation of the passengers' entry permits.[55] Shelton's reasoning reflects Canada's immigration policy in the 1930s. While far more restrictive than Washington's, it was motivated by similar factors, including fear among the public that refugees would create an economic liability and slow the country's recovery from the Great Depression. There was also considerable anti-Jewish sentiment among both the population and the government.[56]

Eastbound

After the US State Department officially declined asylum to the *St. Louis* Jews, Schröder had no choice but to return the ship to Europe. Hurried by a telegram from HAPAG recalling the liner to Germany instantly, so it could be readied to resume its regular cruise schedule,[57] and aware that fuel and supplies were running low, on June 7 Schröder steered the *St. Louis* on an eastbound course. For several days, there were rumors that the ship might receive permission to land the refugees in the Dominican Republic, but that hope eventually waned.[58] The passengers became desperate. A group of men marched on the bridge to force Schröder to change course. He dissuaded them from using force against him and the crew and did not pursue any charges against them. His description of the incident in his official report to HAPAG remains deliberately vague. Only in his 1949 memoir of the voyage does he describe the incident in greater detail and characterize it as mutinous.[59] Resolved not to return his 907 charges to Germany or even so much as enter the North Sea, he concocted a plan to set the ship on shallow grounds off the Southern English coast, pretending that it had foundered, which would have necessitated releasing the passengers into lifeboats to be rescued by British authorities.[60] He did not have to go through with the plan. On June 13, he received a telegram from Morris Troper that the European branch of the JDC had brokered an agreement with Belgium, the Netherlands, France, and Britain to grant asylum to all refugees.

In the course of the eastbound crossing, Schröder kept receiving telegrams from HAPAG assuring him that both its New York and Hamburg offices were doing everything to help the *St. Louis* avoid returning to Cuxhaven. Schröder was not privy to the feverish negotiations that the JDC now redirected toward Europe. At the center of these were two JDC negotiators: Paul Baerwald, chairman-on-leave of the JDC and member of the President's Advisory Committee on Political Refugees, who, at the time, was working in London with the Intergovernmental Committee on Refugees (established as a result of the 1938 Évian conference); and Morris Troper, who was the chairman of the European Executive Council of the JDC and was based in the organization's Paris office. Baerwald had to take into consideration that the JDC was responsible not only for the *St. Louis* Jews, but also for the refugees on the *Flandre* and the *Orduña*. At the same time, he knew that several European leaders, despite personally feeling empathetic to the fate of the Jewish refugees on the Atlantic, had strong concerns about being forced to accept what was then characterized as the uncontrolled dumping of refugees onto European shores. Baerwald expected resistance from Britain because the country was already in the process of accepting thousands of children from Germany on the "*Kindertransport.*"[61] His view was reinforced by Robert Pell, an influential American diplomat and vice director of the Intergovernmental Committee of Refugees, who had been part of the US delegation at Évian (visible on the far right edge in fig. 1.2) and who, based on his knowledge of British politics, noted that the British were further deterred from accepting more Jews because they already felt pressured to respond to the efforts of Jewish organizations working with German and Italian shipping lines to resettle more Jews in British mandate Palestine.

Yet, together with Morris Troper in Paris, Baerwald feverishly negotiated with several European countries on behalf of the *St. Louis* passengers. The strategy that crystallized was to present the *St. Louis* case, in Vincent's characterization, "not as a case of 'illegal dumping' of but as a special exigency involving legitimate refugees."[62] On June 10, HAPAG communicated to the JDC that 743 of the passengers of the *St. Louis* had affidavits for the United States. While this fact was widely known, Vincent points out that it strengthened the JDC's "special exception" approach. That only a small number of migrants lacked such affidavits made it easier for Troper to find asylum for them elsewhere.[63] HAPAG's cable moved the JDC to formulate an official position as to why they were now prepared to put up the funds to help the refugees on the *St. Louis*, the *Flandre*, and the *Orduña* without appearing to favor their cases over those of the countless Jewish migrants who were sailing on other ships. An exception could be made for the Jews on those three ships because most of them had intended to use Cuba as nothing but a way station to the US and had become the subject of Cuba's reversal of policy. Baerwald forwarded the information to Pell, who used it to sway Britain's Lord Winterton, who had headed the British delegation at Évian and promised to lobby the British government on behalf of the JDC's request. On June 12, a meeting took place in London between the JDC, the British government, and representatives of various British private organizations, at the end of which Britain gave its consent to accept a little under 300 of the *St. Louis* passengers.[64] At the same time, negotiations were taking place that swayed France, Belgium, and the Netherlands to accept a share of the passengers.[65] The same day, Schröder received word from Troper of the positive, if still tentative outcome.[66] On June 13, Troper sent another telegram to the *St. Louis*, confirming that arrangements with England, France, the Netherlands, and Belgium had been finalized and advising Schröder that information about the port of landing was forthcoming.[67]

On June 14, the news became official with an article in *The New York Times* informing the world that the four European countries had admitted the *St. Louis* passengers on a temporary basis.[68] On June 17, Troper and other JDC officials met the *St. Louis* at the Schelde estuary near Vlissingen (see fig. 3.7). A few hours later, the *St. Louis* docked in Antwerp (see fig. 3.8). Over the next twenty-four hours,

Figure 3.7. Morris Troper (center) and his wife (with hat) pose with Jewish refugees on the deck of the MS *St. Louis* in the port of Antwerp. Among others pictured are Liesel Joseph, Ruth Karliner, Heinz Gallant, and a person named Windmueller. *Source:* Courtesy of United States Holocaust Memorial Museum.

Figure 3.8. Passengers on deck of the MS *St. Louis* watch while the ship pulls into Antwerp. *Source:* Courtesy of United States Holocaust Memorial Museum.

all refugees were transported to their respective countries of asylum. Holland sent a ferry, the *Jan van Herckel*, to pick up its contingent of 181 refugees. France received 227 refugees and Britain 284. For the transport to Boulogne-sur-Mer and to Southampton respectively, HAPAG had dispatched one of its cargo ships, the *Rhakotis*, which had been provisionally rearranged for passenger transport. The 214 refugees to remain in Belgium boarded a heavily guarded special train for Brussels.[69] At 8 p.m. on Monday, June 19, the last passenger had disembarked the *St. Louis*.

The last-minute acceptance of the *St. Louis* into Antwerp came almost as a relief to Nazi Germany. For HAPAG the damage was done. What began as a lucrative proposition for the company had turned into a considerable liability. The refugee drama had jeopardized the ship's deployment schedule and news reports of threatened mass suicides on board potentially presented a PR problem.[70] A direct return to Germany, which would have meant the concentration camp for the ship's passengers, would only have exacerbated this image problem. Claus-Gottfried Holthusen, the director of passage service, on whose watch everything had transpired, came under pressure.[71] For Goebbels, the ship's voyage became yet another operation that, like Kristallnacht, escalated in ways that now required damage control. When the ship was still on course to Germany, Goebbels and the Gestapo, apparently wary of further negative press, informed HAPAG that the passengers had nothing to fear and would not be taken to camps upon arrival. Then the Gestapo changed course, directing the company to "kindly get rid of the Jews somewhere else and without much ado"[72] and that, going forward, every immigrant returning to German soil would be placed in a concentration camp.[73] Gestapo's Hamburg division chartered a tugboat to meet the *St. Louis* in Cuxhaven to take the passengers into custody. The German Foreign Office instructed HAPAG that, when organizing migrant transports in the future, the company was to avoid such decidedly unwanted results.[74]

Already on June 16, immediately after learning that the *St. Louis* passengers were going to receive asylum in Europe, HAPAG sent a telegram to Captain Schröder, thanking him for his service. Avoiding words like "Jews" and "refugees," the note commended the captain for skillfully steering "your ship, your crew, and your passengers during these critical days."[75] The use of the word *"Passagiere"* (passengers) is consistent with HAPAG's intent, as discussed earlier, to bill the journey as a regular cruise and to conceal its true nature. HAPAG's curious disavowal of the passengers' actual status and of its captain's key role in helping prevent their delivery into concentration camps yet again foregrounds the status of the *St. Louis* Jews—and of refugees in general—as both same and other, as belonging to humanity while also being excluded from it.

Two hours after delivering its Jewish passengers to Antwerp, the *St. Louis* left for New York, from where the ship completed three cruises for American tourists before Schröder, on August 25, received order to return the *St. Louis* to Hamburg due to the impending outbreak of war. On August 29, the *St. Louis* left New York and, while at sea, was caught by the news that on Friday, September 1, Germany had invaded Poland. The crew camouflaged the ship and renamed it *Louise* with Amsterdam indicated as its home port. Schröder successfully steered the ship on a stealth course between Greenland and Iceland to Murmansk, a port in the Soviet Union, which, at that point, was still allied with Nazi Germany. Upon arrival, most of its crew were sent home by train. A skeleton crew repaired the ship, which remained in Murmansk until December 22, 1939, when Schröder successfully returned it to Hamburg without encountering enemy contact. On January 1, the *St. Louis* reached Hamburg, where she was refitted to house German navy crew before being transferred to Kiel. There she was badly damaged by American bombers on August 30, 1944. After the war, the British Occupational Forces permitted the ship to be towed to Hamburg, where it was provisionally repaired and stationed as a hotel and restaurant ship from 1947 until 1950. In 1951 to 1952, the *St. Louis* was broken up.[76]

4

The *St. Louis* Passengers and the Press Coverage of Voyage 98

WHEN THE *ST. LOUIS* docked in Antwerp on June 17, 1939, the clouds of war were already forming over Europe, but no one foresaw that within a year Nazi Germany would invade three of the four countries that had granted asylum to the ship's passengers. Many initially went to refugee camps such as Westerbork, a large facility located in the Netherlands. After the Wehrmacht swept through Holland, France, and Belgium, camps like Westerbork eventually became way stations to concentration camps in the east: 254 of the Jews who had traveled to Cuba on the *St. Louis*—and who, thus, had already been in Havana harbor and in viewing distance of the US coast—died this way. For many others, the years of Nazi occupation meant long periods of living in hiding and staying on the run.[1]

Still, more than two-thirds of the *St. Louis* Jews survived the war and the Third Reich. Many wrote about the trip in letters to relatives and friends or described their impressions in diaries, which chillingly illustrate how the passengers attempted to cope with their uncertain fate. While the westbound crossing was, by most accounts, pleasant enough, once Cuba rejected their landing permits, they officially became refugees.[2] Suddenly, other labels also threatened to impose themselves. Captain Schröder compared the passengers' status as stateless rejects with the condition of homelessness, which is why he titled his personal account of the *St. Louis* voyage *Heimatlos auf hoher See* (*Homeless on the High Seas*). But their situation was even more complex. They were tourists, migrants, refugees, and inmates all at once. It is this contradictory quality—constantly evolving while also staying the same—that the first half of this chapter traces. In no small part does their confusing status owe to the means of their travel, the ocean liner. For them, the *St. Louis* was at once an instrument to escape Nazi Germany's concentration camps and a variant of the camps. But rather than passively accepting their situation, the passengers tried to gain control over it as best they could. They did so by, among other things, sharing their suicide threats and their appeals to politicians with the press, whose coverage of the voyage is the focus of the second half of this chapter.

Tourists—Migrants—Refugees—Inmates: Passenger Accounts of the Trip

The amenities of the *St. Louis* greatly impressed the Jewish migrants. Erich Dublon, who sailed with his family (see fig. 4.1), writes that the ship struck him as a "first-class luxury hotel."[3] Once Cherbourg lay behind them, he waited for the crew to set up the provisional pool (see fig. 4.2). The trip's only flaw, he notes, was its short duration.[4] Of the 373 crew who served on the *St. Louis* on Voyage 98, almost half were cabin crew responsible for looking after the passengers.[5] Captain Schröder took pride in the shipboard service and was confident of the soothing effect the journey across the Atlantic had on the refugees: "Nice weather, good food, the clean ocean air, and an attentive crew ensure the carefree atmosphere on long sea journeys. The ocean makes any memories of life on land fade quickly, even if they are sad. A hospitable ship in the middle of the wide ocean is a different world altogether. . . . Optimism and hope are flourishing."[6] Keenly aware of the traumatic circumstances that brought the passengers on board, he had Hitler's portrait removed from the dining hall during prayer service. Attending to their needs as best he could, he instructed the kitchen crew to include eggs and fish as often as possible, as there was no kosher food on board (see fig. 4.3).

Figure 4.1. Members of the Dublon family pose on the deck of the MS *St. Louis*. Erich Dublon is second from the right, sitting on the railing and wearing a white hat. *Source:* Courtesy of United States Holocaust Memorial Museum.

Figure 4.2. The provisional pool (set up inside a cargo loading hatch) on board the St. Louis. *Source:* Courtesy of United States Holocaust Memorial Museum.

Figure 4.3. MS *St. Louis* cabin-class menu, Sunday, May 21, 1939. Dishes include caviar on toast, bouillon, pan-fried sole, sirloin steak, turkey, asparagus with Hollandaise sauce, sauerkraut, creamed spinach, macaroni, potatoes (mash, boiled, Lyonnaise), cucumber salad and green salad, Californian peaches, chocolate mousse, ice cream, cheese, fruits, coffee, and tea. *Source*: Courtesy of United States Holocaust Memorial Museum.

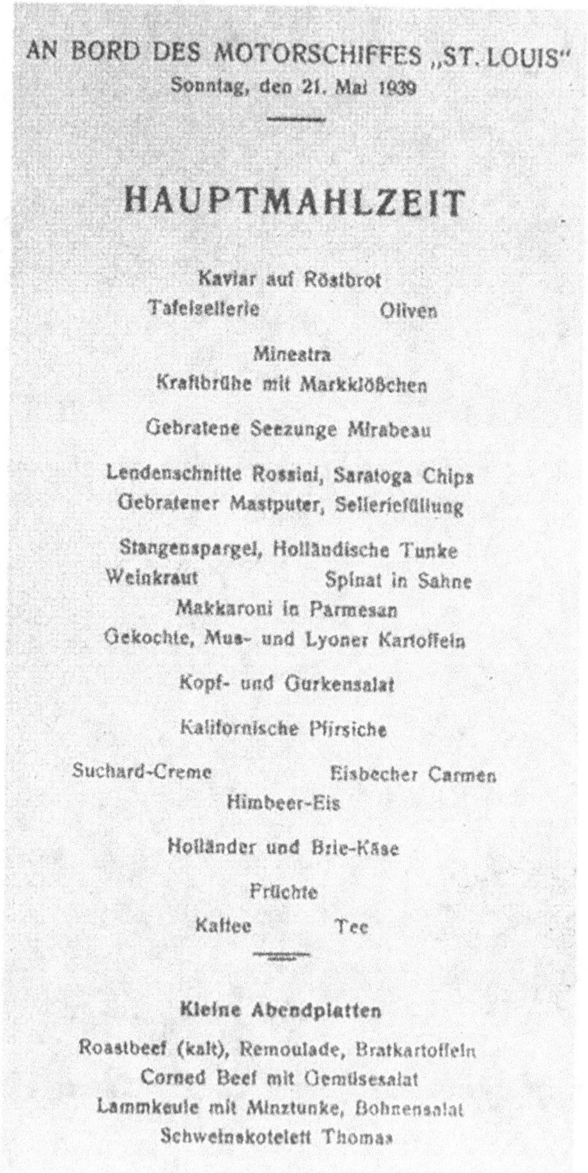

AN BORD DES MOTORSCHIFFES „ST. LOUIS"
Sonntag, den 21. Mai 1939

HAUPTMAHLZEIT

Kaviar auf Röstbrot
Tafelsellerie   Oliven

Minestra
Kraftbrühe mit Markklößchen

Gebratene Seezunge Mirabeau

Lendenschnitte Rossini, Saratoga Chips
Gebratener Mastputer, Selleriefüllung

Stangenspargel, Holländische Tunke
Weinkraut   Spinat in Sahne
Makkaroni in Parmesan
Gekochte, Mus- und Lyoner Kartoffeln

Kopf- und Gurkensalat

Kalifornische Pfirsiche

Suchard-Creme   Eisbecher Carmen
Himbeer-Eis

Holländer und Brie-Käse

Früchte
Kaffee   Tee

Kleine Abendplatten
Roastbeef (kalt), Remoulade, Bratkartoffeln
Corned Beef mit Gemüsesalat
Lammkeule mit Minztunke, Bohnensalat
Schweinskotelett Thomas

The young passengers soon used the ship as their playground. One account describes them as "happy."[7] That he had not yet learned to swim did not keep Sol Messinger from enjoying the pool with his father. Jews had no access to public pools in Germany. Phil Freund was startled when a table steward courteously took his order and even helped him carve his meat. "We have been spat on, beaten up, kicked, and our houses have been set on fire—and now there was a non-Jew who was just really nice."[8] The westbound crossing closely resembled a regular cruise. Nights were filled with costume parties and themed balls, some of which required evening attire (see fig. 4.4 and fig. 4.5). The ship had shops where passengers used on-board currency to buy products they had long missed, such as good tobacco.[9] During warm weather, everyone went to the pool or the sports deck, where the crew organized children's parties. The atmosphere and service would have done HAPAG's cruise brochures proud. The *St. Louis* boasted neither the dimensions nor the extravagant luxury of the era's superliners. But accounts of the Cuba voyage confirm that HAPAG was turning cruising into a middle-class experience.[10] As Dublon's diary shows, passengers were aware of the fact that the *St. Louis* was hurrying to arrive in Havana ahead of two other refugee ships.[11] Yet life at sea helped many of them temporarily forget (or repress) the reason they were on the ship in the first place (see fig. 4.6). This sense of distractedness, brought about by

Figure 4.4. Refugees on board the *St. Louis* dance in the ship's cabin-class social hall. *Source:* Courtesy of United States Holocaust Memorial Museum.

Figure 4.5. Refugees on board the *St. Louis* attend a party in evening attire. *Source:* Courtesy of United States Holocaust Memorial Museum.

Figure 4.6. German Jewish refugee Werner Lenneberg roller-skates on the deck of the MS *St. Louis*. *Source:* Courtesy of United States Holocaust Memorial Museum.

the glamour and the comforts an ocean liner affords, suggests that the *St. Louis* may have functioned like a fetish that, to some extent, covered up a trauma that was both experiential and historical.

Reality started to set in even before arrival in Havana. On Tuesday, May 23, an elderly, ailing passenger, Moritz Weiler, passed away. As Schröder notes, "he had a broken heart because he was driven away from the place where all his life he had worked in harmony with his non-Jewish colleagues. His last wish was to be buried at sea."[12] Right after the burial, a member of the ship's kitchen crew killed himself by jumping overboard at the very spot from where Weiler's body had been committed to the ocean. After HAPAG notified the *St. Louis* by cable that the situation in Havana was uncertain and the news spread among the passengers, Schröder established a committee of passenger representatives from both classes (see fig. 3.2). The members were Dr. Josef Joseph (chair), Dr. Arthur Hausdorff, Herbert Manasse, Dr. Max Weiss, and Dr. Max Zellner. Sally Guttman and Dr. Ernst Vendig joined the committee on the eastbound leg.[13] Most of them were lawyers. The committee had two functions: The captain regularly consulted with its members so as to discuss how certain turns of events might impact the passengers; Schröder also used them to convey HAPAG's orders and his decisions to the passengers. First assembled on May 23, the committee in the weeks to come would assume a crucial function in helping maintain peace and calm on board.

Arrival in Havana afforded the passengers the last moments of normality and harmony. Dublon was charmed by the view onto Havana harbor at dawn: "The city presented itself to us in its full beauty with its towering capitol, the government building, and the palm trees that greeted us in the morning wind. The city is so close that we can make out trolleys and buses" (see fig. 4.7).[14] But everything was about to change. Armed guards arrived and pushed a group of passengers who had already disembarked back onto the gangway and up to the deck. When the *St. Louis* was ordered to anchor in the middle of the harbor, the passengers suspected that something was wrong. With no new information forthcoming and with stifling heat and humidity blanketing the motionless ship, anxiety began to increase. The only positive experience for the passengers during those first two days in Havana harbor was when they were able to spot their relatives drawing near in chartered dinghies. Some wanted to jump overboard and swim to the small boats but were stopped; others

Figure 4.7. A view of Havana harbor, courtesy of Fritz Dieter Vendig, son of Ernst and Charlotte Vendig. *Source:* Courtesy of United States Holocaust Memorial Museum.

tossed gifts from Germany to their families. As one passenger notes, the families "circled the *St. Louis* in dinghies and called out names of people who we then notified on the ship, so they could speak with their loved ones. We were so far away and yet so close. I remember one man shouting to his wife: 'Throw me the child, so at least I can have my child.' Of course, she did not do that, but it was sad. The fathers were able to see their wives and children and could not reach them" (see fig. 4.8).[15] The only exception was the son of deceased Moritz Weiler, who received permission to visit his mother on board.

On May 29, the passengers learned from the Cuban dailies that they had been quarantined and that their landing was by no means secure.[16] When, on May 31, Max Loewe slit his wrists and jumped into the harbor, many on board became desperate. Passengers composed a note to the wife of Cuba's President Federico Laredo Brú, pleading with her to intervene. With Loew's suicide attempt drawing the attention of the press, the ship suddenly assumed a different status. Instead of distracting its Jewish passengers from their dire circumstances, as it had during the crossing, it now distracted the press from covering the

Figure 4.8. The MS *St. Louis* in Havana harbor with dinghies holding relatives of the passengers. *Source:* American Jewish Joint Distribution Committee, Inc. Used with permission.

fates of the many other ships that were cruising the world's oceans with Jewish refugees on board. The *St. Louis* came to stand in for all of them, even though it was a very particular ship and its passengers constituted a particular case. But compared to them, the fate of the hordes of refugees piled into Mediterranean cargo steamers felt less immediate at least to US media, which thus did not cover those stories in nearly as much detail as they covered the *St. Louis*.

It took Loewe's suicide attempt for the other passengers to realize that the world was willing to pay attention to them. At the same time, the nihilism of his act meant they no longer were seen as refined middle-class Jews from Germany, but as desperate souls, people whom the Nazis reduced to a subhuman state and herded into concentration camps. Loew's jump triggered threats of mass suicide among the passengers. The *St. Louis*, too, thus came to be seen as a concentration camp or at least a detention camp. Concentration camps in 1939 had a different function and connotation than the death camps the Nazis would set up just a few years later. But even in 1939 the term signified extreme forms of suffering, torture, and at least the possibility of death. As Messinger notes, "Everyone was fearful that we had to return to Germany. And we knew, my parents knew, all the others knew, that if we returned to Germany, we would be taken into a camp."[17] Schröder recalls a female passenger pleading with him: "Captain, we cannot possibly return to Germany. We have lost everything there and the concentration camp will be our end . . . or the North Sea. If you steer the ship safely to Cuxhaven, you will find about one hundred cabins empty, because we fear the concentration camp more than death."[18] According to Herbert Karliner, 300 families had made plans to jump into the ocean to prevent being taken back to Germany.[19] These threats, as discussed below, would soon galvanize much of the US press in support of the refugees.

The *St. Louis*'s departure from Cuba turned into a spectacle of sorts. As Dublon recounts, "all of Havana was on its feet, thousands of cars have blocked the street to the harbor, from every window people were watching."[20] Members of the JDC told the passengers to remain optimistic.[21] Fearing further suicide attempts, Schröder placed guards on deck and asked the Cuban Navy to escort the ship out of the harbor. The *St. Louis* pulled out at slow speed, its engines stopped intermittently.[22] To contain the spreading of rumors and to give passengers a sense of agency while also trying to keep them calm, Schröder took the passenger committee into his confidence as much as he could. After the *St. Louis* had left Havana, he assured the passengers that negotiations continued between HAPAG, the JDC, and Cuba. He also asked one of the rabbis on board to set up resources for spiritual comfort.

When the ship approached Florida, the mood temporarily improved. Cuba, the passengers were told, was still a possibility, as was the Dominican Republic. Nonetheless, by then the United States had become the main focus. Many believed President Roosevelt would not remain indifferent to their fate. Groups of passengers sent telegrams to Roosevelt, his wife, and other officials, pleading with them to give them asylum. On June 4, the *St. Louis* reached the coast of Florida. Dublon writes that Miami appeared on the horizon with its luxury hotels, skyscrapers, and streets lined with palm trees. "With binoculars, one can even make out individual people. There are many luxury motor yachts around with sport fishermen. They wave towards us. We envy them. A plane, possibly police or U.S. customs, circles us."[23] The *St. Louis* turning away from the Florida coast disappointed those passengers who noticed it, but Schröder's initial course toward Cuba made passengers hopeful.

Also on June 4, the *St. Louis* received news that negotiations between the JDC and Cuba were continuing. As Dublon recounts, "people are enjoying a concert and coffee in the social hall and don't seem worried."[24] The following day, HAPAG sent instructions to stand by for a possible return to Havana. In the evening, word arrived that the refugees had been cleared for landing on the Isle of Pines south of Cuba. But when HAPAG failed to confirm the news, the mood on board rapidly deteriorated again. The passengers, regularly updated by Schröder and the board committee, over several long days and nights were subjected to a roller coaster of new developments, which took a considerable toll on them. During those hours when hope was on the rise, the ocean liner ambience and shipboard service almost restored normalcy. During phases of despair, however, the liner revealed itself as what it really was—a floating prison, which the desperate passengers soon enough considered repurposing as a suicide weapon.[25] On June 6, Schröder ordered crew to stand guard at sixty spots on the ship to keep a tight eye on all passengers.[26] When prospects about the Dominican Republic also faded, panic spread. On June 9, a group of men marched on the bridge. Ready to stage a rebellion, they screamed "We don't want to return to Europe! We're forcing you to turn back! We will set fire on board!"[27] This episode, too, has been misrepresented by popular history (see chapters 7 and 8). Schröder claims that the incident was relatively brief and that he was able to assert control over it without the assistance of any of his crew. That he did not mention any of the instigators by name in his captain's log indicates his empathy with them.

By then, Schröder was already secretly making plans to set the *St. Louis* aground off the coast of Cornwall and, hence, did not feel he was lying when he assured the agitated crowd that he would somehow bring them to England, as long as they did not rush into doing something they would regret.[28] On June 10, the *St. Louis* received confirmation that Cuba and the US declined asylum and that the Dominican Republic was also no longer an option. Dublon writes that the news briefing devastated everyone and that many left the hall in tears.[29] Passengers remained in agony until June 12, when their captain told them there was ground for optimism. But the mood had darkened so much that upon receiving confirmation of their rescue, some refused to believe the good news.[30] By June 14, however, there was certainty that the ship would be allowed to go to Belgium. The passengers composed a telegram to Morris Troper that stated that "our gratitude is as big as the ocean on which we have been floating since May 13."[31] On June 17, the *St. Louis* docked in Antwerp. Dublon notes in his diary that "after completing several formalities and clearing customs and passport control, we get to leave the old tub and step onto firm ground."[32] That the passengers were kept away from "firm ground" and had to spend a month as refugees at sea is chilling proof that international law offers little protection to the stateless.

The Coverage of the *St. Louis* Voyage by the US Press

Max Loew's dramatic suicide attempt instantly caught the attention of the press, which closely covered every aspect of the unfolding drama, including the desperate and tearful exchanges between the *St. Louis* passengers and their relatives. The *St. Louis* quickly became a media spectacle. Every detail of its developing story could be gleaned from the dailies' front pages. On June 1, the American public woke to the *New York Times* headline "Fear Suicide Wave on Refugees' Ship—Officers See Mutiny if the *St. Louis* Sails for Germany."[33] The next day, the *Chicago Daily Tribune* wrote "Jewish Refugee Liner Ordered to Leave Cuba—Must Sail or Warship Will Take It in Tow."[34] On June 6, *The Boston Daily Globe* headlined its coverage with good news: "Exiles Promised Temporary Haven as Cuba Relents,"[35] only to retract it the following day, writing "Cuba Again Bars German Refugees."[36] *The New York Times* had similar coverage. On June 6, it reported in a front-page article that "Cuba Opens Doors to 907 on the *St. Louis.*"[37] On June 7, another front-page story was headlined "Cuba Recloses Door to Refugees; 48-Hour Limit on Offer Expires."[38]

These headlines reflect the fact that, in the months before World War II, there was a heightened interest in the fates of Jews trying to escape from Europe. Still, several other refugee ships were experiencing similar troubles at the time, and while their stories were not outright ignored, they did not receive nearly the same attention as the *St. Louis*. The case was of a different magnitude. Many passengers had American relatives and friends, which partially accounts for the interest from American newspapers. But there are further reasons why the story resonated with the public. Its setting was not some remote refugee camp, nor was the *St. Louis* a small freighter in the Black Sea or the Mediterranean. It was a luxury liner, an object of national and maritime prestige that was popular with tourists in Europe and America. And its dramatic voyage was unfolding right between Europe and the Americas. The ship was big enough and known enough that even under ordinary circumstances would it draw attention in every port it called on. Once it turned into a floating refugee camp, it instantly came to embody a riven world full of absurd contradictions and looming crises.

When the media cover refugee crises, they tend to focus on how the events unfold rather than on the deeper reasons behind them. US press reportage of the *St. Louis* voyage was no exception. To be sure, reporters closely followed the JDC's diplomatic wrangling with Cuba's President Laredo Brú and were eager to obtain information from behind the scenes, no matter the source. Taking front and center in the coverage, however, was the human interest factor.[39] If anything stands out in the quality of the coverage, it is that reporters sought to relay the refugees' shifting fortunes according to the conventions of melodrama. To be fair, the *St. Louis* drama had its own, very strident melos that needed no embellishment from the press. Its distinct emotional texture was shaped by the vagaries of daily negotiations that directly impacted the up-and-down mood of the passengers and their families and friends. Readers vicariously experienced a roller-coaster narrative of hope and despair, acceptance and rejection, suicide pacts and suicide watch, Cuban gun boats and American Coast Guard cutters, good German captains and Nazi villains, and aloof politicians and wailing women and children. Though a melodrama, the *St. Louis*'s journey was not devoid of action or forward thrust. To be precise, strategic mandates turned the ship's course into an alternating pattern of making headway toward prospective safe haven or cruising aimlessly after asylum was deferred or declined and delaying the dreaded crossing back to Europe until that was no longer an option. The tempi and the emotions of this pattern varied like in a symphonic score. The *St. Louis* story, in other words, was inherently melodramatic.

I do not mean to invoke melodrama here in a colloquial way. At issue is a specific cultural formation whose generic tropes, as should become clear, shaped press coverage of the incident in near textbook manner. These include (1) ascribing virtuousness and innocence to the passengers to underscore their victim status and the pathos of their suffering; (2) identifying their situation as precarious, even life threatening, in the eventuality of the ship's forced return to Nazi Germany; and (3) casting efforts to save the Jewish refugees from the clutches of the Nazis as a race against the clock that was shaped by the contrasting logics of "too late" and "in the nick of time."[40]

The melodramatic nature of the unfolding drama can be gleaned just by looking at the front pages of the newspapers, which telegraphed the ship's fortunes as oscillating between salvation and doom. On June 3, *The New York Times* published an article headlined "907 Refugees Quit Cuba on Liner—Ship Reportedly Hovering off Coast."[41] But the article's subheading is even more intriguing. It reads "Rumor that the United States Will Permit Entry Is Spread to Avoid Suicides—Company Orders the *St. Louis* back to Hamburg" (fig. 4.9). The headline mobilizes melodrama in two ways: It plays up the ticking clock factor and it imparts privileged knowledge about the state of affairs to readers, leaving it to them to imagine when and how the drama's protagonists will eventually catch up with the upsetting truth about their situation.[42] Other articles made note of the distrust and outright animosity with which the *St. Louis* was met in Cuba, mobilizing melodrama's trope of victims' undue vilification. On June 1, *The New York Times* reported that harbor police made every effort to keep the boats with relatives away from the *St. Louis* and lit up the ship's anchoring site with giant spot lights.[43] The article's subheading mentions that Cuba will use military force if the *St. Louis* refuses to comply—a fact also widely reported in other newspapers.[44] Some articles foregrounded the transgressive nature of the ship's lingering. *The Boston Daily Globe* wrote "Refugee Liner Fails to Obey Cuban Decree."[45] This is another convention of melodrama's structuring of a protagonist's precarious fortunes, in which transgression is emphasized so that it can be juxtaposed to the victim's innocence, which, if it is not already known, is frequently disclosed in sensationalist manner.

The passengers' refugee status had been an open secret all along, but it became official, as Afoumado argues, after Cuba's rejection of them destroyed their tourist alibi, and it was reinforced by the press's comparisons of them to pariahs. Implicit and explicit invocations of the stereotype of the wandering Jew and other metaphors of abjection abounded in the press. *The Washington Post* on June 5 headlined one of

Figure 4.9. *The New York Times*, June 3, 1939. Source: *The New York Times*. Used with permission.

907 Refugees Quit Cuba on Liner; Ship Reported Hovering Off Coast

Rumor That United States Will Permit Entry Is Spread to Avert Suicides—Company Orders St. Louis Back to Hamburg

By R. HART PHILLIPS
Wireless to THE NEW YORK TIMES.

HAVANA, June 2.—The liner St. Louis, carrying 907 Jewish refugees from Germany whom the Cuban Government refused to permit to land, left Havana Harbor at 11:30 this morning in compliance with a decree signed by President Federico Laredo Bru.

The St. Louis cleared for Hamburg, Germany, according to the Cuban customs authorities. Her distraught passengers hope she will remain somewhere in the waters of the Western Hemisphere while friends, relatives and Jewish relief associations negotiate for their admittance to some other country.

Luis Clasing, agent here for the Hamburg-American Line, refused to discuss the possibilities of a later agreement with the Cuban immigration authorities. He said the ship had left for Hamburg.

"Of course, it might go elsewhere first," he added. "However, we have nothing definite on this."

Nestor Pou, Consul of the Dominican Republic, stated tonight that he had transmitted to Señor Clasing an offer by his government to receive the refugees before the St. Louis sailed. He said the only requirement was the deposit of a bond of $500 for each of the refugees.

Señor Pou said he had notified Lawrence Berenson of the National Coordinating Committee of New York, who is here attempting to solve the situation of the refugees, no reply from either.

So far, he said, he had received reply from either.

President Juan D. Arosamena of Panama has granted special authorization to Dr. and Mrs. Julius Lewith, passengers aboard the St. Louis, to enter his country, it was announced tonight by Dr. Ventura de Llunde, a Havana attorney.

Dr. Lewith, who was a prominent surgeon in Vienna, already has obtained quota numbers for himself and his wife for entry into the United States, according to Dr. de Llunde, and it is planned to transfer them at the first port the St. Louis enters.

The Lewiths have two sons residing in New York.

Dr. de Llunde also said an appeal had been made to the President of Panama to admit all the refugees on the St. Louis, since all have suf-

Continued on Page Four

its articles "Coast Guard Trails Tragic Liner as It Wanders Aimlessly in Florida Waters—Reich Recalls Second Refugee Vessel."[46] The same day, the *Cumberland Evening Times* of Maryland published an article titled "Wandering Jews at Sea After 900 Are Forbidden to Land in Cuba."[47] On June 8, an editorial in *The New York Times* contained the sentence "No plague ship ever received a sorrier welcome."[48] Several op-ed pieces expressed strong empathy with the *St. Louis* refugees and sharply criticized the US for refusing to grant them asylum. On June 11, an op-ed in *The Washington Post* argued, "There are sanctuaries for birds and refuges for wild life everywhere in the United States. But there is no sanctuary for 907 persecuted human beings."[49] One of the most memorable statements came in form of a cartoon published in the *Daily Mirror* on June 6 (see fig. 4.10). It shows the *St. Louis*, as it leaves New York harbor sailing past the Statue of Liberty, whose famous words of unconditional welcome are shown engraved in its foundation. But Lady Liberty ostentatiously averts her gaze and a sign hanging from her raised arm reads "Keep Out."

For the most part, the American press empathized with the *St. Louis* passengers.[50] The illustrious image of a big ocean liner filled with desperate refugees kept interest at a premium. That their suffering

Figure 4.10. *Daily Mirror*, June 6, 1939. *Source:* Newspapers.com.

owed, first and foremost, to their statelessness was reason enough for many readers to believe the passengers should receive asylum in the US. According to Linda Williams, the visibility of suffering in the public sphere could be enough to demonstrate one's worthiness as a citizen.[51] At the same time, there was little commentary on the underlying reasons for the crisis—such as the failure of the Évian conference or the various pressures weighing on Roosevelt. Indeed, the press's heavy focus on the JDC's negotiations with Cuba mirrored the State Department's insistence on finding a Cuba-centered solution to the crisis. On June 2, *The New York Times* reported that HAPAG's Havana Office Director, Luis Clasing, was prepared to fight Decree 937 through the courts but later decided to take no action.[52] The article clearly implies that Clasing intended to place the onus on Cuba. It does not mention the possibility of an intervention by the US. On June 3, the *Chicago Daily Tribune* published a map of Latin America with arrows pointing to four countries that had recently rejected Jewish refugees.[53] The article inadvertently foregrounds the neocolonial framework within which Jewish resettlement had been discussed at Évian. Just two days later, the same paper published an article reporting that the US was considering settling some 30,000 Jews in the Philippines.[54] The article is accompanied by a map of the territory to be settled. This gesture of publicly mapping Jewish resettlement in a geopolitical territory that was remote from the US mainland and yet constituted a zone of vital political interest suggests further parallels to the attitude Europe's colonial powers demonstrated at Évian. On June 18 the *Chicago Daily Tribune* reported on the "happy" outcome of the *St. Louis* drama with the acceptance of the refugees by European nations. The paper, at that point, finds it opportune to stress the role of the US in this outcome, specifically the importance of US immigration quotas in swaying the four nations to accept the refugees.[55]

An American newsreel reporting on the *St. Louis* docking in Antwerp takes an even more drastically editorializing approach. Voice-over narration comments on footage of the ship's arrival, stating that "the liner the *St. Louis*, turned back from Cuba, brings its human cargo to port at last." The voice-over informs the audience about the role the US played in saving the refugees: "through American generosity, they will find at least temporary shelter in France, Holland, and England."[56] That the US could have played a more direct role and spared the passengers weeks of mortal terror by offering them asylum goes unmentioned. A British Pathé newsreel, notable, among other things, for its inclusion of footage of refugees' families swarming the ship in Havana on small boats, is guilty of a similar elision. The film concludes with the voice-over narration stating "so at last the wanderers find rest in lands which cherish freedom."[57] These newsreels indicate that the media rigorously upheld the impression that the role the US and Europe played was to rescue the *St. Louis* refugees. That the ship's voyage reflected the democratic world's complicity with Nazi Germany's stance gets suppressed.

The US press coverage of the *St. Louis* episode allows several conclusions. The way the fate of the *St. Louis* migrants evolved was influenced by the way in which the press covered the story. The passengers came to understand that the outside world's perception of them could impact the outcome of the crisis. In turn, reporting became colored by moral and ideological factors. The public discourse around the *St. Louis* crisis confirms that history and its narration are imbricated with each other. As Martin Jay has argued in a critique of Hayden White's tendency to uphold a residual distinction between the "truth" of historical events and their historical narration and ideological designation, "the factual record is not . . . entirely prior to its linguistic mediation, or indeed its figural signification. What distinguishes the events and facts that later historians reconstruct is precisely their being often already inflected with narrative meaning for those who initiate or suffer them in their own lives."[58] When the process of saving the ship's passengers turned into an international crisis, the ship itself became a spectacle that revealed the contradictory or at least ambiguous function an ocean liner is capable of assuming in moments of political instability. By appearing as an exceptional case, the *St. Louis* deflected from the roots of the quandary surrounding western democracies' attitude to refugees. It boosted the story's moral legibility at the expense of political analysis. In this resides both its virtue and its limitation—its virtue in ensuring that the basic problematic of stateless refugees worthy of rescue and possibly of citizenship became communicated to a broad public; its limitation by deflecting from the political root causes that shaped the Jewish migrant crisis and from the existence of the many other refugee ships that were part of that crisis.[59]

The Coverage of the *St. Louis* Voyage by the German Press

In their mass-market account of the *St. Louis* incident, *Voyage of the Damned*, Gordon Thomas and Max Morgan-Witts claim that German news media gave spin to the *St. Louis* refugee crisis as it was unfolding, but the authors remain unclear about the exact nature and extent of this spin.[60] They claim that the ship's return to Europe following rejection by the US "gave Goebbels' propaganda machine a field day," but they produce no evidence for this claim.[61] Most historians have been skeptical about the authors' "propaganda thesis," which holds that Nazi Germany banked on the Cuba trip to fail so as to use that failure as evidence that Jews are universally unwanted.[62] It ended with four European countries granting asylum to the passengers, a happy ending of sorts that was greeted with relief around the world. Nazi Germany had little reason to feel vindicated by this outcome. Goebbels, who already after Kristallnacht had to contend with an irate foreign press, did not mention the *St. Louis* in his diaries. However, historians who assert that Goebbels ordered the press to ignore the unfolding *St. Louis* drama have unfortunately also failed to cite sources in support of their statements.[63]

To throw light onto this murky area, a survey of news coverage by key German newspapers between May 13 and June 21, 1939, has been conducted for this book. It shows that, while the German press was not completely silent about the Cuba voyage, it only reported it in three short articles, all of which were published in the same publication, the *Hamburger Anzeiger*.[64] The first appeared on June 6 and simply notes that the *St. Louis* was cruising off the coast of Florida under the eyes of the US Coast Guard. The second, published on June 8, notes that American Jews had put up half a million dollars security for the *St. Louis* passengers. Neither of these notices had so much as a headline and their tone was matter-of-fact rather than gleeful. They were buried amid numerous other short notices on a page about miscellaneous events. On June 13, the *Hamburger Anzeiger* ran a slightly longer article under the headline "The *St. Louis* ordered to return." Three concise paragraphs summarize the voyage and mention that the *St. Louis* has been ordered to return to Germany.

This appears to be almost the extent of the coverage of the *St. Louis* in the press of the Third Reich. There is, however, one more item to discuss, published in the official newspaper of the Nazi Party, *Völkischer Beobachter*, on June 3, one day after the *St. Louis* left Havana. On page 5, the paper ran a small article, dated June 2, with the headline "Kuba verhindert Landung jüdischer Emigranten" (Cuba prevents landing of Jewish emigrants).[65] The article states that Cuba's government has denied the landing of a ship carrying 917 Jewish migrants, even though numerous Americans, including a high-ranking union official, have lobbied Colonel Batista to grant asylum to the refugees. The article further states that, according to *The New York Times*, Cuba's official circles are increasingly resistant to granting more Jewish migrants permission to come to Cuba and that the chair of the congressional immigration committee plans to introduce a bill to expel all emigrants residing in Cuba. Although the article misreports the number of passengers on board, its date and content leave no doubt that it is referring to the *St. Louis*. Interestingly, however, not only does the article not identify the *St. Louis* by name, but it also claims that it is a Greek steamer. That the *Völkischer Beobachter* deemed it advantageous to exploit Cuba's rejection of the *St. Louis* is obvious. The paper presents the incident as newsworthy and hastens to exploit the news for antisemitic, anti-union propaganda. But its suppression of the ship's name and falsification of its home flag betrays a notable discomfort with linking the incident to Germany and reporting its actual circumstances—and this at a time when the voyage's outcome was still open-ended.

The article's simultaneous reporting on and censoring of the *St. Louis*'s expulsion from Cuba is consistent with the minimal coverage of the voyage by the rest of the German press. But while these findings decidedly refute Thomas and Morgan-Witts's propaganda thesis, they also illustrate its appeal. That the Nazis would want to draw attention to any news of Jews being expelled or being denied asylum is highly plausible, as they regarded such instances as confirming their worldview. At times, they followed through on this intention, as was the case with the three articles in the *Hamburger Anzeiger*. But the idiosyncratic coverage by the *Völkischer Beobachter* and the fact that no other newspapers informed the public about the *St. Louis* during the period under investigation give pause. In my view, what this shows is that the NS regime fully grasped that propaganda, notwithstanding its vile content, is not an ad hoc game. Goebbels understood that for it to function, a number of factors had to align. Failing that, propaganda became risky and threatened to backfire. When the most dramatic effects of the Jewish refugee crisis became directly linked to Germany and German ships, Goebbels appears to have viewed the crisis as a liability. There are several indications that Goebbels wanted to shield the German merchant marine from any negative connotations. The flag riot on the *Bremen* in New York in 1935, which was a stinging humiliation for Berlin, is early proof of this. Another sign is the fact that the two cruise ships of the NS organization Kraft durch Freude (Strength Through Joy), *Wilhelm Gustloff* and *Robert Ley*, were never considered for the transport of Jewish migrants.[66] Their ideological function as icons of the NS State made this impossible. In fact, on June 2, just one day before the *St. Louis* was expelled from Cuba, the *Völkischer Beobachter* prominently included the *Wilhelm Gustloff* in its heroicizing coverage of the elite NS air force unit Legion Condor, which was returning to Germany on the ship from aiding Franco in the Spanish Civil War.[67]

The regime's ambivalence about the *St. Louis* voyage impacted the news coverage of other refugee ships. One regional North German newspaper published a brief article on HAPAG ordering its liner *Orinoco* with 200 Jewish migrants on board back to Germany from Antwerp, but the article does not mention that the order was linked to Cuba's declining of asylum to the *St. Louis* Jews.[68] The same ambivalence affected Julius Streicher's stridently hateful monthly Nazi pamphlet *Der Stürmer*. It published an article on May 26 about Jewish emigration with the title "Juden wandern aus" (Jews emigrate),[69] but while the article was very likely occasioned by the departure of the *St. Louis* on May 13, it mentions neither the ship nor HAPAG.

In sum, the NS regime's decision not to allow its media apparatus to capitalize in any significant way on the unfolding *St. Louis* drama and on the fact that so many Jewish refugees were sailing the world's oceans in the summer of 1939 refutes Thomas and Morgan-Witts's claim that Goebbels's propaganda machine had a "field day" with rejected Jewish refugees. One hopes that this correction of the historical record will finally cease the stream of claims made in books, articles, and filmed interviews which have paid lip service to the propaganda thesis without ever citing any supporting data for it. Hitler's proclamation at Königsberg that Germany was so intent on ridding itself of its "enemies" that it would put them on luxury liners was beginning to ring hollow in the weeks leading up to World War

II. Nazi Germany's muted and embarrassed response to the *St. Louis* voyage strongly suggests that Goebbels's propaganda machine and the Nazi press found themselves incapable of ideologically recuperating the negative aura that emanated from the *St. Louis* and all the "death ships" in the Black Sea and the Mediterranean.

5

On Shoreless Sea

The *St. Louis* Voyage, the State of Exception, and the Colonial Turn in Holocaust Studies

A PHOTOGRAPH TAKEN FROM aboard the *St. Louis* sometime between May 27 and June 2, 1939, shows a view of Havana harbor with its quay, the Capitol, and other government buildings, where on May 31, 1939, President Laredo Brú's cabinet officially turned the ship's passengers into refugees by declining asylum to them (see fig. 5.1). Although safe land was very close, for most of the passengers it would remain unreachable. Cuba was not the only country to reject them, nor was the cabinet's decision an aberration from the negative tenor of the 1938 Évian conference on refugees. Indeed, the positions formulated at Évian crystallized a dilemma that Europe had been grappling with since the end of World War I, when mass denaturalization and displacement sent thousands roaming the continent in search of statehood. Most nations hesitated to address this crisis. Many were parliamentary democracies and implicitly or explicitly endorsed the "Rights of Man" declaration, but few felt compelled to apply those principles to non-citizens. Hannah Arendt memorably summarized this dilemma as the general condition of the modern refugee: "The conception of human rights, based upon the assumed existence of a human being as such, broke down at the very

Figure 5.1. Photograph of Havana harbor taken from aboard the *St. Louis*, late May/early June 1939. *Source*: Courtesy of United States Holocaust Memorial Museum, courtesy of Fritz Dieter Vendig.

moment when those who professed to believe in it were for the first time confronted with people who had indeed lost all other qualities and specific relationships—except that they were still human."[1]

The twentieth century's first large streams of refugees revealed the hidden difference between nationality and birthright pinpointed by Arendt, and it was the fallout from this phenomenon that eventually put established democracies under pressure when German and Austrian Jews began to flee their homelands in large numbers as a result of Nazi terror. Hitler's antisemitic rhetoric was not exclusively motivated by race. It included accusations by conservative elites that German Jews had participated in a maelstrom of left-wing agitation, strikes, and sabotages that, so it was alleged, had stabbed Germany's World War I front fighters in the back.[2] But NS ideology also tapped into nativist and racist sentiments by portraying the Jews who had migrated from Russia, Poland, and other Eastern European countries as biological pathogens and contaminants that threatened the health and racial makeup of the German nation.

Nativism and racism rooted in colonialism and fueled by eugenics were also coursing through Britain, France, the US, and other democratic nations. Yet Nazi antisemitism went further by elevating the question of national belonging to a matter of "protection of German blood and honor,"[3] a rhetoric Hitler used to justify the usurpation of democracy by dictatorship. As discussed in chapter 1, he accomplished this by declaring a state of exception intended to give the "Führer" supreme power to run the country and protect it from its purported enemies, defined as politically hostile and racially impure. According to political theorist Giorgio Agamben, racial antisemitism, which fueled Hitler's claim to absolute power, identifies Nazism and fascism as the first "properly biopolitical movements that made of natural life the exemplary place of a sovereign decision."[4]

This web of factors figures prominently in debates about the causes of the Holocaust. Do the horrors of Auschwitz and the mass murder of civilian populations by the SS exceed human comprehension or can they be placed into a causal and historical framework? Was the hatred the Nazis unleashed against Jews at home and abroad the root cause of and the driving force behind Jewish mass extermination? This line of inquiry focuses on questions of "deep intention" and a purportedly irrational, "primordial antipathy" driving antisemitism.[5] A different approach asks whether we are to view the Holocaust as a series of politically and socioeconomically caused escalations that could have been averted. This line of thought implies a view of modernity as operating according to a telos of functionality that perversely climaxed in a large-scale industrial mass murder in which no politician, nation, or military intelligence intervened.[6] The functionalist approach, which investigates, among other things, Germany's history and its institutions and economics, has entertained the possibility that the Holocaust, far from constituting civilization's defectiveness, represents the triumph of its functionality. As Zygmunt Bauman put it, "The truth is that every 'ingredient' of the Holocaust—all those many things that rendered it possible—was normal; 'normal' not in the sense of the familiar . . . (on the contrary, the Holocaust was new and unfamiliar), but in the sense of being fully in keeping with everything we know about civilization, its guiding spirit, its priorities, its immanent vision of the world—and of the proper ways to pursue human happiness together with a perfect society."[7]

Each line of inquiry has its established place in Holocaust studies. If my discussion more closely follows the functionalist approach, it is because the historical dynamics of the *St. Louis* voyage prompt us to investigate the mechanics of certain political, economic, and administrative infrastructures that prevented Jews from escaping the "final solution." A look at those infrastructures reveals that the *St. Louis* incident bridges two historical phases of the Holocaust: as a prewar refugee drama, it exemplifies the dynamics of antisemitic expulsion and democratic nations' complicity with it—two intertwined phenomena that preceded mass extermination. But as a tragedy about 254 passengers who, because of those infrastructures of rejection, died in Auschwitz and Sobibor, the ship's voyage remains indelibly linked to the "final solution." The functionalist paradigm, it has been argued, is unable to account for why Germany was the only modern nation that built and ran thousands of concentration camps and set up several camps specifically for the genocide of millions of people.[8] While that question is now something of a commonplace, I wonder whether it is the right one to ask, for it bases the thesis of the singularity of the Holocaust on ignoring rather than taking into account the international community's non-intervention in it.

It is in the interplay between Nazi Germany and democratic countries that we find the reasons for why more Jews were not saved from the Shoah. This interplay centrally impacted the fate of the *St. Louis* passengers. It gives rise to the metaphor of the shoreless sea, which lends both this book and the present chapter its title and which will be explained below. Rather than simply aligning itself with the functionalist approach, however, my discussion critically intervenes in it. Holocaust studies has treated the *St. Louis* episode as a canonized but minor chapter in the Shoah's unfolding, neglecting the fact that it may offer the opportunity to revise our understanding of certain mechanisms that were part of it. One way of beginning this work of revision is to examine the trope of exception, which figures prominently both in the Holocaust and in how we have come to think about it. The NS regime made exception the foundation for its governance by implementing the state of exception as an extra-legislative measure that suspended democracy and ushered in antisemitic laws. Exception also drove the political reasoning by Cuba and the US to *ex*clude the *St. Louis* passengers and, in opposite manner, the reasoning by Jewish refugee organizations to *in*clude the *St. Louis* passengers among those worth saving. Finally, as a principle of historical classification, exception has shaped the logic by which Holocaust studies has conceived of the Holocaust in relation to other genocides, a logic that is now, however, gradually revised by the contributions of postcolonial studies to Holocaust historiography.

These three facets of the trope of exception form the focus of the present chapter. We begin by looking at the significance the state of exception held for the NS regime. The racial underpinnings of Hitler's antisemitism received theoretical grounding in the early 1930s by Carl Schmitt, an established theoretician of the state. Schmitt placed the racial discourses of Hitler's 1925 book *Mein Kampf* into the service of his critique of parliamentary democracy—specifically, the flawed and vulnerable political system of the Weimar Republic. Systematic as it is, Schmitt's defense of the state of exception can function only by bypassing the irreducible ethical foundation on which democracy and justice rest.

The State of Exception in Carl Schmitt's Critique of Weimar Law

Schmitt's 1933 book *Staat, Bewegung, Volk* (published in English by the Plutarch Press as *State, Movement, People*) uses legal theory to justify the elimination of the democratic justice state.[9] Schmitt's argument must be read against the historical background of the burdens placed on Weimar Germany by the Versailles Treaty, the proliferation of political parties, increasing labor unrest, and a certain "internationalization" of society. This latter phenomenon was not specific to Germany, but was felt particularly keenly there with the post-war influx of Jewish migrants from Poland.[10] Germany's increasingly diverse socio-demographics, so Schmitt argues, put pressure on the country's administrative and juridical structure by forcing the legal system to submit to relativization.[11] In legally ambiguous situations, he claims, "every word and every concept soon become contentious, uncertain, vague and unsteady" when such situations are seized by "minds and interests differently conditioned."[12] Administrative and criminal law are haunted by "vague concepts" that are "not norm- but situation-related." Concepts such as "public order and safety," "hardship," "proportionality," "due discretion," and "arbitrariness," are now "so incalculable in case of conflict that they themselves may turn into the worst arbitrariness."[13]

For Schmitt, the advancing contingency of legal concepts was irreversible, because Liberalism and Pluralism have eroded the notion of immutable, calculable scenarios that he regards as the basis for jurisprudence. For Schmitt, the law's capacity for covering in advance all imaginable disputes (a capacity that, as he concedes, was always a fiction to begin with) cannot be revived even as an ideal. Quoting Nazi jurist Roland Freisler, Schmitt thus claims that "a return to strict positivism is out of the question."[14] He concludes, "Thus, the whole application of the laws stands between Scylla and Charybdis. The road forward seems to *lead away from the shore and ever farther from the firm land of legal safety and constraints of the law*, which at the same time is also the land of the judge's independence. The road back to a formalistic legal superstition recognized as meaningless and long outdated historically is not worth considering either."[15] The English translation of this passage comes from the 2001 Plutarch Press edition. For Giorgio Agamben to excerpt the passage in his 1992 book *Homo Sacer—Sovereign Power and Bare Life*, Agamben's English translator Daniel Heller-Roazen chose a different wording. What the Plutarch edition describes as "the road forward [which] seems to lead away from the shore" in Heller-Roazen's translation from the German becomes a condition that "seems to condemn us to drifting on a shoreless sea."[16] As this formulation is more cogent and illustrative, I have adopted its image of the shoreless sea as the central trope that guides my own discussion and lends this book its title. But no matter the specific translation, its meaning as a geopolitical metaphor is integral to Schmitt's ideological world view. For Schmitt, there is only one remedy for the malady it describes. Echoing Freisler, he proposes that the way back to firm land does not involve a reform of the law itself but of those who practice it—in other words, the legal profession.[17] Behind this personnel-based reform of the justice system stands NS ideology's notion of purging the German people of the kind of heterogeneity Schmitt alludes to, with the aim of achieving "an *absolute ethnic identity between leader and following*."[18] For Schmitt, "both the continuous and infallible contact between leader and following, and their mutual loyalty, are based upon ethnic identity. Only ethnic identity can prevent the power of the leader from becoming tyrannical and arbitrary. It alone justifies the difference from any rule of an alien-transmitted will, however intelligent and advantageous it might be."[19] The achievement of ethnic identity, so Schmitt believes, begins by ethnically homogenizing Germany's jurists, for they can best safeguard and continue this process for the whole country.

By positing totalitarianism as the only cure for the weaknesses of Liberalism and Parliamentarism, Schmitt legitimates exactly what he seeks to combat—an exacerbation of the situation he characterizes as drifting on a shoreless sea, the trope that for him symbolizes Liberalism's weaknesses.[20] What Schmitt evokes as a metaphor in his political theory would assume a chillingly literal dimension for the refugee ships traveling the oceans on the eve of World War II. Their voyages were the direct result of how Nazi Germany, by eviscerating democracy, far from exorcised Liberalism's flaws. By exporting the refugee crisis it had created to its democratic neighbors, the NS State hyperbolized the implications of those flaws and promoted them to a near-universal condition for the modern refugee. Democratic nations' refusal to grant asylum to the refugees fleeing the Nazi state made those nations complicit with totalitarianism. Liberal democracy clearly contributed to the creation of the shoreless sea and helped turn the world's oceans into a dystopian structure of existence. It is this dystopia that inscribes itself into the photo of Havana harbor taken from aboard the *St. Louis*, and it does so without having to present us with any views of a boundless ocean limned by the sky.

In his 1942 book *Land und Meer* (published in English as *Land and Sea*), Schmitt turns the ocean into a surface on which he projects the decline of everything he understands as international law.[21] The book's world-historical sketch—seductive yet ultimately reductive in its illustrative verve—paints the English as a people who achieved world domination only through piracy and by terrorizing foreign coastlines. It is no surprise to Schmitt that England has traditionally been a refuge for "liberal and political migration." He contrasts England with both Germany and Russia, two nations he characterizes as "land people."[22] Yet Germany's invasion of Soviet Russia on June 22, 1941, did not deter Schmitt from concocting his fable of the land people and the sea people.[23] If anything, he might have felt confirmed by Hitler's eastward expansion, which was to serve the politics of "Lebensraum" and, thus, of conquering land further away from the sea for the purpose of making the vast Russian territories available for Germans to settle in. In the final pages of *Land and Sea* Schmitt heralds a new era in which "the new *nomos* of our planet grows, unceasingly and irresistibly. . . . Many shall see in it only death and destruction. Some believe themselves to be experiencing the end of the world. In reality we are only experiencing the end of the relation between land and sea, which had held up to this point."[24]

Nazi Germany's invasion of Poland and Russia with their large Jewish populations ceased all consideration of Jewish resettlement. The systematic extermination of Jews in these territories and of the Romani in central Europe had a double goal: to make room for German settlers and to guarantee their safety on a permanent basis by lastingly preventing any partisan activities among the population.[25] The so called "final solution" constitutes the most cataclysmic meaning of being adrift on a shoreless sea, because here, too, the trope's implications extend from Nazism to democratic nations: Britain and the US had information, even photographic intelligence, of the existence of Auschwitz, but decided not to intervene. While the reasons for this lack of intervention differed from the democratic world's resistance to liberalizing asylum, both aspects contributed to how the Holocaust "functioned."

Two aspects of the Holocaust, while intersecting, are often falsely equated. There was the systematic genocide, which was planned for and executed specifically on the Jewish and Romani peoples. It took place in a handful of small-scale facilities, most of which were expressly built for this purpose and were located in secluded areas of Poland (at Chelmno, Treblinka, Sobibor, and Belzec). With the exception of Auschwitz, which was initially founded to house Soviet POWs and Polish intelligentsia and only one part of which was turned into a death camp that lasted until early 1945, these facilities of industrial murder existed only from 1942 to 1943.[26] Then there was the vast system of multi-purpose concentration camps, which were inside Greater Germany and which housed political dissidents, male homosexuals, assorted social "undesirables," Jehovah's Witnesses, and political prisoners from countries under German occupation. This type of facility in fact predates the Third Reich and could also be found in other countries, particularly as an instrument of colonization. By the time the Nazis came to power, several such camps already existed in the Weimar Republic (for the incarceration of political militants). Over the next twelve years, their number would grow considerably. These camps, too, became places of death. It is estimated that between 1933 and 1945, 1.6 million people were incarcerated and 1.2 million perished in them.[27] But death occurred not as the result of planned industrial mass murder, but as the frequently incurred, casually tolerated byproduct of slave labor, systematic neglect, physical and psychological torture, and starvation.

This vast web of facilities, which varied in size and purpose and which were located near large and small towns in Germany, has come to be called the concentrationary system or concentrationary universe. The nomenclature owes to David Rousset, a political prisoner from France, who survived incarceration at Buchenwald and in 1946 published his book *L'univers concentrationnaire* (The concentrationary universe). As Griselda Pollock and Max Silverman explain, Rousset argued that the concentration camp was itself "symptomatic of an extended political logic not confined within it," a characterization by which Rousset intended to invoke "a political system of terror whose aim was to demolish the social humanity of all its actual and potential victims within and beyond the actual sites."[28]

While the Allies' non-intervention in the extermination of Jews and Romani in the Polish death camps merits continued investigation, it seems rather surprising that democratic countries did nothing to save the hundreds of thousands of inmates of the inhumane if much more ordinary concentrationary universe. Political philosophy has argued that it is precisely the more ordinary nature of this universe with its fluid designations as transit camp, prison camp, and labor camp that prevented other countries from being too alarmed by it. Indeed, the camp's "socially constructed ordering of experience"[29] may have been something that some nations, such as the British during the second Boer war of 1899 to 1902, had already come to share with the Nazis. The most provocative formulation of this argument has been submitted by political philosopher Giorgio Agamben, who goes so far as to speak of an "inner solidarity between democracy and totalitarianism."[30] The controversial nature of this thesis deserves more detailed discussion. The figure of exception, as I aim to show, plays a pivotal role within, but also beyond, the dynamics Agamben outlines.

Giorgio Agamben's Theory of Bare Life and the State of Exception

In *Homo Sacer—Sovereign Power and Bare Life* Agamben traces the relationship between sovereignty and its claim to power over human life. The sovereign has supreme power over life by exempting himself from the very rules he issues and safeguards. In the twentieth century, the sovereign governs with the help of the modern state via principles of what Michel Foucault has termed "biopower" and which he has also referred to as "biopolitics."[31] Biopolitics cultivate or eliminate whole populations or portions of them for the purpose of shaping a nation's demographic makeup (see chapter 1). The NS State took biopolitics to an extreme. By declaring a state of exception, it combined the principle of the sovereign with the notion that he should carry extra-legal power over all forms of life until some form of legality can be reinstated (which, in the case of Nazi Germany, never happened). Dividing Germany's population into "superior" and "inferior" races, the Nuremberg laws made Germany's Jews into what Agamben terms a "pivotal referent" of Hitler's sovereign power and the main target of supreme state violence.[32] Agamben shows that it was Schmitt's reasoning which provided the ideological foundation for the racial biopolitics of the NS State, specifically Schmitt's insistence that German law can only be effective if it bases itself on the ethnic identity between leader and followers.[33]

Yet, according to Agamben, racial biopolitics are by no means the exclusive domain of totalitarian regimes. Hannah Arendt deemed the mass extinction of human life in the death camps to be a consequence of totalitarianism (rather than of biopolitics, a concept Arendt did not use).[34] But it was biopolitics that, according to Agamben, enabled totalitarianism in the first place. The modern transformation of politics into biopolitics paved the way for Schmitt to declare ethnic homogeneity the defining criterion of the fascist state. And the historical reality of democratic nations' complicity with Nazi Germany's antisemitic politics of expulsion lends credence to Agamben's claim that biopolitics potentially makes all politics totalitarian.[35] Agamben's conclusion that democracy and totalitarianism possess an "inner solidarity" has been criticized for being reductive. But regardless of whether one agrees with him, Agamben usefully delineates the biopolitical underpinnings of each system and identifies their points of intersection. The refugee crisis triggered by Nazi Germany was both new—in that it turned Jews into racial pariahs who, according to Nazi ideology, *should* not be saved—and just another step in the deterioration of the long-term situation of modern refugees, who, in the eyes of western democracies, unfortunately *could* not be saved.

The conjoining of these proximate—indeed, from the standpoint of the affected refugees, identical—positions suggests that the Holocaust was not a sui generis phenomenon.

Citing Karl Löwith's notion of the comprehensive politicization ("totale Politisierung") of life, which Löwith formulated as part of a critical commentary on Carl Schmitt, Agamben identifies the modern individual's pervasive (bio)political, discursive, and bureaucratic subjectivization by the state as the reason behind the contiguity between democracy and totalitarianism.[36] At issue is a form of domination that Foucault has identified as inherent to modernity and that has enabled the modern state to simultaneously include and exclude its subjects. This phenomenon takes on particularly complex forms with regard to the history of Jewish life in Europe and specifically in Germany, where Jews always enjoyed a double status of being both secular (and thus potentially assimilable) and religious (and thus visible as a minority). The high level of education of German Jews and their propensity for self-organization led to paradoxical relationships with the state that lasted into the period of the Third Reich. The *St. Louis* voyage gives evidence of this type of bureaucratic subjectivization. Several Jewish passengers had learned of the trip through a traditional Jewish organization named Oberrat, the Supreme Council of Israelites of the German province of Baden (founded by the Grand Duke of Baden in 1809 to acknowledge Jews as a religious community). The Nazis declassified the Oberrat as a public body, but they also instrumentalized it as an emigration organization through which they could screen Jews for eventual expulsion.[37]

Examples of this treatment of the individual by the state in the 1930s can be drawn from totalitarianism (the Nazis expelling Jews or ghettoizing them and making them wear the Star of David), from democracy being complicit with totalitarianism (as seen in the Swiss-German initiative to stamp Jews' passports with a "J"), and from democracy acting on its own (foreign immigration authorities' deciding over life and death by granting or denying entry to Jewish migrants). The fluid status of the *St. Louis* passengers as migrants, tourists, refugees, and inmates squarely placed them at the intersection of totalitarian and democratic biopolitics. After racially othering, legally depriveleging, and encamping Jews, the NS State allowed some of them to leave by boat on the condition that they surrender their passports. But the boat did not make them safe. Their rejection by democratic nations extended the NS State's ability to subjectivize them and to classify them as a sort of subhuman biomass, which Agamben has termed "*homo sacer*," or bare life: someone who "can save himself only in perpetual flight [to] a foreign land" and yet who is in "a continuous relationship with the power that banished him precisely insofar as he is at every instant exposed to an unconditional threat of death."[38] Berlin held sway over the fates of the *St. Louis* Jews even as they found themselves on a luxury ship cruising in the Caribbean. So severe were their fears of a forced return to Germany that they threatened suicide.

Does this mean, then, that the *St. Louis* can be categorized as a concentration camp? At first glance, this seems hard to accept. Because it has connected cultures on different continents and enabled millions to start a new life on foreign shores, the ocean liner traditionally carries associations of progress, freedom, and hope. The *St. Louis*, as her service history shows, was no exception. As part of HAPAG's fleet of migrant ships (see chapter 2), the *St. Louis* belonged to what Foucault has characterized as modernity's disciplinary complex, which subjectivizes the modern individual in asylums, boarding schools, hospitals, military barracks, and, last but not least, in a sprawling migration apparatus that included processing facilities and ships.[39]

The status of this disciplinary complex in relation to the study of modernity, fascism, and the Holocaust has been under debate. Recent voices have warned against collapsing modernity's biopolitical apparatus with some of the uses it was put to by totalitarian states. The Holocaust, as Edward Ross Dickinson has pointed out, must primarily be linked to a concrete set of top-down measures (*Maßnahmen*) implemented by and specific to the Third Reich.[40] These measures and the system implementing them are politically and historically distinct from what we broadly call biopolitical modernity. US immigration law, for instance, while certainly meriting discussion in terms of biopolitics, was no tool for mass extermination. "Mass murder," as Dickinson puts it, "is the historical problem; the absence of mass murder is not a problem, it does not need to be investigated or explained."[41] But the absence of mass murder in one country does not foreclose that country's *complicity* in another country's committing mass murder. Nor does it excuse democratic nations' complicity in the dehumanizing and often lethal treatments that transpired in the thousands of camps not expressly designated for industrial mass murder.

The crisis that emerged after Évian and that produced the voyages of the refugee ships on the world's oceans is clear evidence of the unethical or at least highly questionable *Maßnahmen* or policy fiats that democratic nations issued. Many such measures were biopolitical in nature. Some of them, by turning migrants into refugees, assumed an infamous place in the Holocaust's overall timeline.

In this context, it is important to remember that not only was death rampant in the thousands of concentration camps not expressly set up for industrial mass murder, but it also loomed over the many internment camps that, after German troops invaded Western Europe, came to function as deportation camps for the "final solution." It was Arendt who, based on her own experience as a stateless person, already in the early 1940s pointed to the camp's fluid function: "Apparently nobody wants to know that contemporary history has created a new kind of human beings—the kind that are put in concentration camps by their foes and in internment camps by their friends"[42] (see fig. 5.2).

Press coverage of the *St. Louis* voyage shows that, by 1939, the term "concentration camp" was part of public parlance and that it was, in fact, accruing a range of connotations within the categories outlined by Arendt's friend/foe scenario. On June 6, the *Los Angeles Times* ran an article headlined "Cuban Concentration Camp Offered to Liner Refugees."[43] The article reflects the widely held view of concentration camps as mundane transit facilities for housing and quarantining migrants. The same day, *The Washington Post* wrote: "Laredo Brú said the refugees might land if they agreed to live in a concentration camp which would be established on the Isle of Pines and if guarantees were given that their stay would be temporary."[44] But such views competed with more negative uses of the term. An op-ed in *The New York Times*—the same article that stated "No plague ship ever received a sorrier welcome" and "At Havana the *St. Louis*'s decks became a stage for human misery"—noted sarcastically, "Germany, with all the hospitality of its concentration camps, will welcome these unfortunates home."[45] Regardless of their contrasting takes on the concentration camp, these characterizations implicitly draw attention to the power that the state, whether democratic or totalitarian, has held over human lives. Using the *St. Louis* incident to historicize US immigration policy, a 2017 article in the online journal *Vox* foregrounds the state's role as a biopolitical agent: "President

Figure 5.2. Photo of Jewish children at Westerbork, an internment camp that, after the Nazi invasion of Holland, became a deportation camp. Courtesy of Michael Barak, born Michael Fink (back row center with the white shirt and hat). Michael and his parents had arrived back in Antwerp on the *St. Louis* and after the outbreak of World War II were interned at Westerbork as enemy aliens. In 1944, the family was deported to Theresienstadt. Michael's father was passed through several camps and died in Bergen-Belsen in March 1945. Michael and his mother were liberated in Theresienstadt in May 1945. *Source:* Courtesy of United States Holocaust Memorial Museum.

Franklin D. Roosevelt, who a few years later would use an executive order to round up tens of thousands of Japanese Americans and put them in concentration camps, could have ordered that 900 German Jews be allowed to stay. He did not do so."[46] The point here, it should be noted, is not to gloss over the qualitative differences between US and Nazi camps, but to note the lack of action by a democratic state, whose capability of setting up its own prison facilities easily and in ad hoc manner indicates that it would have been just as capable of saving several hundred lives from the camps of an anti-democratic enemy state.

The *St. Louis* on its ninety-eighth voyage oscillated between both functions of the camp outlined by Arendt. In sharp contrast to a concentration camp commander and his staff, the ship's captain and his crew did everything to make life easier for his passengers. Yet, while Gustav Schröder jeopardized his career by trying to prevent their return to Germany, he did not fully escape his place in the disciplinary chain of command, nor was he able to remove his ship from the biopolitical apparatus that enabled what Agamben terms the "inner solidarity" of democracy and totalitarianism. Even if the *St. Louis* cannot be equated with a concentration camp, it was part of the concentrationary complex, which loomed large over every part of the liner's voyage: on its westbound sailing from Germany to Cuba, the ship functioned as the delivery mechanism out of the camps and was thus part of the Nazi apparatus of expulsion; when lying in port in Havana and cruising off the coast of Florida, it functioned as an ambulatory prison, demonstrating that the world's democracies were complicit with the concentrationary complex; and for much of its return trip to Europe the ship functioned as a delivery mechanism back to the camps. Its passengers had reason to be concerned that, barring international intervention, they were headed toward certain death.

Productive as it is, Agamben's theorization of sovereign power and biopolitics has not earned him unanimous approval. Political theorist Oliver Marchart has taken Agamben to task for the heavily eschatological character of his thinking.[47] Agamben, so Marchart argues, defines the concentration camp strictly in topological terms that are too abstract and totalizing.[48] While death camps throw into relief certain aspects of biopolitics and totalitarianism, such functions do not place us at liberty, so Marchart warns, to place Auschwitz on a spectrum of biopolitical facilities including both Guantanamo Prison and suburban gated communities.[49] Agamben's bird's-eye view risks producing false equivalencies and generalizations. For us to relate this debate to the present discussion, we need to note that, while democracies such as the US shared with totalitarian states like Nazi Germany the ability to exert considerable biopolitical power over human life, democratic nations' use of this power in the Jewish refugee crisis must be differentiated from NS biopower and must be assessed with rigor and nuance. Even after the State Department declined entrance to the *St. Louis* Jews, their possession of US immigration quota numbers remained a decisive factor in helping the refugee organization JDC (American Jewish Joint Distribution Committee) broker asylum for them in Europe. Agamben does not discuss the *St. Louis* incident and Marchart rightly charges him with a relative lack of interest in historical detail, especially with regard to examining concrete practices of governance. The synchronic, structuralist nature of Agamben's approach tends toward totalization.[50] Failing to leave any room for the possibility of political action, Agamben's paradigm, as Marchart rightfully argues, risks foreclosing human agency.[51]

Notwithstanding the legitimacy of Marchart's caveats, I concur with Pollock and Silverman that the importance of Agamben's approach lies in successfully disclosing "a more recurrent *logic* of power that reveals itself as a logic of annihilation hidden within certain 'normal' social rituals and modern spaces."[52] In the *St. Louis* crisis, this "recurrent logic of power" emerges especially through the logic of exception, which here structures the double principle of inclusion/exclusion. In its efforts to obtain asylum for the *St. Louis* passengers in Europe, the JDC encountered the same logic of exception that the Nazis had imposed on the Jews and that other countries had adopted—only this time, the logic was mobilized by the JDC itself. In approaching the four European nations that eventually granted asylum to the passengers, the organization realized it was going to have to present the passengers' status as exceptional rather than exemplary. So much did the JDC fear that any impression to the contrary might open the floodgates of asylum claims that, on June 21, 1939, after the refugees had been successfully distributed to the four countries, it felt compelled to release a policy statement against "any such type of enforced and disorderly emigration,"[53] as it characterized the *St. Louis* case:

> the financial and administrative burdens of such "dumped," chaotic, forced, and disorganized emigration are entirely beyond the scope of private philanthropic resources or the facilities of existing organizations. . . . Under these circumstances, the Joint Distribution Committee must place on record that it cannot regard its action in behalf of the St. Louis passengers, and the enormous sacrifices it has made

in the financial commitment undertaken for this relatively small number of persons, as constituting a precedent for any similar action.[54]

At a time when thousands of Jews were trying to flee Germany by land and sea, the JDC felt compelled to emphasize that the *St. Louis* case was a "special problem that required special treatment."[55] To be sure, that the JDC succeeded at all shows that individual agency did make the difference between life and death.[56] Nevertheless, the logic that drove the JDC's strategy gives one pause; it merits the kind of skepticism that fuels Agamben's thinking about the link between democracy and totalitarianism.

Unfortunately, it is Agamben's pinpointing of the permeability between democracy and totalitarianism that Marchart fails to acknowledge in his critique of Agamben, who receives discussion only from the perspective of democratic politics. The problem with this approach reveals itself when considering the JDC's decision to give preferred treatment to the *St. Louis* refugees. In democratic states, so Marchart argues, politics productively mediates between diverse interests by temporarily elevating particular positions to universal relevance. While often messy, this process, Marchart reasons, is the prerequisite for taking concrete action. But the JDC's action on behalf of the *St. Louis* Jews shows that democracy rarely exists in a vacuum and is easily vitiated by totalitarian logic—a phenomenon that Agamben seizes on. In prioritizing the interests of the *St. Louis* Jews over those of other Jewish refugees, the JDC violated the ethical framework in which democracy temporarily elevates certain groups' interests to universal relevance. Needless to say, my argument is not meant as a criticism of the JDC, which did what it had to do to save the *St. Louis* passengers. It is to identify the penetrating force of the logic of exception that is of interest to Agamben. In taking concrete action, the JDC violated precisely the portion of the universal that is never negotiable, not even in democratic politics. That portion is embodied by the "Rights of Man" principle, which is of a higher order than democracy and which nominally informs many democratic nations. According to this principle, the *St. Louis* case should have been treated as a precedent for—rather than an exception to—other asylum cases. This, as we know, is exactly what did not transpire.

Further, while the JDC's taking action resulted in obtaining asylum for the passengers, the exclusion of the many in favor of the few was hardly temporary. It remained the standard operating procedure for Jewish refugee organizations. As such, it prolonged the misery of displacement for Europe's Jews and made the road to the camps, a road that lay ahead for so many, that much harder to avoid. In this light, eschatological thinking of the kind Marchart criticizes in Agamben's argument seem perfectly appropriate.[57]

The treatment of the *St. Louis* refugees by the international community presents clear evidence that the logic of exception, through which the Nazis had firmed their grip on Germany, had found a scandalizing double in the free world's attitude toward Jewish refugees. Exception, whether applied in the negative sense (via the US position that no exception could be made to save the *St. Louis* Jews) or in the positive sense (the JDC arguing that making an exception was the *only* way to save the *St. Louis* Jews), became the single operative logic. Its de facto subordination of human rights to political deliberations designated, in Agamben's suggestive assessment, "a zone in which the distinction between life and politics, between questions of fact and questions of law has literally no more meaning."[58]

Agamben's and Marchart's respective approaches represent opposite agendas of Holocaust studies. Marchart reminds us that theoretical approaches to totalitarianism cannot afford to play fast and loose with historical detail and must rein in the totalizing tendencies that inhere in thought models derived from structuralism; Agamben shows us that, if we want to combat the political apathy that aids the unfolding of genocides, we must subject the Holocaust to a more open-ended inquiry unafraid to compare its symptomatology to phenomena not overtly connected to it. The political stakes behind these methodological caveats have been felt for some time in politics and among historians.[59] In recent years, however, those stakes seem to have been raised further by the shared interest of postcolonial studies and genocide studies in comparing the Holocaust to other genocides. This agenda is germane to the present discussion, for the voyage of the *St. Louis* clearly points to areas of intersection between the Holocaust and neocolonialism. It is here, however, where I have to register my own dissatisfaction with Agamben. While Agamben provides valuable tools for us to debate the political dilemmas and ethical quagmires around the *St. Louis* voyage, placing the incident in relation to questions of neocolonialism gives us no choice but to leave his thinking behind, for he never situates the Holocaust beyond the horizon of Europe.

The MS *St. Louis* and the Colonial Turn in Holocaust Studies

Holocaust studies has long explored historical and epistemological links between Nazi genocide and colonial genocide.[60] Such efforts go back to Hannah Arendt's 1950 essay "Social Science Techniques and the Study of Concentration Camps."[61] The essay places the Holocaust into what Michael Rothberg in his illuminating reading of Arendt characterizes as a "discourse of utility." Arendt analyzes the Holocaust as part of a larger cluster of techniques of domination used during the colonial exploitation in Africa, America, and Australia, where slavery and other forms of forced labor occurred. Yet Arendt instantly sets the Holocaust apart from these colonial genocides, arguing that the building of death camps transcends both conventional antisemitic reasoning and the kind of utilitarian (political, social, and economic) motives behind colonial genocide.[62] For this reason, so the essay concludes, the Holocaust is not worse, but profoundly different in nature from other genocides. While the causes of other genocides can be retraced rationally, the Holocaust, in Arendt's view, remains humanly incomprehensible. Rothberg rightly notes that there is a nagging feeling that Arendt's insistence on the Shoah's non-utilitarianism implicitly paves a path for a "ranking" of genocides.[63] How are other massacres' survivors and their families supposed to make sense of their losses and suffering, not to speak of the nature of their pain, in light of this essentializing distinction? From the perspective of the victims, Rothberg argues, "the nonutilitarian basis of genocide is hardly relevant; ascribed motivation has no bearing on the results of genocidal procedures."[64]

In her 1951 book *The Origins of Totalitarianism*, Arendt doubles down on her distinction between the Holocaust and other genocides. The book paradoxically argues that the Holocaust, while unique, is traceable to colonialism after all, specifically to the Boers' colonization of South Africa. In contrast to the pragmatism of British colonial rule, the Boers' white supremacism, so Arendt argues, existed purely for its own sake. This non-utilitarianism would later resurface as an influence on Nazi mobs.[65] In Rothberg's view, Arendt potentially provides "an opening for a non-Eurocentric Holocaust studies that would not take European categories of utility and humanity for granted."[66] Yet, as Rothberg goes on to say, she lamentably forecloses this path by explaining the Boers' racism as the result of their traumatization upon encountering Black Africans. By positing racial alterity as the psychological root cause for the supremacist mindset that reappeared in the pogrom fever and the "final solution" of the Third Reich, Arendt offers a hermeneutics of the Holocaust that at once summons and disavows colonial genocide. Arendt's intellectual legacy is thus complex. By steering clear of historical determinism, Arendt, as Rothberg concludes, shows the influence of Walter Benjamin's view of history as a loosely woven patchwork of "crystallizing" historical elements. But by positing perpetrator trauma as the root cause for genocide that "boomeranged" back to Europe, she links her concept of history to a figure of etiology that puts enigma in place of illumination.[67]

The boomerang principle also figured prominently in the thinking of Arendt's non-European contemporaries, who engaged questions about the Holocaust from a non-Eurocentric perspective. Like Arendt, Aimé Césaire in his book *Discourse on Colonialism* (1950) identifies Europe as being haunted by the return of genocidal trauma from the colonies.[68] But in contrast to Arendt's claim that genocidal trauma has its roots in an irreducible racial difference between colonizer and colonized, Césaire locates it entirely within the European subject as a *choc en retour*, a jolt to the subject's psyche after years of dormancy:

> And then one fine day the bourgeoisie is awakened by a terrific reverse shock: the gestapos are busy, the prisons fill up, the torturers around the racks invent, refine, discuss. People are surprised, they become indignant. They say: "How strange! But never mind—it's Nazism, it will pass!" . . . and they hide the truth from themselves, that it is barbarism, but the supreme barbarism . . . that sums up all the daily barbarism; that it is Nazism, yes, but that before they were its victims, they were its accomplices.[69]

Like Arendt, Césaire identifies Europe as the site of transference between two genocidal traumas, but with two differences: He expands the notion of the traumatized subject from proto-Nazi perpetrators and paramilitary elites to ordinary citizens and their mundane actions, and he illustrates his concept with an example dating to the early days of the German occupation of France. In other words, by situating the reference point for the return of colonial violence in Europe among the larger population and prior to the "final solution," Césaire avoids relying on the logic of exception that shapes Arendt's reasoning.

This historical and causal reconceptualization of the return of colonial violence goes hand in hand with a widening of the geopolitical framework beyond Africa. France's colonial involvement in Vietnam provides an obvious point of reference for Césaire, but he also mentions Latin America in his list of colonized areas: "I see clearly what colonization has destroyed: the wonderful Indian civilizations—and neither Deterding nor Royal Dutch nor Standard Oil will ever console me for the Aztecs and the Incas."[70] His mentioning of Standard Oil brings into focus the role of the US in neocolonizing Latin America. What happens, Césaire asks, when Europe's work of colonizing half the world appears complete? "The hour of the barbarian is at hand. The modern barbarian. The American hour."[71] For Césaire, Harry Truman's statements that "the time of the old colonialism has passed" and his urging to give "aid to the disinherited countries" are proof of the supplanting of European colonialism through US neocolonialism: "American high finance considers that the time has come to raid every colony in the world.... American domination—the only domination from which one never recovers. I mean from which one never recovers unscarred."[72]

Expanding the historical purview to the role of the US as a neocolonial power enables us to include Latin America—and Cuba in particular—into a more systematic consideration of questions related to the Holocaust.[73] Latin America was a major dialog partner at the 1938 Évian conference on refugees and, as chapter 1 argues, the reasons for Latin American nations' reluctance to grant asylum to Jews can be found in the region's neocolonization by Europe and particularly by the United States. Cuba became a major focus of US political and economic control. In the nineteenth century, US businesses turned Cuba's agriculture into a sugar monoculture that, until the 1959 revolution, made Cuba depend on Wall Street and forced its diversified economy to become an import market for goods from the US. Having helped Cuba become independent from its colonizer,

Spain, the US also began to exert political control over the country.[74] When in the early 1930s a coalition of revolutionaries put Cuba on a political and economic reform course, the US, in a strategy it would repeat numerous times in Latin America, officially remained neutral while secretly protecting its interests by supporting right-wing counterrevolutionaries such as General Fulgencio Batista. As head of Cuba's armed forces in the 1930s, Batista wielded considerable political power over several Cuban presidents—including Federico Laredo Brú, who governed Cuba at the time of the *St. Louis* crisis—before being elected president in 1940 and running a US-backed right-wing dictatorship in Cuba from 1952 to 1959.

As this brief summary shows, neocolonialism evolves through multiple historical stages in the course of which a dispersal of political and economic relations occurs that can produce refracted, at times disorienting power structures involving multiple parties. As Césaire states, "I note that in general the old tyrants get on very well with the new ones, and that there has been established between them, to the detriment of the people, a circuit of mutual services and complicity."[75] Galeano traces this phenomenon in his searing indictment of Cuba's neocolonial oligarchy, who "devastated Cuba's fertile soil" while making frequent trips to Paris and boasting European refinement.[76] This structure produced contradictory interests within the neocolonized nation and generated multiple centers of power. As these tended to compete with one another, they made neocolonial capitals like Havana difficult to read, particularly to outsiders like *St. Louis*'s captain, Gustav Schröder, or Lawrence Berenson and his JDC agents. Cuba also became fertile soil for corruption and bribery, phenomena endemic to all political systems but thriving in neocolonial settings.

Considering Latin America's neocolonized status when assessing the global Jewish refugee crisis helps Holocaust studies move past the field's long-standing epistemological binary, which pits European modernity against the notion of a premodern Africa—a binary exemplified by Arendt's positing that the genocidal violence of white colonizers in Africa returned as Nazi violence towards Jews. What we see with Césaire's non-Eurocentric reconceptualization of Arendt's boomerang effect as a *choc en retour* is that moving past this binary does not mean we must completely forgo conceptual usage of the boomerang effect with its hermeneutic potential. Looking at Cuba's formal triggering of the *St. Louis* crisis, it becomes clear that it was Cuba's history of neocolonial bondage that turned the country into another halfway point from where colonial violence and its US-American neocolonial variant boomeranged back to Europe (and in the process also tainted the US). The result, in this case, was not the "final solution," but the creation of a set of conditions that would make it all the more difficult to escape it.

Cuba's rejection of the *St. Louis* passengers constituted a shock reversal of its policy under which the country, during the mid- to late 1930s, had accepted thousands of Jewish migrants. This reversal is rooted in various aspects traceable to the impact of neocolonialism. The influx of those migrants had been enabled by the head of immigration, Manuel Benítez y González, a corrupt member of Cuba's neocolonial structure who used his office to enrich himself personally. In the wake of Kristallnacht, Benítez's benefactor, Colonel Batista, pledged to increase Cuba's refugee intake, a move that is regarded as a show of support for Benítez (see chapter 2). The administration's abrupt reversal of its immigration policy owed to an internal battle between Benítez and President Laredo Brú, who was afraid to lose ground against both Benítez and Batista and who, in light of the upcoming election cycle, did not want to be perceived as a weak leader unable to protect the country's borders. Laredo Brú was also pressured by Cuba's nativist and pro-Nazi press. While Cuba's immigration policy was never driven by the anxieties that caused other Latin American countries to fetishize and protect "the Hispanic race," Nazi Germany nonetheless appealed to certain circles of Cuba's elite. In the course of the 1930s, Berlin expanded its influence on Cuba by sending envoys to Havana who wooed politicians, administrators, and parts of the press. The new immigration law that was being proposed at the House of Representatives in the wake of Laredo Brú's firing of Benítez was campaigned for with funds from local Spanish merchants and Fascists—two notable power blocks in neocolonized Latin American countries.

For the United States, Cuba's abrupt change in policy was a shock insofar as it terminated the country's de facto liberal intake of migrants, which, as the US knew all too well, stood in contrast to Cuba's official immigration rules. Unwilling to increase its own share of migrants, the US had been using Cuba as a buffer zone and control valve through which to indirectly manipulate the flow of Jewish migrants to the New World. Being subjected to similar political pressures as Laredo Brú and sharing the latter's concerns about upcoming elections, President Roosevelt essentially stared into a mirror when the US found itself unable to sway Cuba to accept the *St. Louis* refugees. By deciding that the US would also decline asylum to the *St. Louis* passengers, Roosevelt amplified the shock of colonial violence, which the eastbound *St. Louis* now carried back across the Atlantic, putting the pressure back on Europe's colonial powers. At Évian, Belgium, France, Holland, and England had advocated for resettling Europe's Jews in territories far outside Europe, even though they hesitated to offer their own colonies for this purpose. Now that a New World colonizer and one of its neocolonized also declined asylum and put the ball back in their court, they were at a loss for a concrete response. The tedious negotiations the JDC had to conduct to bring those four reluctant countries to save the *St. Louis* Jews from concentration camps recall the observation Césaire made about France under Nazi rule—that a colonizing nation's past (and still ongoing) colonial involvement made it ill-prepared to face the fallout of Nazi violence.

The *choc en retour* caused by the *St. Louis* crisis was also felt in Germany. As discussed in chapter 4, NS attempts to downplay the incident show that Goebbels regarded it as a liability. But since Césaire's theorem concerns itself with the impact of violence on a given country's ordinary citizens and infrastructure rather than political superstructure, of interest for us is more how the *choc en retour* registered with, say, the *St. Louis*'s owner, HAPAG, and its employees. As one of Europe's leading cargo and passenger carriers to Latin America, HAPAG helped Jews obtain a new future in Cuba as per a secret for-profit arrangement with the country's corrupt director of emigration. Thus, while HAPAG was a private-sector company, its Jewish migrant business made it both a key player in Cuba's neocolonial political and economic infrastructure and an important part of the NS apparatus of antisemitic expulsion. When the *St. Louis* incident caused these two areas to misalign, HAPAG's director of passage, Claus-Gottfried Holthusen, struggled to deal with the fallout. His position evinces similarity to the European subject who, in Rothberg's words, is "necessarily blind to the social production of his or her own well-being" and who proves "unable to recognize how the violence in the periphery necessary to secure that well-being will migrate to the metropolis and undermine metropolitan well-being."[77]

To be fair, Holthusen's historical role is complicated. As flight and exile became the lesser of two evils for German Jews, Holthusen had little incentive to question the unethical implications of his work. Further, if one is to believe unverifiable claims, Holthusen, by warning the British negotiator that a return to Germany would place the *St. Louis* passengers in acute jeopardy (see chapter 3), crucially aided the JDC in swaying England to accept a portion of them. But even if this was the case, Holthusen's moment of recognition only shows that, in this particular instance, he identified Nazi antisemitism for what it was and decided to deflect its worst impact. There is no evidence that his moment of moral clarity made Holthusen aware of the organic interplay between the Nazi state's antisemitic expulsion and HAPAG's neocolonial trade activities, a business area that overlapped with Holthusen's purview as director of passage.

At issue is what Fredric Jameson has characterized as "cognitive mapping." This term refers to the subject's recognition—or lack thereof—that it participates in the economic transfer of violence between the periphery and the metropolis. Neocolonialism helps normalize this kind of transference by reproducing colonialism's legacy of violent domination within a more humane (read: economic rather than military) register of "free trade" and tourism. When Cuba, by rejecting the *St. Louis*, ruptured the sheen of normality, the result was a variant of what Césaire understands as a *choc en retour*. But since the *St. Louis* case and that of the *Orinoco* remained the only two major disruptions of the synergy between Nazi antisemitism and neocolonialism, HAPAG's key role in making this mechanism function has remained effaced.

Our analysis of HAPAG's and Cuba's role in the *St. Louis* crisis can help us develop a non-Eurocentric understanding of the Holocaust through historical impact models like the boomerang effect. Such models are instrumental in pursuing what A. Dirk Moses has characterized as a transnational historicization of the Holocaust—an approach that can help correct the fallacy that the Holocaust was exclusively a conflict between Nazis and Jews. Bringing a transnational approach to the analysis of the concentrationary universe and mapping that universe onto the global impact zones of colonization promises to further our understanding of the relationship between colonialism and the Holocaust. These inquiries drive what is now called the colonial turn in Holocaust studies.

While the nations attending the Évian conference neither built the death camps nor caused the Holocaust, their refusal to accept Jewish refugees sharply diminished Jews' prospects to escape the "final solution." Democratic nations helped Nazi Germany to create the dystopian territory of the shoreless sea on which dozens of Jewish refugee ships found themselves in the late 1930s. The photograph taken from the *St. Louis* in Havana harbor discussed at the beginning of this chapter aptly visualizes this political and humanitarian scandal.

In closing this chapter on the political and philosophical implications of the *St. Louis* incident, I want us to consider another image that reveals yet another dimension of the shoreless sea. Taken from the final pages of Captain Schröder's autobiographical account of the Cuba voyage, it features a map that charts the meandering course of the *St. Louis* in Caribbean waters (see fig. 5.3). The convoluted line

Figure 5.3. Map charting the course of the *St. Louis* in Caribbean waters. *Source:* Gustav Schröder, *Heimatlos auf hoher See*, p. 47.

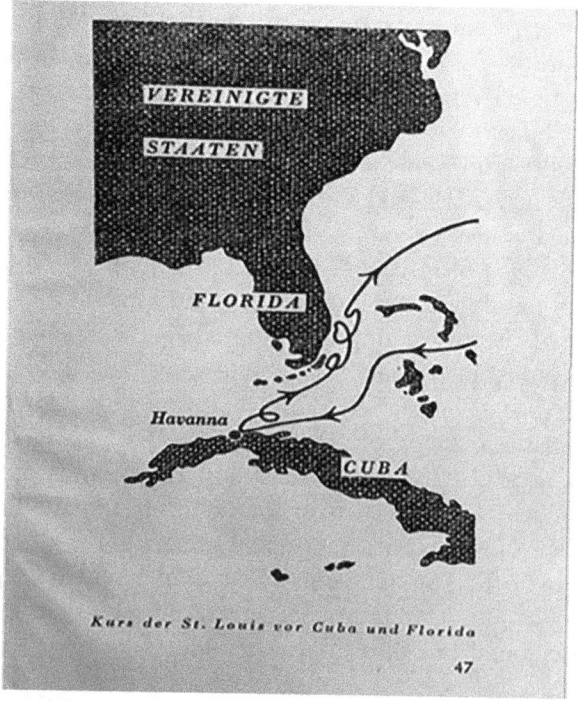

indicates how the ship was moving back and forth between potential safe havens and closed borders, crisscrossing international waters with its passengers suspended between the hope of acceptance and the repeated shock of rejection. As such, the graphic represents the situation of every refugee ship on the eve of World War II, whether they were condemned to cruise through the Black Sea or the North Sea, the Mediterranean or the Caribbean, or idle off the coast of Palestine, Florida, or South America. The map indirectly registers the failure of international politics, diplomacy, and law, not to mention ethics and morality. And it also indirectly points to the disruption of the migrant trade that had connected Germany with countries like Cuba. That this aspect of trade had become something of a spine to HAPAG's Latin American passenger and cargo business in the 1930s can be gleaned from the travel brochures the company issued for its activities in the region (see chapter 2). To the maps featured in those brochures with their boldly designed graphics celebrating existing routes or confidently announcing new ones, Captain Schröder's map, which traces the *St. Louis*'s Caribbean voyage in a single, erratic, and ultimately inverted line, forms a sobering counterpoint.

As soon as the chaotic voyage of the *St. Louis* concluded, the same economic interests that had given rise to it and pushed it along despite all qualms and caveats immediately demanded a return to normalcy. After landing its Jewish migrants in Antwerp, the *St. Louis* headed straight to New York, from where she undertook several Caribbean cruises mostly for American tourists. But the normalcy was short-lived. The migrant business's rapid decline in 1939 became one more manifestation of the shoreless sea. If seaborne migration had turned Jews into little more than human cattle in the years before the war, the termination of HAPAG's activities would deprive them even of that status, which, however uncertain and dehumanizing it may have been, represented at least a chance to escape.

The possibility of turning seaborne travel into a form of escape constitutes the biggest difference among many between the transatlantic Jewish migrant traffic of the 1930s and the Middle Passage by which captured and enchained Africans were sent toward their enslavement in the Americas. Yet postcolonial theorists have paid attention to what Paul Gilroy has termed "correspondences that can be identified between the histories of blacks and Jews," even if these, as Gilroy notes in his seminal study *The Black Atlantic*, "take on a radically different significance after the Holocaust."[78] Gilroy cautions against placing Black and Jewish history into "absurd and dangerous competition."[79] But while he recognizes arguments for the Holocaust's uniqueness, he claims that he decided to not treat it as an obstacle to exploring how Jewish responses to modernity may be relevant to the history of Black life. Factors playing a role in these responses include "escape and suffering, tradition, temporality, and the social organization of memory."[80] Indeed, as Gilroy reminds his readers, "it is often forgotten that the term 'diaspora' comes into the vocabulary of Black studies and the practice of pan-Africanist politics from Jewish thought."[81]

It seems particularly poignant, as Gilroy goes on to say, that Jewish thought, for its part, has largely failed to show commensurate interest in Black history despite the centrality of such phenomena as dispersal, exile, and slavery to Jewish history.[82] And as this chapter has shown, when Holocaust scholars have drawn on the subject of anti-Black racism, the results have been mixed. It thus seems important to conclude our discussion of the relevance of the colonial turn in Holocaust studies to the *St. Louis* voyage by considering race. Counterintuitive as it may seem, given the nature of the ship and its white, mostly middle-class passengers, Holocaust studies should take note of certain correspondences between Voyage 98 and the African slave trade. Both involved for-profit human trafficking, and if the *St. Louis*'s Jewish passengers boarded not as captives, the political conditions that drove them to do so had nothing to do with free will. They spelled racial persecution and exile. While the *St. Louis* only gradually turned into a prison for its passengers, it was an integral part of the concentrationary universe in which over a million prisoners died and through whose lethal jaws 254 of the *St. Louis* Jews passed on their way to the death camps (usually considered separate from the concentrationary universe). Further, the high profile of the *St. Louis* distracted from the fact that, elsewhere in the world, Jewish migrants traveled in extremely hazardous conditions on old, ill-equipped, dirty, and unsafe cargo ships. Many such voyages ended tragically with the refugees drowning, being set out on deserted islands, or being forced to return to their ports of departure, from where they would eventually be deported to concentration camps.

Citing Primo Levi's book *The Drowned and the Saved*, Gilroy asserts that claiming the uniqueness of the Holocaust does not foreclose viewing it as standing "in dialectical relationship with a sense of the ubiquity and normalcy of similar events." Levi, as Gilroy goes on to say, links slavery to both the senseless violence in the camps and to "an argument about the ambiguous insertion of the camps into the normal economic structures of German society."[83] It thus behooves Holocaust scholars to diacritically compare the Holocaust's functionalist aspects to instances of structural racism, such as the slave trade and the enlisting of eugenics for the cause of anti-Black racism in the US. For it was eugenics developed by American scientists for the classification and containment of African Americans that inspired Nazi leaders to develop their own "Rassenlehre" (race science) that became integral to NS ideology and paved the way for the "final solution."

In this regard, the voyage of the *St. Louis* has a unique quality that Jewish migration to Palestine lacks. The involuntary voyage that the *St. Louis* passengers, after their rejection by Cuba, undertook in the Caribbean and along the coast of Florida does not make them the same as Black slaves. It can, however, prompt us to explore what Gilroy terms "correspondences" between the Black and the Jewish diaspora. Arguably, the *St. Louis* voyage brings those correspondences full circle. A pattern emerges whereby certain technologies of racial subjugation, such as eugenics, were developed stateside and became adopted by the totalitarian NS regime on the other side of the Atlantic. That system enlisted the techniques for its own practices of racial discrimination, triggering a large-scale flight to other shores. The centrality of suffering and escape to those experiences of human displacement echo certain aspects of the Middle Passage, the cataclysmic phenomenon that laid the foundation in the "New World" for the historical conditions that would produce modern technologies of racial subjugation in the first place.

The metaphor of the shoreless sea is elastic enough to suggest transhistorical correspondences between different victimized populations, even as details differ from era to era and from one instance of forced migration to another. The colonial turn in Holocaust studies opens new venues for comparing the Holocaust and the forced migration that was part of it with other genocides. Jewish flight to escape Nazi terror never looked like the Middle Passage. It had its own set of terrors and inhumanities. By 1939, the emergence of the Jewish "death ships" on the world's oceans indicated that the biopolitical underpinnings of Jewish migration were shifting dramatically. Prior to the *St. Louis* incident, Jews had reason to believe that they could at least in some cases avert their subtraction from humanity by extracting themselves from the zone of greatest danger. Going forward, extraction and subtraction would overlap ever more closely. This development places Jewish flight into diacritical relation to the genocidal aspects of slavery and, as I will discuss toward the end of this book, to the current mass drownings of migrants in the Mediterranean.

Part II

6

The *St. Louis* Voyage in Popular Memory

Part I of this book concerns itself with the historical contexts leading up to the *St. Louis* voyage, the way it unfolded, and how it prompts us to revise our critical approaches to the Holocaust. The second part analyzes how the voyage has been remembered through different periods, across shifting cultural contexts, and in various media that include autobiography, popular history accounts, film and television, cartoons, and Holocaust memorials. While my earlier discussions of witness reports and the role of the press already questions a hard division between pre-narrated and narrated or "emplotted"[1] history, the texts and artifacts discussed in Part II distinguish themselves in two further ways: all of them were written with historical hindsight (ranging from a single decade to eighty years) and many have reached a large public. I pay attention to the interplay of four factors shaping memory culture: a given text's mode of production, the historical context from which it emerges, its genre of representation, and its reception, which is the most challenging area to analyze. Like any cultural memory, Holocaust memory flows in complex ways, so my discussion of it entails a degree of speculation. At issue is both how a given artifact makes existing memories legible and how it brings to the fore hitherto occluded ones.

The present chapter focuses on literary accounts of the *St. Louis* voyage published from the 1940s to the 1970s. The first comes from the ship's captain, Gustav Schröder, who in 1949 published a short book about the voyage titled *Heimatlos auf hoher See*—referred to from here on by the English title I have given the text in my full translation (see appendix), *Homeless on the High Seas*, abbreviated to *Homeless*.[2] As the print run was likely small, it is doubtful that the book reached a sizable readership in the 1950s. It did, however, find its way into libraries and museums.[3]

West German journalist Hans Herlin obtained a copy of the book and used it alongside other sources for his own account of Voyage 98, which he published in 1961 both in book form and as a high-profile article series in *Stern*, a West German illustrated mass-market magazine. Herlin's account gave public exposure to Schröder's story on a scale Schröder had not enjoyed during his lifetime—he died on January 10, 1959—and it at least temporarily brought the *St. Louis* voyage back into the public mind. Though the book was republished in 1970, Herlin's account is largely forgotten. Nonetheless, I believe it must be accorded a prominent place not only in *St. Louis* memory culture, but also in the way historical reflection on the Third Reich evolved in West Germany. Initially slow to come, West German historical consciousness received a jolt in 1961 by the highly publicized trial of Nazi war criminal Adolf Eichmann and by the West Berlin world premiere of the Hollywood film *Judgment at Nuremberg*.

Along with the popularization of the Anne Frank story and the publication of *Exodus*, Leon Uris's fictionalized foundation story of the nation of Israel, the impact of *Judgment at Nuremberg* would help increase the visibility of the Holocaust also in the US. Mass culture of the 1960s and '70s thus forms the historical context for the stateside emergence of *St. Louis* memory culture, discussed further below. In contrast to West Germany's fledgling memory culture, American consciousness of the Holocaust was firmly shaped by the image of US troops as liberators of Europe's Jews. But the liberator narrative received a blow with Arthur D. Morse's 1967 popular history book *While Six Million Died: A Chronicle of American Apathy*, in which the *St. Louis* voyage is one among numerous case studies of what the book's title bemoans.[4] Though brief, Morse's treatment helped catapult *St. Louis* memory culture into the maelstrom of English-language Holocaust remembrance, which quickly became dominated by US-centric discourses. The book's success set the stage for another mass-market account, Gordon Thomas and Max Morgan-Witts's *Voyage of the*

*Damned.*⁵ Written like a thriller, the book was soon adapted into a large-scale film of the same title (see chapter 7). Both became major reference texts for *St. Louis* memory culture.

Gustav Schröder and the Beginnings of *St. Louis* Memory Culture

After the war, Gustav Schröder's name remained linked to the *St. Louis* in the press and at public events.⁶ In 1947, the illustrated magazine *Revue* published an article that showed Schröder visiting the ship, which was docked in Hamburg harbor in poor condition and surrounded by ice floes (see fig. 6.1).⁷ Readers see a diminutive, tired-looking man in a trench coat standing on the pier and beholding the relic of the liner he once commanded. Another photo shows him touring its bridge, which is littered with scrap, and the eviscerated, cavernous promenade deck (see fig. 6.2 and fig. 6.3). Though Schröder retired as a captain four months into the war and, due to his age, did not have to serve,

Figure. 6.1. Retired Captain Gustav Schröder visiting the burnt and damaged *St. Louis* in Hamburg in February 1947. *Source: Revue*, photo by Albert Cusian.

Figure 6.2. Gustav Schröder standing on the bridge of the *St. Louis* with Hamburg in the background. *Source:* Photo by Albert Cusian; courtesy of Jürgen Glaevecke.

Figure 6.3. Gustav Schröder walking on the promenade deck of the *St. Louis*. *Source:* Photo by Albert Cusian; courtesy of Jürgen Glaevecke.

these photos iconically evoke the returning war veteran who, broken and alone, wanders his old terrain like a revenant.

As Hamburg had been heavily bombed, public space for hospitality and cultural events was in short supply. Despite its poor condition, the *St. Louis* served as a makeshift restaurant and hotel. On one of his visits, Schröder attended a shipboard concert of Johannes Brahms's Fourth Symphony organized by North German radio. Its conductor, Hans Schmidt-Isserstedt, promptly dedicated the concert to Schröder. A photo exists of the conductor being interviewed by a radio reporter with Schröder standing nearby. Schröder was also present when the *St. Louis* was towed from Hamburg to Bremerhaven for breakup in the early morning of April 15, 1950. He observed from the shore how two tug boats struggled to maneuver the hulk onto the Elbe river. The media, too, were on site. A radio reporter asked Schröder for an interview, which gave him an opportunity to recount Voyage 98 to the public.[8]

Already in 1947, prominent Dutch playwright Jan de Hartog had written *Schipper naast God*, a play which had notable similarities to the *St. Louis* voyage and was staged in Europe and the U.S.[9] Translated into German by author Rolf Italiaander, it premiered in Hamburg on September 9, 1949, as *Schiff ohne Hafen* (Ship without harbor).[10] There were only fourteen performances, but the play had a successful 1956 revival there in the theater of prominent German actress and theater director Ida Ehre. Since de Hartog takes considerable artistic license in retelling the *St. Louis* voyage, it prompted Schröder to write *Homeless on the High Seas* to tell the story from his perspective. In addition to chronicling the ship's day-to-day operations, the thirty-six-page book (see fig. 6.4) gives insight into the dilemmas Schröder faced in reconciling his ethical values with his status as a HAPAG employee and an executor of Third Reich law. That he was an NSDAP party member was revealed only in the 2010s with the opening of a chest of Schröder's personal belongings by his surviving family.[11]

Homeless stands in interesting relationship to Schröder's further accounts of the voyage. Unpublished manuscript pages contain details the published book leaves out. There are also the captain's logs Schröder filed for each leg of the journey. From these additional sources we learn that the captain, after hearing that some passengers had formed a "sabotage committee" to prevent the *St. Louis* from returning to Germany, talked two of them into "defecting" and joining the regular board committee. He thus proved himself an adept politician

Figure 6.4. *Heimatlos auf hoher See* (*Homeless on the High Seas*), dust jacket. *Source:* Photo by the author.

uncompelled to resort to using force at the first sign of trouble. It is only by comparing his log entries with the unpublished manuscript pages that we can infer the identity of Schröder's "converts." And none of his accounts identify by name any of the men who tried to storm the ship's bridge.

While Schröder does not hold back on faulting authorities for declining asylum to his passengers, he steers clear of politics. Nor does he criticize HAPAG for rushing the *St. Louis* to Cuba. Indeed, the book more than once commends HAPAG for its actions. Whether he was unable or unwilling, Schröder does not throw light on the reasons for HAPAG's gradually stepped-up efforts to help solve the crisis. Was HAPAG motivated by humanitarian considerations, by pressure from Berlin, or by plain fear of the economic repercussions of having to cancel the New York–based cruises scheduled after Voyage 98? Archival data remains inconclusive about this aspect. Because of the multiple areas in which the *St. Louis* crisis played out, even Schröder was not privy to every detail that shaped the complex behind-the-scenes negotiations. Finally, Schröder does not comment on the JDC's criticism of "uncontrolled dumping" of refugees, though it is certainly possible that he knew about it.

The final sentence in *Homeless* is a reflection of Schröder's worldview, which is that of a passionate humanist, not a political analyst: "We shall never forget the warning to all of humanity that lies in the meaning of the tragic fate of the heavily tried passengers of the 'emigrant ship,' so that cruelty and inhumanity can never again spread anywhere." The only sign of political judgment in this statement is its author's decision to put the words "emigrant ship" in quotation marks. If Schröder portrays himself as a consummate professional, a man in clear possession of a moral compass, and a self-effacing gentleman whose education was shaped by Enlightenment values, this is by no means self-serving. His plan to set the ship aground off the south coast of England demonstrates his willingness to take great risks. Yet he is never self-aggrandizing in his narrative, nor does his account in any way amount to a political defense or ideological recuperation of his position as a representative of Nazi law. The rare moment of self-satisfaction we witness in his book comes with his divulging the strategy of feigning a "ship fire" off the coast of England, which, so he relays with the gusto of someone elated at the prospect of beating the system, "we would 'heroically' extinguish . . . ourselves."

Schröder never tires of inviting solidarity and empathy with the passengers. In fact, it is his identification with them that gave the book its title. This becomes clear in a passage in which he describes his efforts to restore calm in the aftermath of the passenger rebellion: "We were facing nine hundred people who were literally homeless. I, too, started to feel a sense of homelessness. I felt as though every single person on the *St. Louis* had been expelled by the world and was now forced to leave this inhospitable planet—because the ship's crew could not expect any appreciation for their pro-Semitic attitude from the government. But it was exactly this feeling that made me so empathetic toward my passengers in their desolate situation." While it is hard to compare the risk incurred by the ship's non-Jewish crew with the mortal threat the Jewish passengers experienced, Schröder's account shows that he was keenly aware of the punishment the NS regime could administer to anyone perceived as resisting or subverting the state. His circumspection shows in his downplaying of the role of NS personnel on board. For Voyage 98, the NSDAP had appointed one of its members of the rank of "local deputy" (*Ortsgruppenleiter*) to keep an eye on the Jewish migrants. The existence of this person is confirmed in several accounts of the voyage, including by fellow crew members (discussed below), but *Homeless* gives not a word to the NS deputy. Upon completion of the trip, Schröder filed a confidential addendum to his log (see appendix) about the eastbound crossing in which he identifies the NS deputy by the name of Zschiedrich and praises him for helping the crew fortify the bridge and prepare the ship for the eventuality of a passenger rebellion. These comments' confidential status reflects the acumen that people living and working in dictatorships tend to develop. It is unclear, however, why *Homeless* does not mention Zschiedrich, especially given that he apparently did not survive the war.

One explanation may be Schröder's discomfort with questions of guilt. Citing his former high-school teacher's advice to his students, he says, "do not resent one another. . . . Those who do something wrong punish themselves much more than others could." It is important to note, however, that Schröder reserves this comment not for members of the NS regime but makes it in the context of wondering which member of the Cuban government issued the prohibition to land in Havana. Judging Cuba at least as harshly as Germany, he writes, "Here was a state, after all, that definitely disagreed with Germany's laws about Jews and that, against payment, had granted the emigrants temporary stay in its capital." His disenchantment with Havana's port authority and the Laredo Brú administration is understandable. They completely ignored him and made it clear they had no appreciation for his personal efforts to broker a landing. While his decision to sue Cuba for its breach of contract must be commended, the book's lack of criticism of the US for not granting the passengers asylum gives pause. And considering that Germany rather than Cuba was the root cause of the *St. Louis* crisis, the fact that Schröder, four years after Germany's defeat and nearly a decade after terminating his professional career, does not offer a more sustained condemnation of the Nazi state may seem surprising. He does, however, blame the regime for its establishment of concentration camps:

> it makes me even sadder that many of those poor souls, who finally believed themselves in safety in France, Holland, and Belgium, because of the insane war would still end up falling into the hands of criminals and perish. It is more than depressing to think that there were people who first were in a concentration camp, then suffered the *St. Louis*'s odyssey, only to be recaptured and taken away to their miserable deaths in a concentration camp. I only know of a few of the *St. Louis* emigrants who made it to shore and are still alive.

Having been confronted with threats of mass suicide on board caused Schröder to make the existence of concentration camps explicit in his writing. His referencing of camps in a 1949 German book bears significance. And yet, the term "criminals" (*Verbrecher*) with which Schröder describes the NS regime and its henchmen seems slightly too technical, not to mention that it carries associations of otherness. It singles out Nazi functionaries for demonization and "extraterritorializes" them, to borrow a term from Jörn Rüsen, into "a realm beyond the mainstream of German history."[12] As is well known, however, the tendency to place ordinary Germans at a distance from the atrocities of the Nazi era—which is further in evidence in Schröder's use of the word "tragic" to describe the fate of the *St. Louis* passengers—was typical of postwar Germany's struggle to come to terms with the atrocities of the Third Reich. While Schröder's book focuses on the fate of German Jews, it does not reflect on Germany's systematic persecution of those Jews; what it does is provide a vivid record of one particular scenario that was a fallout from that persecution.

As a first-person commentary, *Homeless* markedly rises above the historical amnesia that was the prevailing symptom of a postwar society traumatized by shame, guilt, and the effects of war. Schröder's account is an important primary source that testifies to the plight of Jewish migrants and, within limits, also indicts democratic countries for their complicity with the NS State. Schröder fit the mold of someone whom Germans could point to as proof that not all Germans were bad. Postwar West German memory culture anxiously focused on qualities that either predated or transcended the Nazi period. People prided themselves on their work ethic and on excelling at their jobs. Their respect for the arts and Enlightenment values promised to place them within "a national tradition that could be interpreted as being sharply at variance from Nazi ideology."[13] And some Germans sought to defend themselves by claiming that they had lived in internal opposition (*innerer Widerstand*) to the NS regime.[14] Schröder's bourgeois background and professional handling of the *St. Louis* and its passengers furnished proof of all these qualities. To be sure, his effort to save his passengers from the claws of the Gestapo was motivated by his wish to save lives, but one could also interpret it as a form of quiet, stoic resistance against the regime. Schröder thus largely eludes placement on the scale of guilt that Karl Jaspers designed in the late 1950s in an effort to measure degrees of responsibility Germans assumed for the Nazi period.[15] This is remarkable, given his prominent position as a captain and, even more significantly, as a member of the NSDAP.

Of course, it is precisely Schröder's exceptional status in relation to historical guilt that foregrounds the contradictions of postwar West German memory culture. The qualities that identify Schröder as a "good" German deeply resonated with West Germans during the 1950s and early 1960s, a period marked by reconstruction, the economic miracle, and a muted, many would say repressed, sense of historical awareness, which Jürgen Habermas has characterized as a period of "latency."[16] Despite Schröder's outspokenness, his book cannot be fully divorced from some of the more problematic implications of the cultural context of historical amnesia that shaped the postwar West German public sphere. At issue are certain instances in which Schröder's project inadvertently aligns with the period's conservative tendencies or runs up against some of the overdetermined dilemmas of Holocaust historiography.

One such area is the appendix to *Homeless*. One of its sections consists of telegrams from HAPAG containing updates and instructions for Schröder at sea. They show HAPAG willing to assist their captain in saving his passengers' lives by delaying or averting a return to Nazi Germany. (By June 1939, the NS regime, too, regarded a return of the *St. Louis* Jews to Germany as the least desirable outcome, though evidence of this would not surface until much later.) Yet these telegrams illuminate only one side of HAPAG's role. They support the positive impression Schröder creates of HAPAG, but they say nothing about the more careless—some would say reckless—attitude the company took in the early part of Voyage 98.

Also part of the book's appendix are a series of notes and letters in which passengers shower Schröder with gratitude and praise. Their inclusion has contrasting implications. On the one hand, the sheer existence of statements by Jewish survivors in a German-language book written by a German and published so soon after the Holocaust must be seen as a potential boon to the community of Holocaust survivors who were suffering under their own cloak of silence during the postwar years.[17] On the other hand, when related to the question of historical guilt, the role of these testimonials becomes more ambiguous. *Homeless* has the somewhat problematic effect of creating an impression of solidarity between the captain of the Nazi ship, his shipping line, and the Jewish passengers it transported. An image emerges of an alliance of victims, witnesses, and bystanders, all of whom were in one way or another negatively affected by the evils of the NS regime. To acknowledge that such alliances may have existed is in and of itself not the problem—provided one remains aware that they were fleeting and inadvertent and that their existence risks glossing the differences between the parties affected. *Homeless*, in the final instance, cannot be divorced from the historical moment in which it was published—a period during which West German culture deflected the question of political guilt by presenting ordinary Germans as sufferers and victims of higher circumstances. This tendency remained in evidence in the Federal Republic for decades to come, as the country continued to struggle through the process of sorting out the distinctions between perpetrators, fellow travelers, bystanders, and non-Jewish victims of the NS regime.

The constantly shifting status of the *St. Louis* during Voyage 98 as a transatlantic migrant ship headed for Cuba, a luxury liner cruising in the Caribbean with no immediate destination, a floating prison for temporarily interned refugees, and a delivery mechanism from and to the concentration camps also problematizes Schröder's decision of recounting the trip through the conventions of the travelogue. His difficulties in finding the right scope and tone can be gleaned when retracing his work process. For instance, his unpublished manuscript pages feature a statement he made about the voyage that was not included in the book because, I believe, Schröder may have questioned its suitability. In it he states:

> All told, I would not want to have missed the whole experience, no matter how much it shook me. It was an assignment that left a greater impact on me than a typhoon in the South Sea. Those who appreciate the desperate situation of my passengers and my concern for them will understand. I had to sacrifice many a night's rest. During the whole critical period, from the denial to land in Havana to the time we received permission to anchor in Antwerp, I spent my days taking care of the passengers and my nights writing coded telegrams in English.

While it legitimately documents Schröder's great concern for and tireless efforts on behalf of his charges, the passage is not unproblematic. The reference to a typhoon in the South Sea implicitly likens the *St. Louis* voyage to an adventurous odyssey and thus, at least inadvertently, trivializes the voyage. In this light, the passage's first sentence appears particularly jarring. No matter how grateful the *St. Louis* passengers were to Schröder after the voyage was over, it is certain that none of them shared his assessment that, "all told, [he] would not want to have missed the whole experience." This statement foregrounds the incommensurability of the respective situations experienced by the ship's captain and crew and by the passengers. One reason Schröder may have decided against including it in the final version of the book is that it would have undermined the image of homelessness with which he describes both his crew and his passengers.

The reference to a typhoon in the South Sea also prompts comparisons to Schröder's earlier book, *Fernweh und Heimweh* (Wanderlust and homesickness). At first glance, the relationship between both books seems innocuous. The earlier book mostly features impressions from some of Schröder's other sea voyages, which contain descriptions of the ocean, the weather, and marine wildlife. But if those impressions are mundane, the context in which Schröder gained them is not. They occurred during trips he undertook on assignment for the Nazi organization KdF, which organized cruises and other vacations exclusively for NSDAP party members. These trips were ideological in that they intended to attract new members to the party and reward existing ones for their loyalty. To be sure, Schröder was not employed by KdF directly, but by HAPAG. Yet HAPAG chartered the *St. Louis* to KdF, which meant that Schröder, ultimately, worked for the Reich on those trips.

The second half of the unpublished excerpt seems similarly problematic, because within the concise space the passage affords him, the captain's description of his own hardship threatens to eclipse that of his passengers. As mentioned, I deem such descriptions legitimate, for Schröder should be commended for his valor, tenacity, and compassion. Fortunately, the published book shows that Schröder found ways to relay his personal situation even more vividly than in the excised passage and at places in the book where such inserts seem more appropriate. Given his acumen and tact, it is quite possible that Schröder recognized some of the problems I identify here.

As *Homeless* anticipates many of the contradictions of postwar West German memory culture, one is tempted to ascribe a pioneering role to the book. But because of its slender size and lack of a proper publisher, its direct cultural impact had to have been modest. *Homeless* filtered into *St. Louis* memory culture more indirectly through remembrances of Voyage 98 in the media and by constituting one of the sources of Hans Herlin's book and article series on the *St. Louis*, which in every regard was a high-profile publication. It is thus all the more astounding that Herlin's account, too, has been nearly forgotten and to this day occupies only a minor place in the historiography of the *St. Louis* voyage. While Herlin first published his story in book form in January 1961, it gained exposure mainly because it also ran as a series of articles.[18] But while the book was republished in 1970, it was never translated into English. German-language historians have dismissed Herlin's account as too apocryphal in its details to be taken seriously. Though space limitations keep me from performing a detailed analysis, I deem such a charge to be only partly warranted. My main interest is in gauging the cultural significance of Herlin's narrative in the context of its time. What role did it play for *St. Louis* memory culture at a moment when West German consciousness about the Nazi era entered a new phase?

Remembering the *St. Louis* in Early 1960s West German Mass Culture

In January 1961, Herlin published his book *Kein gelobtes Land: Die Irrfahrt der St. Louis* (No Promised Land: The *St. Louis* voyage) with the Hamburg publisher Henri Nannen (see fig. 6.5). The print run and popularity of the book are hard to determine in hindsight. Significant, however, is that just months after its publication, Nannen republished the book as a series of articles under the title "Das Rote J" (The red J) in the illustrated mass magazine *Stern*.[19] Founded in 1948, *Stern* quickly evolved from a society gossip rag to a magazine for ambitious photo journalism with a social consciousness edge (somewhat comparable to *Life* in the US). By the late 1950s, *Stern* had a circulation of over one million and was estimated to reach over four times as many readers, because it was part of the standard magazine selection offered in hair salons and the waiting rooms of

Figure 6.5. Gerhard M. Hotop, *Kein gelobtes Land* (No Promised Land), first edition, dust jacket. *Source:* Photo by the author.

medical practices. Branding itself as an forum for quality journalism, *Stern* was the ideal platform for Herlin's article, but the article was also a good fit for *Stern*, given the magazine's interest in investigating controversial aspects of German history.[20] Herlin by then had already made a name for himself with entertainingly written books on aspects of German and world history, one of which was a bestselling account of the travails of a German U-boat crew during World War II.[21]

Reading Herlin's capsule summary of the *St. Louis* voyage in the inside flap of the dust jacket of *Kein gelobtes Land*—which also serves as the introductory paragraph of "Das Rote J"—makes it clear that the author does not presume any knowledge on the part of his reader about the incident. By 1961, Schröder had been deceased for two years, de Hartog's play was no longer in reruns, and West German historical memory had just turned its attention to another war-era maritime disaster, the sinking of the NS cruise liner *Wilhelm Gustloff*. Carrying 9,000 passengers (including some NS troops and medical staff but mostly civilians fleeing Soviet troops advancing from the east), the *Gustloff*, as the ship was called, was torpedoed in the Baltic on her way west by a Soviet submarine on January 30, 1945. The nearly complete loss of life made the sinking the largest maritime disaster in history. As most of the casualties were mothers, children, and old people, their victim status was overdetermined, which led to the fact that the incident firmly lodged itself into German historical consciousness. Here was a tale of wartime suffering that, as it seemed, showed the perpetrator nation as victim, similar to the "firestorm" aerial bombings of Dresden by Allied forces that unfolded just two weeks after the sinking of the *Gustloff* and that resulted in large-scale loss of civilian life. Spawning commemorative events already in the 1950s, the disaster occupied a far more prominent place in West German memory culture about World War II than the *St. Louis* incident. The film adaptation of the sinking, *Nacht fiel über Gotenhafen* (Night fell over Gotenhafen), a melodrama cast with some of West German cinema's top stars of the period, premiered in February 1960, a year before Herlin published his *St. Louis* story as a book and *Stern* ran it in serialized form.[22]

And yet, the retitling of Herlin's story from the book's poetic "No promised land" to the article series' more suggestive and accusatory "The red J," which refers to the NS regime's marking of Jewish passports, was very much in tune with the next step that historical consciousness in the Federal Republic was about to take. In April, the Adolf Eichmann trial commenced in Jerusalem and was closely covered by West German media, and in December the Hollywood film *Judgment at Nuremberg* had its world premiere in West Berlin. Eichmann's claim that he only followed orders when committing his crimes indirectly put all of Germany on trial. *Judgment*, too, made its representation of the Nuremberg war crimes trial all the more personal for ordinary Germans by casting popular star Marlene Dietrich and Austrian-born Swiss actor Maximilian Schell. Herlin, for his part, makes clear at the outset of his article that the true victims of the Third Reich were the Jews: 900 women, children, and men having to flee their homeland on a luxury ship; the red "J" in their passports branding them as Jews; and the sobering fact that only a fraction of them would survive (a claim reflecting what was known about the number of survivors in the 1960s).

Herlin tells his readers that in preparation for the article, he and his researcher, Carl-Heinz Mühmel, conducted a global search for surviving passengers and for documents corroborating their stories. In fact, the article's inaccuracies seem less egregious than its poor reputation among historians would suggest. In contrast to Thomas and Morgan-Witts, Herlin makes no claims that Berlin wanted the *St. Louis* voyage to fail so as to prove that Jews were universally shunned. "The Red J" is also laudably devoid of any pulp tales that the ship was an instrument of Nazi espionage. Herlin had access to Gustav Schröder's book and made good use of it. He relays the main details of the voyage with accuracy and gives correct information on the distribution of the passengers to other countries; he accurately identifies key members of the crew, such as the steward Leo Jockl and Schröder's first officer, Frisch (misidentified in other accounts as Ostermeyer, someone who served as first officer on the *St. Louis* on previous trips, but not on Voyage 98); and he supports his account with information from surviving passengers. All this makes "The Red J" a significant retelling of the *St. Louis* voyage for a mass readership that was only just beginning to prepare itself for a serious, sustained engagement with the most difficult aspects of Germany's past.

That Herlin's account heavily draws on interviews does, however, become a problem, for many of the interviewees' statements cannot be verified. Herlin bases numerous details—indeed, whole tangents of the story—on his interview with Jan Lüttgens, who, we are told, was a clarinetist in the shipboard orchestra. Like Leo Jockl and Paul Bendowski, the ship's photographer and print shop manager, Lüttgens died many years ago.[23] It is through Lüttgens that we learn of the Heymanns, a family of mother and four children who, according to Herlin, travel to Cuba to reunite with the family's father, who is already waiting for them in Havana. The passenger roster of the *St. Louis* lists three Heymanns and two Heimanns. None of their first names coincide with the names used by Herlin. This is frustrating, because the Heymanns serve Herlin to relay important details about the arduous process to which German Jews were subjected to receive permission to migrate.

His readers have to take Herlin's word for what the book presents as fact.[24] Herlin claims that Laredo Brú demanded that Benítez share the profits from Jewish migrant visas with him and also coveted the funds the JDC had offered Cuba for the *St. Louis* Jews.[25] Easier to verify is Herlin's description of the infrastructure that turned Jewish migration from Germany to Cuba into a transnational money-making machine.[26] Readers learn that a Cuban consul in Germany demanded $1,000 for a visa and several consuls issued numerous passports for a hefty fee. Importantly, however, Herlin suggests that the center of corruption was Europe. He faults German travel agencies for proposing unethical but profitable migration schemes to the Gestapo. The shipping lines also had their own agents, so-called passage solicitors, who placed themselves in front of cafés, consulates, and office buildings to sell passage to desperate Jews.[27] When the *St. Louis* arrived in Cuba, HAPAG's Havana agent, Luis Clasing, was eager to turn the ship around quickly because hundreds had booked passage on it to travel to Germany.[28] Apparently, Clasing was willing to bribe a person Herlin describes as the president of the Immigration Committee of the Cuban congress with the sum of $5,000 to ensure disembarkation.[29] While the source of this information is unclear, Herlin seems to have interviewed Claus-Gottfried Holthusen, HAPAG's director of passage. Holthusen told Herlin that the JDC brought him into a phone conversation with the British government in which he painted a bleak picture of what would happen to the passengers if they had to return to Germany.[30]

Even more central to Herlin's account than Holthusen and the Heymanns is board musician Jan Lüttgens, who almost becomes the story's main narrator. Lüttgens recounts that JDC agent Lawrence

Berenson advised the *St. Louis* passengers in Havana to affix a crucifix to their clothing if they wanted to disembark, because Cuba's president had signaled that he would allow all Christians to come ashore with or without landing permit. Lüttgens claims that four passengers opted to pass for Christian, but he fails to address that none of the passengers who actually disembarked were in need of using that ruse. Lüttgens further told Herlin that he urged Arthur Heymann's sister, Stella—with whom, as he alleges, he had a coy romance—to follow Berenson's advice.[31] The crucifix vignette plays no role in any scholarly account of the voyage, but it is not unimportant. While it may be fictitious, it references the broader reality of the Nazis pushing Germany's Jews into hiding and forcing them to commit acts of self-denial. It is particularly the melodramatic aspects of Herlin's popular history account that make the *St. Louis* migrants enter West Germans' historical imago through an emotionally charged discourse of belonging—and this at a time when Zionism was becoming a central vector in German–Israeli relations and in Holocaust memory. This is not the only time that melodrama serves Herlin's didacticism. Another anecdote by Lüttgens foregrounds the need to compare the respective fates of Jewish and non-Jewish Germans during the war with greater nuance. During embarkation in Hamburg, Lüttgens witnesses how NS agents pull Stella out of the processing queue for interrogation. Stella's mother looks on with dismay. About the mother, Lüttgens says, "The woman just stood there, speechless and dismayed. Several years later I would see a face like that again: my mother's face, when we rescued her from the rubble of our house after the big raid on Hamburg. The first time I saw such a face was back at the pier. Her whole fate was readable in it. But I did not yet understand the language in which it was written."[32] Lamentations about the hardships non-Jewish Germans suffered as a result of allied bombing campaigns on cities like Hamburg have figured prominently in Germany's attempt to come to terms with its past. Yet the scene Lüttgens describes does not have to be read as an instance of competitive victimhood. It implies that the wartime and immediate postwar suffering Germany's civilian population incurred was at least partly the result of Germany's persecution of its Jews. Whatever else one may want to say about Herlin's account, its ability to expose a mass readership to a vividly told story about German antisemitism and Jewish suffering by making postwar West

Germans identify with the Jewish migrants lends the book and the article in *Stern* historical and cultural significance.

Both versions of Herlin's account are accompanied by a wealth of photographs. They are significant because they document the everyday horrors of antisemitic persecution in prewar Germany. The *Stern* article features photos of a park bench carrying an "only for Aryans" sign, of Jewish passports stamped with a "J," and of the Jewish passengers boarding the *St. Louis* in Hamburg and later looking out of the ship's portholes in Havana harbor, after the ship had become their prison. Herlin also includes photos taken by passengers while in Havana. One captures a view of the unreachable pier, another shows a dinghy filled with relatives trying to make contact, a third shows the lucky few who were allowed to disembark, and a fourth records Captain Schröder dressed in civilian clothing going ashore in the hope of meeting with Cuban officials. The article even includes a copy of the *Daily Mirror* cartoon that attacked the hypocritical attitude of the US toward the migrants (see chapter 4).

One crucial difference between the book and the article version of Herlin's story merits commentary. The article series is firmly embedded within West German commoditized culture, which testifies to the country's economic reconstruction. *Stern*'s myriad print ads for consumer goods ranging from shampoo and champagne to electric kitchen aids and new car models surround and, at times, threaten to swallow Herlin's story of Germany's victimization of Jews. But while the commercial framework may prompt charges about the passive consumption of Holocaust history, the magazine publication mode arguably counterbalances such consumption through one particular feature—the Letters to the Editor section, of which *Stern* published at least one edition in response to Herlin's article. One letter comes from a former *St. Louis* crew member who confirms the veracity of Herlin's account and emphasizes that the crew treated the migrants well. Another confirms Herlin's information about the greedy disposition of German travel agents who drove Jewish migration as a for-profit business. A third letter comes from a non-Jewish wife of a Jew who mentions that she carried the Star of David along with her husband and their children. This letter writer had no involvement with the *St. Louis*, but Herlin's article prompted her to share her wartime experience. Finally, one letter writer faults the US for rejecting the

St. Louis passengers. The writer claims that prohibiting the *St. Louis* Jews from landing and leaving them to their own horrific situation enabled the US to place Germans in a bad light.

Even this statement, despite its misconceptions, indicates the dialogic aspect of mass-market publishing. What began with a Dutch play, which was inspired by the *St. Louis* voyage and which, in turn, prompted the ship's captain to write his own account of it, continued with the first truly popular, mass-market narrative of the voyage. Once it emerged into the West German public sphere, it prompted readers to share their own memories. "The Red J" helped spawn an expanding web of memories from diverse perspectives. This expansion continues in US culture remembering the *St. Louis* voyage in the late 1960s and '70s.

From Voyage 98 to *Voyage of the Damned*

To understand how *St. Louis* memory culture developed in the United States, we must first consider the factors that by the late 1960s and early '70s made a popular history treatment of the *St. Louis* voyage a timely proposition. The 1950s still constituted a period of relative silence about the Holocaust in the US, though obviously for different reasons than in West Germany. US troops participated in the liberation of the concentration camps, but the evidence of ineffable suffering they found initially marked Jewish survivors as "Other" to an American culture dominated by WASP values. While popular culture in the 1940s acknowledged that Jews were part of American society, it did so strictly via discussions of antisemitism—in other words, within the framework of debating America's social problems.[33] Notwithstanding those pro-integrationist voices, however, because of the legacy of the Holocaust, Jewishness remained at variance with the postwar spirit of optimism.[34] But the popular successes of the films *The Diary of Anne Frank* (1959), *Exodus* (1961), and *Judgment at Nuremberg* and the coverage of the Adolf Eichmann trial by the US press shifted the status of Jewishness in the US.[35]

The Eichmann trial, as Alan Mintz points out, had several repercussions. To begin with, it cemented the status of Jews as the Holocaust's official victims. No longer constituting a taboo, Jewish martyrdom now became something America's Christian majority could relate to because of the centrality the Christian faith accorded to martyrdom. But the figure of the martyr was counterbalanced by that of the survivor. Concentration camp survivor Elie Wiesel's story lent prestige rather than shame to the community of survivors. It also drew attention to the situation of Eastern European Holocaust survivors and their offspring still living in the Soviet Union. For Americans, comparisons between persecuted Jews and the victims of Stalinism fit into the context of the ongoing Cold War rivalry between the US and the USSR.[36] But while the Eichmann trial raised the profile of Jews in relation to the Holocaust, it also despecified the Shoah by turning it into a history lesson of what humanity was capable of in general. In this vein, the Holocaust came to serve as analogy in left-liberal polemics against the negative effects of American politics in the 1960s, particularly regarding systemic racism at home and the war against civilian populations abroad as part of the nation's military engagement in Vietnam.[37]

It was at this moment of increasing ambivalence about US politics that remembrance of the *St. Louis* incident reemerged in American culture. Arthur D. Morse's *While Six Million Died: A Chronicle of American Apathy* read the Roosevelt administration's decision to decline asylum to the ship's passengers as evidence of America putting its own interests above those in need of help. For historians of the *St. Louis* voyage, Morse's book is of limited use. The brief chapter he devotes to the *St. Louis* references no historical sources. Morse interviewed JDC agents Cecilia Razovsky and Lawrence Berenson but leaves out any discussion of Berenson's flaws as a negotiator. Either Berenson was uncomfortable reflecting on those flaws or Morse did not want to discuss them because it would weaken his thesis about Washington's apathy. The chapter does not mention that Berenson's reluctance to seek the State Department's assistance contributed to Cuba's terminating negotiations. Attempting to shift blame away from Berenson, Morse charges the State Department with underestimating Cuba and even warning Ambassador Wright that Cuba was bluffing in its demands.[38]

While Six Million Died paved the way for more elaborate treatments of the *St. Louis* voyage. Gordon Thomas and Max Morgan-Witts's *Voyage of the Damned* retold the story in book length and in a manner approaching novelization. Using a literary technique known as figuration, the authors render complex constellations into subjective positions, which they ascribe to individual historical participants. Figuration became a common strategy in 1960s New Journalism but has been criticized for its failure to achieve historical rigor when dealing with the topic of genocide.[39] As C. Paul Vincent notes of *Voyage of the Damned*, its blending of "well-documented discourse with unsubstantiated and speculative commentary"[40] has cast doubt on its accuracy: "Lacking footnotes and with the historical-fiction writer's propensity for fabricated dialog and ascribing motives, the book is exciting but of little use for scholars."[41]

The success of Morse's book and the literary evolution of long-form journalism would only have encouraged Thomas and Morgan-Witts to draw on such fiction genres as melodrama, horror, and espionage. Paperback editions published after the release of the film adaptation added the overtly melodramatic branding tag "A Shocking True Story of Hope, Betrayal, And Nazi Terror" (see fig. 6.6). The problem with Thomas and Morgan-Witts is not that it is sensationalist and that it uses melodrama. Those aspects, as discussed in chapter 4,

Figure 6.6. *Voyage of the Damned*, dust covers for hardcover edition (left) and paperback edition. *Source:* Public domain.

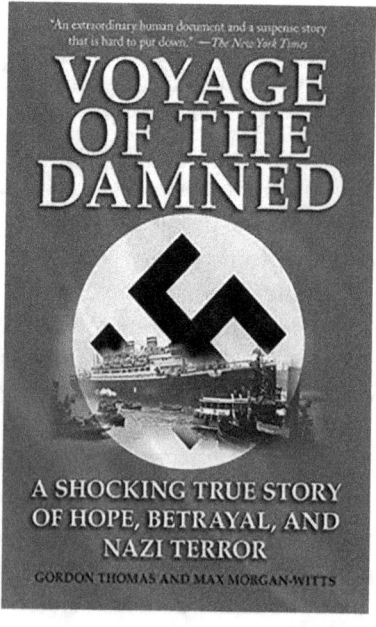

are an inherent part of the way the *St. Louis* voyage unfolded. What warrants objection is that the authors use sensationalism and melodrama to disguise their own inability to substantiate their speculative, pandering claim that the Nazis had planned the voyage to prove no other nation wanted the Jews. The book alleges that Propaganda Minister Joseph Goebbels, Nazi second-in-command Hermann Göring, and military intelligence chief Wilhelm Canaris secretly met at the Hotel Adlon, Berlin, to discuss how Germany could exploit a large Jewish migrant transport "to the full for propaganda purposes." Thomas and Morgan-Witts do not explain the nature of this purpose. Giving the appearance of paraphrasing NS leadership through indirect speech, they write that "the German nation could be told that [the voyage] was part of the general 'housecleaning' operation; the world at large could be told that here was clear evidence that Germany was allowing Jews to leave unharmed and unimpeded."[42] The authors cite no historical source for this claim. Instead, readers are told that Britain's Foreign Secretary received a message from the British Consul in Havana alleging that "*St. Louis* and its passengers would become the excuse for a Nazi propaganda campaign."[43] Not only does the existence of this message remain undocumented, but it also passes off one person's suspicion of Nazi propaganda as evidence for its existence.

In the same vein, the book recounts how, prior to boarding the *St. Louis* in Hamburg, one of the passengers, Aaron Pozner, sees that the ship is flying the Nazi swastika, which, to Pozner, "symbolized the party's control over the *St. Louis*. He understood by instinct what the captain disbelieved, that the ship was a pawn of the Nazis."[44] The authors base this statement on Pozner's diary, which, as they say, survived when Pozner perished in the Holocaust. But again, they do not give us factual evidence of the NSDAP's control over the *St. Louis*. They merely give us Pozner's understandably fear-stoked conviction that this is the case. In contrast to Herlin and Morse, Thomas and Morgan-Witts put partial knowledge and subjective impression center stage. They admit that some of the events remain difficult to explain, which is part of the appeal that *Voyage of the Damned* holds. Unfortunately, the authors turn figuration into an alibi for their untenable speculations, for which they enlist the voices of actual Holocaust victims. And they use Pozner's paranoia to assign him a place in their kaleidoscope of Jewish identities easily consumable by a 1970s US readership. If Pozner epitomizes the prototypical Holocaust victim,

Max Loewe, who jumped overboard in Havana harbor, is depicted as a victim-hero, a fierce fighter who does not give up even when fate seems to have irreversibly turned against him and his family. His attempted suicide could be regarded as a declaration of defeat and his defiant shouts "Murderers! They will never get me!" and "Let me die!" are not relayed in any other accounts of the voyage. The authors are, of course, correct that his jumping overboard became the clarion call for reporters: "[The reporters] had seen enough to draw a graphic picture of the ship 'that shames the world.'"[45]

If the book's Jewish characters remain anchored in historical fact, the details surrounding other characters are less easy to verify. The depiction of HAPAG agents and NS deputies in particular confirms the long-standing pulp appeal of anything having to do with Nazi Germany. For instance, if an espionage plot that had the *St. Louis* carry microfilms back to Germany really transpired, as Thomas and Morgan-Witts claim it did, the weight they give it is disproportionate to its historical significance. Several pages describe in lurid detail how Robert Hoffman, assistant manager of HAPAG's Havana office, carried off one of his "biggest espionage coups" by putting American defense secrets on microfilm and getting the NSDAP deputy on board the *St. Louis* to take them to Germany.[46] We also learn that already on Monday, May 15, more than a week before *St. Louis*'s arrival in Cuba, HAPAG's Havana office director, Luis Clasing, initiated talks with Benítez to avert the impact of Laredo Brú's Decree 937 and that these revolved around bribing Laredo Brú and Benítez. About Benítez the authors write that there had been "periodic and handsome kickbacks from HAPAG, and this Monday . . . Clasing arrived with $5000 in small bills. The agent explained that Hapag didn't want the 'problem' of taking the *St. Louis* passengers back to Europe, and . . . was happy to make Benítez this 'gift of friendship' to ensure that the 'problem' would not arise."[47] As with most other details, the authors cite no source for this exchange, though given that Herlin, too, mentions the sum of $5,000 in connection with Clasing's briberies (though without identifying Benítez), it is possible that Thomas and Morgan-Witts drew on Herlin's similarly unsupported account without acknowledging as much.

Thomas and Morgan-Witts's list of interviewed crew members is short and includes no one who had a key role in the events. This criticism is shared by former members of the crew of the *St. Louis*.

A document exists in the HAPAG archive in which its author, Kurt Vogt, who was Third Officer on Voyage 98, and several other crew members take Thomas and Morgan-Witts to task for not interviewing them and for including numerous errors in their book.[48] Some of Vogt's corrections, such as regarding the actual name of the first officer, align with existing archival data. On other aspects, such as the identity and character of the Local Gestapo Group Leader on board, Vogt provides privileged information.[49] In other ways, however, Vogt's document undercuts his claim to authoritativeness. Some of his assertions show that neither he nor the co-signatories had full knowledge of the situation on board. He states that in his function as a nautical officer he had no knowledge of the *Orduña* and the *Flandre*. In light of his responsibilities and rank, this is astounding. Even more puzzling is his assertion that there never was a passenger rebellion. More understandable is his claim that no plan existed to set the ship aground off the coast of England. Schröder shared this plan only with a select few, and evidently Vogt was not among them.[50]

The lore that has sprung up around Thomas and Morgan-Witts's claims over the years indicates the blurring between historical memory and historiography proper. Some of the authors' claims have clouded our understanding of the *St. Louis* voyage for decades. At the same time, the authors' structuring of their account through anecdotes and subjective impressions suggestively illustrate the bureaucratic inertia, complicity, opportunism, avarice, and cowardice that made the situation for the *St. Louis* passengers more difficult. While its sensationalism lends the book an aura of fabrication, the authors' use of melodrama at least in some instances helps them explore moral questions of guilt and responsibility in a literary mode. And apocryphal though it may be, the book's sensationalist depiction of Hoffman's and Clasing's briberies in essence corresponds to the information we now have of the profit motif that guided HAPAG's Jewish migrant business. In that context, even flawed assessments such as Vogt's are of interest. Vogt's response to Thomas and Morgan-Witts, defensive and partly misinformed though it is, is evidence of a larger culture of denial about HAPAG's culpability. Defensive and misinformed responses are just as much a part of *St. Louis* memory culture as are truthful witness reports and lucid historiographic assessments.

Figure 7.1. *Voyage of the Damned*: the MS *St. Louis* prior to its Hamburg departure. *Source:* ITV Studio/Timeless Media Group/ITC Entertainment/AVCO Embassy Pictures, 1976. Fair use.

7

Voyage of the Damned on the Big Screen

*V*OYAGE OF THE DAMNED was the first and, for many decades, the only cinematic retelling of the *St. Louis* voyage. Critics have further identified it as "the first post-Holocaust American film to focus on the Holocaust from a purely Jewish perspective."[1] Beyond this pioneering status, it is precisely the film's qualities as a commercial film—the use of spectacle, stars, and such lowbrow film genres as horror, melodrama, and the disaster film—that enable it to reference hitherto overlooked aspects of the fateful trip, such as the biopolitical framework in which it took place and the mercantile logic that shaped the Jewish migrant traffic. And, as I will show, it is those same qualities that also make the film "speak" in unexpectedly eloquent manner to broader issues of Jewish diaspora and Jewish myth. My discussion, as will become clear, remains keenly aware of the caveats against commercial cinema's glossing of history and, more specifically, the culture industry's reductive approach to the Holocaust. But rather than focusing only on the film's shortcomings and dismissing it for its commercialism, in this chapter I argue that *Voyage* stands in intriguing relationship both to history and to film history. The way the film stages its transatlantic drama about Jews, Nazis, and the Americas on the eve of World War II tells us much about US society—and US and transatlantic film culture—in the 1970s.

Voyage was one of the most high-profile films of 1976. Based on a pre-sold property, Gordon Thomas and Max Morgan-Witts's popular history book of the same title, and boasting a high-profile cast of American and international actors, the film was nominated for three Academy Awards and five Golden Globes, but it received mixed reviews and did poorly at the 1977 box office. Released the same year as the popular sitcom *The Love Boat* and three years before the landmark TV miniseries *Holocaust*, and showing intertextual connections with films as diverse as *The Diary of Anne Frank* (1959), *Ship of Fools* (1965), and *The Poseidon Adventure* (1972), *Voyage* illuminates our understanding of the mid-'70s film and media landscape in the US and Europe, which was marked by cross-fertilization between multiple modes of production and media spheres. Its large-scale format and prominent US distribution through AVCO Embassy made *Voyage* appear to be a big Hollywood release. Yet the film's roots are on two continents and stretch across several media. It is a British–American co-production made by a predominantly British crew. It was shot on soundstages in London, on location in Spain (with Barcelona standing in for Havana), and on an Italian ship—and, perhaps most surprisingly, its production history is firmly anchored in television. *Voyage*'s hybridity on every level—as an industrial product, a genre film, a star vehicle, a narrative, a visual text, and a political commentary—reflects the industry's rapidly evolving understanding of the commercial logic and artistic potential of international co-productions and it illustrates the trans-medial work not only of stars, but also of producers.

Production History

After Thomas and Morgan-Witts's book became a bestseller, producer Robert Fryer acquired the film rights. Fryer started in wartime theater, then worked as a casting director for CBS in the early 1950s before developing a distinguished record as a stage producer. From the late 1960s on, he also produced films in the US and Britain, including *The Prime of Miss Jean Brodie* (1967), *Myra Breckinridge* (1970), and Stanley Kubrick's *The Shining* (1979). Fryer had originally intended *Voyage* as an ABC Movie-of-the-Week, but the budget exceeded that of telefilms and the project's commercial viability was initially in doubt.[2] He found financing with British film and television mogul

Lew Grade, whose association with British production companies had generated several landmark British (and some US) TV series since the late 1950s.[3] One of the film's two writers, David Butler, wrote teleplays for British historical dramas and miniseries, including *The Duchess of Duke Street* (1976) and, later, *Disraeli* (1978), and *Lord Mountbatten: The Last Viceroy* (1986).[4] These productions exemplify "quality television" by combining middlebrow drama with historicism and educational value. Their focus on the British Empire and its institutions has earned them the label of "heritage film." Some of Fryer's work—the 1974 TV adaptation of *Great Expectations* (Fryer's first collaboration with Grade), but also the more political *The Prime of Miss Jean Brodie*—likewise falls under this category, which I discuss below in relation to *Voyage*.

The credits of Stuart Rosenberg, the director of *Voyage*, link the film to both American television and cinema, especially the auteur cinema that blossomed in the late 1960s and early '70s and that became known as "the New Hollywood."[5] These were the industry's nadir years in which producers were so desperate to reconnect with rapidly changing audience demographics and tastes that, for a brief period of time, they opened the door to unpedigreed filmmakers and their offbeat projects. Like Robert Altman, the New Hollywood's patron saint, Rosenberg started out in 1950s TV, directing episodes for *Decoy* (1957–59), *Naked City* (1958–63), and the courtroom series *The Defenders* (1961–65), for which he won an Emmy in 1963. Success as a film director came with *Cool Hand Luke* (1967), a chain-gang drama starring Paul Newman that, like Altman's *M.A.S.H.* (1969), appealed to the youth market for its anti-establishment sensibility. While Rosenberg's early '70s films reflected the experimental tendencies of the New Hollywood, he never lost touch with the venerable tradition of genre filmmaking—and in doing so, he honored genre cinema's own capacity for social critique. For instance, Rosenberg's 1961 film *Question 7* is set in East Germany and focuses on the son of a minister who, in order to gain admission to a conservatory, has to disavow his Lutheran faith to please the East German State. This story about totalitarianism and religious discrimination thematically prefigures *Voyage*.

When *Voyage* premiered in late December 1976, the American public had already been introduced to what one may term the film's low-culture televisual counterpart. On September 17, ABC had aired the first of three pilot movies of what would become the long-running hit show *The Love Boat*. I do not mean to be facetious by making this comparison, nor am I claiming that there is any significant overlap between the creative concepts, teams, and casts of *The Love Boat* and *Voyage*. Nonetheless, both entities afforded audiences during the 1976 to 1977 season two versions of maritime-themed popular culture set on ships, each in its own way engaging with the travails of a large dramatis personae of passengers on a cruise liner. While *Voyage* outgrew its television roots in scale and appearance, in order for it to compress the individual stories of its multiple characters into a feature film plot it had to borrow from serialized television, a medium then widely considered culturally inferior to film. The film partakes in the convention known from some ocean-liner-themed films but especially from cruise-themed TV shows of introducing the main cast via the initial embarkation sequence before it adopts the formula known from some historical epics but, again, used more widely by TV of fleshing out the narrative arc with individual character vignettes. Given that the industry, as I show below, was not content to link *Voyage* solely to art cinema, but sought intertextual connections to middlebrow and lowbrow film genres, it is legitimate to position *Voyage* and *The Love Boat*, despite their obvious differences in theme and mood, within the same patterns of cultural consumption. Just as *Schindler's List* was indelibly shaped by the pop culture provenance of its central creator Steven Spielberg, the creative concept behind *Voyage* positions the film squarely at the intersection of film and television.

In addition to television, New Hollywood auteurism, and genre films, theater and European art cinema are further influences on *Voyage*.[6] Several of the film's cast members had stage pedigrees, while others rose to prominence in prestigious European and international art films. A closer look at the film's cast illuminates how the film constructs meaning by referencing diverse media, modes of production, genres, and film cycles.

Casting, Narrative, Genre

In contrast to the seemingly random, spectacle-driven cast-of-thousands approach of many large productions of the 1960s and '70s, Fryer's casting for *Voyage* was well thought through and effectively helps the film build its diegetic world. Several cast members situate the film in relation to art cinema. Max von Sydow, who plays Gustav Schröder, the captain of the *St. Louis*, had found fame in Swedish films directed by Ingmar Bergman and Jan Troell, though by the mid-1970s, he had also begun to appear in such Hollywood films as *The Exorcist* (1973) and, co-starring with Faye Dunaway, *Three Days of the Condor* (1975). Oskar Werner, the introverted and nervy Austrian stage and film actor who plays one of the ship's passengers, Egon Kreisler (the husband of Dunaway's character, Denise), was best known for his performances in *Jules and Jim* (1962) and *Fahrenheit 451* (1965). But his casting also evokes the Nazi-themed ocean liner film *Ship of Fools* (1965), Stanley Kramer's prestige adaptation of Katherine Ann Porter's novel about the naïve conjectures of a group of self-absorbed passengers on a sea voyage from Veracruz, Mexico, to Bremerhaven, Germany, in 1933. This film, too, boasts an all-star cast in a very similar dramaturgical setup to *Voyage*. José Ferrer, like Werner, appears in both *Ship of Fools* and *Voyage*, playing a glib, callous Nazi in the former and a corrupt Cuban immigration director in the latter. Both films' intertextual links foreground their central tropes, including that of the ship as symbol of a world incapable of averting or escaping the threats of fascism or, indeed, as a symptom of the world's complicity with it. Fryer cast big European names in supporting roles, such as James Mason as government official Juan Remos, Fernando Rey as Cuba's president Laredo Brú, and Maria Schell as another Jewish passenger. In addition to Dunaway, the cast also includes American actors Sam Wanamaker, Julie Harris, and Ben Gazzara. All three are associated with the New York stage and had been involved with morally serious and artistically ambitious dramas. Wanamaker acted on Broadway in the 1940s before going to Hollywood. In the early 1950s, he left for England out of fear he might be blacklisted for his leftist leanings. In *Voyage* he plays Carl Rosen, whose real-life counterpart jumped overboard while the *St. Louis* was in Havana harbor. Rosen's wife, Lili, is played by Lee Grant, whose history as a de facto victim of the Hollywood blacklist is well remembered and lends her tragic role in the film additional weight.[7]

The art cinema and highbrow theater intertext in *Voyage* serves two functions: First, it endows the film with the kind of moral gravitas and artistic cachet that mainstream films about the Holocaust seek to project in an effort to dispel charges of profaning the subject matter; second, it helps shape certain narrative and dramatic tropes. Particularly in its second half, which shows the *St. Louis* aimlessly cruising in Caribbean waters following the expulsion from Cuba, the film shows its passengers overcome with confusion, disappointment, despair, and rage. The threat of having to return to Nazi Germany prompts some to wax philosophically while others lapse into near-catatonic depression. In such scenes, the already sputtering and stalling narrative is further slowed to showcase wistful soliloquies in which characters reflect on their situation and their lives. Oskar Werner's Egon Kreisler, for instance, is mired in self-loathing and passivity for much of the voyage before his wife pulls him out of it and he helps the captain quell a rebellion by angry passengers.

The film's paralyzed or quietly despondent characters evoke what Gilles Deleuze has identified as the crisis of the action image in American cinema of the 1970s. During this period, films associated with the New Hollywood deployed heightened realism, emphasized setting over plot, slowed their narratives, and borrowed from art cinema, a tendency that Deleuze and others have read as a response to the country's political and cultural crises.[8] However, whereas the European cinema generated a completely new narrative form, which Deleuze, in reference to World War II Italian art films, has termed "time image" and which radically suspends narrative sequencing in favor of a crystalline structure of equal possibilities, the action image in American films did not break with chronology.[9] Rather, as Christian Keathley has explained, Hollywood films pushed their protagonists to a crisis point at which they shockingly recognize their lack of viable options for action.[10] In *Voyage*, this shock befalls not only some of the *St. Louis* passengers, but also the ship's captain, whose character arc, closely following the ship's voyage, exemplifies what Robin Wood has delineated as a narrative paradigm in New Hollywood films: "The protagonist embarks on an undertaking he is confident he can control; the sense of control is progressively revealed as illusory; the protagonist is trapped in a course of events that culminate in disaster (frequently death)."[11]

Voyage ends on a note of relief with the ship's admission by Belgium, but not without acknowledgment that hundreds of passengers failed to escape the lethal reach of the Gestapo when Germany invaded Western Europe just months after the voyage's conclusion.[12] The film's transposition of this ambiguous outcome onto narrative, style, and atmosphere constitutes its clearest affinity to the mood of early 1970s American cinema. In *Voyage*'s bleakest moments, its aesthetics approximate the action image's devolution into the more radical time image. For instance, to introduce the big costume ball sequence, the film shows passengers gradually populating the dance floor not in real time, but by means of a dissolve. Their hovering between presence and absence renders them ghostlike creatures, which is further accentuated by them donning carnival masks. When the ship's band plays "Vienna, City of My Dreams," the dancers' spectral quality intensifies.[13] As if summoned by a call from the past, they all freeze. Then they collectively turn toward the musicians and ever so slowly and eerily move in on them (see fig. 7.2). The music envelopes them in their memories. They realize that their status as stateless refugees positions them outside time and space. The scene's overall effect fits Thomas Elsaesser's eloquent definition of Deleuze's time image: "Time appears to be neither linear nor chronological, it envelops the characters and the landscape, or layers the image like

Figure 7.2. *Voyage of the Damned*: Masked passengers attending a costume ball freeze when the orchestra plays "Vienna, City of My Dreams." *Source:* ITV Studio/Timeless Media Group/ITC Entertainment/AVCO Embassy Pictures, 1976. Fair use.

a memory of a thought, rather than leading to action, with its calculable consequences, its exact timing, and purposeful bodily motor coordination."[14]

In the film's otherwise conventional style, the dissolve, along with lengthy character close-ups, stands out as "artsy." Though not absent from classical Hollywood, it is a marker of modernist cinema and conveys ambiguity and complexity. The dissolves in *Voyage* tend to function both as syntactic bridges and to create an oneiric effect. Several dissolves beautifully lyricize the ship at the center of the film in its precarious, forlorn position after having been rejected by Cuba and seemingly moving in multiple directions at once (see fig. 7.3). Another dissolve follows the scene of Moritz Weiler's sea burial (which also begins with a dissolve and combines image and sound in layered, lyrical manner). After lowering the coffin into the ocean the crew give Weiler a final salute. The music swells and the film cuts to an extreme long shot that displays the *St. Louis* as but a small speck on the vast ocean (see fig. 7.4). This long shot powerfully visualizes Carl Schmitt's metaphor of the "shoreless sea," which Schmitt invoked to lament what he perceived as an erosion of juridical standards in Weimar Germany, but which, as discussed in chapter 5, must ultimately be read as the literal consequence fleeing seaborne Jews

Figure 7.3. *Voyage of the Damned*: Multiple dissolves of an aerial shot of the *St. Louis*. *Source:* ITV Studio/Timeless Media Group/ITC Entertainment/AVCO Embassy Pictures, 1976. Fair use.

Figure 7.4. *Voyage of the Damned*: The *St. Louis* as a tiny speck on the open ocean. *Source:* ITV Studio/Timeless Media Group/ITC Entertainment/AVCO Embassy Pictures, 1976. Fair use.

suffered because of the suspension of juridical rule under the Nazis and the democratic world's complicity in it. The long shot of the ship, in turn, dissolves into a close-up of José Estedes, an influential and worldly-wise Cuban lawyer, who explains to Morris Troper, the head of the Jewish refugee organization JDC, that the passengers' fate is anyone's guess, as they have become pawns in a political game.

Estedes is played by Orson Welles, whose tendency to fabulate about life's many risks and uncertainties is part of his star persona. By contrast, Ben Gazzara's Morris Troper copes with the crisis through physical externalization. His face contorts in disbelief or outrage and his body movements signal his frustrated urge to overcome the stasis that marks the intractable crisis. Sam Wanamaker, too, plays his character's suicide attempt (discussed further below) with great physical intensity. Many films feature introverts and extroverts side by side. But in *Voyage*, those types represent contrasting approaches to performance, which, in turn, imply different narrative orders. What comes to mind in this context is Paul Schrader's adage that in American movies protagonists work to solve problems whereas in European ones they probe dilemmas. Its contrasting use of Werner and Gazzara shows how *Voyage* effectively hedges both sides by using a double strategy. First, it embeds its diverse performance styles into the genre of melodrama, a category that inherently oscillates between stasis and action and that accommodates different tempi and moods. Second, the film draws in equal measure on acting as a craft and on its stars' elaborate personas, which serve as narrative shorthand. For instance, Werner's portrayal of Kreisler as a melancholic skeptic showcases his acting skills but also draws on his earlier role in *Ship of Fools*. In both films, Werner plays medical doctors who, beset by existential fears, disparage themselves and doubt their purpose as professionals, husbands, and responsible citizens of the world. Star performance has its own intertextuality.

Something similar holds for Gazzara in his own register, though his star presence in *Voyage* is less informed by any past film roles (however memorable some of these may have been) than by his revered status as a Method actor. That his Troper is American is more important than his being Jewish. As I discuss in detail further below, it serves the film to exonerate America from its historic failure to save the *St. Louis* Jews.[15] That the unfolding crisis puts Troper on the brink of failure does not, however, align him with the characters of the New Hollywood whom Thomas Elsaesser discusses in his well-known essay on that cinema's pathos of failure.[16] In contrast, say, to Jack Nicholson's Bobby Dupea in *Five Easy Pieces*, Troper is far from unmotivated. Similar to Captain Schröder, he is not paralyzed from within, but held back by external forces. The pathos of their failure is not the result of internal malaise, which, in itself, is a response to a horrific, irresolvable situation. Nor is spatiotemporal progression altogether absent from the film's narrative. If movement is punctured by stretches of slowing or going in circles, these phases owe to impediments caused by antagonists. In fact, the reason *Voyage* can present the ship's meandering with such dramatic verve is that it taps into the historic episodes' actual nature as a race against the clock (see chapter 4), deftly immersing viewers in melodrama's competing scenarios of "too late" and "in the nick of time."[17]

Voyage, with few exceptions, expresses the pathos of failure through a slowed action image rather than allowing its narrative to come to a complete standstill. While it temporarily freezes some of its characters in enigmatic close-ups and stilled tableaux, those images' textual autonomy is in question. Can they hold their own against the narrative thrust in which they are embedded or do they become mere citations for a post–New Hollywood media consumer immersed in television? After all, in television, a character's close-up reaction (identified by Deleuze as the "affection image") is a bread-and-butter device, whose rhetorical impact the medium knew how to heighten for the miniseries *Holocaust* at the same time that it would subordinate the series' dramatic flow, like that of any other show, to commercial breaks.

Voyage's hybridity also extends to genre. As noted, the film uses melodrama's fluid narrative dynamics and elastic performance registers to modulate between time and movement, paralysis and action, and crisis and hope. But this is not the only genre the film partakes in, as is evident in its advertising campaign. While the British trailer showcases the stars in their costumes to brand the film as a lavish period picture, the French and American trailers stress the historical angle, while also signaling that there is drama and romance. The US trailer references the so-called propaganda thesis, which forms the specious core of Thomas and Morgan-Witts's book and holds that Berlin all along intended for Cuba to reject the *St. Louis* Jews to reinforce Nazi claims that Jews were universally unwanted. But the film's paratexts, especially the poster art, reorient attention away from history and toward the offerings of genre entertainment. One such poster (see fig. 7.5) places a tagline (also used in the US trailer) beneath the film's title. It reads "It lasted 30 days . . . You will remember it as long as you live."[18] While the line references the historic nature of the ship's voyage, the color drawing suggests a different meaning. It depicts the ship listing heavily to one side with the terrified passengers staring into a stormy ocean while trying to maintain their balance (the *St. Louis* on its trip to Cuba encountered no inclement weather). The drawing slyly suggests that *Voyage* may be a disaster film, one of the decade's signature film cycles that included *The Poseidon Adventure*, a big-screen spectacle about a group of passengers attempting to escape from a capsized ocean liner that had been struck by a gigantic wave. The sensationalist poster for *Voyage* suggests that the ship at its center might suffer a similar fate. The cast of characters of *The Poseidon Adventure* and the fact that some of them plan to travel to Israel after the ship's arrival in Greece offer further intertextual links. Shelley Winters's character, a Jewish matron on her way to see

Figure 7.5. *Voyage of the Damned* publicity poster. *Source:* ITV Studio/Timeless Media Group/ITC Entertainment/AVCO Embassy Pictures, 1976. Fair use.

her grandchildren, embodies the general theme of courageous Jews imperiled at sea on their way to the Promised Land and thus, at least obliquely, references the story of the Jewish refugee ship *Exodus*.

A further link to the disaster genre comes with the casting of Faye Dunaway, who is clearly recognizable among the figures positioned in the poster's foreground. Dunaway did not appear in *The Poseidon Adventure*, but two years before *Voyage* she had a principal role in *The Towering Inferno*, about a skyscraper that had caught on fire. Dunaway's casting also reinforces the branding of *Voyage* as a period picture about the 1930s. She had helped popularize the decade's style in her iconic portrayals of the gangster moll Bonnie Parker in *Bonnie and Clyde* and the misunderstood femme fatale Evelyn Mulwray in *Chinatown*. She lent both characters the same sense of mystery she brought to her portrayal of Denise Kreisler in *Voyage*.

In conjunction with casting, film style thus opens up a further area of discussion about *Voyage*'s hybridity. How does a film's "look" function vis-à-vis questions of realism or, more specifically, historicism, and what ideological implications does style have for a film's treatment of its theme? Its production history and generic framework place *Voyage* within the terrain of lowbrow mass media (television, mass market paperbacks publishing) and such popular genres as the melodrama and the disaster film, while its prestige cast, its serious subject matter, and its branding as a history lesson signal its middle-brow-to-highbrow aspirations. If the film elevates melodrama to a kind of middle ground on which it stages its subject matter narratively and dramatically, its stylistic makeup places it within the realm of the historical film. Yet this catch-all category is of little use. Hence, my discussion below focuses on a set of generic features that have been discussed more specifically as heritage cinema.

Voyage of the Damned and Heritage Cinema

Heritage films appear across a variety of genres and, as Lutz Koepnick points out, involve "the production of usable and consumable pasts, of history as a site of comfort and orientation."[19] In 1950s England, television afforded the postwar public reassuring glimpses into the country's elite conservative institutions, but in the late 1960s, heritage films like *The Prime of Miss Jean Brodie* began to critique those institutions. The success of the 1981 TV miniseries *Brideshead Revisited* sparked a renaissance of the heritage genre. Britain, however, is not its exclusive home. While Koepnick, for instance, focuses on films about the Nazi period made in reunified Germany, heritage treatments also prominently operate in late 1960s and '70s Hollywood films set in the 1930s. In addition to *Bonnie and Clyde* and *Chinatown*, these include the Depression-era comedy *Paper Moon* (1973), the musical *Cabaret* (1973), the disaster film *The Hindenburg* (1975), and the Woody Guthrie biopic *Bound for Glory* (1976), among others. Pop culture of the 1970s was suffused with 1930s period iconography. One of the most popular TV shows was the long-running Depression-era family series *The Waltons* (1972–80).[20]

Stories about the "red decade" appealed to the social consciousness and anti-establishment sensibility that characterized the movie industry in the 1970s. But 1930s period style was also very photogenic. That visual beauty could even be brought to cinematic treatments of fascism and antisemitism became clear with the global success of two Italian-made period dramas, Vittorio De Sica's *The Garden of the Finzi-Contini* (1970) and Bernardo Bertolucci's *The Conformist* (1970). Aided by the cinematography of Vittorio Storaro, Bertolucci and De Sica lifted the heritage film from middlebrow period drama into art cinema, but this did not impress Saul Friedlander, who in *Reflections on Nazism* discusses the emergence of what he provocatively labeled "Nazi chic."[21] At issue is a fascination with opulent imagery and grand gestures, the showcasing of pageantry, and an obsessive pairing of kitsch with death: "Attention has gradually shifted from the re-evocation of Nazism as such, from the horror and the pain—even if muted by time and transformed into subdued grief and endless meditation—to voluptuous anguish and ravishing images, images one would like to see going on forever."[22]

Friedlander's comment reflects the distrust that proponents of modernism have expressed against mass culture. They regard entertainment cinema's spectacle-oriented historicism and its promise of direct access to historical experience as proof of the "nefarious effect of an all-encompassing ideology of textuality, form, and commoditization."[23] The first to identify the pitfalls of commercially oriented Holocaust films was Annette Insdorf, whose 1983 book *Indelible Shadows: Film and the Holocaust* begins with Eli Wiesel's warning that the Holocaust was becoming "a phenomenon of superficiality."[24] Concurring with

Wiesel, Insdorf asserts that "people shrug off the complexities of history to embrace the simplification offered by film."[25] On the other hand, Insdorf recognizes popular cinema's important cultural role in remembering the Holocaust. This ambivalent position also guides her take on *Voyage*. She appreciates the film for its diverse dramatis personae, which dispels the myth that all Jews were upper class and which, by including two former concentration camp inmates, points to the horrors to come; and she praises it for indicting the bartering to which Cuba subjected the refugees and foregrounding the world's "crass blindness to their plight—even by the American government."[26] But she concurs with reviewers who criticized the film for the limitations of its Hollywood treatment. *Voyage*, so Insdorf argues, contorts the events it depicts into a string of histrionic star turns that, "shown in huge close-ups, non-stop dialogue, and a surging musical score," prevent the drama and the protagonists from achieving nuance and depth.[27]

While I accord greater value to the film's star casting than Insdorf does and while my discussion below aims to identify areas of nuance and depth in the film, there is no gainsaying that, as a high-budget period drama, *Voyage* exemplifies spectacle-oriented cinema's promise of direct access to historical experience. The film's use of slow dissolves and superimpositions and its sustained close-ups capturing characters unable or unwilling to communicate do not run counter to the middlebrow philosophy of heritage cinema, but play into it. These attributes, as Koepnick argues, include the privileging of setting over narrative and of mise-en-scène over editing. While the film's Cuban sequences were shot in Barcelona and look somewhat generic, the producers secured an actual ocean liner, the *Irpinia*, which was of similar age and size to the *St. Louis* and which the cinematography exploits in handsome long shots. Some of the interiors of the *St. Louis* were meticulously rebuilt on soundstages in London and thus also raise the film's level of authenticity, as do the cast's costumes and hair styles. *Voyage* takes its historical subject seriously enough to generate what Koepnick terms a "museal" gaze that transforms the past into an object of consumption.[28]

Koepnick argues that the museal gaze has a fetishistic effect. It turns "the lost victim into a tableau vivant [and] obscures the asymmetries of heritage transfer," a process whereby heritage cinema "makes the resurrection of history possible."[29] His points are well taken. Yet the museal gaze in *Voyage* retains a measure of ambiguity. Several elements in the film run counter to realism's effect of authenticity and thereby foreground the farcical nature of the *St. Louis* voyage. To begin with, the ship at the center of the film is no mere historicist spectacle. It is only superficially an appropriate stand-in for the real *St. Louis*. In contrast to the *St. Louis*, which had the no-frills functional look of a passenger-cargo combi liner of its era, *Irpinia*, as a result of having undergone decades worth of refits and updates, sported a white hull and was equipped with several outdoor pools (*St. Louis* only had a provisional pool—see fig. 4.2). While still projecting a certain nostalgia in its appearance, the ship, by the 1970s, looked exactly like what it was—a leisurely cruise liner for the tourist market. By fetishizing the *Irpinia* for her beauty, *Voyage* does not necessarily do its subject matter a disservice. The film arguably foregrounds the disingenuousness with which the operator of the *St. Louis*, the Hamburg America Line, designated the Jewish refugees as tourists so as to downplay the reality of antisemitic expulsion and forced resettlement that was the reason for the "cruise." In other words, the film's departure from historical verisimilitude inadvertently identifies the voyage's farcical dimension, while its representation of the passengers as victims of international cowardice and red tape throws into relief the democratic world's biopolitically motivated complicity with the NS State's politics of Jewish expulsion. And the film poignantly shows how the Jewish passengers, too, bought into that very illusion of being tourists or "proper" migrants until Cuba turned them into refugees. For the film to convey their bizarre situation through dramatic means thus almost seems to call for what Insdorf characterizes as "histrionic star turns."

But the most intriguing heritage cinema aspect in *Voyage* is the film's use of music. Weiler's sea burial on the crossing to Cuba is accompanied by Jewish prayer music. Music also accentuates the class spectrum among the passengers. The tourist-class restaurant features a Jewish "kapelye" playing Klezmer-inflected music, while the first-class passengers get to listen to the main band playing big-band standards. As with the producers' decision to have the *St. Louis*, which was an instrument of antisemitic expulsion, be played by the *Irpinia*, a ship that, by the time the film was shot, was readable as a kind of European version of the Love Boat, the effect of this museal treatment is contradictory. It fulfills conventions of realism, but also subtly pushes up against them. In one particular scene both tendencies play out simultaneously. At issue is a fictional plotline depicting a shipboard romance between Anna, the Rosens' daughter, and Max, a member of the ship's crew, that ends tragically with their suicide pact. As Anna struggles with the prospective separation from Max upon arrival in Havana, their nocturnal on-deck tête-à-tête is underscored by faint music, the Rogers and Hart tune "Blue Moon." On one level, "Blue Moon" serves the retrograde effects of the museal gaze. A period-specific love theme for the Jewess Anna and the gentile Max, the song becomes what Koepnick in his analysis of recent German films about the Nazi period has characterized as a signifier of the transgressive bonds between Jewish and gentile Germans. *Voyage* is not a German film, but, having been shot and released during the year of the US Bicentennial, it has been read as an apology to all the Jews whom the US and the democratic free world did not save from the Nazis. And it allows this conciliatory sensibility to infuse its portrayal of the relationship between Anna and Max. Their romance, I believe, can thus be compared to the German-Jewish bonds that, in the films Koepnick discusses, express post-unified German cinema's wish-fulfillment fantasies of German-Jewish integration. In *Voyage*, too, representations of the past serve a social phantasm of the present.[30] The implication, as Koepnick finds, is one of historical obfuscation, and it plays out specifically with regard to the use of music: "Jews as much as non-Jews become German, not because they commit to shared rights and beliefs, but because popular music sutures what is different into a unified whole."[31]

If read along these lines, Anna and Max's romantic love theme functions to disavow, in Koepnick's words, the fact that "Jews might have experienced the same places and times in fundamentally different ways than non-Jews."[32] But while the lovers' suicide pact can be read as a melodramatic denial of those fundamental differences, it can also be read as the ultimate protest against the Nazis' erection of false and antisemitic boundaries between Jews and gentiles. From this perspective, "Blue Moon" becomes a signifier not of German-Jewish integration, but of the insurmountable obstacles placed between Jewish and gentile Germans. Three aspects speak for the fact that "Blue Moon" does not gloss over the difficulty of German-Jewish integration, but, on the contrary, identifies integration precisely as what it is—an impossibility and a wish-fulfillment fantasy. First, there is the song's very selection. "Blue Moon" is a rather unlikely choice to match the film's setting because American jazz music was legally prohibited in Nazi Germany, and that law also applied to German ships.³³ Thus flouting historical accuracy, the song makes the realist framework of the romantic bond between Anna and Max debatable. Further, the film's use of "Blue Moon" evinces a striking similarity to a German song of the period. The melody of the verse is almost identical with the middle verse of "Ganz leis' erklingt Musik" (Softly the music plays), one of the Nazi era's most popular songs. Since the tune Anna and Max hear the band playing is unaccompanied by singing, it briefly accommodates a near-complete overlap between an Anglo-American and German frame of reference.³⁴ While a German song seems more appropriate to the setting, its implications are no less utopian than those of "Blue Moon." The theme that both songs share plays exactly at the moment when Anna and Max start dancing by the lifeboats and Anna drops Max's date gift, a white carnation, to the floor. This foreshadows her loss of virginity to Max, but since their lovemaking is immediately followed by their taking poison, it defines their union solely through death, and thus, as something unachievable by the living.

The out-of-place status of "Blue Moon" has a third trans-diegetic function. It expresses the film's critical view of America's historical role in the Holocaust. The well-known second line of "Blue Moon," "you left me standing alone," even though it remains unsung, hints at America's letdown of the refugees, whose enchanted dancing to the song at the costume ball suggests their tragically misguided trust in the US as a beacon of justice and hope. While the social critique embedded in *Voyage* is ultimately more muted than in the films of the New Hollywood, it is this muted quality that accounts for the complexity the film achieves in the ambiguity of its museal approach to the past. This ambiguity reflects what Koepnick characterizes as heritage cinema's tension between heeding historical authenticity and telling stories that challenge hegemonic cultural assumptions.³⁵ On the one hand, *Voyage*'s representation of the *St. Louis* passengers caters to the common view of persecuted Jews as a human collective. On the other hand, the film is, as Insdorf notes, interested in exploring various differences between the passengers. To explore those differences, we turn to three areas that have thus far received scant critical attention—the film's use of melodrama, its depiction of Jewish myth, and its commentary on colonialism.

Melodrama and Jewish Myth

Michael Rothberg has cited *Schindler's List* (1993) as a prime example of the quintessentially American logic of engaging history through mass cultural circulation of its realist, melodramatic imitation.[36] While critical discourse has identified melodrama as one of the key liabilities in mass culture's representation of the Holocaust, the *St. Louis* voyage, as this book argues, was from the beginning strongly imbricated with melodrama both in the way the trip unfolded and in how the media covered it. Reporters had no need to embellish when they characterized the events as a conflict between virtuous victims (and their allies) on the one hand and conniving villains on the other. Yet the conflict's subtending connotations deserve further commentary. Melodrama's mode of pathos, as Linda Williams has argued, is complex.[37] While suffering implies passivity, it is often in tension with such emotions as anger and rage, two sentiments that tend to be associated with active rather than passive modes of behavior. The active–passive tension that subtends suffering can be traced through numerous texts and myths about the Jewish diaspora. Michael Walzer has discussed the significance of suffering to the Exodus myth and its eschatological correlative, messianism. Because of its origins in disenchantment, messianism links suffering to a longing for destruction, an eschatological impulse so great as to include even the destruction of the self.[38] But because the successful endurance of suffering aided the survival of the Israelites, suffering also remains linked to tropes of positivity, which include hope, optimism, and the willingness to be patient and proactive, to provide and accept leadership, and to "join in covenants and constitutions [and to] aim at a new and better social order."[39]

Jewish suffering in *Voyage* includes proactive and destructive elements that respectively align with Exodus and messianism. The film's use of melodrama thus turns active and passive modes of character behavior into narrative and mythological coefficients. The ship's passengers first experience the doldrums of despair before converting despair into action. While some of their acts are self-destructive, the fact that the ship avoided returning to Nazi Germany compels the film to convert messianism into the catharsis of survival and liberation. Rather than presenting messianism and Exodus as mutually exclusive, then, the film fluidly connects both, and it does so through a specific trope—the act of cutting. Following Moritz Weiler's death, his widow Rebecca performs the Jewish ritual of "kriah"—the rending of a garment in both grief and anger—by tearing the seam of her sleeve on her blouse. Karl Rosen, upon realizing that the *St. Louis* is leaving its berth in Havana harbor without letting passengers discharge, slashes his wrist with a razor and jumps overboard. Taking her father's attempt on his life as a visionary act of self-liberation, his daughter Anna decides to follow him into what she assumes is his death. While she chooses poison rather than a blade, her successful suicide and her father's attempted suicide cause Lili Rosen to cut off her hair at the roots.

Even as the film stages these characters' slicing, tearing, and cutting as messianic acts of self-destruction, it already implants into them the potential for a conversion to actions that, in the spirit of Exodus, are directly or indirectly liberating. Some of these acts and their consequences are a matter of historical record: Max Loewe's (Rosen's) spectacular suicide attempt sparked the media's attention through which the world learned about the *St. Louis* Jews. And if, by contrast, the scene of Lili Rosen cutting off her hair is fictitious, it does not merely pander to audiences' taste for sensationalism and histrionics. Just when Lili is about to lay waste to her coiffure, a horrified Denise Kreisler interrupts her. Unable to stop Lili, Denise sarcastically offers to assist her with the cutting to make her see the consequences of her pointless self-defiling (see fig. 7.6). The struggle between the two women pushes self-abjection almost into a grotesque register. But when Lili eventually breaks down and sobbingly buries her head in Denise's chest, the shot of the two women is reminiscent of a Pietà pose in which Denise has now assumed the position of cradling mother (see fig. 7.7).

The film here mutates into the subgenre of the maternal melodrama, while the scene's exalted nature, which involves physical struggle and the wielding of scissors, foregrounds the affinity between the melodrama and the related "body genres" of horror and psychodrama. In fact, prior to her dramatic interaction with Lili, Denise has a horrific experience of her own. She witnesses Karl Rosen's suicide attempt at close range and in a manner that is evocative of 1970s horror films, specifically the then novel genre of the slasher film. When Rosen storms on deck holding up his slashed wrist in a hysterical fit

Figure 7.6. *Voyage of the Damned*: Denise forces Lili to look at herself in the mirror. *Source:* ITV Studio/Timeless Media Group/ITC Entertainment/AVCO Embassy Pictures, 1976. Fair use.

Figure 7.7. *Voyage of the Damned*: Denise cradles a despairing Lili. *Source:* ITV Studio/Timeless Media Group/ITC Entertainment/AVCO Embassy Pictures, 1976. Fair use.

of rage and despair, he collides with Denise. For a moment, it appears as though he may be stabbing her (see fig. 7.8). Their clash soils Denise's white dress with his blood (fig. 7.9). While technically not the target of a slasher attack, the horrified woman nonetheless takes on the appearance of someone slashed, or rather, of the character of "the final girl," who ends up eluding the slasher's deadly reach. This is not where parallels to the slasher genre end. Similar to the final girl in a slasher film, Denise is masculinized by her experience without diminishing her feminine features.[40] This combination of masculine and feminine traits, in turn, enables Denise to become more proactive (something the Exodus myth usually ascribes to male figures), while allowing her to retain her capacity for performing feminine, quasi-maternal acts.

Rather than merely aiming for visual excess, the scene between Denise and Lili demonstrates the film's creative use of genre to probe the deeper implications of Jewish myth. The scene is a prime example of what Peter Brooks has termed the "aesthetics of astonishment."[41] At issue is the concentrated gestural summing up of moral virtue in a self-conscious register of representation, a phenomenon Brooks defines

Figure 7.8. *Voyage of the Damned*: Carl Rosen collides with Denise. *Source:* ITV Studio/Timeless Media Group/ITC Entertainment/AVCO Embassy Pictures, 1976. Fair use.

Figure 7.9. *Voyage of the Damned*: Denise's blood-soiled dress. *Source:* ITV Studio/Timeless Media Group/ITC Entertainment/AVCO Embassy Pictures, 1976. Fair use.

as "the moral occult." Enabling melodrama to place moral value at a premium and to express moral virtue through heightened emotions, the moral occult points to melodrama's seventeenth-century origins as a reaction formation against the waning of stable moral (and spiritual) values in an era of advancing epistemological and juridical uncertainty. Another response to those uncertainties, and specifically to the absence of verifiable divinity, is the Jewish myth of Exodus with its account of earthly liberation through divine deliverance.[42] If melodrama in *Voyage* thus lends expression to the self as the only knowable moral center—as it does in the scene between Denise and Lili at a moment when the world seems bereft of all moral values—this "heightened personalization and expression of the self," which Williams identifies as central to melodrama,[43] also points to its intersection with Jewish myth. In *Voyage*, melodrama helps Jewish myth negotiate the tension between constructive and destructive tendencies.

But if the scene between these two Jewish women is so insistent on averting Lili's self-destruction and, indeed, on negating destructiveness as a value, this is not for Lili's but for Denise's sake. For it is Denise who, along with her husband Egon and Morris Troper, enables the film to use melodrama and Jewish myth to stage its ideologically motivated redemption of America. As the film's female lead, Denise embodies survival and, thus, the spirit of Exodus. And because Denise is played by one of the decade's biggest American movie stars and in an earlier scene gets excited by American music, her survival is itself coded as American (and, as I will argue shortly, must be read as a correlative to the fictionalized role of Morris Troper). But for Denise to inhabit this status, the film must first humanize her by pulling her down from her ice queen pedestal (a dynamic also at work in other Dunaway films, such as *Chinatown* and the 1975 *Network*). By saving Lili from herself, Denise enacts the moral occult. She declares her true moral virtue, though her moral growth already began with an intervention at the costume ball. Realizing that "Vienna, City of My Dreams" has made everyone melancholic, she orders the band to play an upbeat dance from the Americas, a conga. Denise thus prompts her fellow Jews to leave Europe and their memories of their past lives behind.

Denise's transformation rubs off on her husband, who, after having been chided by his wife for being passive, pulls himself together and takes a lead in averting the ship's hijacking by other passengers. While the passenger rebellion was factual, Thomas and Morgan-Witts blatantly misrepresent it as a sustained physical altercation in which the rebelling passengers disable the first officer and, thus, become the eschatological version of a Jewish covenant.[44] The film adaptation mythologizes the incident further by making Egon Kreisler a key figure in the rebellion, even though his real-life counterpart, Fritz Spanier, did not participate in it. Neither was Spanier a member of the passenger committee and suicide watch, which both the book and the film identify as another instance of Jewish covenant. But while Spanier was never even asked to join the committee, his counterpart in the film is approached by the captain only to decline the request for help. This is to paint Kreisler as a loner who will eventually come around to helping the community in need. By devising Kreisler this way, the film dismisses collective agency, coded as European and embodied by the rebellious but chaotic group of passengers, and replaces it with individual agency, coded as American and embodied by Kreisler assuming the role of reluctant hero. The film's use of Oskar Werner here convincingly demonstrates the protean hermeneutics of star casting. The actor's Austrian nationality and heritage evoke associations with the complacency of Austrians before the country's annexation by Nazi

Germany; his upper-class airs recall the myopia of Western Europe's assimilated, cultured Jews, whom Hannah Arendt criticized in her 1940 essay "We Refugees" and who are the subject of De Sica's film *The Garden of the Finzi-Contini*. Yet Werner's laconic predisposition and aloof nature are also perfectly compatible with American mythology, for they evoke America's reluctance to get involved in conflicts and crises, as embodied by a long line of anti-heroes ranging from Humphrey Bogart's Rick Blaine in *Casablanca* to Gene Hackman's reluctant priest-leader in *The Poseidon Adventure*.

On the one hand, depicting the Kreislers as initially failing to see the Nazis as the threat they are before waking up and springing into action is a way for the film to show its audiences what America can do—or rather, what it could have done to save more Jews.[45] On the other hand, the fact that *Voyage*, like *The Poseidon Adventure*, includes a traditional savior figure reveals that its social critique is offset by conservative tendencies, which are marked by the ideologically compensatory function of offering reassurance to 1970s audiences that all is not completely lost and that there are still capable leaders in the world.[46] *Voyage*'s central savior figure is not, as one commentator argues, the ship's Christian captain, but Morris Troper, the head of the Jewish refugee organization American Jewish Joint Distribution Committee (JDC).[47] The real Troper indeed had a key role in saving the *St. Louis* Jews. But the film's heavily editorializing treatment of him goes far beyond exploiting this fact and veers into tendentious territory. In *Voyage* Troper is a portmanteau character of two JDC officials: the actual Troper, who never visited Cuba during the *St. Louis* crisis, but who famously secured asylum for the refugees in Europe, and Lawrence Berenson, the JDC's New York-based negotiator in Cuba. The decision to fold both into a single character likely owes to the fact that Berenson's flawed negotiations with Cuba's president do not cast him in a favorable historical light. Excising Berenson from the story and transplanting Troper to Cuba has several effects to be discussed in detail below. By removing Troper from his tedious, unshowy diplomatic legwork in Paris and making him a melodramatic savior figure on the refugee drama's frontline, the film converts the incident from a political conflict into a humanitarian crisis readable in moral terms. In doing so, it favorably revises the role of the US in the incident and it reshapes both the eschatological and the reparative elements of Jewish myth for the political agenda of post-war Zionism.

The latter received a momentous boost with the 1958 publication of Leon Uris's foundation myth novel *Exodus*, which is widely credited with reinvigorating Americans' identification with Israel.

Ben Gazzara, who plays Troper, does his part in transforming political into moral conflict.[48] Given Gazzara's affiliation with the New York Actors Studio, one might expect a Method-inflected performance aiming to give the character's frustrations the requisite nuance. But Gazzara does not play Troper that way. Script and direction make the actor draw on a limited lexicon of rote expressions from the repertory of melodrama and the soap opera. Upon learning that the *St. Louis* Jews are on the auction block, Troper's face becomes a reactive canvas that represents the world's moral indignation about the fate of the refugees. The real Morris Troper, no less than his colleague Berenson in Cuba, had long been aware of the underlying logic of bartering that shaped Jewish refugee politics of the period. For the film to acknowledge this, it would have needed to move Troper not only back to Europe, but closer to European art cinema. But *Voyage* does not want Troper to spend time "probing dilemmas," to reference Schrader's gloss on the difference between European and American cinema. Its revisionist agenda mandates that Troper become an old-fashioned American movie hero—someone who tries hard to solve problems and someone, too, who both possesses moral certainty and is unafraid to advertise it. Given the breakdown of the Cuban negotiations and the failure of the Evian conference the previous year, Gazzara's performance closely follows melodrama's purpose, which is to provide moral orientation.

That *Voyage* so thoroughly redesigns Troper as a character reveals an underlying urge to historically and ideologically revise the role the US played in the *St. Louis* crisis. Troper functions in a similar way to Oskar Schindler in *Schindler's List*—as a savior figure. When such figures save Jews, they implicitly also help the complacent free world, which tolerated the Nazi pogroms and the genocide, save face. Even as figures of historical record, Schindler and Troper are poised to assume their roles in the playbook of melodrama: The savior's action does not address the actual wrong (the Holocaust and the world's complicity in it). By saving a small number of Jews, his action addresses only one effect of the wrong.[49] The real Troper's keen grasp of resettlement diplomacy is a matter of historical record. But rather than showing those skills in action, and throwing light on the JDC's ethically debatable manner of bargaining, *Voyage* transforms in-the-weeds diplomacy into moral grandstanding. In Cuba, Troper is outraged. Toward the end of the film, when we briefly see him back in Europe, he acts like a mendicant who doggedly haunts one hall of government after another to beg for mercy on behalf of the refugees. The real Troper and his aides engaged these governments in a far more complex manner—which, however, does not easily lend itself to spectacle.

But what kind of politics does this shift—away from politics and toward morality—conceal? Roosevelt's refusal to allow the *St. Louis* migrants into the US necessitated Troper's efforts in the first place. The film, however, turns Troper into a figure who, while he happens to be Jewish, is first and foremost an American and, thus, represents America's resolve to step in and save the Jews. This spin not only seeks to redeem the US, but also tries to retroactively align the prewar *St. Louis* incident with America's postwar—or, more specifically, post-1967—agenda. When the US, during the Cold War, turned Western Europe into a bulwark against the Eastern Bloc, it also consigned a special role to Israel vis-à-vis the Arab world. When the *St. Louis* crisis unfolded, Israel did not yet exist. But by the time *Voyage* was made, relations with Israel had long been fortified, while those between the US and Arab countries had become fraught with US concerns about the destabilizing potential of Arab states' radical factions and the generally increasing clout of oil producing Arab nations. Whether views that Israel had come to be of vital strategic importance to the US were merely manufactured or ultimately legitimate cannot be debated in these pages. The fact was that such a view became prevalent both in the US and in Israel in the wake of the 1967 Six-Day War.[50] I do not mean to claim that these factors are all precisely traceable in the Morris Troper of *Voyage*. But the moral virtuousness and urgency signaled by Gazzara's performance implicitly accommodates Judaism's shift away from the eschatological messianism of the 1930s, '40s, and '50s and toward Exodus. As such, it is highly compatible with US–Israeli relations since 1967 without, however, probing their deeper political implications.

The foundation of Israel, which furnished long-standing Jewish settlement efforts in Palestine with a framework of nationhood and national politics, is but one piece of a larger picture and longer history of settlements that have placed different populations in fraught relationship with each other. The expulsion of German Jews in the 1930s already evinced two distinct but interrelated facets of displacement: that of driving Jews from the European continent to European colonies, protectorates, and mandates, and that of subjugating and potentially also displacing the peoples of those territories. To unearth this broader dynamic, which has been buried underneath the drama of saving Europe's Jews, we must expand the historical context in which we have thus far investigated the *St. Louis* incident beyond the horizon of totalitarianism to the history of colonialism. The Nazis, of course, were acutely aware of colonialism in their attempt to make their European neighbors, many of them colonizing nations, complicit in their racism and antisemitism. In this expanded context, Cuba holds a key position. Its economic ties to the US made the country an important trade hub in the Americas and a key destination for HAPAG and other shipping lines to land Jewish migrants. But Cuba's history of colonization goes back to Spanish colonial rule and includes the Middle Passage. Does *Voyage* reference those histories? As I will argue next, the film does not fail to draw attention to the refugees' status as human cattle, and it references, however inadequately, Cuba's subordinate relationship to industrialized nations, particularly the US. But to what extent the film conceals or exposes colonialism's longer history and its relationship to the Holocaust is a question that, as we shall see, begs a detailed response.

Voyage of the Damned and Colonialism

As a mainstream refugee drama and product of the liberal entertainment industry, *Voyage* both critically reflects on and reinforces the colonialist underpinnings of the historical episode it depicts. This is already evident in the film's representation of Cuba, which the film reduces to a generic tropical setting embodied by the stand-in location of Barcelona, a city belonging to Cuba's former colonizer. The film treats Cuba's role in the *St. Louis* drama with what can be characterized as condescending liberalism. It reproduces colonialist presumptions even as it feels obliged to critique them.[51]

When Morris Troper complains to José Estedes about the complacency of local officials and that all one can obtain in Cuba is "bananas, cigars, and whores," Estedes reminds Troper that Cuba has no monopoly on corruption. Several scenes show Cubans rebuffing Nazi officials who try to bribe them. Nonetheless, the film depicts Cuba as a place of bordellos, shady backroom deals, smiling fruit and vegetable vendors, gamey streetwalkers, and rhumba and salsa bands. As Estedes explains to Troper, "You can afford to be sophisticated. We are poor and primitive. We must sell what we have." With such proclamations, Estedes becomes a cinematic tour guide of sorts. He joins several Cuban officials in explaining Cuba's refugee policy to Troper and the film's viewers, who learn that the pressures weighing on Cuba's president are similar to those affecting Roosevelt. The film wants to suggest that Cuba is really no different from first-world countries that have contributed to the Jewish migrant crisis. And from negotiations between immigration director Benítez and HAPAG officials we learn that the German shipping line has happily profited from Benítez's corrupt scheme. Ultimately, however, it is Cuba the film blames for the fate of the refugees, and it does so simply by making Cuba's politicians shoulder the burden of explaining the intricacies of the country's immigration policy. The US does not come up in any of those discussions and US politicians are absent from the film's dramatis personae.

Of greater interest is how the film depicts the Jewish refugees from Europe in the colonial setting. This aspect, too, is rooted in melodrama and the museal gaze and, thus, evinces a similar ambiguity to the film's use of music discussed earlier. The film's approach is both Eurocentric and critical of Eurocentrism and it begins with the ocean liner, a type of ship that historically represents European and US involvement in Latin America. The presence of the *St. Louis* in Havana marks the contrast between the industrial and the developing world, an effect that is only exacerbated by the film's misrepresentation of the liner as a white cruise ship. When it shows the *St. Louis* lying isolated in the middle of the harbor, the film suggests that white Europeans are not safe from suffering tragedy.

Voyage critiques those Europeans for their Eurocentrism, but it does not resort to the heavy-handed didacticism with which the script saddles José Estedes. The film uses a subtle combination of dialogue, mise-en-scène, and choreography, all of which it brings to bear on one character, Denise Kreisler. When the *St. Louis* arrives in Havana, Denise says to her husband, "Egon, you know something, it's not Berlin." Both retain their feeling of cultural superiority even as they are made to suffer the repercussions of that very mentality. The *St. Louis* Jews' complex cultural status, which is defined both by relative privilege and by terror, abjection, and betrayal, finds artistic expression in the film's costume ball scene. The three styles of music the band plays, European waltz, American big-band music, and Latin American dances, function as political coordinates that situate the passengers who dance to them between European privilege, antisemitic expulsion, and a naïve trust in America's willingness to save them. The freezing of their dance moves triggered by "Vienna, City of My Dreams" shows them being haunted by their status as refugees. When Denise, sensing the waltz's chilling effect on her fellow Jewish passengers, requests that the orchestra play a conga, she does not merely try to improve the mood. The conga prompts the Jewish migrants to leave their ghostly Old World shells behind and get ready for their New World reincarnation, which leads to—or at least through—Latin America. Denise thus gets the Jewish diaspora back on course by literally jumpstarting it. Yet, if we view the scene through colonialism's racial differential, we do not see any Jews on the dance floor. We see genteel European society renewing itself by seizing on other civilizations and appropriating their music. The fact that in 1939 Cuba's government temporarily banned the conga for fear it would incite excessive reveling and street fighting only heightens the sense of European privilege. The *St. Louis* Jews get to enjoy what Cuba's population was barred from. Further, by dancing a Latin American folk dance, the European passengers appropriate and invert the lower class's practice of behaving like gentry during carnival. But the fact that the freedom afforded by carnival is temporally limited foreshadows the Jews' own resubjectivization to the mechanisms of their oppression.

Finally, it is in the film's depiction of the passengers' reactions to their abruptly changed status from tourist to refugee that we glimpse certain links between the Holocaust, racism, and colonialism. By showing how different passengers absorb this realization in different ways—ways that align with messianism and Exodus respectively—the film locates colonialism at the heart of the Jewish refugee community. To understand this, we briefly recall our discussion of the perceived difference between Nazi genocide and colonial genocide. As outlined in chapter 5, Hannah Arendt was the first to link colonial genocide to the Holocaust, but her Eurocentric notion of genocide ultimately leads her to categorize African victims of colonial genocide as different from Jewish Holocaust victims, since in her view colonial genocide was initially utilitarian, whereas the Holocaust was nonsensical from the outset.[52]

The racializing differential through which Arendt distinguishes between the victim categories of white European Jew and non-white Other historically resurfaced in only slightly displaced manner *within* the community of Jews affected by the Holocaust. There were the wide-eyed, shorn, emaciated concentration camp inmates who register the ravages of the Shoah in their eyes and on their bodies and who carried the label of "Muselmann."[53] A signifier of human existence on the lowest level, the label also had connotations of non-whiteness. And then there were Jews who did not have outward marks of destruction and managed to retain a sense of optimism and fighting spirit. The *St. Louis* undertook her historic voyage several years prior to the "final solution," during which such figures as the *Muselmann* emerged. Yet, perhaps buoyed by its historical hindsight position, the film's characterization of the ship's passengers seems to echo the Jewish community's internal victim differential.

For Carl Rosen, the encounter between Europe and its colonial other plays out very differently from the Kreislers'. While they consider Cuba a mere way station en route to what they believe is a temporary exile, Rosen, after learning that he will be denied this reprieve, faces up to the finality Cuba signals in its rejection of him. His act of jumping overboard in Havana harbor turns Cuban waters into a locus where the fate of victims of past genocides converges with that of Europeans earmarked for another mass killing. If read through Walter Benjamin's theses on the philosophy of history, Rosen's suicide attempt constitutes a moment in which the European and the colonial subject temporarily and "in a flash" appear contiguous. Such moments refute the notion of history's sequential flow, which generates misleading comparisons between genocides and their victims. There is no historical record indicating that Rosen's real-life counterpart, Max Loewe, intended his suicide attempt as an expression of solidarity with legions of murdered slaves or that he believed that the only use Jews had for the tropics was as a place to die. It was, however, in Cuba where the prospect of death began to loom large for the *St. Louis* Jews.

By attempting to terminate his life in a sudden burst of mad rage, Rosen enacts the effects of what Egon Kreisler upon departure in Hamburg characterizes as the "temporary madness" of antisemitism. Rosen demonstrates what effect this madness can have on its victims—with the notable difference that he refutes the notion of the "temporary." By performing what he believes is the only solution to escaping what would come to be characterized as the "final solution," he shows the Kreislers what history has in store for them. His theatrical self-abjection makes Rosen a taboo figure among his fellow passengers. Like the monster in a horror film, he represents the return of the repressed. As mentioned, when he emerges on deck like a whirling dervish, razor in hand and blood splattering on those with whom he collides, he looks like a slasher (see fig. 7.10 and fig. 7.11). Yet his fellow passengers must be protected from Rosen not because he tries to kill them, but because, leading by example, he shows them that they may already be dead, or moribund. It is in this sense that Rosen becomes an instantiation of the *Muselmann*, the embodiment of the victimized Jew as subhuman other—or at least he becomes Hollywood's version of it. One may object that Rosen does not seem nearly as abject as a *Muselmann*, because his abjection is mental and self-inflicted rather than the result of externally inflicted torture written onto his body and his mind. Yet, within the dramatic

Figure 7.10. *Voyage of the Damned*: Carl Rosen storms on deck. *Source:* ITV Studio/Timeless Media Group/ITC Entertainment/AVCO Embassy Pictures, 1976. Fair use.

Figure 7.11. *Voyage of the Damned*: Carl Rosen continues to slash his wrists on deck. *Source:* ITV Studio/Timeless Media Group/ITC Entertainment/ AVCO Embassy Pictures, 1976. Fair use.

universe in which the film charts different characters' responses to Nazi persecution, Rosen embodies the starkest effects of dehumanization. His abysmal despair is the root cause for his taboo status. Other passengers must be shielded from him because he may contaminate them. And those whom he affects, like his wife Lili, must be saved from enacting his destructiveness on their own bodies.

Rosen's suicide attempt and other scenes of messianic self-destruction, such as Lili's self-defilement, not only theatricalize violence, but also foreground violence's irrationality. Their acts demonstrate that because something does not make sense does not mean it is not real and won't come to pass. Messianic Jews do not need factual evidence of the "final solution" to make the Holocaust a real possibility for Exodus Jews. The violence they register on their own bodies and through their acts is what those invested in Enlightenment notions of rationality and progress try to repress or attempt to cast back into an earlier age of savage wars and wars against "savages." The loss of humanity the *Muselmann* projects in his consummate torture puts him in proximity to the victims of colonial genocide. But since he does not essentially differ from his fellow passengers, he implicates them in the fate that his violent acts anticipate. As their collective response to "Vienna, City of My Dreams" at the costume ball reveals, none of them can escape their abject status. As the film indirectly places them in relation to the historical trauma of colonialism, they become revenants of sorts, mnemonic markers of humanity's genocidal biopolitics.[54]

The real *St. Louis* passengers used their suicide threats to give their pleas for asylum more weight, but the film neglects this aspect because, one assumes, it would have required a stronger focus on the role of the US toward which those threats were directed. And while Rosen's desperate rejection of Enlightenment values allows us to chart correspondences between the Holocaust and the victims of colonial genocide, his behavior also locates the freedom to act, however self-destructively, on the side of the European subject. That subject can only indirectly testify to the existence of the victims of colonial genocide who remain locked in their role of passive, silent subjects of history. But the tale of Rosen's leap into the harbor may form part of a long-term dialectic that can eventually give voice also to the victims of other genocides. One might imagine this dialectic to unfold along the lines of what Michael Rothberg has termed "multidirectional memory," a process whereby the remembrance of one event triggers the recollection of other events and by other subjects, who may recognize parallels to their own experience, but whose voices have remained subaltern. The prominent circulation of the *St. Louis* episode in popular memory would seem to afford memory's expansion in multiple directions.

8

Germany Revisits the *St. Louis* Voyage

Die Ungewollten — Die Irrfahrt der St. Louis (The Unwanted — The Voyage of the *St. Louis*)

OVER THE PAST SIX DECADES, Holocaust remembrance has become a central component of German political self-understanding. After launching an extensive reparations program for Israel and Jews all over the world in 1952, West Germany became one of Israel's closest economic partners and political supporters. Since the 1970s, the state—initially that of West Germany and, since 1990, reunified Germany—has continually increased its role as custodian and sponsor of Holocaust remembrance. Germany's federated states (*Bundesländer*) have integrated the history of Nazi Germany and the Holocaust into school curricula. Federal, state, and local governments have rededicated the sites of former concentration camps as Holocaust memorials and turned some of them into educational centers. Local administrations have raised awareness of how their communities' pasts have intersected with the Holocaust. Private and government-sponsored initiatives have furthered Holocaust remembrance by organizing memorial events, honoring Holocaust survivors, and sponsoring exhibitions and other cultural events. And public (state-subsidized) broadcasters have thematized the Holocaust in their radio and television programming.

Except for the West German government awarding Captain Gustav Schröder the Federal Cross of Merit in 1957, the *St. Louis* voyage, until recently, has played almost no role in any of these efforts. This vacuum was filled by mass culture. As Schröder's and Herlin's books fell into obscurity (even though Herlin's was republished in 1970), it was mainly the 1976 German translation of Gordon Thomas and Max Morgan-Witts's 1974 US bestseller *Voyage of the Damned* and its 1976 film adaptation, released in West Germany in 1977, that helped keep the *St. Louis* voyage in German popular memory.[1] The fictionalizing aspects of the book and the film have obscured as much as they have illuminated the circumstances and unfolding of the voyage. As this chapter will show, however, such tendencies are not limited to commercial mass culture. They are also evident in the 2019 feature-length film *Die Ungewollten—Die Irrfahrt der St. Louis* (The unwanted—the voyage of the *St. Louis*),[2] a product of German public television. The film is historically significant as the first high-profile retelling of the incident in German-language culture since Herlin's account, and the first feature-length narrative film about the subject since the screen adaptation of *Voyage of the Damned*; its treatment of the *St. Louis* voyage reflects Germany's highly evolved self-image as a successfully reunified nation considered one of the world's most stable and liberal democracies, not the least because of its vigorous efforts to work through its totalitarian and genocidal past. But Germany's national imago not only shapes but also burdens the discursive logic of *Die Ungewollten*. This tension accounts for the film's revisionism.

The primary goal of *Die Ungewollten* is to bring an updated retelling of the *St. Louis* voyage to contemporary German audiences and, in doing so, incorporate *St. Louis* memory culture into the larger fabric of Holocaust remembrance. But since the voyage's unfolding also revealed the democratic world's complicity with the NS State's anti-Semitic politics of expulsion, it presents the film with a second goal. Depicting the ship's trip as a drama about refugees being denied safe haven allows *Die Ungewollten* to formulate an implicit plea for solidarity with current migrants and an indirect defense of Germany's liberal but increasingly controversial migrant policy.

Media coverage of the current migrant crisis has frequently invoked the *St. Louis* voyage. In 2018, newspaper and magazine reports on the ship *Aquarius*, which crisscrossed the Mediterranean with African migrants after rejection from several countries, referenced the *St. Louis* as a precedent.³ One article even features interviews with former *St. Louis* passengers.⁴ The article concludes that "what links both refugee ships is an ocean of tears."⁵ The *St. Louis* voyage has also been mentioned in critiques of current US immigration policy. Urging the US not to stop accepting Syrians displaced by their country's civil war, a 2015 article compares those refugees to the *St. Louis* Jews. It, too, includes statements by surviving passengers who, despite their ambivalence about the Arab background of many current migrants, declare that world history must not repeat itself by tolerating human suffering.⁶ A 2015 *Time* article places the US rejection of the *St. Louis* into a broader history of failed appeals of refugee ships to various countries.⁷ In 2017, criticism of President Donald Trump's Muslim travel ban also invoked the *St. Louis*. One article, titled "How America's Rejection of Jews Fleeing Nazi Germany Haunts Our Refugee Policy Today," features a photo of a crying woman aboard the *St. Louis* as the ship is forced out of Havana.⁸ Another article places the *St. Louis* incident into a longer history of anti-immigration legislation.⁹ And at the time of Trump's controversial travel ban but without explicitly referencing it, the German magazine *Der Spiegel* published an article about the *St. Louis* that focused on its Captain Schröder and that closes by referencing a passage from Schröder's account of the voyage, in which the captain proclaims that the *St. Louis* voyage should serve as a warning for posterity.¹⁰

Die Ungewollten aired four years after Chancellor Angela Merkel decided not to block the influx of large numbers of migrants from Afghanistan, Iraq, and Syria into Germany, and Merkel's 2015 in-the-moment call of "Wir schaffen das!" (We can do this!—meaning: we are able to absorb those refugees) provides a crucial context for the film. Merkel presented her decision primarily as a humanitarian gesture. Yet the inscription of the right to political asylum in the 1949 West German "Grundgesetz" (Basic Law) is widely read as an ethical-historical response to the legacy the Third Reich created by triggering two refugee crises, that of Jews fleeing Germany and Europe before and during the war and that of migrants of German origin fleeing the territories the Soviets occupied after defeating Nazi Germany.¹¹

Germany thus links its current refugee policy to the lessons it claims to have drawn from the past. Yet the film's indirect plea for solidarity with present-day migrants is troubled by the fact that most of those migrants are Muslims, whom German society struggles to integrate. Apart from being targeted by right-wing anti-Muslim demagoguery, Muslims in Germany encounter distrust simply because they are not Christian and not white. Just as significantly, most Muslim migrants hail from countries that have difficult relations with the nation of Israel, for which Germany has declared unwavering support and which has been a steady point of reference in Germany's efforts to come to terms with its Nazi past and with the Holocaust.[12] Israel's policy against Palestinians has long been controversial. While the history of the Israel–Palestine conflict is too long and intricate to assign the role of aggressor solely to Israel, the Netanyahu government's control of Palestinian territories has been compared to colonial-style occupations and has been criticized not only by Islamic nations. Leftists and postcolonial academics in Germany and Europe have joined nations of the Global South in condemning the systematic resettlement of Israeli Jews in the West Bank as a new instance of colonialism and Israel's militarily and architecturally enforced isolation of Palestinian territories and heavy policing of Palestinians as a form of apartheid. The discomfort felt in Germany when it comes to questioning Israel's handling of Palestine markedly increased in 2019, during the months in which *Die Ungewollten* was in production. On May 17 of that year, the German parliament formally condemned the Palestinian-led BDS (Boycott, Divestment, Sanctions) movement, a campaign for justice and equality of Palestinians in Israel, as anti-Semitic and voted to cut off funding for any organization actively supporting BDS.[13]

Of interest to the present discussion is how the political context outlined above shapes the way *Die Ungewollten* retells the *St. Louis* incident. Proceeding from the assumption that Germany has fully "mastered" its past, *Die Ungewollten* seeks to combine the discourse of Holocaust remembrance with an implicit humanist defense for a liberal migrant policy in the present. But those two projects are at odds with each other because of the political realities that underscore them. It is precisely the self-assuredness the film projects of Germany having worked through its Nazi past that increasingly appears in a critical light. At issue are, among other things, debates that compare the Holocaust to other genocides and, in doing so, present a challenge to the German state's position as custodian of Holocaust memory.[14] As one commentator has recently observed, Germany's Holocaust remembrance has begun to feel "static, glassed in, as though it were an effort not only to remember history but also to insure that only this particular history is remembered—and only in this way."[15] *Die Ungewollten*, as I will discuss in detail, enacts this "glassed in" approach to history through its mobilization of the conventions of the docudrama and its depiction of the ship's voyage and its passengers, captain, and crew. This depiction is shaped as much by the industrial context, which saw the commercialization of television in the 1980s and '90s and has culminated in post-millennial "event" television, as by a mentality that can be traced back to 1950s West German cinema. Conspicuously absent from the film are discourses of working through the past pioneered by the West German left in the 1960s and specifically by the New German Cinema of the 1960s to '70s.

Of further interest is how the film's use of archival footage, which conveys the week the *St. Louis* spent in Havana, reflects what Masha Gessen has characterized as a strong interdiction in German culture against "de-singularizing the Holocaust."[16] As coming to terms with the atrocities of the NS State is central to Germany's political self-legitimation, any understanding of the Holocaust about other genocides, Gessen explains, "can [be] and is being perceived as an attack on the very foundation of this new nation-state."[17] Attempts at "de-singularizing the Holocaust" thus tend to be dismissed or, as is the case with *Die Ungewollten*, are concealed behind a more dominant discursive logic which, as I demonstrate, is heavily if unselfconsciously Eurocentric.

Die Ungewollten as Docudrama

Die Ungewollten premiered on German network television's Channel 1 (Das Erste) on Monday, October 21, 2019, in the 8:15 p.m. primetime slot. It was the evening's third-most-viewed item, garnering almost 10 percent of the viewership.[18] Within the German media landscape's offerings, *Die Ungewollten* served the slot of quality television, a category traditionally comprising literary adaptations, period dramas, non-fiction films, or, as with *Die Ungewollten*, docudramas. With Ulrich Noethen in the role of Captain Schröder and Britta

Hammelstein in the role of female passenger Martha Stern, the film features two actors well known to German audiences. The film's director, Ben von Grafenstein, has several documentaries and fiction films to his credit and is listed as coeditor of *Die Ungewollten*. As we shall see, the editing is as essential to the film's docudrama approach as the reenactments, the archival footage and photographs, and the talking head interviews with surviving passengers.

In docudramas, fact and fiction complement each other and, in some cases, critically reflect on each other.[19] While pre-1980s German docudramas effaced drama in favor of education,[20] the gradual commercialization of German television has shifted the emphasis away from a modernist/reflective/didactic mode and toward drama, mimesis, and spectacle.[21] The rise of what has been termed "historical event TV"[22] has rendered the representation of Germany's past problematic. In contemporary German media, history returns as a nostalgic event presented through a citational treatment of past styles and fashion, as if displayed in a museum.[23] Further, large-scale, spectacle-oriented treatments of pivotal, often traumatic moments of German history turn the broadcast into an event of its own, in which television functions as a ritual medium.[24] *Die Ungewollten* does not compare in scale with the most high-profile examples of historical "event television," but the network's decision to retell the *St. Louis* incident eighty years after it occurred aligns with the "remembrance boom" that characterizes this form of TV.[25]

German networks tend to farm out the production of scripted films to independent firms. Even so, the production company of *Die Ungewollten*, Ufa Fiction Productions, followed a concept developed by the network's in-house editors specializing in creating docudramas.[26] This is communicated in the press notes for the film, which the network issued to media outlets ahead of the broadcast premiere. They summarize the story, list the cast and crew, including statements by the producer, the director, and the principal actors, and feature caption comments by surviving passengers interviewed in the film.[27] The press notes also prominently feature a statement by the network's in-house docudrama team about their editorial approach. Their mission, as they say, is to combine reenacted scenes with archival materials and interviews to enable viewers to process a given topic rationally and emotionally.[28]

In a preface to the press book, the network's director of programming, Volker Herres, claims that the archival images of the *St.*

Louis that the team selected for the film "especially in the present time evoke associations and images" (rufen natürlich gerade in der gegenwärtigen Zeit Assoziationen und Bilder hervor).²⁹ As the above-cited articles that associate the *St. Louis* voyage with the current Mediterranean migrant crisis show, Herres was not the first to make such associations. In fact, *Die Ungewollten* can be read as responding to them. However, Herres quickly points out that the 1939 context was utterly different.³⁰ Instead of reading Captain Schröder's role in saving the *St. Louis* refugees as an inspiration for Germany to develop a politics of solidarity with current migrants, Herres focuses only on Schröder's humanitarian motivation to save his passengers. His actions, so Herres claims, can teach us how enormous empathy can grow from a seemingly hopeless situation.³¹ Schröder's conscience, Herres goes on to say, made him defy injustice despite his vulnerability to being blackmailed by the regime (he had a wife and handicapped son at home) and despite his NSDAP membership, which came not only with privileges but also with obligations.³²

Schröder's own account of the *St. Louis* voyage at least in part confirms Herres's impression of him as not being overtly politicized. While Schröder, as I discuss in chapter 6, alludes to NS officials as "criminals" and, in one passage, condemns concentration camps, he withholds criticism of the NS State as a whole. And his book clearly shows that the personal and professional risks he took by delaying the *St. Louis*'s return to Europe owed primarily to his professional sense of responsibility for the safety of his passengers. Yet there is also Schröder's outspoken warning to posterity, mentioned earlier, with which he concludes his account of the voyage. In contrast to the article in *Der Spiegel*, which abridges the warning and, in doing so, depoliticizes it, the network fully excerpts the quote and positions it rather prominently in the press notes: "But we shall never forget the warning to all of humanity that lies in the meaning of the tragic fate of the heavily tried passengers of the 'emigrant ship,' so that cruelty and inhumanity can never again spread anywhere."³³ Given the applicability of this statement to the current migrant crisis on the Mediterranean and given its prominent placement in the press notes of *Die Ungewollten*, it surprises that the film ignores the statement's spirit by keeping its plea for solidarity with current migrants rather indirect.

The press notes thus bring the rhetorical contours of the film into view. While covering the same historical incident as *Voyage of the*

Damned, Die Ungewollten has a different focus. *Voyage of the Damned*, while about a German ship, is not really about Germany, which is why it treats Schröder as but one part of its ensemble cast and accords him relatively little prominence. *Die Ungewollten*, by contrast, has been conceived as a specifically German history lesson, but one that is "politically safe" and taught in the televisual classroom of post-millennial "event TV." The film inscribes its viewer not as an analytical individual but as an emotionally engaged "we."[34] The double focus on education and entertainment has, as noted, long been a hallmark of German docudramas. But as Paul Cooke has pointed out, television's "impulse to create a community of viewers rooted in a shared understanding of the German past"[35] has become more effective through TV's "eventization," that is, by television assuming what Dayan and Katz have termed a community's "ceremonial center."[36] This evolution of the medium has, according to Cooke and with further reference to Dayan and Katz, the additional effect of representing past historical traumas in an integrative and reconciliatory manner.[37] The impulse to reconcile history with itself (by smoothing over its thorny contradictions) and with the present (exemplified, for instance, by Germany's particular understanding of what type of historical responsibility arises for the country from remembering the Holocaust) is clearly evident in *Die Ungewollten*. Instead of using tensions and ellipses, the film works toward building a unified meaning. Its flamboyant aesthetic of fast-paced editing and emotionalizing music is characteristic of the faux dialectics of "event TV."[38] The various fragments, shards, and ruins (such as the ship itself) the film displays as spectacle constitute the ingredients for the filmic Schröder's gaining of consciousness, which the film mines for narrowly humanist purposes.

The Captain, his Ship, and his Crew

Die Ungewollten begins with the camera following a man as he walks toward a ship docked at the end of a long quay. The view of the ship ahead of him is blurry. Soon, however, we see him standing directly in front of it (see fig. 8.1), dwarfed by its dilapidated port side that rises before him like a towering ruin. The film reinforces the impression that the ship is all but a wreck by displaying a series

Figure 8.1. *Die Ungewollten*: Captain Schröder (Ulrich Noethen) on a postwar visit to the *St. Louis*. *Source:* © ARD 2019. Fair use.

of black-and-white photographs that depict the same man standing on the ship's derelict bridge and walking its decks like a revenant. (These are the photographs from the illustrated magazine *Revue* that show the actual Gustav Schröder on one of his postwar visits to the ship—see figs. 6.2 and 6.3.) Then, just as fluidly, it returns us to high-definition color footage of the man, now positioned at the front of the ship and looking up to the bridge (see fig. 8.2). His voice-over identifies the ship as the *St. Louis* and implies he is its former captain, Gustav Schröder, who commanded the liner on its historic voyage to Cuba. He states that the trip compelled him to choose and to act, even though his choices risked affronting the NS State. Following his comments, the film features archival footage of Nazi marches and pogroms and microfiche newspaper articles that covered the *St. Louis* voyage. The images rotate in rapid succession, as if driven by a machine. The film speeds up footage of marching brown shirts and burning synagogues to the dark, percussive beat of synth sound. Yet, just like the dilapidated ship Schröder visits, these images are artifacts of the past displayed for fleeting consumption, like an illustrated history book for readers to leaf through.

Figure 8.2. *Die Ungewollten*: Schröder overlooking the ship from its bow. *Source:* © ARD 2019. Fair use.

The film "glasses in" history right from the start with its central protagonist revisiting his old ship. As a stand-in for the *St. Louis*, the producers of *Die Ungewollten* rented MV *Funchal*, a Portuguese liner that, at the time of filming, had been taken out of service and was laid up in the port of Lisbon, Portugal, where the film was shot.[39] It appears that the *Funchal* remained in port for the film shoot, which explains the striking absence of intermittent establishing shots of the ship on the open ocean, an engrained convention of ocean travel films. The use of an actual ship lends authenticity to *Die Ungewollten*, an approach it seems to share with *Voyage of the Damned*. That film's realism, as discussed in the previous chapter, has certain ambiguities that harbor anti-realist implications and inadvertently foreground the farcical nature of the *St. Louis* voyage. By contrast, the cinematography of *Die Ungewollten* and the mise-en-scène's digital manipulation of the ship subsume its material objecthood under the film's rhetorical designs. The early shot, which shows Schröder facing the ship's side before stepping on board to retrace his memories of the fateful 1939 voyage, is deliberately disorienting. The hull's rusty expanse exceeds the boundaries of the frame and becomes a signifier of traumatic, unformed memory, which threatens to overwhelm the remembering subject and suggests that facing the past is a challenging task. By contrast, the closing image, a long shot of Schröder walking toward the camera as he exits the pier, gives us a full view of the liner behind him (see fig. 8.3). The ship looks as dilapidated as at the beginning. But Schröder has turned his back on it and is gaining distance from it, which suggests that his revisiting the past has been successful.

The way the film here positions Schröder does not merely suggest that mnemonic clarity has been obtained. It also conflates that clarity with the idea that history can be fully understood. By limiting a clear display of the ship as a whole object to the ending, *Die Ungewollten* makes the *St. Louis* a symbol of the successful reassemblage of historical memory, implying as it does that working through the past is not an ongoing but a finite task. Paradoxically, the film's emphasis of the materiality of rust and wreckage to signify Germany's defeat and postwar proneness function to deny the viewer a clue of history as "other," as something that transpires partially outside the film's system of signification.

The old press photographs *Die Ungewollten* borrows show that the *St. Louis* was in poor condition after the war. And Schröder, as records show, visited the ship more than once in the late 1940s. Of interest to us, however, is that *Die Ungewollten*, with full hindsight knowledge of the Holocaust, crafts the Schröder of 1939 as a role model for Germans to work through the past. The film equates historical responsibility with personal conscience and enacts this

Figure 8.3. *Die Ungewollten*: Schröder walking away from the ship at film's end. *Source:* © ARD 2019. Fair use.

equation through its dramatization of the captain's relationship to his passengers and crew. The desperate Jewish migrants corner him on deck and intrude into his cabin to confront him with their demands. Unable to escape their company, he comes to share in their misery. This triggers his gaining of consciousness, which makes him delay the ship's return to Germany. To accomplish this goal, the film asserts by fictionalizing the historical record, he takes his first officer into his confidence and, in the latter's approval of his actions and authority, finds confirmation that he is doing the right thing.

Die Ungewollten thus mobilizes traditional patriarchal norms reminiscent of West German entertainment cinema of the 1950s, derogatorily labeled "Papa's Kino" by the Young German filmmakers of the 1960s. From the late 1940s to the early '60s, West Germany's efforts to come to terms with the legacy of the Third Reich were uneven and slow to come.[40] Films that negotiated questions of historical guilt often did so through portrayals of middle-aged men, whose age closely linked them to Germany during the Nazi period and whose authority and moral integrity would be challenged by younger men, only to be deemed an asset at the end. When intergenerational stories migrated to television in the 1960s, they further sublimated the oedipal striving of the rote postwar film plots.[41] Plots shifted from the family as a site of conflict to the working world in which middle-aged police inspectors and other professionals spar with their junior partners. But the pattern remained the same: The patriarch's authority is challenged, which foregrounds his flaws and weaknesses before he eventually proves that his experience is of value to the younger generation.[42]

Yet, for portrayals of besieged patriarchal authority, West German film and television scarcely drew on the figure of the captain (or other merchant marine and navy personnel). When such figures did appear, it was again to stage scenarios of victimhood. Key examples are the two adaptations of the sinking of the Nazi cruise liner *Wilhelm Gustloff* by a Soviet submarine: Frank Wisbar's 1960 West German melodrama *Nacht fiel über Gotenhafen* (Night fell over Gotenhafen) and the incident's 2009 retelling by German television, *Die Gustloff* (The Gustloff), as well as Wisbar's 1958 U-Boat drama *Haie und kleine Fische* (Sharks and small fish) and Wolfgang Petersen's 1981 adaptation of the World War II U-Boat novel *Das Boot*.[43] Each film uses the ship's physical distance from Germany to signal its commander's and crew's ideological remove from the worst aspects of Nazi rule.⁴⁴ Their strong sense of responsibility for crew and/or passengers and their being merely a small part of the larger chain of command, whose purpose, so these stories claim, was to defend Germany rather than support Hitler, makes these captain figures into ideological placeholders. West German audiences could project onto them their own feelings of victimization and defeat.⁴⁵

Although the real Gustav Schröder was far too complex to fit this mass cultural mold, the version of him imagined by *Die Ungewollten* combines vestiges of these earlier characters.⁴⁶ But what purpose might such patterns have for a film intent on dealing with the past head on and by centering on a character whose probity from a German perspective was never in question? Interestingly, *Die Ungewollten* makes no effort to establish Schröder's honorability upfront. As he boards the wreck of the ship he used to command, he appears almost sinister and in need of illumination. This makes sense historically to the extent that the real Schröder's visit to the wreck took place prior to the founding of the Federal Republic and before any process of confronting the past could have been brought underway. At that point, history's heroes shared proximity with its villains. Both resided under the shadow of collateral damage and devastation that was the legacy of the Third Reich. Indeed, Schröder had to prove his innocence in an Allied court after the war. But in the half-century that followed, he received several honors, culminating with his induction into Yad Vashem in 1993. Media coverage of the 2018 discovery of his NSDAP membership did not damage his reputation.⁴⁷

By setting its framing narrative in the immediate postwar period, *Die Ungewollten* capitalizes on the trajectory of Schröder's reputation. It depicts the postwar Schröder as a mysterious, even slightly sinister figure. But by opening on Schröder, the narrative mobilizes the so called primacy effect, which, as defined by Johannes von Moltke, "causes us to give the first character we encounter the benefit of the doubt."⁴⁸ Through this tension, *Die Ungewollten* performatively distances the character from the audience, creating a gap that the film proceeds to fill by moving its viewers from mere alignment with the character to allegiance to him, to use von Moltke's terminology.⁴⁹ The film reveals Schröder's moral virtuousness through several devices. Repeated close-ups of his face construct what Carl Platinga has termed the "scene of empathy": The camera gives viewers privileged access to Schröder's emotions, often in moments of private introspection. However, Schröder's face is not very communicative, so its semantic function depends on how other characters respond.[50] When the Nazi steward Otto Hendrich refuses to pick up passenger Martha Stern's broken lunch plate from the floor of the lido bar, Schröder stares at him in a manner that can be read as castrating.[51] When Stern begs Schröder not to return the ship to Germany, he remains expressionless. Even when confiding in his first officer that he plans to put his passengers into lifeboats once the *St. Louis* is close to a Florida harbor and, later, that he plans to run the ship aground off the coast of England, his mien remains neutral. The film maintains this ambiguity by showing Schröder reprimanding his First Officer Ostermeyer for permitting two passengers to disembark in Havana.[52]

To turn Schröder into a *Vorbild*, a role model for whom helping refugees is a moral imperative, the film shows how the captain earns the loyalty of his crew. Over several scenes, Ostermeyer's role evolves from following his Captain's orders to becoming his loyal junior partner and confidant—almost a surrogate son. The change from alignment to allegiance begins with Ostermeyer reluctantly agreeing to Schröder's plan to set the passengers in lifeboats close to Florida. It continues with him helping his captain ward off the passenger rebellion. When a group of men attempt to storm the bridge to force Schröder to take the ship to Canada, Ostermeyer backs up his besieged boss by announcing that the Canadian government has also refused to accept the refugees. The scene is fictional, since that decision was not made public until after the *St. Louis* arrived in Antwerp. But Ostermeyer must deliver the news only after Schröder tensely solicits his information. His defense of the captain is implicit rather than explicit. In another fictional scene, which follows the passenger rebellion, Hendrich urges Ostermeyer to seize command of the ship. Ostermeyer's surprisingly muted response further delays certainty about his allegiance to Schröder. In the following scene, Ostermeyer asks Schröder why an NSDAP member jeopardizes his job and family by protecting Jews. Schröder's response that saving lives is a moral imperative prompts Ostermeyer's moral growth, so the scene implies. Thus, when Hendrich, in another fictional moment, urges Ostermeyer again to take command of the ship, Ostermeyer sharply warns Hendrich that he is risking arrest for mutiny. When Schröder tells Ostermeyer he has been uncertain of him, Ostermeyer responds that this is all part of getting to know one another.[53]

The following scene completes Ostermeyer's growing allegiance to the captain. When Schröder informs the passengers that they do not have to return to Germany, Ostermeyer delivers a note to Schröder in front of the passengers about the specifics of their disembarkation that makes them believe the captain. This time, Ostermeyer defers to the captain to announce the news, but his messenger role is nevertheless crucial. Whereas his earlier announcement about the Canadian government's rejection of the refugees implicitly indicted the democratic world for its selfishness, his latest dispatch signals the world's redemptive potential. Ostermeyer is thus not only a scripted historical figure who, so the film in a not entirely credible manner suggests, merely witnesses Nazism and other nations' complicity with it; by joining his captain in helping the passengers obtain asylum, he also becomes an allegorical representative of the present generation of Germans, whom the film through its history lesson prompts to reflect on the European Union's callous indifference to refugees—the "Fortress Europe" mentality (see discussion in the epilogue).

But what exactly does *Die Ungewollten* tell us about the significance of the historical legacy of the *St. Louis*? If the film's commissioning network conceives of the ship's voyage as a history lesson only to warn us in its press notes not to take that lesson too far, what does this say about the lesson's purpose? There is more to be said about the film's rhetorical structure. As a docudrama, the film supplements its reenactments of events with interviews and archival materials. Their selection and arrangement yield further insight into how the film intends us to view history as a "lesson" of the past.

The Archive and the Work of Mourning

Die Ungewollten embeds talking heads and archival footage into a scripted narrative that makes all elements cohere rather than foregrounding history's enigmatic nature. About fifteen minutes into its narrative, it features a series of black-and-white photographs of the voyage with passengers cheerfully posing for the camera and children playing on deck. Their function is to bring audiences closer to the trip's mundane details and underscore the passengers' idiosyncratic status as tourists, migrants, and encamped refugees. Yet the implications of such images tend to shift with the context in which they are embedded.

The first time *Die Ungewollten* uses those images is in combination with an interview with passenger Gisela Knepel, portions of which accompany the photographs in voice-over. Taken by actual passengers, the photographs constitute popular memory. Yet how the film weaves them into its narrative undercuts some of popular memory's qualities. The film withholds basic information regarding the taker(s) of these photographs. Were some or all of them taken by Knepel herself, as the film seems to suggest by pairing their display with her voice-over? Instead of clarifying this, the film stages its fictional account of the photographs' origin. It embeds their display into a reenacted scene in which Martha Stern, the film's main female protagonist, asks fellow passengers for permission to take their picture. While the reenactment intends to show how popular memory originates around survivors documenting their own stories, it links many such documents to a single individual who, it must be noted, has no historical counterpart among the *St. Louis*'s actual passengers.[54]

The film thus subsumes two of popular memory's essential and closely interrelated features—its origin in the lived experience of the multitudes and its documentation of them as heterogeneous—under its unifying didactic fiction. The reenacted scene suggests that Martha chooses her objects randomly, but the photographs do not hint at the heterogeneity that a random sampling of motifs might foreground. The ship's class division would be one example of this heterogeneity. Yet neither the photographs nor the reenactments make class division palpable.[55] Reducing the black-and-white photos to impressionistic tokens undermines their status as artifacts of popular memory and homogenizes the passengers. The same holds for the sequences featuring footage from Nazi marches and burning synagogues. It is little more than atmospheric embellishment, and its informational value is further diminished by the images' fast-paced editing accompanied by synthesizer sound. This technique prioritizes ambience over analysis. As such, it follows a certain tendency among post-millennial German films whose makers have deliberately, even self-righteously, replaced the leftist historiographic practices of the New German Cinema with a "diffuse, but distinctly new feeling for history."[56]

Rather than conveying a sense of history's internally contradictory nature by highlighting its gaps and frissons, *Die Ungewollten* uses archival snippets to conceal those gaps. The film aims to assign the archive a blandly illustrative role so as to compensate for history's aporias, rather than identifying archival findings as those aporias' material foundation. Analyzing history in its heterogeneous nature—whether in the form of photographs, film fragments, or potentially contradictory witness positions and historians' diverging assessments—mandates that it be apprehended "from the bottom up." West German memory culture in the 1960s and '70s adamantly embraced this agenda and developed a specific approach to dealing with it—the process of *Trauerarbeit*, which translates to "mourning work." As a specific aesthetic-discursive mode of historical inquiry, mourning work, in Thomas Elsaesser's characterization,

> is an acknowledgment of spectatorial divisions in representation, an exploration of the rifts as well as the continuities between past and present, a sensitivity for the intensities and resistances that individual memory opposes to the public images and public discourses about history. More a telling of the stories that go against the grain of the master-narratives of world-political events and charismatic careers, *Trauerarbeit* marks the gaps that occur, and the very obtuseness with which people live their own participation in what posterity comes to regard as significant.[57]

This definition of *Trauerarbeit* represents the opposite approach to how *Die Ungewollten* features interviews with survivors and deploys sundry archival materials. The film's talking heads demonstrate little plurality of experiences and viewpoints.[58] They mostly reiterate long-established historical facts. There is a marked discrepancy between the film's declared agenda of teaching viewers the meaning of historical responsibility and its concrete pursuit of this agenda. The use of archival materials documenting and narrating the week in which the *St. Louis* was in Havana is particularly instructive in this regard. This twenty-five-minute segment typifies the docudrama's strategy of using archival material to convey historical detail in economical manner. But the film's use of archival footage reveals the vicissitudes of this approach. It also demonstrates how the film systematically glosses over an important historical context of the *St. Louis* incident: colonialism. To understand this problematic, we need to focus on the film's depiction, through archival images, of its central object, the ship.

Colonialism as Structuring Absence

Media coverage of the *St. Louis* episode was extensive. Yet *Die Ungewollten* consistently supplements its archival materials with footage unconnected to the incident. Reenacted scenes of Schröder rushing the *St. Louis* to Havana in the hope of landing his passengers before the arrival of two other refugee ships, the French *Flandre* and the British *Orduña*, are illustrated with archival footage of two ocean liners at sea with one seemingly pursuing the other. The editing implies that the footage is taken from aboard the *St. Louis*, but the funnel livery reveals that the ship belongs to the NS organization KdF, possibly *Wilhelm Gustloff* or *Robert Ley*. The footage further misleads because the *St. Louis* never was within sight of *Flandre* and *Orduña*. *Die Ungewollten* blithely subordinates the archive to entertainment cinema's trope of the sea chase. This disregard for the *St. Louis* as the central referent continues in the Cuba segment. It features footage of several ships that the film suggests are the *St. Louis*, even though the latter is only briefly shown (see fig. 8.4).

Figure 8.4. *Die Ungewollten*: MS *St. Louis* in Havana harbor, part of historical footage that includes multiple ships. Source: © ARD 2019. Fair use.

This use of archival footage follows a practice James E. Young has identified as the intention to signal proximity to a past reality to repress evidence of the constructedness of said reality: "by calling itself a slice of the reality it now signifies, or an extension of it, documentary montage claims rhetorically to be unmediated and determined solely by the larger reality from which it has been torn."[59] Through its montage of archival footage, *Die Ungewollten* creates the effect of what Roland Barthes in *Mythologies* characterizes as "the decorative display of *what-goes-without-saying*."[60] Treating specific ships as interchangeable representatives of the ocean liner as an iconic ship type has, of course, been a widespread practice in nonfiction and fiction films. Often, the results are innocuous enough. But how *Die Ungewollten* partakes in this practice has direct bearing on the film's historicization of the Holocaust.

The Cuba segment begins with footage of the French liner SS *Bretagne*, a colonial liner that we are led to believe is the *St. Louis* entering Havana harbor (see fig. 8.5).[61] The film soon cuts to aerial shots of one of Havana's main avenues and the harbor with another ship in the distance. Moments later we see that same ship docked at the quay (see fig. 8.6). The film again implies that this is the *St. Louis*, when in fact it is the SS *Pennsylvania*. This is not the last time the film shows the *Pennsylvania*. Because the ship's service is specific to the Cuba segment's overall logic, it merits further commentary below. After a reenacted scene of the aborted disembarkation of the *St. Louis* passengers, *Die Ungewollten* features footage of the *St. Louis* anchored mid-harbor and surrounded by small boats. The film seamlessly combines this footage with a US newsreel about the *St. Louis* crisis. This newsreel is a staple in many TV reportages about the *St. Louis* voyage. It likewise misrepresents the *St. Louis* through another, unidentified ship. Further archival footage shows yet another unidentified ocean liner and a car departing from the quay next to it. Because the editing suggests that the car carries Schröder, whom we just saw leaving the *St. Louis* in a reenacted scene, we are falsely led to believe that this liner, too, is the *St. Louis*. The Cuba segment ends with footage showing the actual *St. Louis* being escorted out of Havana harbor by a flotilla of small boats (see fig. 8.7). But to pad this footage, the film once again adds footage of the *Pennsylvania* (see fig. 8.8) without, however, identifying the ship by name.

Figure 8.5. The SS *Bretagne*, built in 1922 as *Flandria*, was a colonial liner operating between France, the French Antilles, and other parts of the Caribbean. *Source:* © ARD 2019. Fair use.

Figure 8.6. The SS *Pennsylvania*. *Source:* © ARD 2019. Fair use.

The film's obfuscating treatment of ocean liner footage has contradictory implications. Though it violates historical facts, it suggests the importance of the ocean liner as a ship type to nineteenth- and twentieth-century mass transport, a prominent part of which was migration. And by establishing this context expressly about the *St. Louis*, the film foregrounds the ocean liner's role as an instrument of biopolitics, the principle that not only governed

Figure 8.7. The MS *St. Louis* leaving Havana. *Source:* © ARD 2019. Fair use.

Figure 8.8. The SS *Pennsylvania*. *Source:* © ARD 2019. Fair use.

migration but also drove the mass expulsion and extermination of Jews by the Nazis. Though technically not a concentration camp, the *St. Louis*, by helping facilitate this mass expulsion, became part of the overall logistic and institutional apparatus of Nazi anti-Semitism, which has been termed the concentrationary universe.[62] But while *Die Ungewollten* lets us glimpse this context, the film's attempt to make several other ocean liners stand in for the *St. Louis* without stating their actual identities also has a less salutary consequence: It forestalls any possibility of linking the Holocaust to other historical phenomena—especially to colonialism and neocolonialism, which, in the case of the *St. Louis* voyage, directly intersected with the Holocaust because of Cuba's role. As discussed in detail in chapters 3 and 5, the Cuban government's rejection of the *St. Louis* migrants did not simply owe to Cuba's often-cited corruption and political intrigues. The circumstances behind it must be assessed against the country's neocolonization by the US—which helped create domestic power structures that furthered political instability and corruption in the first place—and by considering the eagerness of companies such as HAPAG to collaborate with corrupt neocolonial officials to capitalize on the Nazis' antisemitic politics of expulsion.

Die Ungewollten, however, treats Cuba strictly as an example of other nations' moral failure to save the Jews. It does not probe Latin America's neocolonization, which was the framing context for Cuba's corruption, and this refusal is nowhere more apparent than in the film's decontextualizing use of footage of Havana harbor and its ships. By suggesting those ships are the *St. Louis*, *Die Ungewollten* erases the key role they had in Cuba's neocolonial trade relations with countries such as France—the home country of the *Bretagne*—and particularly the US. The film's use of the *Pennsylvania* is exemplary in this regard. Built in 1929 together with its two sister ships SS *California* and SS *Virginia*, the *Pennsylvania* operated for the Panama Pacific Line on the trade routes to Latin America that US President Roosevelt had sought to boost with his Good Neighbor Policy. The three liners were, in fact, labeled the "good neighbor fleet." The *Pennsylvania* was also a designated US mail carrier. After the US terminated its mail route subsidies in mid-1937 and the Panama Canal tolls increased the following year, Panama Pacific Lines discontinued servicing the route. The US Maritime Commission took over all three ships, gave them a refit, and placed them under contract with McCormack Lines for service to Brazil, Uruguay, and Argentina, a route they would continue to serve well into the 1950s. For this service, the *Pennsylvania* was renamed *Argentina* in 1938. Its refit included replacement of the double funnels with a single, sleeker one.

Just as the *St. Louis* was part of the concentrationary complex, the *Pennsylvania* was part of the Good Neighbor Policy, the effects of which, as is well known, by no means decreased the political and economic hegemony of the US in the region. The way *Die Ungewollten* uses the *Pennsylvania/Argentina* entirely erases this context. As the *Pennsylvania* by 1939 had already changed name and appearance, the footage we see of the ship cannot possibly date from that year. By subsuming the *Pennsylvania/Argentina*, which serviced Latin America before, during, and after the *St. Louis* crisis, under its own narrative of that crisis, the film severs the events it depicts from the historical and political factors that shaped them. It presents a vital episode of the NS State's antisemitic expulsion entirely from a European perspective on the Holocaust and its pre-history. Said perspective has traditionally deprivileged or outright ignored such historical phenomena as colonialism and neo-colonialism—factors that have frequently intersected with and compounded antisemitism. The particular manner in which this lacuna then finds thematic and aesthetic expression in *Die Ungewollten* evinces affinities to mythmaking. It literalizes what Jacques Derrida observed as the phenomenon by which mythological structures have "whitened themselves out,"[63] which is to say they shape consciousness precisely by effacing their racialized logic.

By subordinating all footage of Havana harbor and its ships to its retelling of the *St. Louis* incident, the film transforms visual referents of Europe's and North America's neocolonial relationship to Latin America into signifiers solely of German–Jewish relations. This approach reflects the narrow parameters Germany has established for Holocaust remembrance, in which the Holocaust is more or less exclusively a conflict between Nazis and Jews and its prehistory entirely shaped by antisemitism. Yet the archival footage the film relies on to visualize its remembrance cannot be fully reduced to its vision of the Holocaust. The images of the ships in Havana harbor also link to other memories and other facets of history, which complicate canonized ways of remembering the Holocaust because they indirectly reference important historical circumstances behind Cuba's rejection of the *St. Louis* Jews. Colonial history cannot be excised from the film's archival images, even though *Die Ungewollten* does not consider that history to be relevant to its subject. The film's use of archival footage constitutes a specific version of the dynamics within image-based Holocaust memory culture, which, as Georges Didi-Huberman has shown, oscillates between reminiscence and forgetting, wish and refusal, and knowledge and non-knowledge.[64] And because these dynamics follow a Eurocentric logic in *Die Ungewollten*, the film struggles to use its retelling of the *St. Louis* voyage to pledge solidarity with current migrants, many of whom represent European society's racial, ethnic, and religious Other.

A History Lesson with Qualifications

Die Ungewollten constructs a history lesson with a double agenda. Its retelling of the *St. Louis* incident eighty years after it occurred constitutes a high-profile contribution to the culture of Holocaust remembrance in Germany. But the film also indirectly suggests that Germany's historical responsibility for the plight of the *St. Louis* migrants might inform Germany's (and Europe's) response to the current migrant crisis. *Die Ungewollten* draws inspiration from Merkel's humanitarian battle cry, "We can do this," because it wants to remind us that we have done this before. But network editor Volker Herres's simultaneous evocation and disavowal of a link between the current migrant crisis and the *St. Louis* voyage is a chilling indication of the forces that police any comparison between Jewish refugees and current migrants, many of whom also flee totalitarianism and the various effects of neocolonialism. One reason may be that such comparisons risk opening the Pandora's box of relating the Holocaust to other genocides—the film's erasure of colonialism as one of antisemitism's most impactful coefficients suggest as much. The correspondences that would emerge in the process could potentially upend the way Germany remembers the Holocaust. Read against such a "risk" and the fears and interdictions it triggers, the principled resolution that informs *Die Ungewollten* devolves into a defeatist caveat: Just because we have done this before does not mean that we can—or should try to—do this again.

9

The *St. Louis* Voyage and Grassroots Historical Revisionism

Robert M. Krakow's Independent Film *Complicit*

"THIS IS OUTRAGEOUS!" exclaims US President Franklin Delano Roosevelt, who, while on trial for refusing to grant asylum to the Jewish refugees of the *St. Louis*, is charged with placing political ambition over humanitarian considerations. Roosevelt's outburst is one of several climactic moments in the sixty-four-minute independently produced film *Complicit*, written by Robert Krakow and directed by Michael Ivan Schwartz. Its centerpiece is the twenty-five-minute-long *Voyage of the SS St. Louis: The Trial of Franklin D. Roosevelt*, a stage play written by Krakow, head of the SS St. Louis Legacy Project.[1] The organization dedicates itself to remembering the ship's journey and the death of 254 of its passengers in the Holocaust as a result of Cuba, the US, and Canada refusing to provide safe haven to the passengers. *Complicit* prefaces the play with a documentary segment, also written by Krakow, which relays the main aspects of the *St. Louis* voyage to viewers. The segment uses a combination of archival footage and talking head interviews with surviving passengers, historical experts, diplomats, and members of the State Department. Some of these elements are also interspersed between the play's scenes.

A mock trial of a revered US president already constitutes a fascinating outlier within American Holocaust memory culture. But it is the involvement of the US State Department, which invited Krakow to stage his play as a reading on its own premises, that renders the play and its filmed performance unique. In fact, Krakow's play catalyzed the State Department into organizing a full-fledged ceremony commemorating the *St. Louis* incident. An earlier performance of the play at the National Archive in Washington, DC, was attended by a member of the State Department, who brought it to the attention of Hannah Rosenthal, Secretary of State Hillary Clinton's Special Envoy to Monitor and Combat Antisemitism. Rosenthal lobbied Clinton to invite Krakow to stage the play at the State Department and to organize the memorial ceremony around it. It took place on September 23, 2012, with Krakow's play being performed the following day. That performance is what *Complicit*, which was completed in 2014, centers on.

Complicit ends with a Q&A, which followed the performance of the play, between surviving passengers who were in attendance and members of the State Department, for whom the play was performed. One of the highlights of *Complicit* is the formal apology to survivors of the *St. Louis* voyage issued by Deputy Secretary of State William Burns. The US had already acknowledged its role in the *St. Louis* incident three years earlier with a Congressional Resolution approved on June 6, 2009, the seventieth anniversary of the day the US officially declined asylum to the *St. Louis* Jews. The resolution admitted to America's guilt in rejecting the ship's passengers and pledged to raise awareness about the fateful decision and to assume historical responsibility for the future.[2] But it was the events hosted by the State Department three years later that gave passengers and their offspring official retribution.

Following the play's staging at the State Department, Krakow took two years to complete the film. By featuring both the play and the State Department event that occasioned and framed its performance, *Complicit* constitutes the convergence of two distinct, at times antithetical, strains of Holocaust memory culture. One is defined by what is commonly termed popular memory. It comprises a spectrum of diverse grassroots voices that have shaped Holocaust memory from the bottom up as a response to the dearth of official commemorations of the Holocaust in the 1950s, '60s, and '70s. Grassroots remembrances tend to revolve around testimonials from survivors and witnesses, but also feature the discourse of amateur historians. And they include efforts by activists like Krakow, whose own findings and warnings against historical amnesia at times carry an element of revisionism. As is on display in Krakow's scripted mock trial of FDR, such efforts engage audiences with untold stories and revelations of hidden truths.

This grassroots form of Holocaust remembrance exists alongside more official, state-sponsored memory culture, which had its beginnings in postwar Europe but took hold in the US with President Jimmy Carter's establishment of the President's Commission on the Holocaust on November 1, 1978. Carter's initiative resulted in the founding of the United States Holocaust Memorial Museum (USHMM) in Washington, DC, which has played a major role in US Holocaust remembrance and is the destination of millions of Americans and foreign visitors each year. The museum opened in 1993. In *Complicit* we see state-sponsored memory culture not merely coinciding with, but also openly embracing and institutionally integrating grassroots memory culture—and this not despite but because of the latter's explicit, even confrontational, critique of the government. This is not as surprising as it sounds. With the 2009 Senate Resolution about the *St. Louis* voyage, the US had already joined the ranks of other nations that have acknowledged their historical failure to intervene. But by inviting Krakow and offering to host the staging of his play at the State Department, Clinton's office signaled that it was ready to revise America's long-standing image of being a safe haven for refugees. The State Department's intention to come clean is laudable, given that the country's status of having served as the liberating endpoint of Jewish migration has traditionally helped offset its tainted status as endpoint of the African American diaspora.

But despite its provocative project of putting a former US president on trial, *Complicit* is not exactly an anarchist text. It is guided by the spirit of reconciliation and consensus. The film does not show Burns's apology until late, whereby it functions as a climax of sorts that seals America's official recognition of its historical guilt. But the logic of this climax is not as straightforward as it looks. The film begins with an official apology to the *St. Louis* Jews, albeit one issued by a foreign head of state. On November 7, 2018, Canadian Prime Minister Justin Trudeau addressed the House of Commons in Ottawa to express his regrets that his country in 1939 refused to grant asylum to the ship's passengers. Opening with television footage of

Trudeau's speech, *Complicit* holds up the northern neighbor of the US as a paragon of moral and political integrity, an ideal to which the US must aspire and which, as the film implies, it has yet to achieve (see fig. 9.1). Only later do we learn about the State Department event, which actually predates Trudeau's speech by four years.

Why accord Canada's gesture primacy, when it came after the one made by the US? One of the reasons, we can assume, has to do with Trudeau's status. Canada evidently wanted to give its apology the highest national and political stage. Krakow, his audience, and the *St. Louis* survivors had to make do with Burns, who was filling in both for his immediate superior, Hillary Clinton, and for President Barack Obama. And while Trudeau's speech was shared with the Canadian public on national television, Burns's would have fallen into oblivion, if it had not been recorded in *Complicit*. But there are further reasons for why the film reverses its timeline of commemorative events. Although its central conceit is the trial of FDR, the film is ultimately interested in a different kind of culprit. The bottom-line charge, as signaled by the film's title, is complicity as such, whose adjective the film presents as a dictionary entry—COM·PLIC·IT—and which it

Figure 9.1. Canada's Prime Minister Justin Trudeau addressing the House of Commons in Ottawa, November 7, 2018, to apologize to the *St. Louis* passengers. *Source: Complicit* © The SS St. Louis Legacy Project, 2014. Used with permission.

defines as the act of being "involved with others in an illegal activity or wrongdoing." Trudeau's cogent characterization of complicity by using Canada's example handily illustrates the point for the film, while also leaving room for US memory culture to stage its own process of reckoning.

The opening credits display the film's title, and a subheading announces the subject at hand: "The untold story of why President Roosevelt and the State Department refused safe haven to Jewish refugees under Nazi tyranny." That Krakow's play ends without a verdict for Roosevelt signals its intention to appoint its viewers as the jury. It further implies that our deliberations should regard FDR's fateful decision less as a crime and more as a history lesson prompting us to hone our own sense of ethics and justice. In other words, the play stresses the processual nature of assuming historical responsibility and it identifies this process as inherently American. The US may not be perfect, but the film implies that the country's willingness to learn from its mistakes endows it with a capacity for self-renewal. This view has in fact informed much of American cinema, and there is no better genre to display it than the trial film. Its performative debating of case laws as a means of reconciling moral with juridical principles presents moviegoers with a vision of a nation able to grow in the name of justice and freedom. Thus, while Canada sets the moral bar in *Complicit*, the film's historical revisionism takes place within the broader ideological project of American self-renewal.

Complicit follows a five-part dramatic structure with an identifiable arc. Each part has its own title: "I. Night of Broken Glass"; "II. A Ship Without a Home"; "III: The Question of Guilt"; "IV: Atonement"; and "V: Inspiration and Remembrance." This sequence is by no means unique to the example at hand. It reflects the standard script that historical narratives about the *St. Louis* voyage, and especially popular, non-academic accounts, tend to adopt. Its underlying rationale is that retelling the story contributes to a project of reconciling the present with the past. How exactly *Complicit* inscribes reconciliation into its structure is something to be discussed in detail below. But to do so, we first need to address what role the film accords the United States in the *St. Louis* drama and in the escalation of the Jewish refugee crisis. *Complicit* is part of a tradition of films investigating America's response to the Shoah. They either raise the question of failed intervention or use the persecution of the Jews in Europe to analogize failures and inequities on the part of the US (such as the racism against African Americans). In this sense, the film participates in what has been termed the "Americanization" of the Holocaust, a term referring to the partial assimilation of Holocaust memory to American history and culture or, in Lawrence L. Langer and Alvin Rosenfeld's words, a "process by which a catastrophic European event became an American moral touchstone."[3] Not surprisingly, this process is highly political, as the establishing of similarities and differences between two different continents and their seemingly separate histories is ideologically contested.[4]

America on Trial

The Holocaust, as Michael Rothberg has noted, has impacted not only Europe's societies and cultures. It began to function some time ago as an "anchor of American modernity, part and parcel of postmodern culture and economics."[5] Part of this phenomenon has entailed putting America on trial for the Holocaust. The film that established this practice is Stanley Kramer's 1961 dramatic fiction film *Judgment at Nuremberg* about the Nuremberg Nazi war crimes trials (1945–49). The film is significant for our discussion not only because, like *Complicit*, it is a courtroom drama, but also because it demonstrates how Holocaust memory culture developed institutionally. Going into release when the Adolf Eichmann trial in Jerusalem was nearing conclusion, *Judgment* has been lastingly linked to the question of institutional, national, and universal guilt in committing genocide. Distributor United Artists held the film's premiere in West Berlin at a venue close to the recently erected Berlin Wall. Berlin's then-mayor, Willy Brandt, who in 1969 became West Germany's first Social Democratic Chancellor and ushered in a process of political atonement for Nazi Germany's crimes, took the event as an occasion to position West Germany in relation to its past and its present. Addressing the opening-night audience, Brandt directly linked Germany's Cold War division to the legacy of the Third Reich and asserted that the film's West Berlin premiere served as a reminder of this legacy. Feeling a sense of shame was, according to Brandt, what West Germans had to accept in order to start the process of coming to terms with the past.[6]

Judgment climaxes with the impassioned "not guilty" plea of defense lawyer Hans Rolfe (Maximilian Schell) on behalf of Ernst

Janning (Burt Lancaster), a Nazi judge on trial: If Janning is guilty, so Rolfe insists, his guilt is "the world's guilt. No more and no less." The film, as Judith E. Doneson has pointed out, is the first American film to place guilt both with Germany and with the international community of democratic nations.[7] It particularizes guilt by charging top Nazi administrators like Eichmann, who ran concentration camps, but also judges like Janning, who sent Jews to those camps. At the same time, it universalizes guilt in a manner explained by director Kramer: "Who among us may judge others; who among us is so innocent if we are so sure of the guilty?"[8] But the film can be perceived through yet another lens. Like other films made in the aftermath of the McCarthy witch hunt and during the Civil Rights era, *Judgment* indirectly references America's battles with racism, human rights violations, and various anti-democratic issues. Screenwriter Abby Mann selected two victim stories that are easily applicable to 1950s and early '60s America. One is the sterilization of a member of the Communist Party, whose political stigma was instantly recognizable to US audiences; the other is a case of perceived violation of "racial hygiene." Revolving around the criminalization of Jewish–gentile intercourse, the story implicitly references American fears of miscegenation between whites and African Americans. (Kramer further alludes to racism in America by casting the role of a military policeman securing the courtroom with a black actor.)[9]

In contrast to *Judgment*, which alludes to domestic issues indirectly, *Complicit* openly dismantles America's savior image by questioning FDR's motives and exposing antisemitism within the State Department. The courtroom drama on which the film centers both assumes and reinforces the contested nature of history. With the dictionary-style announcement of its title, the film signals its anchoring in language and its investment in the specificity of texts and their interpretation. Centrally revolving around the art of rhetoric as a key for the acclamation of truth, *Complicit* proceeds from the assumption that "what is remembered of the Holocaust depends on how it is remembered, and how events are remembered depends in turn on the texts now giving them form."[10]

Krakow's play blends overt fabrication (the improvised theatrical setup, the use of amateur actors playing the dramatis personae) with actual historical materials. These include newspaper articles, government reports, transcripts of correspondences between officials, and photographs of actual events and persons. This "performed actuality" approach places the play in the tradition of subversive modernist agitprop culture, such as the 1920s "Proletkult" movement and the plays of Bertolt Brecht and Erwin Piscator, which mixed documentary with fiction for their didactic messages.[11] The legacy of these works continued to shape postwar representations of the Holocaust, particularly in the medium of theater, as can be seen in the success of German dramatist Peter Weiss and his play *The Investigation* about the 1965 Auschwitz trial in Frankfurt, West Germany. Weiss's play became known for its discourse of objectivity, carried by the use of photographs, testimonials, and other historical materials. Weiss, however, has been charged with mystifying his own objectivist perspective by suppressing the fact that it, too, relies on fabrication. Krakow's approach appears more successful, as his play makes no effort to conceal its fabricated nature, though the effect, as discussed below, is somewhat undermined by Krakow's use of documentary footage in *Complicit* that accompanies the play.

Krakow frames his play as a piece of fiction that references reality. He appropriates the conventions of commercial, mostly fictional theater by giving the play its own playbill (see fig. 9.2). It is titled *Voyage of the SS St. Louis: The Trial of Franklin D. Roosevelt* and lists Krakow as its author. After showing the playbill, the film announces the first two members of the play's dramatis personae: Prosecutor: Supreme Court Justice Oliver Wendell Holmes (1902–1932) (see fig. 9.3); Council for the Defense: President John F. Kennedy (January 20, 1961–November 22, 1963) (see fig. 9.4). Scripted drama often bases itself on historical characters. But their introduction through photographs and a voice-over commentary indicating their significance as government officials opens up the discourse of actuality. Following courtroom drama conventions, the play stages the proceedings, including the opening statements by the prosecutor and the defense, and the questioning of their respective witnesses and, eventually, of the defendant, as rhetorical set pieces. Their didacticism lies in identifying America's failed rescue of the *St. Louis* Jews as a story of compromised principles.

The play presents its own production as improvised. In fact, what we see is more of a reading than a staged play. The actors assemble in front of an audience consisting of members of the State Department (see fig. 9.5). Cast members hold copies of the play in hand, from which they read their parts either seated or standing up. The only other item on stage is a screen that, in the tradition of agitprop art,

Figure 9.2. Playbill for the September 24, 2012, performance of *Voyage of the SS St. Louis: The Trial of Franklin D. Roosevelt*. Source: Complicit © The SS St. Louis Legacy Project, 2014. Used with permission.

Figure 9.3. Actor playing prosecutor Supreme Court Justice Oliver Wendell Holmes. *Source: Complicit* © The SS St. Louis Legacy Project, 2014. Used with permission.

Figure 9.4. Actor playing council for the defense John F. Kennedy. *Source: Complicit* © The SS St. Louis Legacy Project, 2014. Used with permission.

Figure 9.5. The cast of *Voyage of the SS St. Louis: The Trial of Franklin D. Roosevelt* on stage. *Source: Complicit* © The SS St. Louis Legacy Project, 2014. Used with permission.

features images of the historical persons appearing in the play and various exhibits illustrating the statements of prosecutor, defense, and witnesses. When the prosecutor charges Roosevelt with failure to save the Jewish refugees from the concentration camps and with hedging his bets with political opponents and the electorate to win a third term, we see newspaper headlines about the *St. Louis* projected on the screen. In a talking head interview, Krakow summarizes Roosevelt's questionable motives. We see newspaper headlines projected, including "Third Term for Roosevelt Sought by Mine Workers," "Third Term Backed by Cabinet," and "Six Governors Boost FR for Third Term." When Holmes states that Roosevelt's rejection of the passengers suggested to the world that the Jewish community was expendable, we are shown photos of murdered concentration camp inmates. Defense attorney Kennedy reminds the court in his opening statement that Roosevelt persuaded Congress about the danger of Nazi aggression and guided the allies to historic victory. We see a projected image of a headline reporting Nazi Germany's surrender.

One of the film's most intriguing elements is its illumination of the role Joseph H. Kennedy played as Roosevelt's Ambassador to the UK (January 17, 1938, to October 22, 1940). In the play, Kennedy is a witness for the prosecution. Holmes labels him "Hitler's best friend in London." Holmes confronts Kennedy with a report from the German Foreign Ministry (its cover shown on the courtroom screen) about Kennedy's meeting with Germany's Ambassador Herbert von Dirksen, during which both men discuss the Nazi persecution of the Jews. Holmes accuses Kennedy of having used antisemitic epithets against Jews and having confided in Harvey Klemmer, one of his London aides, that "individual Jews were alright, but as a race they stink. They spoil everything they touch. Look at the movies!"

One of the key witnesses for the prosecution is Cordell Hull, Secretary of State from March 1933 to November 1944 (see fig. 9.6). Hull refers to the 1924 US Immigration Act to defend the State Department's decision to deny Captain Gustav Schröder's request of June 5, 1939, to provide safe haven for his passengers. Holmes then puts Hull through a series of questions as to why his office explored no other ways of saving the refugees. To each alternative Holmes mentions—placing them in Alaska, declaring them temporary workers, admitting them as per emergency executive order on humanitarian grounds—Hull answers in the negative, citing existing law as the obstacle. The interrogation peaks when Holmes confronts Hull with his rejection of the offer from the governor of the Virgin Islands to welcome the *St. Louis* Jews. Holmes forces Hull to read a transcript of an explanation he had given to Henry Morgenthau, secretary of the treasury. In it Hull explains that the *St. Louis* passengers did not qualify for the issuing of tourist visas to the

Figure 9.6. Actor playing Cordell Hull, Secretary of State, 1933–44. *Source: Complicit* © The SS St. Louis Legacy Project, 2014. Used with permission.

Virgin Islands because they were unable to provide a return address. In response, Holmes asks Hull polemically whether Buchenwald or Dachau would have been valid return addresses—a point that instantly causes the defense to object (sustained by the judge). *Complicit* reinforces Holmes's point by inserting an images of concentration camp inmates. Holmes also charges Hull with refusing to help the *St. Louis* Jews for fear of drawing attention to the fact that his wife, Frances Fitz, came from an Austrian Jewish family, as that might have compromised his own political career in the US.

Laying the groundwork for putting Roosevelt on the stand, Holmes confronts Hull with the fact that the president denied asylum to the refugees on Hull's advice while, at the same time, removing himself from the decision (bound to be unpopular with part of his constituency) by having Hull implement it. Through Holmes the play pinpoints two causes for the rejection of the *St. Louis* refugees—Roosevelt's own antisemitism and his political ambition, which caused him to make discreet preparations to run for a third term. Holmes goes on to cite an exchange between Roosevelt and Montana Senator Burton Wheeler from August, 1938, in which Roosevelt expresses his concern about the marriage of his secretary of state to a Jewish woman: "In contrast to Mrs. Hull, we know there is no Jewish blood in our veins. A lot of times these people don't know if they are Jews or not." Krakow uses this exchange for a biting attack on the hypocrisy not only of Hull but the whole administration. Says Holmes: "It's a terrible thing to be Jewish, isn't it, Mr. Hull? To have Jewish blood in your veins. One wonders how your wife and her family would have fared under Hitler." The film inserts a photograph of Hitler. Holmes addresses the judge and the court (including us, the audience, through the appellation "Members of the Jury") to formulate his charge: the refusal of FDR's administration to grant asylum to the *St. Louis* Jews "set the tone for the American government's response to the refugee crisis during World War II. It was a case of political ambition over humanitarian need. And it sent a clear message to Adolf Hitler that the Jewish people were expendable." The film accompanies Holmes's statement with the famous newspaper cartoon of the Statue of Liberty averting its eyes from the *St. Louis* sailing past it. Here Krakow's play is clearly in the tradition of morally driven, politically trenchant agitprop, which supported characters' monologues and onstage proclamations with photographs, cartoons, and other imagery.

Put on the stand by the defense, Eleanor Roosevelt asserts that her husband cared greatly about the welfare of America's Jews and received overwhelming electoral support from them in turn. Then the prosecution begins its questioning of her husband (see fig. 9.7). After allowing the defendant to extol his historical merits (in lieu of giving the stage over to a cross-examining defense counsel), Holmes accuses

Figure 9.7. Actor playing Franklin D. Roosevelt. *Source: Complicit* © The SS St. Louis Legacy Project, 2014. Used with permission.

Roosevelt of appointing Joseph Kennedy as ambassador to the UK to please the antisemites among his constituency: "Antisemites vote too, don't they? You heard Kennedy quoted as saying that the US population harbored antisemitic feelings; that's an important voting bloc, Mr. President, isn't it, especially when you're running for a third term? You appointed Joseph Kennedy not in spite of his Jew hating but because of it!" And, addressing the court, Holmes summarizes: "The appointment of Kennedy was a brilliant political tactic: It appealed to isolationists, Irish Catholics, German Americans, and most of all to the Jew haters; it was the beginning of his successful run at a third term."

Roosevelt defends himself by saying he was a great friend of the Jews and that he appointed Felix Frankfurter to the Supreme Court and Henry Morgenthau as head of the Treasury Department. But Holmes promptly takes the reference to Morgenthau as an opportunity to seize on the State Department's questionable refugee policy. As Holmes tells the court, Morgenthau so disapproved of the State Department's handling of Jewish refugees that he urged Roosevelt to relocate the Refugee Affairs Office from the State Department to the Treasury after having commissioned an in-depth study on the State Department's failings in helping Jewish refugees. At this point, the film interrupts the court proceedings for Hannah Rosenthal (see fig. 9.8), Hillary Clinton's Special Envoy to Monitor and Combat Antisemitism,

Figure 9.8. Hannah Rosenthal, Special Envoy to Monitor and Combat Antisemitism, addressing the cast of the play and its audience. *Source: Complicit* © The SS St. Louis Legacy Project, 2014. Used with permission.

to read out the damning title of Morgenthau's study: "Report to the Secretary on the Acquiescence of this Government in the Murder of the Jews." She quotes Morgenthau's summary of the report: "One of the greatest crimes in history, the slaughter of Jewish people in Europe, is continuing unabated. I am certain no effective action will be taken by this government to prevent the complete extermination of the Jews in Germany and that this government will have to share for all time the responsibility for this extermination." Holmes adds one more name to the list of culprits—Breckenridge Long, head of the Visa Division, who in a 1940 memo wrote, "We can delay and effectively stop for a temporary period of indefinite length the number of immigrants in the US; we can do this by simply advising our consuls to put every obstacle in the way and to require additional evidence and to resort to various administrative devices which would postpone and postpone and postpone the granting of visas."

In a talking head interview that is part of *Complicit*'s documentary section preceding the trial, one of the surviving *St. Louis* passengers, Judith Steel, recounts how after the refugees were returned to Europe, she and her parents came to France, which would soon be occupied by Nazi Germany. While she was able to hide with the help of the French Resistance, her parents one day were arrested by Vichy police and deported to Auschwitz. Given that the *St. Louis*'s passengers failed with their asylum pleas in the New World, Steel's account strongly implicates the US in the murdering of 254 of the passengers by the Nazis. This historical guilt is what the State Department decided to confront by hosting the commemoration ceremony that included a staging of Krakow's play in the presence of surviving passengers and members of its office. As this gesture constituted a political recognition for Krakow and the SS St. Louis Legacy Project, it is fitting that the film accords it special significance by devoting a whole section or "act" to it, titled "Atonement." Atonement is a standard component of Holocaust memory, but in *Complicit* it is a gesture that is framed by (and that helps catalyze) the convergence of the two strains of Holocaust memory culture: grassroots memorial activism and state-sponsored memory culture.

The Convergence of Two Holocaust Memory Cultures

The most prominent part of the "Atonement" chapter and constituting a climax of sorts in the film is Burns's apology speech (see fig. 9.9).

Figure 9.9. Deputy Secretary of State William Burns apologizing to the St. Louis passengers. *Source: Complicit* © The SS St. Louis Legacy Project, 2014. Used with permission.

The film prepares its viewers for the speech with two commentaries. The first is a talking head interview, provided for the film by Stuart Eizenstat, Special Adviser to the Secretary on Holocaust Issues, who notes the emotional impact of Burns's speech on those present in the room. The second is an address Hannah Rosenthal gives at the ceremony. *Complicit* previews a brief excerpt in its documentary section, where it functions to prepare viewers for Roosevelt's trial. Rosenthal mentions that the contested status of America's role in the *St. Louis* incident reached all the way into the daily lives of survivors, who, as was the case with Rosenthal's own parents, struggled to agree on how "good" a president Roosevelt was, given that "he sent back ships," as her father put it. In the second excerpt, featured after the trial, Rosenthal continues to emphasize the importance of grassroots memory culture, but now explicitly frames it as the discourse that has been missing from and ignored by the state.

> When is it gonna be time for our country, who sends me around the world to tell other countries how they have to face up to their role and responsibility—when is it time for

us to do that, and do it on an official basis? Not just in a best-selling book *In the Garden of the Beast*; not just by a play that we hope will be shown from shore to shore, in this country and around the world; not just in newspaper articles, not in other books. But when is it going to be discussed in the halls of the State Department? And the answer is—tomorrow.

Rosenthal's assessment is at once critical and laudatory of the State Department. As such, it bears the hallmark of the liberal democratic nation state. By allowing its critics to bite the hand that feeds them, the democratic state legitimizes itself as rightful custodian of its people, prepared to protect the free flow of ideas so the nation can remain a dynamic entity capable of adapting and improving. Deputy Secretary of State Burns's speech is in the same spirit. Anticipating Trudeau's address in rhetorical structure and content, it begins by rehearsing the story of the *St. Louis*'s voyage and the plight of its refugees: "Having made it so close to our shores, nearly one third of the men, women, children of the MS *St. Louis* perished half a world away in Auschwitz and other camps." Burns acknowledges America's guilt and responsibility. "In the spring of 1939, the dangers were visible to those clear-eyed enough to see these. Warnings were already clear for those who cared to listen to the voices of Stephen Wise and others. And yet the US did not welcome these tired, poor, and huddled passengers as we had so many before and would so many since. Our government did not live up to its ideals. We were wrong." Burns must be commended for his adamant apology. But the speech is noteworthy for two further aspects: Burns's wording that the US did not welcome the refugees as it "had so many before and would so many since" implies that the *St. Louis* crisis was an isolated occurrence. Further, his framing of the crisis reflects the limitations of traditional Holocaust memory discourse. That discourse, as argued in this book, has failed to address the colonialist logic that shaped the Évian conference, where European powers sought to resettle Germany's Jews in areas of what is now called "the Global South" while, at the same time, shielding their own colonies in those areas from Jewish migration. The same logic guided the US when it denied the *St. Louis* Jews entry into the US Virgin Islands and, instead, used Cuba as a buffer to slow down the stream of US-bound migrants.

Burns's claim may have been genuine that the US is committed to responding in proper manner "next time the world confronts us with another *St. Louis*, whether the warning signs are refugees in flight or ancient hatreds resurfacing." But how credible can such a claim be, given that we have barely begun to assess the Holocaust in relation to colonialism and given, too, that we are over a decade into the escalation of the refugee crisis at the US–Mexico border? Much has been written about the United States' neocolonization of Latin America, a history that in part accounts for why so many Latin Americans flee their impoverished countries to come to the US. Yet analytical comparisons between the United States' record as a neo-colonizer of Latin America and its fortress mentality both during the *St. Louis* crisis and at the present moment do not figure prominently in historical discourse.[12]

Complicit is a successful, and rather astounding, instance of grassroots Holocaust memory culture. It documents how a nonofficial, revisionist act of remembrance succeeded in gaining recognition and support from the state. The state's public gesture of atonement and apology to the invited survivors meant the world to them, but the State Department's assumption of the role of host let the government shape the parameters in which the state's atonement took place. In contrast to *Die Ungewollten*, a film made by public German television discussed in chapter 8, neither *Complicit* nor the play embedded in it was conceived as a mouthpiece for the state. As mentioned, however, *Complicit* has its own lacunae. If I discuss those now in closing, I remain mindful of the film's unquestionably salutary mission and the overdetermined implications of the institutional framework in which Krakow was allowed to stage his rapprochement with the State Department.

The agitprop approach *Complicit* uses effectively debunks Hull's defense and demystifies the US government's historical role. But the film's treatment of Burns has the opposite effect. Krakow's exhaustive assemblage of expert opinions includes no critical commentary on Burns's speech. Though far from disingenuous, the speech, as mentioned, reproduces long-existing lacunae about the way the US has used Latin America for its political goals. And while *Complicit* deploys archival materials with great efficiency, Krakow, in order to show the *St. Louis*, draws on some of the same footage as *Die Ungewollten* and promptly incurs similar problems. We recognize the same excerpt from a US newsreel that shows several passengers on a ship talking to people on the pier. While this scenario "neatly" invokes the plight of the *St. Louis* passengers, the ship it shows is not the *St. Louis*. The footage cannot function as historical evidence. Krakow includes footage of a second ship that also resembles the *St. Louis* and that even belongs to the same shipping line. It is the SS *Patria*, which HAPAG had commissioned to serve routes to Latin America (see chapter 2). Similar to *Die Ungewollten* misrepresenting the *St. Louis* through the SS *Pennsylvania*, a colonial ship belonging to Roosevelt's Good Neighbor Fleet, misidentifying the *Patria* as the *St. Louis* ignores the neocolonial framework in which the rejection of the *St. Louis* passengers in the Americas took place and perpetuates a Eurocentric understanding of the Holocaust as being a conflict strictly between Nazis and Jews. We fail to see that the forced resettlement of Jews was part of a much broader context of neocolonial trade relations with Latin America in which HAPAG embedded its for-profit migrant traffic. And the front cover of the playbill for *Voyage of the SS St. Louis: The Trial of Franklin D. Roosevelt* features not the MS *St. Louis* in its background image, but the SS *St. Louis*, which was a US American ship built in 1894. The film's use of archival materials is one more instance that demonstrates the pitfalls of deploying a seemingly objective, non-fiction discourse as part of an agitprop approach.

10

The *St. Louis* in Multidirectional Memory

Robert M. Krakow's grassroots independent film *Complicit* prompts us to revise our assessment of the *St. Louis* incident. In this chapter I continue this search for alternative viewpoints by analyzing texts that either feature polyphonic accounts of the *St. Louis* voyage or whose own polysemic structure encourages the pursuit of such accounts. As I will argue below, the novel *Heretics* by Cuban crime author Leonardo Padura, the cartoon *The St. Louis Refugee Ship Blues* by graphic novelist Art Spiegelman, and the installation *The Wheel of Conscience* by architect Daniel Libeskind share a concern with what Michael Rothberg has influentially defined as multidirectional memory.[1] They locate remembrance of *the St. Louis* in various places and, by facilitating dialog between these locations, they enable memory to course through heterogeneous and unexpected channels.[2]

For Rothberg, multidirectional memory is epistemologically productive and politically salutary in its attention to "the dynamic transfers that take place between diverse places and times during the act of remembrance."[3] Its dialogic, cross-referential, and negotiable mode sharply differs from competitive memory, in which historical narratives vie for dominance in a zero-sum struggle for validation. Memory tends to be associative, working through displacement and substitution. In this sense, as Rothberg argues, memory is "fundamentally and structurally multidirectional."[4] (Attempts to hierarchize and police memory discourses tend to be politically reactionary.) Displacement and substitution also figure prominently in the mnemonic processing of historical trauma and, more specifically, in helping us trace one trauma through another. For instance, when postcolonial thinkers in the postwar period recounted incidents of repressive colonial violence, they at times included references to Nazi warfare, torture, and encampment. Conversely, accounts of Nazi treatments have triggered memories of violence suffered at the hands of colonial powers. For Rothberg, these associations constitute particularly cogent examples of multidirectional memory. He perceives a connection between the rise in Holocaust awareness in the years 1945 to 1962 and the first wave of decolonization during the same period. As this book has been arguing, colonialism and neocolonialism were among the factors that helped enable the Holocaust. With both phenomena linked in complex ways, it is not surprising that the Holocaust would come to figure prominently in postcolonial discourse, specifically in its various literatures.

Cuban writer Leonardo Padura's novel *Heretics* entwines remembrance of the Holocaust and of centuries of antisemitic persecution with a vivid chronicle of Cuban history from the 1930s to the 2000s.[5] Padura's literary genre of choice is the detective novel, in which he has established himself as an acclaimed author. The genre's key components—the mystery, the sleuthing, the flashback, the piecing together of bits of seemingly disparate information—have an affinity to memory's tenuous, apocryphal, contested, and ultimately multidirectional mode. And the heterogeneity of protagonists and historical locations Padura envisions for his readership neatly foregrounds the condition by which multidirectional memory comprises an archive of spatially and temporally dispersed sites. Padura consistently places these sites and the dramatis personae that populate them into stimulating dialog.

Leonardo Padura's *Heretics* and the Transversal Archive

Heretics is part of a series of detective novels that center on former policeman-turned-private eye Mario Conde. While hard-drinking and holding to his personal code of honor, Conde, a Havana native, is not exactly hard-boiled. In contrast to romantic and/or cynical loners Philip Marlowe and Sam Spade, Conde respects the limits of self-reliance, has a steady girlfriend, and enjoys socializing with a group of friends. But what Conde shares with the protagonists of Dashiell Hammett's and Raymond Chandler's novels is a profound disenchantment. Conde's is rooted in having been born into a postwar Cuba that developed from a repressive, corrupt dictatorship into an ultimately no less repressive socialist autocracy. Born in 1953, Conde's upbringing was tainted by the bleak reality of ever-diminishing opportunities. Padura describes his protagonist as being part of a lost generation and turns his biographical details into a rich portrait of a country battered by successive waves of domination.

In *Heretics*, Conde is tasked with locating a lost Rembrandt painting that had come to Cuba in 1939 on the *St. Louis* as an heirloom of the Kaminiskys, a fictitious Jewish family that undertook the trip to escape Nazi Germany. Family father Isaiah Kaminsky hoped to use the painting to bribe Cuban immigration officials into letting his family disembark. The painting came ashore, but without the Kaminskys, who returned to Europe on *the St. Louis* and were eventually rounded up by the Nazis and murdered in Auschwitz. The dramatic events in Havana harbor that paved the way for the Kaminskys' doom were witnessed from ashore by Isaiah's brother, Joseph, and Isaiah's son, Daniel. His parents had sent Daniel ahead to join his uncle, who had been living in Havana for some time. After experiencing the trauma of his family being declined asylum and later learning of their deaths in Auschwitz, Daniel renounces the Jewish faith and grows up as a member of an ethnic and religious minority in Batista's Cuba. One year before the Cuban revolution, adult Daniel and his wife move to Miami. In 2007, Daniel's American-born son Elias returns to Cuba and seeks out Conde to solve the mystery of the lost painting. Into this framework, Padura installs multiple story lines that blend the detective plot with historical fiction. The book's lengthy middle section imagines the Dutch master Rembrandt van Rijn creating the painting that is the novel's subject with the collaboration of a young Jew. After being branded a heretic for acting as the maestro's model and assistant, the assistant flees with it to Poland, where in the chaos of antisemitic pogroms the painting falls into the hands of the Kaminskys' ancestors. The novel's third part resumes a depiction of present-day Cuba. Conde's investigation of Joseph Kaminsky's granddaughter by adoption, a member of Havana's nihilistic punk subculture, serves the author to depict the corrosive impact of current forms of greed, corruption, and

US economic imperialism. *Heretics* thus transcends the detective genre. A little like D. W. Griffith's historical epic *Intolerance* (2017), each of its parts concerns itself with how political totalitarianism, religious orthodoxy, and unbridled capitalism produce specific formations of repression, but also generate different forms of resistance.

Padura's description of the fateful week the *St. Louis* spent in Havana harbor aligns with historical facts. The author commendably foregrounds the complex factors that shaped Cuba and other Latin American nations' immigration policy. For instance, as Conde learns in the course of his investigation, Cuba's domestic Nazis and nativists directed their ire not exclusively toward Jews, but also toward Jamaican and Haitian laborers who had been essential to Cuba's agrarian labor force. The country had recruited them en masse so it could honor its export obligations to the US. When the economy no longer permitted their employment, they met with racist vilification. Placing these groups alongside the Jewish protagonists, if only fleetingly, is one among many details by which Padura links the history of antisemitism in Russia, Europe, and the New World with New World nativism, racism, and neocolonialism. The different temporal, diegetic, and mnemonic realms of the story are accentuated in different ways by the cover designs of some of the book's editions. The US paperback stresses the side-by-side existence of the book's narrative planes about *the St. Louis*, the Jewish diaspora, and the seventeenth-century Dutch painting milieu (see fig. 10.1); the British edition stresses the sinister glamour of *the St. Louis* as a Nazi ship (see fig. 10.2); the original Spanish-language edition (and also the cover of the German edition, not shown here) emphasizes Padura's interest in memory as unstable and crumbling, as conveyed by a photo of a detail of the interior of a decaying Spanish colonial mansion (see fig. 10.3).

Heretics' strongest virtue is its fluid combination of individual and collective histories. They emerge through Elias's musings about his father's and uncle's lives in Havana, through the conversations between Elias and Conde, and as part of Conde's own effort to lift the mystery of the lost painting. By combining information about the Jewish diaspora with impressions of seven decades of life in Cuba, the novel blurs the line between history, memory, and projection. As Elias in the narrative present explores the ramshackle house in the poor section of Havana in which his father had grown up, he imagines Daniel's life under the tutelage of his uncle Joseph. A lyrical

Figure 10.1. Leonardo Padura, *Heretics*; US Paperback edition, © Farrar, Straus and Giroux. *Source:* Public domain.

passage describes how Elias ascends "the sordid steps" of a large nineteenth-century house on Calle Compostella, formerly owned by "apocryphal counts," where Joseph, recently arrived, "had put a bed, a table, a sewing machine, and his leatherworking tools and where, for almost fourteen years, his nephew Daniel had lived."[6] Then Elias climbs to the second floor, the former sojourn of *la mulata* Caridad Sotolongo, Joseph's lover and the mother of Ricardo, whom Joseph would adopt and who would take on the Kaminsky name. Padura conveys to his readers that the lives that once unfolded between those walls were mostly stories of survival, yet the habitat's decayed state eerily invokes the struggles and the despair its erstwhile tenants experienced—a despair that the exiled Jews shared with the subjects

Figure 10.2. Leonardo Padura, *Heretics*; British edition, © Bitter Lemon Press. *Source:* Public domain.

of neocolonialism. On the second floor, "life had seemed to stop in the persistent and painful poverty of those who are crammed together without hope. By contrast, the third floor, the building's most noble back in its day . . . had lost the ceiling and part of the balconies and warned of the irreversible fate awaiting the rest of the structure."[7]

Two things about the passage are notable: First, the crumbling building is not only a signifier of Havana's decay under neocolonialism, communism, and decades of US-led economic embargos, but it also, within the context of the Kaminskys' trajectory, indirectly evokes some of the waystations of Jewish exile in Europe, marked as these were by burning roofs and smashed windows. That Latin America, among other locations, assumes a place in the Jewish diaspora is something

Figure 10.3. Leonardo Padura, *Herejes*; Spanish-language edition © Tusquets Editores S.A. *Source:* Public domain.

Hannah Arendt indicates in her 1940 essay "We Refugees," when she characterizes Latin American cities as places where Jews simply go to die. But as discussed in chapter 5, because Arendt does not account for the impact of neocolonialism, she does not explore the deeper connections between neocolonialism and the Jewish diaspora in the years leading up to the Holocaust. Padura's novel fills this gap.

Second, by relaying to us the years of Daniel's upbringing in Cuba through Elias, who was born in the US and never knew the earlier waystations of his father's life, the passage renders memory of the Jewish diaspora fragile, even "fabulistic."[8] This becomes clear early on, when Padura compares Elias, as he ascends the stairs to his father's former abode, to a blind man "who needs to cautiously and exactly measure each step."⁹ If spatial and temporal distance hampers the son's memory so as to make him appear handicapped, the mental construct he crafts of his father's life evokes associations with ruins: "Making the most herculean effort, the foreigner tried to imagine . . . leaning over the no-longer-existent wall of the third floor [to watch a catfight between a black Cuban woman and a Sicilian immigrant], and later he insisted on seeing him go up to the rooftop. . . . But he couldn't."¹⁰

In addition to casually reminding us here and elsewhere of Cuba's racial hybridity, Padura's prose renders remembrance a practice that holds loss and recovery in precarious balance. In doing so, the author complicates the notion of the archive. It is marked by gaps, blind spots, loss, doubt, and speculation no less than by evidence, presence, certainty, and proof. In other words, it is not only fragmented and incomplete, but also has a quality Rothberg defines as "transversal" because of the plurality and heterogeneity of its locations, forms, functions, and capacities.¹¹ For Elias to retrace his father's steps is challenging because he himself is disconnected from Jewish memory and has but a tenuous sense of the diaspora, even though he is a true product of it. As he explains to Conde:

> I myself feel at times that I don't belong to any place, or that I belong to many; I'm like a puzzle that can always be taken apart. I suppose I am North American, the son of a Polish Jew who commanded himself to be Cuban among other things while here so that he wouldn't suffer from being uprooted and other pains, and of a Catholic Cuban, the daughter of immigrants from Galicia, Spain, who at decisive moments took on her husband's pragmatism when he decided that the best thing was to be Jewish again, and so she converted.¹²

Elias's self-description shows that, while he is no heretic himself, heresy is one of the factors that has shaped his life. It is the central figure through which the book frames its characters' and its readers' understanding of how to resist totalitarianism, dogmatism, and persecution. Upon learning of his family's ultimate fate after Cuba expelled the *St. Louis*, Daniel becomes convinced that there no longer is a god and that all one has is one's own capacity for making decisions. About god, he concludes that the commandments against killing, stealing, and coveting could turn Jewish history into "nothing but a series of agonies." Further, "The end result of that sentence had been, undoubtedly, the suffering of the most horrifying of the holocausts."[13]

Notably, this passage at once compares the Shoah to other genocides (by placing the noun in plural and lower caps) and sets it apart from them (by making it superlative). And the narrative places the victims of different forms of totalitarian oppression in proximity to each other. As Daniel becomes unbelieving, irreverent, and rebellious against "a suspicious divine plan overflowing with cruelty," he also becomes "more Cuban and less Jewish."[14] But as the friends he and his wife leave behind in 1958 and subsequent generations of characters in the book come to understand, instead of providing respite from disenchantment, being Cuban constitutes but a different form of it. The reader encounters Conde and his friends as survivors of a succession of autocratic systems and living in the present vacuum of whatever low-end consumerism the West's political and economic isolation of Cuba allows them to enjoy. Notwithstanding their differences, what Conde's generation shares with that of Cuba's nihilistic teen punk subculture is profound disillusionment. Both groups live in the moment and use any tonic they can access to alleviate their languishing under the privations inflicted on them.

Padura does not treat Daniel's upbringing from the eve of World War II through the 1940s as a self-contained narrative. The book's early chapters toggle back and forth between the fateful week in which the *St. Louis* passengers beg in vain for asylum, and life in Havana in 2007, when Conde receives his assignment from Elias. The book becomes a multigenerational saga of political corruption, economic impoverishment, and systemic disregard for the rights and concerns of common people. The circumstances of rescue denied, which split the Kaminisky clan into those doomed to sail toward the Holocaust and those allowed to go on living at the margins of a foreign land, find a correlative of sorts in that land's underdevelopment as relayed to us through the often squalid details of the life of a former policeman. While many private eyes (fictional and real) got their start on the police force, the fact that neither Conde nor some of the story's Jewish characters still work in their erstwhile professions has a special meaning—it is a mark of exile. The settings Padura conjures are haunting because the characters in them—be they Jewish exiles or native Cubans—evince startling correspondences in their struggle for survival. About Conde we learn, "The option to make a living clawing at the walls wasn't easy and caused that stellar exhaustion, the feeling of constant uncertainty and irreversible defeat that frequently gripped the former policeman and drove him, with one rough push, against his will and desires to hit the streets looking for old books that would earn him, at least, a few pesos to survive."[15] The last sentence foregrounds another trait Conde shares in common with many Jews, at least those of an earlier exilic generation—a strong bibliophilia, which provides intellectual and spiritual respite from the ravages of one's life and which also, in some cases, allows for new social ties to form among the like-minded. This is not to mention that books are among totalitarianism's most feared enemies, as they have a way of nurturing heretics.

Another thing Conde shares with Elias and, indirectly, with his father, is a nostalgia for the past. Elias's wanderings through his father's decrepit Havana childhood home, which faintly allude to the ravaged habitats of the Jewish diaspora in Europe, complement Conde's nostalgic memories of when he was a boy and his grandfather Rufino instructed him in cockfighting, "a sentimental education adequate for surviving in a world that looked very much like a cockfighting arena."[16] While stopping short of making an explicit comparison, the passage hints at correspondences between the dangerous worlds of pogrom-ridden Krakow or Nazi-ruled Berlin and the dog-eat-dog world of lower-class Cuban society—especially when bearing in mind that these settings are perceived through the eyes of a terrified child.

As the story continues, the parallels become more explicit. In the late 1950s, as social discontent about the Batista regime was reaching critical mass, Daniel's friends schemed a plot to overthrow the dictator. Its failure caused a violent backlash against the student movement and Daniel lived in fear of being linked to his revolutionary friends. We learn that his fear, which had been dormant for years, was becoming unbearable, causing him insomnia and making him wait to hear the police at the door. Readers will recognize this sentiment as central to the Jewish diaspora. It constituted a regular part of Jewish life in Nazi Germany, but then Daniel continues to experience it under Batista. And the same feeling is commonly associated with life under Stalinism and other communist autocracies.

One of Daniel's friends, Pepe Manuel, who was sought by the Cuban police, took refuge with his godfather, a fighting-cock breeder named Pedro Pérez, on the man's secluded farm. As Elias recounts this detail to Conde, *Heretics* continues to build its associations between different eras and political systems through multidirectional memory. Conde realizes that Pedro Pérez, the cockfighter who hid Elias's father's revolutionary friend, had been one of his grandfather Rufino's best friends. This triggers childhood memories in Conde of him visiting the very farm that, unbeknownst to him at the time, was serving as a place where people hid before going into exile. Again, Padura links distinct histories through intertwined stories of persecution.

Heretics is a work of popular modernism. Padura links the different planes of historical trauma through the tools of realist narrative. The goal is to guide the reader in ways that, basic as these may be in comparison to high modernist literary techniques, negotiate historical baggage by offering clearly legible moral and political frameworks. While Conde had been vaguely aware of the *St. Louis* incident before Elias tells him about the Kaminskys, learning the details makes him feel ashamed of his Cuban countrymen, who allowed themselves to be manipulated into virulently opposing Cuba granting asylum to the *St. Louis* refugees. Elias puts him at ease by explaining to him the larger political context for Cuba's decision, which involved internal Cuban politics as well as pressure from the US (unfortunately, Padura remains vague on the details). Elias further assures Conde that, while his father had to witness his parents leave Cuba on the *St. Louis* never to see them again, Daniel ultimately came to reject resentment and "preferred to be Cuban and forget about the pettiness that can show up anywhere."[17] Once the war was over and the refugee streams gradually subsided, Daniel, so Elias tells Conde, had a carefree passage into adulthood because, as the book suggests, for a Jew the reemerging inclusivity of civilian life offset the reality of the country's autocratic structures. Jews, Padura writes, were but one among many peoples from all over the world who came to live in postwar Cuba. This instilled into Daniel "a fullness" none of his people had been able to imagine since Sephardic Jews had been permitted to come to Amsterdam.[18]

While this passage conveys a sense of the country's relative postwar stability, it already prepares the reader for the fact that this world, which was far from perfect but in which life seemed livable, would soon undergo further radical changes by the rise of Castro. Talking to Conde about this period, Elias tells him that Joseph lost his cash assets after the new government decreed a change of money that would leave every Cuban with only two hundred pesos. Conde indicates that he is all too familiar with the repercussions of the late 1950s regime change, which resulted in large-scale poverty.[19] A few pages earlier, Padura had already painted a detailed picture of what regime change meant for a Jewish immigrant like Joseph. As Elias explains to Conde,

> Uncle Joseph, as opposed to my father, wanted to continue being what he had once been, but everything around him had changed: the country where he lived, the family he had once had, the way of practicing his religion . . . In the end, not a single rabbi was left in Cuba, almost no Jews were left. . . . So he must have felt like a shipwrecked man . . . like a real shipwrecked man, without a compass or any hope of touching on dry land, because that land had disappeared centuries before, as all Jews know well.[20]

In *Heretics*, multidirectional memory is expansive. Padura describes Joseph Kaminisky not only as the proverbial last Jew left in place when a new regime comes into power; he also compares him to a shipwrecked man with no compass and no hope to reach land. The parallel to the democratic world's post-Évian refusal to alleviate the Jewish refugee crisis, which I have discussed through the metaphor of the shoreless sea, becomes only more haunting with Padura's assertion that for Jews there had been no saving land for centuries—not even through the advent of communism.[21]

Meta-Narration and Meta-History in *The St. Louis Refugee Ship Blues*

The metaphor of the shoreless sea is also at the heart of Art Spiegelman's one-page cartoon *The St. Louis Refugee Ship Blues*, in which the artist's familiar Maus character, a stand-in for Spiegelman, addresses the readership of the cartoon's publication venue, the *Washington Post*, about the *St. Louis* voyage.[22] One of the cartoon's images explicitly visualizes the metaphor by displaying a tiny refugee ship on a vast ocean. But Spiegelman does not merely want to retell the events of the voyage. Like other art sponsoring multidirectional memory, *The St. Louis Refugee Ship Blues* has as much to say about the historical moment of its creation as about the event it recalls. Like Padura, Spiegelman allows mnemonic processes to connect different periods for comparison. But unlike Padura, Spiegelman performs a form of artistic navel gazing. In addition to stimulating memory, he self-consciously interrogates his chosen medium's ability to do so by critically reflecting on its checkered history of covering political failures and humanitarian tragedies.

By the time Spiegelman published *The St. Louis Refugee Ship Blues*, his *Maus* comics had achieved broad popularity and literary canonization. *Maus* relays Spiegelman's father Vladek's memories as a Holocaust survivor as told to his son, Spiegelman's avatar Artie. Serialized from 1980 to 1991 in Spiegelman's own avant-garde comics magazine *Raw*, the material reached mass exposure through its republication in two volumes, the 1986 *Maus: A Survivor's Tale*, subtitled *My Father Bleeds History (Mid-1930s to Winter 1944)*, and the 1991 *Maus II: A Survivor's Tale and Here My Troubles Began*.[23] Since, in Padura's novel, violating the ban on graven images constitutes one of the central forms of heresy, Spiegelman's decision to retell the Holocaust through the lowbrow medium of comics and as an Aesop-style animal fable could well make him one of Padura's protagonists. But idolatry constitutes only one of Spiegelman's offenses.[24] A possibly even more serious one is that *Maus* resists classification on every level.[25] Artie's frustrations about his interlocutions with his father provide both a narrative framework for and an incursive commentary on Vladek's story. This double structure has *Maus* partake in a set of classic binaries, such as between high and low art, fact and fiction, and *histoire* and *discours*.[26] About himself Spiegelman has observed, "I don't know how to refer to myself—author, artist, cartoonist, historian. They are all words trying to surround actuality. I think of comics as co-mix, to mix together words and pictures."[27] *Maus*, as Dominick LaCapra has pointed out, blurs the boundaries of history (the Holocaust), ethnography (contemporary Jewish culture and survivor culture in particular), and autobiography (which explores the relationship between individual and collective trauma).[28] Spiegelman's work thus breaks multiple taboos. As Michael Rothberg has noted in his discussion of traumatic realism, Spiegelman "heretically reinserts the Holocaust into the political realm by highlighting its necessary imbrication in the public sphere and in commodity production."²⁹ *Maus* stands for art's obligation to reflect on form, content, and discursivity all at once. Its aesthetic reflexivity consistently extends to discourse analysis.³⁰

My reading of *The St. Louis Refugee Ship Blues* owes to these insights and, specifically, to the conceptual framework LaCapra uses for his analysis of *Maus*. According to LaCapra, Spiegelman's comic constitutes a problematization of identity in four partially overlapping areas—with regard to the artist and his relation to the text, within the genre of the text, in the text's relation to its readership, and in the text's work and play.³¹ Not only can this framework be usefully applied to the *St. Louis* cartoon, but, as I will argue below, it also constitutes the terrain on which *The St. Louis Refugee Ship Blues* erects its edifice of multidirectional memory. To begin with, if *Maus*, as Joshua Brown has noted, "is an oral history account and also an account of an oral history,"³² *The St. Louis Refugee Ship Blues* can be characterized as a cartoon account, but also an account of cartoon history—or, more precisely, a history of the political cartoon. While a few cartoonists mustered the courage to criticize the Roosevelt administration for its refusal to accept the *St. Louis* Jews, the profession as a whole, in Spiegelman's view, failed to follow suit. The intention behind *The St. Louis Refugee Ship Blues* is to alert readers to these shortcomings. The cartoon lays this out in four rows of four to five images each, supplemented by speech bubbles attributed to Artie, who surveys a sampling of political cartoons for the reader that reference the *St. Louis* crisis in various ways.

Artie assumes the function of a lecturer or, rather, a museum guide giving a gallery talk that takes audiences through an assemblage of drawings. This ploy enables Spiegelman to perform an abrasive auto-critique of a profession in love with its reputation for being outspoken and fearless. We learn from Artie that some cartoonists, such as Jerry Doyle, while not completely ignoring the *St. Louis* Jews, trivialized their dilemma. Doyle's drawing, as presented by Artie, shows a group of American college graduates sitting on the ship "Alma Mater" and looking at a factory on shore with a sign saying "No Jobs—Quota Filled." Jesse Cargill, another cartoonist, blandly urges his readers (and presumably the *St. Louis* Jews) to take shelter in Christ with the Protestant hymn "Rock of Ages, Cleft for Me." These words headline Cargill's drawing, in which a sword (with "hatred and intolerance" written on it) cuts through the globe traversed by a vessel flying a flag with the words "refugee ship." Artie's sarcastic verdict: "As a cartoon trying to make a clear point, it didn't quite—um—cut it." Referring to himself as a "cartoonist-American, whose parents survived Auschwitz," Artie tells his audience that he is proud that at least a few of his colleagues were outspoken in their indictment of the lack of empathy that turned the *St. Louis* journey into a tragedy. He turns his attention to the cartoon "The Wandering Jew" by Edmund Duffy. Its title sits atop a drawing of the *St. Louis* from which arises a cloud in the shape of a ghostly figure with a knapsack and a staff. Artie praises the image as "haunting and prophetic." Artie's sampling also includes Fred Packer's well known cartoon, discussed in chapter 4, of the Statue of Liberty averting its eyes from the *St. Louis* and telling the ship to keep out. While Artie acknowledges that using the Statue of Liberty as a motif is a cliché, he stresses that it is "the right cliché" to use.

Its instructional mode makes *The St. Louis Refugee Ship Blues* more overtly didactic than *Maus*. The fact that the cartoon's first image displays not a drawing but an actual black-and-white photograph of the ship, accompanied by a caption telling us that the "Roosevelt administration's refusal to let those refugees in has come to symbolize America's indifference to the Nazi genocide," suggests that Spiegelman does not want to waste any time meditating on the historical event itself. He sets it apart from the cartoon proper in its facticity, signaled by the change in mediums, as a prologue to what follows. And while what follows is also about history—the historical failure of cartoons to address the *St. Louis* incident—Spiegelman's commentary, we realize, expands its focus from the cartoonist profession to the artist's readership. He makes the cartoon serve as a warning to them not to become complacent in the face of current humanitarian tragedies of the kind that give rise to political cartoons in the first place.

This is where *The St. Louis Refugee Ship Blues* links the Holocaust to contemporary refugee crises. One of its images, located toward the end, tells readers that, since 2003, 48,000 people have fled to the US to escape political, religious, and ethnic persecution but have been "detained by the Department of Homeland Security in harsh prison-like facilities for months, even years, often without an immigration court review." The image shows a large group of people, the "huddled masses," standing before the Statue of Liberty, which, with a steely grin on her face, offers them orange jumpsuits and handcuffs. The next image links this new refugee crisis back to the *St. Louis* by mentioning the work of famous cartoonist Herblock (short for Herbert Lawrence Block), who in 1939 drew a two-image panel titled "Tragedy at Sea," which shows the ship's voyage to be a result of political hypocrisy. The top image displays a shipwreck at the bottom of the ocean with a caption stating "Failure of Machinery." The image below shows a ship titled "refugee ship" that, as mentioned earlier, is lost on the vast ocean. Its caption reads "Failure of Man." It is striking that the artist, rather than showing us a group of miserable passengers (in the manner of the "huddled masses" of the previous image), links the refugee drama directly to a visual of the shoreless sea. Given the metaphor's endurance, it is perhaps no surprise that Spiegelman's cartoon, like the film *Voyage of the Damned* before it, promptly draws on its by now perhaps clichéd meaning. But Spiegelman, like Padura after him, uses the imagery to refer to incidents and situations that happened long after the *St. Louis* crisis. It becomes an idiom of multidirectional memory.

Spiegelman expresses his solidarity with recent waves of refugees by suggesting that "the failure of man" is ongoing. He makes this clear already in the image of the Statue of Liberty handing out orange jump suits to the huddled masses. An important detail of the drawing shows Artie leaning into it from above and, in the manner of early animated cartoons that show Mickey Mouse literally flowing from Walt Disney's pen, completing it by drawing the huddled masses himself. The gesture of Artie abandoning his detached position of gallery guide and picking up pen and paintbrush has several implications. To begin with, it establishes a crucial continuity between *Maus* and *The St. Louis Refugee Ship Blues*. *Maus* goes to considerable length to argue that the children of survivors remain entangled in the historical trauma their parents suffered. It wants to educate younger readers about the Holocaust, lest we let something like it happen again. *The St. Louis Refugee Ship Blues* presents a correlative to this mission. By committing to keeping memories of the *St. Louis* alive for future generations and by linking the ship's voyage to contemporary refugee crises, Spiegelman, in a "the-personal-is-political" message, appeals to the moral conscience and political consciousness of fellow Jews (and liberal Americans in general): the complacency that helped kill so many Jews is happening again, although this time the targets are not Jews.

That Artie directly involves himself in the cartoon's creation is also a response to the complacency of his profession. Above the cartoon's top row of images, Spiegelman announces that what follows was prompted by his realization that only a small number of cartoonists addressed the *St. Louis* crisis effectively. The final two images trace this kind of meekness all the way to the present. Following the "Tragedy at Sea" image, Artie bemoans the fact that these days political cartoons only go for bland "topical 'laffs' " and "editorial cartoonists are dying off even faster than the newspapers that hire them." Artie cites one exception to this trend, a July 21, 2008, *New Yorker* cover titled "The Politics of Fear," which satirizes right wing projections about Barack Obama as an Arab politician (with an image of Osama bin Laden on the wall) and Michelle Obama as an Angela Davis-style armed black militant. But the penultimate image of *The St. Louis Refugee Ship Blues* repeats the earlier motif of a group of boat people looking at a factory with a sign stating "No Jobs—Quota Filled"—except that it now identifies the huddled masses in the boat as "Unemployed Editorial Cartoonists" and describes the ship, which is shown to be made of folded paper, as the "Ship of Damn Fools."

With *The St. Louis Refugee Ship Blues* Spiegelman weds the self-questioning of Jewish identity, which we encounter in *Maus* through Artie's ambivalence toward his father, to a questioning of his profession. But as in *Maus*, any criticism is tempered by an acknowledgment that the sheer complexity of the issues makes passing judgment on one's kin, whether familial or professional, nearly impossible. Spiegelman ends the *St. Louis* cartoon with an image of Artie, who, with the look of resignation on his face, sighs and admits that it is hard to say the right thing—by which, we assume, he means both what cartoonists say in their cartoons and what he can say about his fellow cartoonists.

The fact that some of the cartoonists Spiegelman criticizes for their failure to bear political witness to the *St. Louis* crisis are not Jewish suggests a parallel to the role that *Maus* assigns to the non-Jewish Poles in the Holocaust. But in commenting on the non-Jewish Poles, the artist's well known anti-essentialism shines through: "We've all become that. . . . The Poles were the victimized witnesses."[33] His comment also seems to bear out that, with *The St. Louis Refugee Ship Blues*, Spiegelman can explore new paths of inquiry that lie beyond the oedipal issues that loom so large in *Maus*. While the Artie of

Maus, as LaCapra attests, is unwilling or unable to question his own role as an interrogator or to extend his criticism of his father also to himself, the Artie of *the St. Louis* comic tries to set a personal example of what makes a good political cartoonist while, at the same time, acknowledging how hard it is to do so. It seems that Artie, by the time he appears in *The St. Louis Refugee Ship Blues*, has mastered some of his own demons by acting on his resolution to become a "good-enough secondary witness."[34] For Spiegelman, this presumably constitutes the first step in helping prevent post-Holocaust genocides and refugee crises.

If Spiegelman's central project is, as Rothberg has argued, the discursive production of Jewish identity articulated through the trauma of disappearance,[35] *The St. Louis Refugee Ship Blues* arguably expands on this project even as it eliminates the artist's father, Holocaust survivor Vladek, from its narrative. The cartoon's straightforwardness is deceptive, because on closer inspection, it links the trope of disappearance to more contexts than does *Maus*. In one fell swoop, it connects the historical tragedy of disappearing Jews with contemporary tragedies of refugees who, by drowning in the Mediterranean or perishing in the treacherous border region between the US and Mexico, likewise disappear and, further, with editorial cartoonists, whose failure to call out these tragedies loses them their jobs and makes them disappear from the public sphere. Last but not least, the ostentatious riffing the comic's title performs on the pre–World War I popular jazz song "The Saint Louis Blues" also links its discourse of disappearance to the history of enslaving and murdering Blacks (a prominent line in the song is "Ma' man's got a heart like a rock cast in de sea").[36] As such, Spiegelman's cartoon can be read as a response to Paul Gilroy's lament in *The Black Atlantic* that too few connections are being charted between the Holocaust, the Middle Passage, and African American history (see chapter 5).

Finally, the auto-critique Spiegelman articulates in the *St. Louis* comic also includes a jab at the advancing commercialization of the newspaper business. Already in *Maus*, as Rothberg finds, Spiegelman self-consciously satirizes his cartoon's "entanglement in the marketplace."[37] *Maus II* creates a subversive graphic match between the stripes of Vladek's prison uniform and the stripes of the book's bar code imprinted on its back cover. *The St. Louis Refugee Ship Blues* elevates this kind of insider rebellion against the commoditization of the Holocaust to the level of theme—the threat of disappearance of the profession of cartoonists is closely connected to the commercialized nature of publishing, which coerces cartoonists to become bland and go for easy laughs. Like in *Maus*, disappearance is caused by its seeming opposite—overabundance—and can be traced back, as Rothberg does, to the workings of the culture industry. (Disappearance as overabundance created by the media has, as the epilogue of this book discusses, also directly impacted the making of *Havarie*, a German experimental non-fiction film about contemporary refugees.) The discursive and semiotic dilemmas Spiegelman incurs by publishing his work from within the culture industry are hard to bypass, particularly if one's medium is cartoons. If Spiegelman attempts to do so by rebelling against the industry from within, architect Daniel Libeskind seeks to avoid those dilemmas altogether by working in the medium of sculpture, which, like painting, is part of the fine arts and, as such, encourages contemplation rather than consumption. But as we shall see, Libeskind, too, is keenly aware of the implications of exhibiting his *St. Louis*-themed installation in the public sphere. Memorials, too, are subject to specific conditions and parameters within which remembrance is articulated and received by the public.

Materiality, Abstraction, and Placement: Spaces of Memory In and Around Daniel Libeskind's *The Wheel of Conscience*

Commemorating the *St. Louis* voyage has become a tradition that is enacted especially on anniversaries of the incident. Initially, the organizing of remembrances mainly fell to survivors and their kin, but over the years an increasing number of Jewish organizations have taken a role in *St. Louis* memory culture, such as by partnering with municipal and state bodies to dedicate plaques and build memorials. In 2010 the Canadian Jewish Congress (CJC)[38] opened a competition for a memorial that would specifically foreground Canada's role in the events. The proposal of Polish-born American architect Daniel Libeskind won the selection process. The memorial's designated site was the Canadian Museum of Immigration at Pier 21 in Halifax. Similar to Ellis Island in the US, Pier 21 for many decades served as Canada's gateway for millions of immigrants. It would have been the port of entry for the *St. Louis* passengers, if Canada had given them permission to land. While the *St. Louis* never directly appealed to Canada for landing permits, what weighs on the country's conscience is that its political leaders at the time were unreceptive to an asylum plea made by other Canadians on behalf of the passengers.[39] Libeskind titled his memorial *The Wheel of Conscience* and unveiled it on January 20, 2011. Unfortunately, the installation soon suffered a technical defect because its electrically powered mechanics were negatively affected by environmental factors due to the museum's proximity to the sea. Eventually, it was removed for repair, but after it was repaired it remained inaccessible to the public as the museum limited its exhibition space while undergoing renovation.[40] The decision to bar access triggered protests and queries as to whether a search for a better permanent home should be launched.[41] Ultimately, the memorial returned to its original site, where it has remained (see figs. 10.4 and 10.5).

Described on Libeskind's website as a "kinetic installation," *The Wheel of Conscience* consists of a steel drum that sits up vertically

Figure 10.4. *The Wheel of Conscience* by Daniel Libeskind; © Canadian Museum of Immigration at Pier 21. *Source:* Canadian Museum of Immigration. Used with permission.

Figure 10.5. *The Wheel of Conscience* by Daniel Libeskind; © Canadian Museum of Immigration at Pier 21. *Source:* Canadian Museum of Immigration. Used with permission.

and houses four electrically powered steel discs of differing sizes that interlock via cogs.[42] The smallest gear, titled "Hatred," drives the installation by transferring its power to a larger wheel, titled "Racism," which turns a yet larger one named "Xenophobia." Its cogs engage with those of the largest wheel, titled "Antisemitism." This one, in turn, engages with the inside casing of the steel cylinder that functions as a rotating ribbon on which the story of Voyage 98 is conveyed in three sentences: "On May 13, 1939, more than nine hundred Jews fleeing Nazism departed Hamburg, Germany, aboard the ocean liner St. Louis, desperate to find refuge somewhere in the free world. Cuba, the USA and finally Canada turned the ship away. The St. Louis was forced to return to Europe, where more than a quarter of the passengers perished in the Holocaust" (see fig. 10.6).

A black-and-white photograph of the *St. Louis* covers the face of the steel drum and thus stretches across the four wheels. Their cogs make the wheels visible as discs that are stenciled out from the photograph. As the discs rotate in different directions, they subject

Figure 10.6. *The Wheel of Conscience* by Daniel Libeskind; © Canadian Museum of Immigration at Pier 21. *Source:* Canadian Museum of Immigration. Used with permission.

the image of the ship to a process of disintegration and reintegration. A glass plate that covers the face of the drum causes viewers to see their own reflections superimposed on the rotating discs. In a gesture similar to other memorials, such as the Vietnam Veterans Memorial in Washington, DC, the backside of the drum has the names of all passengers of Voyage 98 written on it. The outside of the drum's casing displays a map of Canada's east coast. An arrow with the words "Access Denied" written above it symbolizes the position of the *St. Louis* and points toward the location of Halifax on the coastline.

Using denotative elements such as written language, a photograph, and a map, *The Wheel of Conscience* is highly communicative about the key facts of the voyage, the passengers' fates, and Canada's role in the affair. Yet it does not merely aim to inform. It alerts viewers to the factors that caused the incident by inviting them to ponder the interplay of the moving discs that represent these factors. The unfolding chain of associations is complex, implying that history itself is constituted by moving parts. On one level, the interplay of hatred, racism, xenophobia, and antisemitism creates a chain of associations that leads to the *St. Louis* incident, with the words on the rotating steel ribbon narrating the fateful result for the ship and its passengers. On another level, however, Libeskind's construction implies that hatred, racism, xenophobia, and antisemitism are semi-autonomous historical phenomena (their foundations rotate around their own axes). This uncouples them from the specifics of the *St. Louis* crisis.

Padura's novel and Spiegelman's comic each use the *St. Louis* voyage to reference specific historical contexts and occurrences (such as Cuba's authoritarian treatment of its citizens or the Department of Homeland Security's lack of empathy for asylum seekers). Libeskind's memorial is more minimalist and open-ended. The focus is on the vectors of political dysfunction as such, not on any events they have generated since the *St. Louis* incident. In addition, the design downplays the fact that the smallest disc, "Hatred," is the mechanism's originating force. This enables a tracing of the chain in reverse, starting with the largest wheel, "Antisemitism," and ending with the word "Hatred." But either way, the design makes clear that the respective vectors the discs display all interlock, whether directly or indirectly. For instance, while the "Antisemitism" disc engages with the "Racism" disc only indirectly, we still associate both phenomena with each other (as we should, given that antisemitism has racist components).

In contrast to established conventions of remembrance, such as the dedication of plaques or the renaming of streets, Libeskind's approach makes visitors encounter *The Wheel of Conscience* not simply as a memorial but as a work of art. As is typical of the three-dimensional medium of sculpture, the installation engages viewers' full sensorium to stimulate the intellect and emotions in rich manner.[43] On the level of ratio, the play of metaphors generated by the rotating discs prompts one to contemplate the relationship between the syndromes they name and questions of history, politics, and human rights. Viewers may wonder under what circumstances democratic governments become enablers of totalitarian regimes. But Libeskind aims beyond engaging the intellect. Because *The Wheel of Conscience* is an installation, it stimulates bodily sensation alongside intellectual cognition. For instance, it inscribes viewers standing in front of the memorial into its aesthetic-discursive realm via their own reflections. Lest one is under the assumption that the *St. Louis* crisis was solely the fault of politicians and diplomats, the memorial makes its viewers realize that the ship's voyage took place under the eyes of the public. Not only are visitors learning about the historic public that in 1939 watched the *St. Louis* crisis unfold, but they see themselves in the role of that public by apprehending their own countenance in the work. By placing its viewers into the role of witnesses to historical trauma, *The Wheel of Conscience* creates what recent scholarship on memorials has termed "difficult knowledge" and "knowledge that does not fit."[44] As it prompts us to remember the ship's historic journey, it warns us that the political apathy and lack of empathy that impacted the *St. Louis* passengers can repeat itself. It inures us to current humanitarian tragedies without naming any specific ones.

The installation thus combines overt didacticism with subtle pedagogy, the latter facilitated by a layered, unstable aesthetic that makes the act of witnessing both an oneiric and an unsettling experience. This is what *The Wheel of Conscience* shares with Padura's novel and Spiegelman's cartoon. The aspects that intrigue Libeskind—the fragility of memory and the fear of disappearance—are the same ones that help constitute multidirectional memory in Padura and Spiegelman. Libeskind describes these qualities as follows: "I thought, how does that image of that ship that people have in their heads—how does it fracture, fragment and disappear from reality because of the callousness of the machinery which drives not only bureaucracy or the ship but the machinery of forgetting?"[45] The memorial renders knowledge difficult in several ways. It addresses visitors both as individuals and as members of a public. That it reserves its largest wheel for antisemitism indicates that it imagines this public to include Canadians. Antisemitism was not only the reason the *St. Louis* Jews had to flee Germany, but also the main catalyst for Canada's decision to decline asylum to them.[46] The memorial prompts Canada to confront its restrictive, racially and biopolitically motivated immigration policy during the 1930s, which resulted in the country's infamous "none is too many" attitude toward Jewish immigration. As such, it falls into the category of public artworks that are "purposefully commissioned to tell stories not comfortably incorporated into national or post-national identity narratives."[47]

The choice of the Canadian Museum of Immigration at Pier 21 as the exhibition site for *The Wheel of Conscience* underscores this strategy. The museum's status within Canada's overall national memorial culture makes its functioning as the site for the memorial the first significant step in a decade-long process of national reckoning, which culminated with Prime Minister Justin Trudeau issuing an official apology to the *St. Louis* Jews on November 7, 2018, in the Canadian Parliament. While such gestures are important and must be respected, only time will tell if they are more than token efforts designed to recuperate the state's historical role and to seek closure where none is warranted. The CJC's CEO Bernie Farber has gone on record stating that "the *St. Louis* is not a moment frozen in historical time but is rather a part of the continuum of human experience and must be owned by all of us if its memory is to have any value today."[48] If read in relation to the conceptual parameters of multidirectional memory I have applied to Padura's and Spiegelman's works, Farber's statement can only mean that memorials such as *The Wheel of Conscience* are only as credible as the current refugee policy of the nation that exhibits them as part of their national memory culture.

But there is more to say about the exhibition site of the *St. Louis* memorial. It bears repeating that Pier 21 is an immigration museum, not a Holocaust museum or monument. *The Wheel of Conscience* is neither the sole nor even the main destination for visitors coming to Pier 21. Like most of Libeskind's works, it has garnered press coverage, yet many visitors may be unaware of its existence and encounter it almost by chance when entering the museum to learn about the history of immigration into Canada. But the memorial counters any impulse to perceive the *St. Louis* voyage as a freak occurrence, a one-off tragedy. It reminds viewers that the ship's journey was a drama of migration and it makes them realize that for Jews the statuses of migrant, refugee, and camp inmate closely overlapped.[49] To place a narrative about rejected refugees into the context of migration is to suggest that flight and migration are phenomena that share correspondences and, thus, homologous or intersecting structures of memory.

Exploring the gray zone between voluntary and involuntary migration, Libeskind's installation foregrounds migration as an area equally impacted by the state's calculated biopolitics, the cowardice and complacency of international diplomacy, and the mercantile logic of international trade. In the historical period under discussion, the ocean liner was the main site on which these factors converged and shaped the passengers' status. A sign of its thoughtfulness is that Libeskind's memorial invites visitors to contemplate precisely this complex historical function of the liner. It does so by virtue of both its specific materiality and its exact location within the museum. A sculpture's material can have a decisive impact on the metaphors it generates.[50] Libeskind's choice of steel for the memorial's casing and back wall courts associations with the hulls of steam ships and ocean liners. The installation strikes a careful balance between concreteness and abstraction, allowing for a certain freedom of association. The steel is not only the material from which ships are built. Representing the foundation of the industrial age, it becomes a metaphor for the unique status of the Holocaust as an industrial form of murder. The significance of the quality of roundness for the installation, instanced by the drum-like shape of the casing and the reliance on wheels, suggests further associations with industry. As cog wheels, the rotating discs help evoke the industrial age and its valorization of machines that transcend human agency. But as Libeskind himself has indicated, they may also allude to the wheels of bureaucracy, which were partially responsible for the fact that the *St. Louis* drama, despite its many turns, unfolded as a series of mutually reinforcing diplomatic failures.

Further, as rotating discs, each of which carries portions of the photograph of the *St. Louis*, the wheels metaphorically tear the ship to pieces by destroying its unified image. A correlative to Padura's use of language in *Heretics*, the process suggests that memory about the *St. Louis* voyage is fragile, heterogeneous, and contested, but it also does something else: It demystifies the ship's position as a glamorous, secure means of transport for migrants. As discussed in chapter 4, at issue is a certain fetish-like status the *St. Louis* assumed both for the Jewish passengers traveling on it and for the US press, which, by focusing only on the *St. Louis*, neglected the fate of so many other refugee ships.[51] Add to this the impression that the rotating discs renounce any unified historical narrative (the three sentences on the drum's metal rim constitute but a bare-bones summary) and instead position *the St. Louis* as a compendium of intersecting political, economic, and sociocultural constellations. What the memorial ultimately displays, then, is Libeskind's analytical, materialist view of history.

Both the installation's materiality and its abstract qualities allude to the ocean liner and embed it in multiple intersecting contexts (modernity, industrialization, the biopolitics of mass migration, and the

Holocaust). On this level, the memorial provides a notable contrast to the overwhelming concreteness of all the other ships that are on display in the museum's permanent exhibition—either as stunningly handsome miniatures or in the form of meticulously crafted replicas of steerage cabins or through a wealth of photographs. To be sure, these exhibition pieces make visitors encounter the many facets of migration in sensual manner without romanticizing immigrant travel by trivializing its hardships. But they cannot help but endow migrant ships with a seemingly neutral, perhaps even innocent, instrumentality. To all this, Libeskind's *St. Louis* memorial provides a perfect counterpoint. Its haunting combination of material concreteness and semantic abstraction generates multiple intersecting metaphors and constitutes an intriguingly minimalist model for multidirectional memory. These qualities become enhanced by the place the museum has assigned the piece, in its foyer just to the right of the main entrance. Visitors can take a close look at it prior to redeeming their admission tickets but also have to pass by it on their way to and from the gift shop or the bathrooms. The memorial is thus positioned in public space, its location shrewdly using the processual character of conventional museum culture to its advantage.

If memorials are sites and objects of mnemonic activity, Libeskind's *St. Louis* memorial affords viewers ways to take this activity into multiple directions. Not only does it help them gain a better understanding of the historically fraught nature of migration and the tainted role Canada played in the Jewish refugee crisis, it also—in its own minimalist way—undermines any impulse to treat the *St. Louis* incident as distant history in order to avoid comparisons to the contemporary global migrant crisis. That crisis, it should be clear, is a refugee crisis only because western industrial nations have allowed it to turn into one. If involuntary migration serves as a gauge for global politics in crisis, Libeskind's *St. Louis* memorial instills a nagging sense that the past is prologue.

Epilogue

"With Whose Blood Were My Eyes Crafted?" Philipp Scheffner and Merle Kröger's *Havarie* (2016), the Mediterranean Migrant Crisis, and the *St. Louis* Voyage

IN 2015, MIGRATION TO Europe from Northern Africa and the Middle East skyrocketed to dramatic proportions.[1] Large streams of migrants from Syria, Eritrea, Libya, Iraq, and Afghanistan reached Europe via the Balkans, Greece, and Turkey. In addition, close to a million crossed the Mediterranean in small, overcrowded boats, willing to risk their lives on the perilous journeys to Greece, Italy, and Spain. Displaced by civil war and famine, many Syrians and Africans also applied for asylum in the US and thus added to the growing stream of Latin Americans who crossed the dangerous Darien Gap on their way north to the US–Mexico border, where fortified urban crossing points forced them into hazardous desert territory. On both sides of the Atlantic, the migrants' precarity caught the attention of the public. The mass drownings in the Mediterranean in particular received extensive media coverage and generated widespread horror. At the same time, concerns emerged over whether the prospective host countries would be able to absorb the large number of new arrivals. Both in the US and in Europe, the political right instrumentalized the crisis to stoke xenophobia and nationalism. In Germany, Chancellor Angela Merkel's historic 2015 decision to allow two million migrants into the country indirectly triggered the significant increase in popularity of the right-wing party AfD (Alternative für Deutschland—Alternative for Germany).

Liberal politicians and NGOs have called for more flexible and progressive immigration policies, and similar arguments have found their way into the popular press. And, as discussed in chapter 8, numerous articles in English- and German-language publications have linked the plight of today's migrants to that of the *St. Louis* Jews, some even featuring interviews with survivors of the voyage. In the US it is traditionally Jewish Americans who, because of the legacy of the Holocaust, have advocated for a progressive migrant policy. Headlines such as "Closing Our Doors" and "How America's Rejection of Jews Fleeing Nazi Germany Haunts Our Refugee Policy Today" have appealed to America's historical responsibility.[2] Most articles, however, place humanist pleas over incisive political and historical analysis. For instance, an article on the migrant ship *Aquarius*, which crisscrossed the Mediterranean in 2018, voices moral objections but fails to draw attention to the underlying reasons for the "Fortress Europe" mentality. The writer is content with invoking the courage of the captain of the *St. Louis*, Gustav Schröder, as a counter-example.[3] Another article simply states that what links both ships is "an ocean of tears."[4]

But no matter the degree of their politicization, comparisons between the *St. Louis* voyage and today's mass migration tend to distract from the fact that their respective media coverage impacted both crises in opposite ways. The same kind of attention that worked in favor of the *St. Louis* Jews has become a crushing liability for the Mediterranean migrants. Shaped by the economics of network, cable, and satellite TV and by digital "prosumer" culture's expectation of total access, coverage of the precarity and plight of Mediterranean migrants has been inflationary. If anything, it has numbed the public instead of rousing its interest. Given the crucial role the media play in shaping public opinion about migrant and refugee crises, several questions pose themselves at the end of this book: What capacities and functions should we look for in contemporary media and media practices, whether used in journalism or art, that have the potential to reframe, historicize, and politicize migration? How can media productively compare different historical instances of migration? How can new media forms help educate the public in how to look past mass-mediated stories of suffering and help foster solidarity with the migrants? Last but not least, what new directions must the theorization of media and art take to be able to effectively critique media representations of migration?

The final case study of this book is *Havarie*, a 2016 experimental film to which these questions are relevant. While *Havarie* is about migrants on the Mediterranean and makes no mention of the *St. Louis*, my discussion of it seeks to locate aesthetic-discursive areas that enable us to place both crises in relation to each other. By exploring the role of media in offering a discourse of migrant awareness that is not strictly about the *St. Louis* but that can be read to include it, I once more trace the workings of multidirectional memory. As the latter developed as a theoretical concept with reference to the history of decolonization and within what has been termed the colonial turn in Holocaust studies (see chapter 5), my own approach, too, is guided by postcolonial theory. I follow Paul Gilroy's call for exploring correspondences between the Holocaust and other genocides, including but not limited to the Middle Passage—comparisons, in other words, that identify colonialism either as a direct cause of mass murder or a framing condition for the failure to prevent it.

While it was Nazi antisemitism that triggered the Jewish refugee crisis and caused the Holocaust, the racial biopolitics that made European nations complicit with antisemitic expulsion and that had a key role in preventing Jews from escaping the death camps are reemerging today. We see those biopolitics inform current calls for the fortification of Europe and North America against the influx of racial, ethnic, and religious Others. What links today's fortress mentality to that of the past are the effects of colonialism and neocolonialism. In the late 1930s and early '40s, colonialist thinking directly or indirectly caused many nations to shut their borders to Jews. In the twenty-first century, colonialism's legacy and neocolonialism's abiding grip on the Global South are the causes of the current migrant crisis. I should note that my critical approach to these phenomena reaches beyond diagnosis. I take it to be reparative. This dimension emerges through the engagement with an innovative media artifact such as *Havarie* and by theorizing the film's pedagogic potential. *Havarie*, as I argue below, suggests new frameworks through which we can map forced migration across different eras and contexts; it teaches us to critically engage with the current migrant phenomenon rather than allowing us to passively witness it.

Subverting the Eurocentric Gaze

Over the past decade, the splendid vista of the open ocean as it may be experienced, for example, by Mediterranean cruise tourists from aboard a large ship, has been disturbed by an unsettling bit of reality—the presence of stateless migrants floating precariously in small boats in the swells. The experimental nonfiction film *Havarie*, written by Merle Kröger and directed by Philip Scheffner, revolves centrally around this moment of disturbance. *Havarie* temporally extends a brief amateur cell-phone video that was shot from aboard the cruise ship *Adventure of the Seas* and that focuses on a dinghy with migrants floating in the Mediterranean hoping to reach the coast of Spain. The film's minimalist aesthetics turn it into a meditation on both the divisions and the linkages between the migrants in the dinghy and the passengers aboard the *Adventure of the Seas*, a maritime representative of Euro-American political and economic hegemony. After encountering the video on YouTube, Scheffner and Kröger interviewed its maker, Terry Diamond. Unable to trace the migrants Diamond had filmed, Scheffner interviewed others who had undergone a similar experience. He obtained recordings of the radio traffic of the rescue operation and interviewed crew members both from the *Adventure of the Seas* and from a container ship that had a history of carrying migrants as stowaways. He used the audio materials to engineer a complex soundscape for the film. Scheffner's extension of the three-and-a-half-minute video to the length of ninety minutes reflects the approximate time it took the Spanish coast guard to rescue the migrants in the dinghy.[5]

Part of a recent spate of migration-themed films, *Havarie* charts new aesthetic paths in its attempt to uncouple migration from the status of spectacle. The film has already garnered considerable attention from film and media scholars.[6] Several theorists have commented on how its minimalist visuals and layered soundtrack succeed in making spectators develop political solidarity with the migrants rather than having mere empathy. Johanne Villeneuve and Debbie Blythe analyze *Havarie*'s intricate soundscape as a means of grasping the Mediterranean as a plurivocal aquatic space. Drawing on theories of the disembodied voice and vocal performance, they argue that *Havarie*'s sonic mapping opens up new ways for spectators to rethink their relationship to migrants as one of ethical cohabitation.[7] Alena Strohmaier and Lea

Spahn discuss *Havarie* as facilitating a multi-sensory, immersive form of spectatorship that mobilizes viewers' precognitive engagement with moving-image media. This engagement, so the authors claim, prompts spectators to suspend the subject–object divide in their encounter with the on-screen migrant dinghy.[8]

While critical discourse has thus attended to how *Havarie* compels viewers to engage the migrants in a more sustained way than facilitated by the glut of media and TV news images of migrant boats, some commentators read the film as a meditation on the irreducible differences between the cruise ship and the dinghy. Nilgun Bayraktar, for instance, finds that the stillness of the image, once we link it to clandestine migration, "defies cosmopolitan notions of escape, tranquillity and rest; instead, it elicits a sense of precariousness and uncertainty—conditions that mark the experiences of refugees and undocumented migrants in detention camps, on dinghies, or stowed away in containers or trucks."[9] And as Anat Tzom Ayalon argues, the fact that the film shows neither the faces of the migrants nor of Scheffner's interviewees prompts reflections on the unknowability of the other, forcing one "to reflect on one's blindness and deafness while watching the other."[10]

The common ground I find in these critical takes encourages me to approach *Havarie* as a kind of meditative template that prompts us to revise the self–other binary with its subtending sets of oppositions. These include white vs. non-white, European vs. non-European, Christian vs. non-Christian, citizen vs. migrant—and, last but not least, present vs. past. *Havarie*, as I shall argue, prompts us to put different temporal planes in relation to one another, so as to compare different histories of migration, which, despite their specifics, share colonialism and neocolonialism as framing conditions and flight and genocide as consequences of those conditions. The site of this activation of viewers' mnemonic faculty is a particular segment of *Havarie* that, while frequently noted, has yet to attract sustained analysis—the mid-film pan, during which the camera temporarily relinquishes its gaze onto the migrants and turns toward the cruise ship from where the filming proceeds. Below, I centrally concern myself with a discussion of this pan and how it subverts the Eurocentric looking relations in which the film partakes. My methodological approach is informed by two of postcolonial theory's ongoing anti-Eurocentric projects. The first is to break down politically fraught categories of identity that have been shaped by and, in turn, help reinforce the geopolitical chasm and pervasive power differential between the prosperous West and the Global South. The second is to better understand and promote the reparative role of cultural memory—both in its function of invigorating the bonds between victims of colonial violence, displacement, and deracination and in its potential to create points of contact even between unrelated cultures.

For the Caribbean poet and theorist Édouard Glissant, the need to cope with the loss of traditions and severing of lineages in the wake of the Middle Passage has resulted in the salutary rejection of the very concept of roots. Influenced by Deleuze and Guattari, Glissant replaces the singular root (with its essentializing Eurocentric baggage) with the rhizome, a web of liminal connections not associated with territorial possession.[11] In related manner, difference for Glissant is not the fixed mark of disparity between two or more essences. He reconceives the processes of cultural formation that are central to anti-essentialist identity through a concept he terms "Relation"—a philosophy of cohabitation that is politically productive because it considers everyone an other.[12] At the heart of Glissant's rejection of Enlightenment concepts of legibility is his notion of opacity, which is both an ontological and epistemological concept, as Glissant's exegete, John E. Drabinski, notes.[13] Consisting of interrelated facets that involve the production of memory without referencing what precedes it,[14] the colonized subject's obscuring of meaning from the colonizer and even from itself,[15] and the uncoupling of epistemic processes from teleologies of certainty and finitude,[16] opacity has an anti-Eurocentric, anti-Enlightenment logic that is central to Glissant's anti-colonial agenda: "We demand the right to opacity [le droit à l'opacité]. Through which our anxiety to have a full existence becomes part of the planetary drama of Relation: the creativity of marginalized peoples who today confront the ideal of transparent universality, imposed by the West, with secretive and multiple manifestations of Diversity."[17]

How does Glissant's theory help us compare different histories of migration, such as the Middle Passage and the current migration across the Mediterranean, despite their differences? What are the stakes in subsuming the respective subjects of these migrations under Glissant's category of "the planetary drama of Relation?" To be sure, the migrants in *Havarie* have left the African continent of their own accord, in contrast to the Africans of the Middle Passage, who were victims of genocidal colonialist capture. But how free a choice, we must ask, is the decision of subjects who embark on an extremely hazardous, quite possibly fatal sea journey to a new land, where they, even in the slim eventuality of safe arrival, will be instantly encamped and legally, politically, and culturally othered? The difference between the Middle Passage and the Mediterranean migrant crisis is not, I believe, one between forced and voluntary migration. It resides in gradations of force and in both cases this force owes to the effects of colonialism and neocolonialism.[18] Correspondences do not end here. The Africans of the Middle Passage were bereft of their identities on their way to becoming slaves; the migrants in *Havarie* are so-called *harraga* who strategically destroy their official identification documents to secure asylum in Spain. It is precisely this voluntarist element that gives their voyage the character of a retracing of a specific consequence of the Middle Passage: Both journeys share a contingency between the erasure of the past and the possibility of beginning again in radically new manner—radical because of the potential to reshape, over time, the body politic and culture of the country of destination.

From the perspective of continental philosophy, the representation of the migrant dinghy in *Havarie* as a distant and blurry presence certainly constitutes a "crisis of figurability."[19] But what significance does this crisis assume in the framework of decolonization? The migrants' decision to define their existence on their own terms by becoming "harraga" accords with how the film lends them a presence that, while visually precarious, is insistent, even quasi-hypnotic. Their distant, blurry, slightly changing position makes them readable either as one or as multiple subjects. The illusion of their visual proliferation implicitly mitigates against the impression of their fragility. They acquire opacity in Glissant's sense, summarized by Drabinski as "a resistance to certain senses of knowing and understanding that would seek to absorb, reactivate, and possess."[20] In related manner, *Havarie* works against assumptions that hold Mediterranean migration to be synonymous with tragedy and death. While it is possible to feel skeptical about the migrants' fate, the film's anti-positivist representation of them floating on the open sea and refusing to disappear may also be read as advocating for their right to self-determination—both during their sea rescue and upon being subjected to the vicissitudes of the asylum process that awaits.[21] The strategies by which migrants elude deportation certainly partake in the above-mentioned quality of opacity. And the strategies they develop to survive in the interstices of European society warrant reassessing through Glissant's concept of Relation with its radical postulation that *everyone* is Other.

As critical concepts, opacity and Relation also pertain to a discussion of *Havarie*'s mid-film pan, which, as the filmmakers have pointed out, explicitly places the European citizen-tourist and the stateless migrant in relation to each other.[22] The film subverts the Eurocentric looking relations it uses by infusing the act of observation with an ethics of accountability. Two questions arise with regard to the pan. First, how does the pan's execution relate to Diamond's complex subjecthood as being both a white European and a citizen of Northern Ireland, one of the few European countries with a recent history of colonization? Below, I discuss Diamond's subjecthood and his execution of the pan through Donna Haraway's theorem of situated knowledges. Second, how does the pan connect the cruise ship rescue scenario to other historical scenarios of migration? I will argue that the pan's semi-abstract visuals stimulate viewers' mnemonic faculty in ways similar to those found in certain kinds of modern art. I then discuss the way *Havarie* prompts viewers' mnemonic faculty to connect different scenarios of migration, many of which have involved traumatic experiences of flight and statelessness, in terms of Michael Rothberg's concept of multidirectional memory.[23]

The final part of this epilogue explores correspondences between multidirectional memory and Glissant's concepts of opacity and Relation through the voyage of the *St. Louis*. I ended my discussion in chapter 5 by arguing that the ship's transatlantic trajectory retraces part of the geopolitical coordinates of the Middle Passage and, despite the latter's political and economic particularities, hints at some underlying commonalities attributable to colonialism and neocolonialism. As mentioned, the need to diacritically compare the Holocaust and the Middle Passage has long been acknowledged by postcolonial theorists. My discussion will conclude with thoughts on how an analysis of *Havarie* through Glissant's and Rothberg's frameworks can contribute to this project by triangulating the *St. Louis* voyage and the Middle Passage with the Mediterranean migrant crisis as instances of forced migration.

Terry Diamond's Video and the Negotiation of the Self–Other Binary

Terry Diamond's wife had given him the Mediterranean cruise as a wedding anniversary gift.[24] The *Adventure of the Seas* is one of many ships that nowadays cater to middle-class tourists like the Diamonds. It is the backbone of a business model of mass tourism that was pioneered in the US in the 1970s by such corporations as Royal Caribbean (which operates the *Adventure of the Seas*) and Carnival Cruise Line, but that caught on in Europe only in the 1990s.[25] Of course, when compared to the migrants in the dinghy, Diamond's privilege as a white middle-class person is obvious. Yet, as a citizen of Northern Ireland living in Belfast, Diamond is part of a population that remains under British rule. He belonged to the youth branch of the Irish Republican Army and was directly involved in the Troubles, an armed conflict between Irish nationalists, who fought against Northern Ireland remaining under British control, and unionists, who sought to maintain England's power over the region, which England secured through state violence.[26] Diamond was unable to escape these punitive conditions—as he mentions in an interview, he spent time in prison and at a young age saw his best friend shot by the British police. This experience of helplessness shaped his attitude toward the migrants adrift on the ocean. Near the end of the film, we hear his voice as he describes his response to spotting them in their dinghy:

> They were a distance away from the ship. You sort of tried to zoom in to get a clear understanding of what you were actually physically looking at. And then you realized, my God there's, there's human beings in this? You know, you start to try and imagine why they're there. What's driven them to there. To a certain extent, you start to try and put yourself in their position. But you can never replicate that. You can only assume that it has been something that has been drastic enough to drive people to do that sort of thing.[27]

When Scheffner, commenting on Diamond's response to laying eyes on the migrants, states that all of this was "part of the atmosphere, part of the baggage with which he [meaning Diamond] was looking at the boat,"²⁸ what Scheffner presumably means with "baggage" is Diamond's growing up as part of an externally ruled national minority and his brush with the violence used against this minority.

As a European postcolonial subject, Diamond is in a hegemonic position. He enjoys the limited material benefits of decolonization, while his memory of colonial oppression continues to shape his worldview. The form of traveling his hegemonic status affords Diamond warrants theorization through a theorem Glissant relates to opacity and Relation—that of errantry. In contrast to discovery or conquest, errantry is a form of traveling that "is no longer the locus of power but, rather, of pleasurable, if privileged, time. The ontological obsession with knowledge gives way here to the enjoyment of a relation; in its elementary and often caricatural form this is tourism."²⁹ But Glissant further relates this form of travel to the postcolonial subject's state of internal exile as someone who remains marginalized because their "solutions concerning the relationship of a community to its surroundings" remain only partially realized. In this context, errantry has a compensatory function. It "tends towards material comfort, which cannot really distract from anguish."³⁰

Diamond's cell-phone video registers his state of internal exile. Of particular interest is his professional background as a surveillance specialist. It constitutes a hegemonic form of visual control that, however, appears to be fragile because of the anxious manner in which he trains his cell-phone camera on the migrants. By panning to the cruise ship, he then acknowledges his presence to the scenario. Donna Haraway has argued that the way we use vision and the insights we gain from it are never neutral. Aiming to wrest techniques of the observer away from the techno-scientific apparatus of white patriarchy, Haraway wants to replace its disembodied conquering gaze—the view from "nowhere"—with embodied vision and knowledge, or the "view from a body."³¹ If these "situated knowledges" constitute a new kind of seeing, one that acknowledges its embodied nature and embraces its answerability, the concept helps us to further understand Diamond's visual acknowledgment of the position of relative power and agency he occupies. "Vision is always a question of the power to see," Haraway goes on to explain, "and perhaps of the violence implicit in our visualizing practices. With whose blood were my eyes crafted?"³² Technologies of vision thus index social orders and practices of visualization: "How to see? Where to see from? . . . What to see for? Whom to see with? Who gets to have more than one point of view?"[33]

Diamond first pans to the right toward the ship's stern, then he pans 180 degrees left for a forward view of its starboard side. Then he pans away from the ship and comes to rest on the dinghy in the middle of the ocean. In its motion, the pan acknowledges, and thereby implicitly destabilizes, the divide between European tourist and African migrant. His documenting the migrants' existence without objectifying them and his acknowledging his material base without assuming a glibly celebratory position (the selfie pose) registers his desire to create a space of ethical cohabitation for him and the migrants. His decision to film the migrants certainly conveys his curiosity about them. Yet, as his quoted comment above indicates, he readily acknowledges his inability to put himself in the migrants' position. Even more noteworthy is that his limited knowledge about the migrants' motives for abandoning their own habitat compels him to judge their decision in good faith. His attitude aligns with that of the errant traveler who, in Glissant's characterization, "plunges into the opacities of that part of the world to which he has access."[34] Errantry, as Glissant's comment suggests, is bound up with failure, but here we are to understand failure as a salutary coefficient of rejecting Western epistemology's totalizing ambitions. By foregrounding elements of risk and contingency, the film transvalues failure's conceptual implications. This begins with its title, which in German means accident or collision and, more specifically, shipwreck.[35] While we know that a shipwreck does not occur, *Havarie* plays with the possibility that it may.

The Aestheticization of the Pan in *Havarie*

Diamond's original pan lasts about twenty seconds. In *Havarie*, it takes eight minutes. Handheld camera movement traditionally functions as indexical proof of the existence and agency of the filmmaker.[36] Yet Scheffner's extension of Diamond's pan does not merely shift the locus of meaning from one filmmaker (Diamond) toward another (Scheffner). The aesthetic effects produced by the lengthening of the pan stimulate viewers and give maximum interpretive agency to them.[37] One of the first things we notice in *Havarie*'s slowed-down pan is the subtle doubling of the image of the migrants in the dinghy (see fig. E.1) and of the tourists on the cruise ship (see fig. E.2). The unstable phenomenology renders migrants and tourists similarly fragile. This correspondence suggests that both types of passengers share one and the same world in ways that their different positions—the cruise tourists high up on the towering passenger ship and the migrants way below in their tiny dinghy—seemingly belies. (It is, however, precisely this vertical differential that, as I shall argue later, is unstable to the point of being random and as such points to a broader political instability.) Further, the left pan foregrounds the optical effects generated by the sunlight meeting the lens. These effects inject the realist view of the ship with garish pink and dark green hues. First we see the ocean and sky being pierced by a flash of light (see fig. E.3). As the camera moves left, the flash appears toward the middle and brightens, before the image as a whole turns a deep pink (see fig. E.4). Then the film oscillates between a dark green (see fig. E.5) and a saturated pink (see fig. E.6). Then the pink hue becomes less intense and the bright flash moves toward the right-hand corner (see fig. E.7). Before the camera pans away from the cruise ship again, we see what is perhaps the most striking optical effect, a set of light beams that hit the water next to the ship and produce a field of sparkles (see figs. E.8

Figure E.1. *Havarie*. *Source:* © Pong film 2016. Used with permission.

Figure E.2. *Havarie. Source:* © Pong film 2016. Used with permission.

Figure E.3. *Havarie. Source:* © Pong film 2016. Used with permission.

Figure E.4. *Havarie*. *Source:* © Pong film 2016. Used with permission.

Figure E.5. *Havarie*. *Source:* © Pong film 2016. Used with permission.

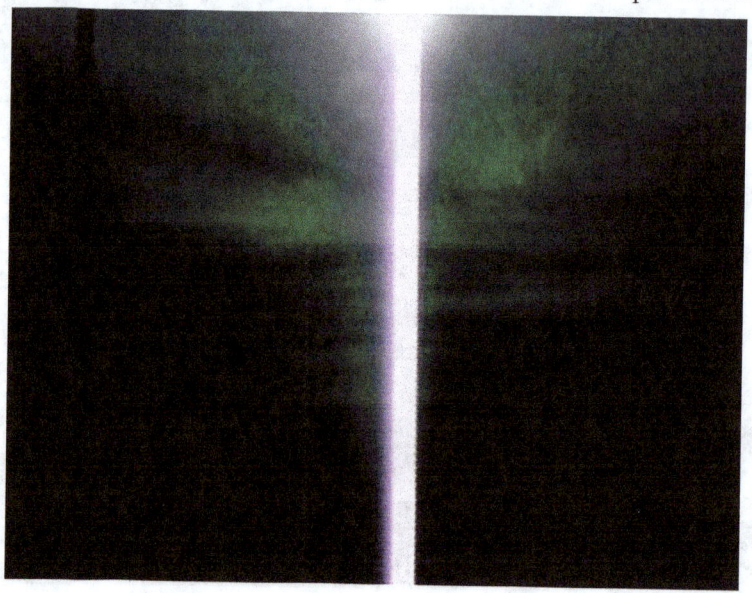

Figure E.6. *Havarie*. *Source:* © Pong film 2016. Used with permission.

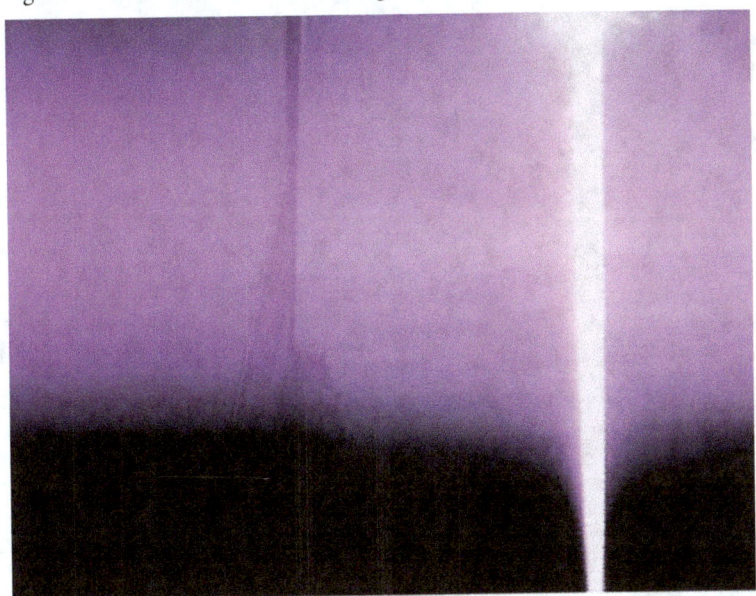

Figure E.7. *Havarie*. *Source:* © Pong film 2016. Used with permission.

Figure E.8. *Havarie. Source:* © Pong film 2016. Used with permission.

Figure E.9. *Havarie. Source:* © Pong film 2016. Used with permission.

and E.9). These effects are already fleetingly noticeable in Diamond's video, but *Havarie*'s segmentation of the footage into what are almost individual frames elevates them to the order of spectacle and gives us time to take them in.

Reading the extended pan as a series of individual frames—despite the fact that movement between them never fully ceases—has a purpose. My discussion of the spectator's perception of these slowly moving images is guided by film theory's recent proposition of the mobile frame as a composite of two kinds of movements. One kind refers to pro-filmic content captured by the camera, while the other, as Jordan Schonig has claimed, refers to the frame's status as an aesthetic surface.[38] This surface, so Schonig argues, citing David Bordwell, displays movement "as a series of expanding, contracting, and labile configurations."[39] The affinity between camera movement and human perception encourages a reading of the pan as an expression of Diamond's desire to map pro-filmic reality, a gesture interpretable as his spur-of-the-moment filmic "confession" of being implicated in the power differential between the cruise ship and the migrant dinghy.[40] But *Havarie* allows us to move beyond this common reading of camera movement. Its lengthening of the pan aestheticizes movement as such. This quality of the mobile image accentuates the self-implicating quality of Diamond's pan but, more importantly, it introduces an element of abstraction that heightens the images' associative—and, more specifically, mnemonic—potential. To rehearse this process in detail, it is useful to compare *Havarie*'s aestheticized pan with a form of modern art that has already been discussed for its mnemonic quality—pop art. As I'll discuss below, the aesthetic effects of the lengthened pan resemble the aesthetics of certain works of pop art visually. But before doing so, it is worth addressing how the mode in which Scheffner has appropriated and processed Diamond's video evinces broader conceptual affinities with pop art.

Among the qualities pop art became famous for was its appropriation and eye-popping defamiliarization of realist images circulating in popular culture and news media. Scheffner himself appears to allude to pop art's affinities with Diamond's video when, in a conversation with his interviewer, he describes the effect of the pan on the viewer: "The pan was the moment where I felt 'Pow!' . . . The pan puts you into a position, and suddenly you understand your position. And that's the beauty of the image."[41] In the minds of many, "Pow!" invokes the speech bubbles in comic strips, which became the subject of Roy Liechtenstein's paintings. In my view, however, *Havarie*'s aestheticization of the pan is most reminiscent of the work of another leader of pop art, Andy Warhol. What *Havarie* shares with Warhol's paintings is the visual referencing and emotional negotiation of anxiety caused by traumatic loss. A prominent example of this are Warhol's silkscreens of celebrities linked to death, and in particular several paintings showing Jackie Kennedy as a grieving widow. That these paintings bear no iconic resemblance to *Havarie* is not relevant. Of interest is the way in which, for instance, the silkscreens commemorate a traumatic event in US history through aesthetic surface qualities. While the inflationary volume of media coverage of Kennedy's assassination had a numbing effect on the public, some have argued that the seriality and formal composition of Warhol's silkscreens foreground obsession and repetition *as* cultural conventions and thus constitute a viable alternative to commemorating trauma.[42]

Three aspects warrant a comparison between Warhol's silkscreens and Scheffner's film. First, both artists have based their works on already existing sources (for Warhol, *Life* magazine's coverage of the First Lady; for Scheffner, Diamond's cell phone video). Second, in both cases, the artistic processing of realist source imagery wrests the images away from their circulation in dominant media. By taking the finished work to alternative spaces of reception, Scheffner, like Warhol before him, intervenes in the dominant view of history as constructed by mainstream news. And third, by forgoing a conventional documentary treatment in favor of an experimental one, Scheffner unleashes the hidden potential of Diamond's video. His slowing down of Diamond's footage has an effect similar to what we see in Warhol's silkscreen panels. Particularly in the mid-film pan, the segmentation of the original footage into a series of individual aestheticized images—images notable for their aesthetic surface qualities rather than their pro-filmic content—produces an emotional charge.[43]

Just as in pop art, however, the production of affect in *Havarie* is complex. The ambiguities of the image (between depicted content and surface aesthetics, narration and stasis, and minimalism and plenitude) generate emotional ambivalence toward the subject represented. *Havarie* troubles viewers' conventional role of passive, disengaged witnesses to TV coverage of the Mediterranean migrant crisis. The film prompts viewers to perceive its cinematic space as bridging the self–other divide—as a space, in other words, that is shared by tourists and migrants and, for that matter, by citizens and foreigners. In doing so, the film prompts viewers to reflect on the contradictory attitudes toward migrants. Shaped by Enlightenment values and the historical prominence of social market economies that have sought to raise standards of living for the working class and have traditionally favored unionization, European society defines itself via discourses of solidarity. In contrast to this spirit of solidarity, many EU member states have developed extensive security apparatuses to protect their borders, a move that has been termed the "Fortress Europe" mentality.[44] This contradiction heightens a second one, between the continent's Christian ideals and the decidedly secular political pragmatism with which the EU fortifies its borders. *Havarie* subtly foregrounds these contradictions and the moral predicaments they generate by subjecting viewers to the epistemological self-inquiries eloquently articulated by Haraway: With whose blood were my eyes crafted? How to see? Where to see from? Whom to see with?

One way in which *Havarie* bridges the self–other divide is by projecting the migrants' precarity back onto viewers. The conduit for this transference is the cruise ship, which takes on ominous connotations because of the pan's heavy stylization. The frame alternately brightens and darkens, the shaft of light that travels through the image looks like a bolt of lightning, and the beam that hits the water next to the ship like a rain-like cluster looks otherworldly. These flourishes produce an unsettling, even subtly apocalyptic ambience, giving the impression that the ship may be at the center of a disturbance. This impression is reinforced by the audio that plays over these images, a recording of the radio communication between the ship and the Maritime Rescue Unit. We hear a voice telling the *Adventure of the Seas* that the unit will arrive in the area of deployment in about forty minutes (see figs. E.10, E.11, and E.12). Scheffner plays this audio over the images not of the dinghy but of the cruise liner, as if the latter is the one in need of attention. The effect is enhanced by audio from the cruise ship listing the number of people on board: "Passengers 3,781; crew 1,165; altogether 4,946 passengers aboard." The question that arises is not only how the liner contrasts with the dinghy, but what both may share.

Figure E.10. *Havarie*: ". . . to inform you of arrival in about 40 minutes." *Source:* © Pong film 2016. Used with permission.

Figure E.11. *Havarie*: ". . . in the zone of deployment." *Source:* © Pong film 2016. Used with permission.

Figure E.12. *Havarie*: "I will calculate this more precisely, but approximately 40 minutes to there." *Source:* © Pong film 2016. Used with permission.

While this question invites rich speculation, I believe it is most productively pursued if placed within the framework of comparative histories. One point of investigation is whether the fate of the migrants in the dinghy was at some point in the past shared (and may thus be shared again) by others, including European cruise travelers. But to address this possibility, we first need to determine how the film establishes a historical mode of inquiry. In a canonized argument, art historian Thomas Crow has identified a set of mnemonic processes at work in pop art and, more particularly, in Warhol's silkscreens. The key feature of the silkscreen process is its inherently impoverished reproduction of a preexisting image, which constitutes both the image's look and the foundation for its reproducibility. This link between technique and function and the silkscreen image's characteristic tension between presence and absence was, so Crow argues, something Warhol seized on in his portraits of dead or deathly ill celebrities, so as to "come to terms with the sense of loss, the absence of a richly imagined presence that was never really there. . . . The screened image, reproduced whole, has the character of an involuntary trace: It is memorial in the sense of resembling memory, which is sometimes vividly present, sometimes elusive, and always open to embellishment as well as loss."[45]

Reminiscent of pop art's tendency to keep loss in play with its opposite, embellishment, the aestheticized quality of *Havarie*'s pan accords with Glissant's notion of memory as opaque, which, in Drabinski's characterization, comprises "erasure, trace, struggle, proliferation, accumulation, knowing, and the unknowable—all at once."[46] Further, the opaque quality of the pan's undulating visuals has affinities to the ebb and flow of mnemonic processes that Michael Rothberg seizes on in his concept of multidirectional memory. While for Rothberg, memory's dialogic, cross-referential, and labile mode makes it "fundamentally and structurally multidirectional," dominant media discipline this flow into "competitive memory" to have their historical narratives participate in a zero-sum struggle for validation.[47] By contrast, the stylized pan of Scheffner's liminal, experimental film—which reflects pop art's insistence on keeping loss in play with its opposite, embellishment—plays into memory's non-hierarchical nature, which, as Rothberg asserts, works through displacement and substitution.[48]

Displacement and substitution also figure prominently in the mnemonic processing of historical trauma and in the tracing of one trauma through another. But if multidirectional memory performs these mnemonic processes via the "interlacing of memories in the force field of public space,"[49] how exactly can traumatic memories of a specific event be related to *Havarie*'s pan to the cruise ship? For Rothberg, as discussed in chapter 10, multidirectional memory attends to "the dynamic transfers that take place between diverse places and times during the act of remembrance."[50] This quality accords with certain philosophical understandings of history, particularly Walter Benjamin's notion of loosely connected historical constellations. These, so Benjamin argues, can on closer inspection illuminate history in a different way. When the historian comes upon certain tensions within a historical constellation, such encounters can produce a burst of associations that crystallize into what Benjamin terms "monads" (Monaden). According to Benjamin, this approach to historical thinking rejects the notion of history as a linear cause-and-effect chain and instead seizes on looser correspondences between different periods and events.[51]

That this approach to history has an aesthetic dimension—in other words, that it invites visualization—can be inferred from Rothberg's definition of the monad: "Benjamin's crystallized constellations provide an *image* of encounter in which different temporalities collide and in which movement and stasis are held in tension."[52] But if we read the pan in *Havarie* as a Benjaminian monad, an aesthetic-discursive site that makes another historical trauma linked to migration visible to the viewer, what past event might the pan be said to reference? It is here that the voyage of the *St. Louis* reenters the picture or, more precisely, our minds.

The Dinghy and the Cruise Liner

A photograph (fig. 3.6) shows the *St. Louis* leaving Havana on June 2, 1939, and taking its passengers into an uncertain future caused by democratic nations' complicity with Germany's expulsion of Jews. The photo, if compared to the pan toward the cruise liner in *Havarie*, demonstrates the function of Benjamin's monad as an associative cluster that allows us to place two historical constellations in relation to each other by reversing certain elements between them. In *Havarie*, it is the dinghy with the stateless migrants floating on the open ocean that epitomizes despair and abject isolation to the tourists looking on from the big cruise ship. In the photo of the *St. Louis*, it is the big ocean liner that signifies abjection. The white European refugees it carries are victims of racial antisemitism compounded by the consequences of Cuba's neocolonization. Deprived of citizenship and rejected by the world, they are being watched by people escorting the liner out to sea in their dinghies or waving them goodbye from ashore. In both scenarios, the onlookers have a rightful place in the world while those they watch do not. Another photo (fig. E.13), which was originally published by a US newspaper and which has long been part of *St. Louis* memory culture, even more startlingly visualizes the monad's heuristic powers. It shows relatives of the passengers surrounding the *St. Louis* in small launches and dinghies, hoping to catch sight of their loved ones. The view of the ship's starboard side eerily corresponds to the view of the starboard side of the *Adventure of the Seas* in *Havarie*. Its placement of the big passenger ship in the

Figure E.13. Newspaper coverage of dinghies ringing the *St. Louis* in Havana harbor. *Source:* © Central Press. Public domain.

same frame as the dinghies makes the links to the scenario captured in *Havarie* even more pressing.

In Benjamin's well-known explanation, the monad's power is quasi-combustive. It involves a flash-like moment of recognition that "blasts open" history's continuum.[53] This flash is what *Havarie* potentially triggers. The film's defamiliarization of the cruise liner activates multidirectional memory, which may include images such as the press photo of the *St. Louis* in Havana harbor, images that have long existed "in the force field of public space," to use Rothberg's formulation. The mnemonic capacity of images thus resides in their intersection with other memory cultures—including *St. Louis* memory culture, which has been developing for over eighty-five years. When memory cultures intersect, they can help us relate events to each other in unforeseen manner and they can help us search for connections between different historical constellations. In performing this task, the historian contributes to illuminating what Glissant terms "the planetary drama of Relation." One way of doing so is to place different sets of historically persecuted peoples in relation to one another by diacritically comparing the causes of their displacement and the modes and trajectories of their journeys. Like other postcolonial thinkers, Glissant is not ignorant of the persecution of the Jews. His remarks on errantry include a notable passage that indicates that the uniqueness of the Jewish diaspora is not lost on him:

> The persecuted errantry, the wandering of the Jews, may have reinforced their sense of identity far more than their present settling in the land of Palestine. Being exiled Jews turned into a vocation of errantry, their point of reference an ideal land whose power may, in fact, have been undermined by concrete land (a territory), chosen and conquered. This, however, is mere conjecture. Because, while one can communicate through errantry's imaginary vision, the experiences of exiles are incommunicable.[54]

Keenly aware of the exile's ineffable despair, Glissant acknowledges every exile's desire for—and entitlement to—a home. To what extent that desire should lead to the establishment of a home*land* in the form of a nation state is something the Caribbean theorist leaves open. His world view and his philosophical project leads us to assume that he is invested in forms of existence that pose a vital alternative to nation states, for it is nation states that have historically been responsible for colonialism and that have committed genocide.

In contrast to the journeys Europe's Jews took across the Black Sea and Mediterranean toward Palestine to escape Nazi terror, the *St. Louis* voyage did not transpire in conjunction with projections of a future Jewish state. It exemplifies the open-endedly diasporic nature of Jewish culture. And, as this book has argued, it has much to teach us about the links between antisemitism and colonialism. Its trajectory compels Holocaust studies to expand its investigation of the antisemitic persecution of the Jews in the 1930s and the world's indifference to it from Europe to Latin America. This shift, in turn, markedly qualifies the epistemological status of colonialism within Holocaust studies. In 1951, a consideration of colonialism served

Hannah Arendt to make sense of the "final solution" by locating its roots in the Boers' and in Imperial Germany's genocidal treatment of their colonized African populations.[55] The *St. Louis* voyage forces us to relate the Holocaust also to the (neo)colonization of Latin America with its own genocides and histories of forced migration exemplified by, but not exclusive to, the Middle Passage. As my discussion of *Havarie* and the *St. Louis* incident through postcolonial notions of opacity and Relation has aimed to show, this change in perspective involves a shift in thinking away from a Eurocentric *pensée continentale* and toward a postcolonial—in this case, Caribbean—*pensée archipélique*, to borrow Drabinski's terminology.

As Rothberg's work on multidirectional memory has shown, continental philosophy engages in a ranking of genocides at the top of which it places the Holocaust. Like all genocides, the Holocaust represents an irrecuperable trauma. But continental thinking, as Drabinski explains, reads this irreparable rupture through Eurocentric preoccupations with ontologies and essences.[56] Those preoccupations seem to resurface in the perceived need for the Jewish people to establish roots, whereby the establishment of a concrete territory, as Glissant surmises, has come to compete with the notion of an ideal land as a utopian point of reference. The distribution of the Jewish people across the globe is evidence that there is nothing relativizing or dispossessive about reading the Jewish diaspora through the kind of archipelagic thinking that Glissant formulates in his theorization of the Middle Passage. Glissant, too, conceives of genocide as an irrecuperable trauma. But as his analysis of Caribbean culture has taught him, the way to negotiate the irreversible damages of the horrors of colonial mass murder and forced migration is to continue one's existence in diaspora's ever expanding wake. This creolized mode of existence affords the descendants of genocide's victims a chance to enter into systems of Relation that have the potential to overcome the destructive effects of colonialism and, by extension, the toxic presence of imperialism on world politics.

An application of this argument to Jewish history meets with the obvious caveat that Jews are not Africans. Their displacement and suffering differed from that which Africans incurred during the Middle Passage. It would be presumptuous, to say the least, to expect Holocaust survivors, most of whom were Europeans, to recast their trauma in anything but European terms. But how the trauma of the Holocaust is processed already changed with their children, the Second Generation. Citing the novelist Melvin Jules Bukiet, *The New York Times* recently pointed out that, "if a chasm opened in the lives of the First Generation, they could nonetheless sigh on the far side and recall the life Before . . . but for the Second Generation there is no Before. In the beginning was Auschwitz."[57] This circumstance has created its own set of inner turmoil for those affected. However, the fact that the Second Generation was forced to begin life as Jews in an ex nihilo state in which all aspects of the past had to compete with the far more immediate realities of post-traumatic existence makes that generation more comparable to other peoples who somehow managed to come out the other side of mass extermination, such as Afro-Caribbeans. To be sure, in contrast to the latter, the children of Holocaust survivors had a vast reservoir of memories at their disposal. But the fact that none of those memories were firsthand laid the seeds for a process of cultural rejuvenation marked by hybridization. This process is being continued by the Third Generation and its expansive hybridizing thrust is reflected in the changing socio-demographics of US American Jews, who are more secular, more open to marrying outside of the Jewish faith, and more willing to at least consider the possibility that the Holocaust, while unique, has not been the only trauma of mass displacement and decimation. My discussion of the cartoon *The St. Louis Refugee Ship Blues*, by Art Spiegelman, still a member of the Second Generation, has tried to make this clear.

That the persecution of Jews has not led to the same kind of creolization that transpired for Afro-Caribbeans is a historical fact. But the longue dureé history of the Jewish diaspora, which significantly predates the twentieth century and its framework of nation states, has no lack of affinities to Glissant's theory of Relation. There is a good reason why postcolonial scholars have let themselves be guided by Jewish history in their theorization of other diasporic formations. It evinces an even greater sprawl than Afro-Caribbean culture and its generative powers have been hugely impactful. It would be no exaggeration to call it one of humankind's great carriers of civilizational progress and hope.

It will take many more mnemonic images such as those furnished by *Havarie* to demonstrate the protean possibilities of entering into Relation. This despite the fact that the frequent invocation of the *St. Louis* in mainstream press critiques of the "Fortress Europe" and of

US immigration policy suggest that a comparative approach to forced migration is already a mundane practice. The poet Amanda Gorman has recently sketched out correspondences between Mediterranean migration and the Middle Passage. Her description is broad enough to allow for the inclusion of the Jewish migrant crisis: "these two occurrences," Gorman writes, "share the cruelty and global apathy that allowed them. And the result is fundamentally similar: humans denied their homes, their humanity, and, far too often, their lives."[58]

Part III

Figure A.1. Captain Gustav Schröder. *Source*: Courtesy of United States Holocaust Memorial Museum.

Appendix 1

Introduction to Gustav Schröder and His Accounts of Voyage 98

The documents published in translation in these appendixes are accounts of Voyage 98 written by Gustav Schröder. The central source is his slim book *Heimatlos auf hoher See* (*Homeless on the High Seas*; see appendix 2). A second source is several unpublished manuscript pages related to the Cuba voyage, given to me by Schröder's grandnephew Jürgen Glaevecke. As there is overlap between the unpublished pages and the published book, I have not included them in full. Instead, wherever an interesting discrepancy between the published and unpublished version appears, I have inserted translated passages from the original manuscript and linked them to the relevant passages in the published text via footnoted annotations. The other two accounts of the trip (appendix 3) consist of translations of the captain's logs, which Schröder was required to file with HAPAG as an official record of the eastbound and westbound legs of the voyage. The third log is a brief confidential addendum to the second log.

Gustav Schröder

A brief biographical sketch of Schröder has to suffice to illustrate his background and career. My account owes to two sources, Schröder's grandnephew Jürgen Glaevecke, with whom I have had an illuminating conversation and correspondence about Schröder, and Heinz Burmester, who was Schröder's colleague at HAPAG before the war and who wrote an authoritative biographical article about Schröder.[1]

Schröder was born on September 27, 1885, in the north German town of Hadersleben, located in a small swath of land that, after Germany's defeat in World War I, was given to Denmark and has remained Danish. His father was a high-school teacher. Schröder left high school at the age of 16, after completing his junior year, to begin his seafaring career. He got his start as a seaman on a tall ship, the non-commercial full-rigged training ship *Grossherzogin Elisabeth*, on which he sailed from 1902 to 1903. His slight build made it difficult for Schröder to continue on other large sailing ships, which was a prerequisite for obtaining the rank of helmsman. He doggedly worked his way up on the HAPAG passenger liner *Deutschland* (where the company's legendary director, Albert Ballin, on a brief inspection tour, met Schröder and encouraged him to reapply to HAPAG after having obtained the higher rank), the small fore-and-aft schooner *Albert*, and eventually the freight barks *Titania* and *Bertha*, which were large enough to afford Schröder with necessary training credentials. After attending navigation school, Schröder obtained the helmsman qualification at the end of 1908.

Through further schooling, and after having spent over four years as crew on sailing ships, he earned his captain's license in early 1912 and was promptly hired back by HAPAG, for which he sailed as third officer on cargo steamers around the world. In that capacity, he found himself in India at the beginning of World War I and was interned there for five years by the British. He used the time to co-found a male chorus and a gymnastics club and he taught languages, navigation, and astronomy to fellow inmates. When the Spanish flu reached the camp in 1918, Schröder helped out as a nurse assistant. He did not return to Germany until 1920. By then, his north German hometown of Hadersleben had become Danish with the Versailles treaty. Hoping that Hitler would reclaim their territory, its inhabitants eventually founded a Danish counterpart of the NSDAP. It is unclear, however, whether this moved Schröder, who did not return there but settled in Hamburg, to seek NSDAP membership. The second, perhaps more plausible, reason is that in Nazi Germany, all merchant mariners were expected to join the party. Not doing so could jeopardize one's career.[2]

Having settled in Germany, Schröder married Elsa Färber in 1921. Two years later, their mentally disabled son Rolf was born.

The Versailles Treaty had almost completely dismantled the German merchant fleet after the war, but HAPAG was able to employ Schröder on the steamer *Frankfurt*, whose diminutive size spared it from being used as war reparation. As discussed in chapter 2, however, by the mid-1920s, HAPAG was able to bypass the worst effects of the Versailles Treaty. After sailing as cargo officer on the HAPAG freighter *Steigerwald*, Schröder between 1926 and 1935 sailed as either second or first officer on increasingly large ships, including SS *General Artiga*, SS *Gera*, and SS *Hansa* (formerly *Albert Ballin*)—and also on the MS *St. Louis*. Despite Schröder's captain's license and his extensive expertise as a navigator—he regularly contributed articles on navigation to a professional journal—he had to wait for several years until HAPAG promoted him to the rank of captain. The world economic crisis had caused much of the merchant marine to lie fallow in the early 1930s and there was a backlog of promotions at HAPAG.

In 1935, Schröder sailed as first officer on the *St. Louis* for a cruise to Madeira that promoted cruise tourism organized by the NS organization KdF (Kraft durch Freude—Strength Through Joy) and that also included two other German liners, *Oceana* and *Der Deutsche*. It was the first of ten cruises on which Schröder served on the *St. Louis* in that capacity. In 1936, HAPAG promoted Schröder to captain and gave him the command of a small freighter, *Kyphissia*, but the following year, his outstanding service record as officer on the *St. Louis* for the KdF cruises prompted HAPAG to reassign him to captain the *Oceana*, with which he would undertake fifty weeklong cruises for KdF in 1937 and 1938. His successful command of the *Oceana* earned him promotion to substitute captain for HAPAG's quartet of fast transatlantic liners *Hamburg, Deutschland, New York*, and *Hansa*. In February and March 1939, Schröder for the first time sailed on the *St. Louis* as captain, taking the ship on two transatlantic crossings to New York. He retained command of the ship for the rest of the year and, indeed, his remaining career, first on the historic voyage to Cuba and then on three cruises, one to the Caribbean, one to Bermuda, and one to Halifax. As mentioned in chapter 3, shortly before the war Schröder received order to return the *St. Louis* to Europe. After evading the British blockade by taking the ship to Murmansk and eventually returning it to Hamburg on January 1, 1940, Schröder retired from active captain's duty and went to work for the German Nautical Observatory for several years. In 1950, Schröder officially retired from active professional life and spent his remaining years editing and publishing his diaries from his earlier trips. On February 4, 1957, he received the Bundesverdienstkreuz am Bande (Federal Cross of Merit on Ribbon) for his "service to people and country through his rescuing of emigrants" (Verdienste um Volk und Land bei der Rettung von Emigranten). He died on January 10, 1959, and is buried in a cemetery near the river Elbe. In 1989, the City of Hamburg named a street after him (Kapitän-Schröder-Weg). In the early 1990s, several former *St. Louis* passengers wrote to Yad Vashem in Israel to induct Schröder into the "Righteous among the Nations." They stress in their letters that by helping the passengers the way he did, Schröder risked his career and his well-being. Yad Vashem inducted him in 1993.

Homeless on the High Seas

Homeless on the High Seas was not the first book Schröder published. In 1940, after he had returned the *St. Louis* to Germany and had moved from captain's duties to lending the German Maritime Observatory his expertise as a navigator, he began transforming decades of seafaring diaries and notes into publishable form. In 1941, he published his first book, *Fernweh und Heimweh* (Wanderlust and homesickness). The 237-page book compiled impressions ranging from Schröder's early seafaring career on tall ships to his service for HAPAG, including his fifty trips he made with the *Oceana* for KdF. After publishing *Heimatlos auf hoher See* in 1949, which was specifically about his Cuba voyage on the *St. Louis*, in the 1950s Schröder published two more books, in which he recycled some of his earlier memories as a seafarer and which appear to have focused mostly on his tall-ship period and his observation of maritime animal life. In the early 1950s, he published *Mein Albatros und andere Tiergeschichten* (My albatross and other animal tales) and in 1956 *Unter Segel um die Welt* (Around the world under sail). These books reflect his love of nature and of seafaring, and testify to his desire to express himself through the medium of literature, even though his literary skills were those of an amateur with a proclivity for impressionistic formulations.

While Schröder's love of the ocean and of seafaring also seems to have informed his first book, *Fernweh und Heimweh*, that book awaits closer assessment. Its contents and the fate of its publisher may have been a factor why Schröder had to publish his account of the Cuba voyage without an actual publisher, using what appears to have been a print-on-demand facility (the long-defunct Becker Druck, Berlin). Schröder published *Fernweh und Heimweh* with the once-illustrious publisher Rütten & Loening. Founded in Frankfurt am Main in 1844, the company was one of the most prestigious publishing houses in Germany for much of the nineteenth century and into the 1930s. (Among other titles, the company held ownership of Struwwelpeter, the classic collection of illustrated educational parables for children.) In 1936, its Jewish owners, as a result of the Nuremberg Laws, sold the company to a non-Jewish publisher, who moved it to Potsdam and eliminated its roster of notable Jewish authors. It is this new iteration of the company that published *Fernweh und Heimweh* in 1941. The book's thematic focus on seafaring adventures, maritime life, and nature was compatible with the kind of literature that NS ideology deemed worthy supplements to its broader ideological framework of romanticizing nature and promoting self-sustaining masculinity. An additional factor for the book's appeal to its "Aryanized" publisher appears to have been that it included detailed descriptions of the many cruises Schröder undertook as a captain for KdF. Burmester points out that, while Schröder's accounts of those cruises did not glorify the NS State that provided the superstructure for KdF, they reflected the satisfaction he took in the fact that, by fulfilling his professional duty, he could help make cruise tourism accessible for middle-class Germans.

We do not know whether this circumstance became a direct liability for Schröder after the war and proved an obstacle for him to publish his account of the Cuba voyage. The fact is that with the defeat of Nazi Germany, Potsdam came under Soviet military governance and the publisher of *Fernweh und Heimweh* was entrusted to another publisher that purged many of its contemporary titles, including Schröder's book. This aspect—along with the fact that the division of Germany into two countries in 1949 caused a rift in the German-language publishing scene—may have added to the challenges for Schröder to find an established publisher for *Heimatlos auf hoher See*.

Figure A.2. Title page of *Heimatlos auf hoher See* by Gustav Schröder. *Source:* Public domain.

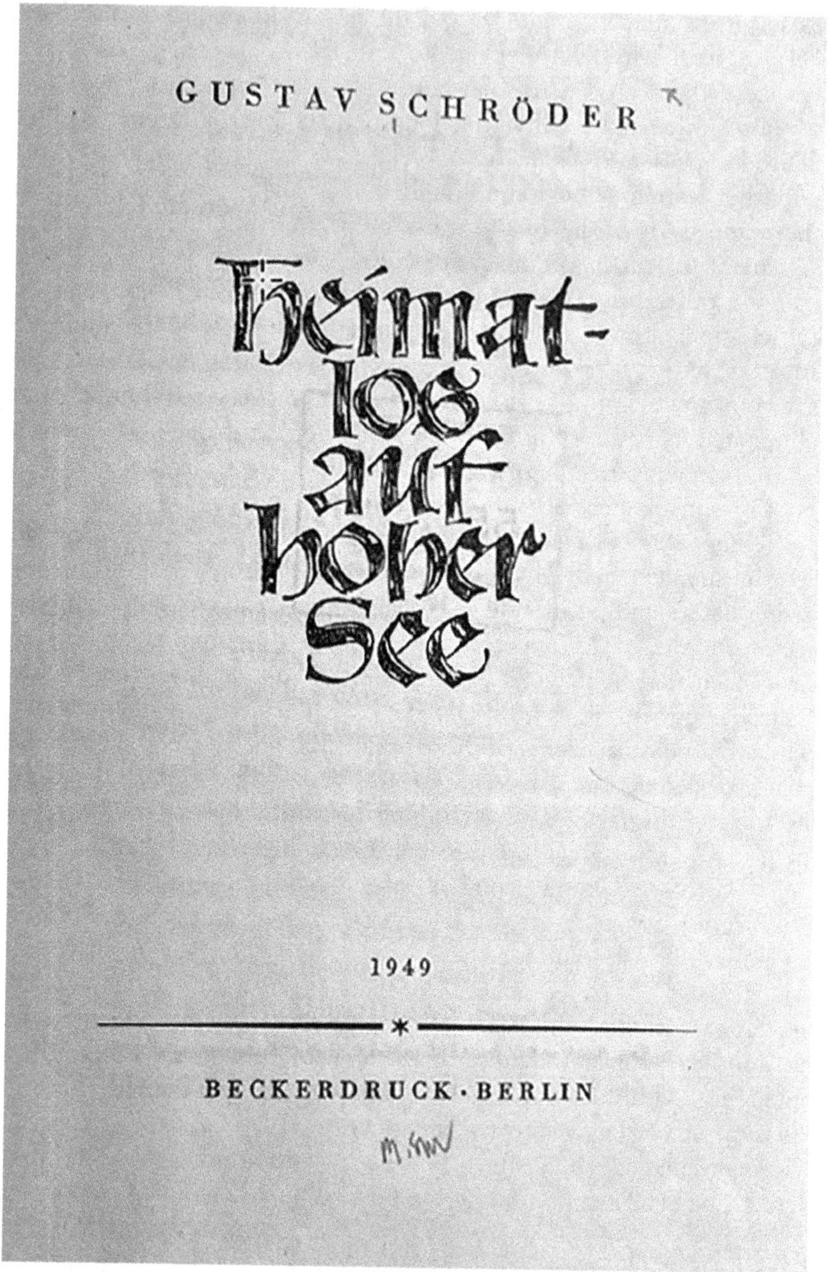

GUSTAV SCHRÖDER

Heimat-
los
auf
hoher
See

1949

BECKERDRUCK · BERLIN

Appendix 2

Homeless on the High Seas (1949)
by Gustav Schröder, translated by Roy Grundmann

The Subject

In June, 1939, the *St. Louis* of the Hamburg America Line was scheduled to undertake cruises from New York. But before that, in May, she was deployed to transport 900 emigrants from Hamburg to Havana. Because Cuba's government declined permission to land, the voyage turned into an adventure for the ship.[1] The international press followed the story much more closely than it had covered earlier, smaller yet similar endeavors.

The drama *Schipper naast God*, written by the Dutchman Jan de Hartog and superbly translated and edited for the German stage by Rolf Italiaander under the title *Schiff ohne Hafen* (Ship without harbor)[2] caused me to recall those events that I had already forgotten during the long war. I do not know what specific incident inspired the dramatist to write this play, set on a small Dutch steamer carrying 146 emigrants. After several failed attempts to land, the captain who is responsible for these people realizes that no country is willing to accept his unlucky passengers. He sinks his own ship in proximity of the US Navy in order to force the warships to rescue the stateless and declare them shipwrecked so they get taken to land. The play excels in depicting the desperate mood of the emigrants and the concerns and challenges faced by those in charge of the ship that I had similarly experienced. Despite the play's sparse staging, it was highly dramatic and devastating.

The following factual report by no means intends to compete with the artistry of the poet. It is a straightforward chronicle of my experiences as the captain of the *St. Louis* with the 900 emigrants. I want to go on record that the Dutch play is not a representation of the voyage of the *St. Louis*, as many seem to believe after reading news items to the contrary. The crew depicted in the play commit acts of violence against the passengers. This is something that never happened on the *St. Louis*. The passengers were not harmed in the slightest. The foreign press confirmed this.

Already before *St. Louis*'s departure from Hamburg there was talk that the landing in Havana might cause problems, despite the fact that each passenger had purchased an entry visa signed by the Cuban immigration office. There were rumors that certain disruptions and changes in domestic politics could prevent a landing. From the beginning, the passengers were thus a bit nervous. Nonetheless, most seemed to be convinced that they would never see Germany again. Touching farewells took place. Some looked relieved; others left their old homeland with a heavy heart.

But soon enough, nice weather, a pure sea breeze, good food, and attentive service created the carefree mood characteristic of long sea voyages. Once at sea, the burdens and the sadness of life on land evaporate like tiny bubbles. A hospitable ship crossing the wide ocean in a stretch of calm weather is another world altogether. That was the case here as well. Optimism and hope blossomed and no one was upset.

As we came closer to our destination, the big city we were approaching cast its shadows over us. Telegrams alluded to problems at disembarkation. In addition, an old teacher, Moritz Weiler, became ill and apathetic. It broke his heart that he had been forced to leave the place where he had worked all his life in harmony with his colleagues.[3] The ship's medic, Dr. Glauner, led me to the patient. One no longer sensed his will to live. Moritz Weiler's last wish was to die at sea. He passed away the same day. Together with his widow, I sent a telegram to his son, who lived in New York, so that he could pick up his mother in Havana.

The passengers were concerned that a dead body on board could further jeopardize the landing. And so, in accordance with his widow, we quietly buried the deceased at sea. Unfortunately, his would not remain the only death. Hardly had we completed the funeral ceremony and restarted the engines when a young man from the Baltic, who worked in the kitchen with his brother, jumped overboard from the same spot at the railing where the coffin had been placed. I immediately turned the ship around, had a lifeboat lowered, and the whole scene illuminated with spotlights, but to no avail. All our boat retrieved was the rescue buoy with its water light. We had to lock up his brother, because he too was trying to end his life.

Prohibition to Land

We moored the ship at the pier in Havana as scheduled at 4 a.m. and immediately began with disembarkation in order to preempt any bans preventing us from landing.[4] We could not believe our eyes when armed guards in uniform appeared, forcing those who had already disembarked back on board and occupying the gangway. The emigrants came very close to forcing their way onto land. Their anger was all too understandable. Here was a state, after all, that definitely disagreed with Germany's laws about Jews and that, against payment, had granted the emigrants temporary stay in its capital. But now, after having received the money, Cuba refused to accept the passengers at the very moment they were about to disembark? I don't remember all the paperwork I completed, all the in-person appointments I went to, and all the telegrams I sent asking for help. The success was nil.

Cuba Does Not Relent

During the five days we were anchored in Havana, no passenger was allowed to go ashore. And their many relatives, who had come to the capital to meet them, were not allowed to visit them on board. Only the son of Herr Weiler, who had died at sea, received permission to visit his mother, thanks to my lobbying and assurances. But not one of our many petitions had been able to move the government officials to permit the landing. Nobody—no committee and no influential American citizen—succeeded in changing their minds. Cuba did not relent. But I never learned the reason. I engaged legal counsel and sued the government. I told the lawyer that, in my opinion, the government's attitude is comparable with that of a man who invites a guest for a meal only to force him to wait in the lobby before having him thrown out. I spent much time waiting in the offices of the palace and the government. I requested an audience, but no one received me or Herr Clasing, HAPAG's local agent. A representative of the Joint

Committee assured the disappointed passengers that despite of all the difficulties, everything humanly possible was being done to avoid a return to Germany.[5] But the words "return to Germany" shouldn't have been uttered. That was a psychological faux pas! The concern among the passengers grew. Several people tried to commit suicide.[6] A lawyer, Dr. Max Loew, slashed his wrists and jumped overboard, oddly enough from the same spot on deck where the earlier funeral and suicide had taken place. Two of my brave sailors immediately jumped after him and brought him, who was fighting so hard for his death, back on board, leaving Dr. Glauner enough time to save him. His condition and the suspicion that he had gone mad garnered sympathy for him. He was permitted ashore and was transferred to a hospital. But I was unable to arrange for Dr. Loew's wife and children to accompany him. The Cuban immigration authorities remained unsympathetic. I pointed their lack of sympathy out to them when I submitted a new request, proposing to house the emigrants in a small town or on a small island.

The response I received came in the form of an ultimatum. I was ordered to remove the ship from the harbor at once; otherwise, the ship would be removed by force. Again, I went ashore and, with the help of the local German diplomat, I negotiated that the departure be postponed until the following day in order to allow us to take on water and provisions.

On board I had the following statement posted:

"The Cuban government forces us to leave the harbor tomorrow. This departure, which is scheduled for 10 a.m., does not mean that negotiations have been terminated. It is the prerequisite for the Joint Committee to be allowed to step in. The ship management will remain in contact with all organizations and government offices and is trying everything to obtain permission to land. We will remain in the proximity of the American coast."

Another post said:

"The ship management has requested that the gentlemen listed below represent the interests of the passengers: Dr. Weiß, H. Manasse, Legal Counsel Dr. Joseph, Legal Counsel Dr. Zellner, Legal Counsel Dr. Hausdorff. Ship management will update these gentlemen on all measures. The passengers are asked to rely exclusively on statements, which the ship management releases through the formed committee."

My managers of the ship's various divisions received the following directions:

"Due to the uncertain situation in which our passengers find themselves, the atmosphere is very tense. Everything must be done to calm them down. So far, our crew has kept up good manners in treating the passengers. Please ensure that **all** crew members respond to the passengers in calm, polite manner. Questions about the next port destination must always be answered by referring to the posted statements.—Inform every crew member about these instructions."

All three statements are given here in slightly abridged form.

Whereto?

And then we put to sea. Numerous dinghies accompanied us with relatives shouting, "Don't despair!" But many did despair. I, too, was depressed. I had never experienced such a melancholy departure. The women in particular were restless due to the lack of any posted destination. "Captain, where are you taking us?" For the first time in my life, I was unable to answer this question. But in close cooperation with the board committee, I tried everything to make these unhappy people reach a new home. I had orders from HAPAG to do everything in my power for the passengers.

I even had the idea to attempt an illegal landing on the coast of Florida. The passengers were on standby for disembarkation. I had arranged that with the board committee. And so, one fine morning, we entered one of the small ports, just to test whether or not this move was being anticipated and whether measures to address it were under way. A small immigrant ship may have tried this before us, because when entering the harbor, I immediately noticed that we were being observed. When we reached our place of anchorage, planes and Coast Guard cutters approached us to prevent us from landing. So, I steered the ship back out of port.[7] Staying close to the coast to keep the passengers calm and distracted, I took a southwest course toward Havana. During lunchtime, when everyone was assembled in the dining hall, I turned away from the coast until land was out of sight. When the sun was highest, I slowly changed the course to north-northeast; that way, no one was able to notice that we were once again moving away from Havana, where hopes for us to land were still kept alive. Personally, I no longer believed in this possibility. I tried to take a northward stealth course, because it appeared that a new option had just emerged in New York. But by late afternoon, when the sinking sun left no doubt about our going north, everyone became concerned again.

In those days of uncertainty, I decided, among other things, to permit Herr Manasse to send a telegram to the US press that conveyed the atmosphere on board in blunt terms. It triggered a flood of wires from Havana, New York, Hamburg, and God knows where. Some told us to turn by, others to stay put and wait. Yet others tried to give us courage and indicated that tireless efforts were underway to find a solution. We could only shake our heads in disbelief. Appreciative as we were, we wondered what could possibly be so difficult about that. The whole problem could be solved with a stroke of the pen. One of the telegrams announced that officials had permitted us to land on the Cuban island Pinosa. The telegram was signed "Centro Israelita." We stopped the ship and requested official confirmation. After a while, news came that the decision had not yet been made. Nothing came of it. A long telegram from the master of a large Masonic lodge asked me to come to New York and lie at anchor. With the help of influential Americans, he would put up any sum necessary. The intention was to appeal to the US Congress to ask for "quick asylum" for the *St. Louis* passengers. I answered asking that the required sum be deposited with HAPAG New York. Nothing came of this either.

Back?

When it became clearer and clearer that landing in America was hopeless, we had no choice but to expedite our return. Our supply of engine oil, provisions, and water permitted no further cruising around. Soon enough, the corresponding order arrived. Port of destination: Cuxhaven—which, however, I kept a secret because I was determined not to go there. A voyage through the North Sea seemed very dangerous, if not utterly unfeasible, given the mental constitution of the passengers, who kept lapsing into despair. With the help of the gulf stream and the dark nights, I had already maneuvered the ship to the exit of the Florida Strait. For the moment, I decided to steer toward a point that was equidistant from New York, Havana, and Haiti, so that in case of positive news, I could return to one of these points as quickly as possible. It is near Bermuda. At the same time, I focused all my thoughts on a landing in England. I remember that in those days I had exchanged telegrams with the banker Warburg in New York without, however, learning anything positive. On June 7, the following telegram arrived:

"As landing in Cuba remains undecided, we are trying St. Domingo, where landing is possible, pending availability of funds required for immigration." This plan, too, failed. Gradually, one no longer knew whether to trust any news at all.

Worrisome Days

In the midst of all this hopelessness the collaboration with the board committee turned out to be extremely valuable. The committee received a boost through the addition of S. Gutmann [sic] and Dr. Ernst Vendig.[8] Without our daily briefings, I don't think I would have been able to cope with the nerve-racking situation on board. Each day, we sent several telegrams to Hamburg in order to inform the directorship about the critical atmosphere on board and finally bring our odyssey to an end. The contents were composed in German. At night, I translated the telegrams into English, because that was the language of our secret code. This was followed by additional enciphering. That is how I passed the bleak nights, during which I could not have slept anyway.

In addition to the board committee, there was a spiritual comfort committee, founded by Gustav Weil, which provided assistance during the numerous nervous breakdowns. The doctors on board had to take care of other patients. At times, the spiritual support team sought my help. They brought the desperate passengers to see me and I had to comfort them. When all words of succor failed, we resorted to telling a white lie by promising a landing in England. During this time, Mr. Weil and I became friends. I also recall that Leo Haas and his wife came to me during those days, and the words of this fine woman still ring in my ear: "Captain, we really cannot go back. We've lost everything and the concentration camp will be our end—or the North Sea. If you take the ship to Cuxhaven, you will likely find 100 cabins empty, because we fear the concentration camp more than death." Others told me something similar.

There were some men who had been in a concentration camp. When I asked them about their experiences, they looked around furtively, as if they feared people listening in. I asked if it was forbidden to speak about that. They gave me a look of embarrassment and fell silent. My dear Captain, it is true that I don't dare talk about it, because who knows what awaits us. But trust me, better dead than having to experience that again. Their eyes betrayed a terrible fear of returning there, but also a resolve to do everything for a rescue. Any empathetic look into such desperate eyes remains something unforgettable.

It did not really surprise me, then, when a concerned couple, traveling with their children, told me about a sabotage committee that was meeting below in the ship. The couple had overheard discussion about a plan to bring about a catastrophe in the North Sea. The idea was to set fire to the ship, but other actions, to be tried even sooner, were also being discussed—such as mutiny. At that moment, the only thing I could do was to advise them to form an anti-sabotage committee that could check on the arsonists. I would have loved to have a serious word with those arsonists but they sensed that their cover had been blown and started to keep a low profile. I had no choice but to keep the bridge fortified and to place the whole ship under close surveillance.

The Crisis

On the day of our anticipated noontime arrival at said point of equidistance, I awoke at sunrise sitting in my leather chair. I must have fallen asleep around 4 a.m. after having completed all telegrams. Unfortunately, cruising in the middle of the Atlantic with 900 passengers, whom no nation in the world wanted to accept, had turned out not to be a dream. And I felt unease at the realization that I would no longer be able to maintain discipline on board by holding up any hope for a landing in the West.[9] It was now my sad duty to tell the passengers the truth that there was no longer any hope of a landing in America. Last night's telegrams had confirmed that. The East, too, showed no sign of acceptance. From New York the following message came: "We regret . . . but we consider the response of the Joint Committee accurate." That response read: "We are doing everything humanly possible to help you. We ask that you keep up hope and ensure you that all our organizations here and abroad are working for you day and night."[10] I knew that no one, including myself, could take this telegram as anything but America's final refusal and that today was a day of the most critical order. After I visited the bridge to plan the course for entry into the English Channel, I made the rounds through the ship. There was despair everywhere. Querying looks met me at every turn. In front of the dining hall, I ran into two gentlemen from the board committee, Dr. Joseph and Dr. Zellner, who likewise could no longer keep calm. I handed them the telegrams, telling them, "No more hope expected from the West. I am asking the committee to meet me at 10 a.m." "How can I tell my child?" Dr. Joseph asked me. Dr. Zellner added, "Captain, I am no coward, but I dread going through the North Sea." Quietly, I whispered into his ear, "Me too." But as I continued on my way, a saving thought entered my mind so suddenly that I stopped in my tracks. I thought of a plan that had to be worked out at once. The First Officer was still asleep because of his late shift the night before. So I went to the Chief Engineer, an early riser who was having his morning coffee. I had come to the right person. Upon my request, he immediately phoned orders to his officer on watch to increase the engine's RPMs, adding quite a few. Then I took the phone to notify the officer on the bridge about the increased speed. After that, we had enough time to discuss my plan.

In case we would be denied landing outside of Germany and in order to avoid the catastrophe that was looming in the North Sea, we intended to gently set the ship aground off England's sandy south coast at low tide and at night or during fog. We would pretend the engine had broken down, stage a sizable fire on board, and land all passengers with the lifeboats. After that, we would "heroically" extinguish the fire ourselves. Following the removal of the shipwrecked passengers, we could refloat the ship at high tide and with the help of a tugboat. We'd officially have to operate only on one engine, and after relieving the tugs of their duty, we would telegraph them our goodbyes and take course to the nearest "port of refuge." I had already picked a spot for this maneuver. There were several possibilities between Plymouth and Dover.

The Chief Engineer gave me a lot of good advice in preparing the plan. As arranged, he never divulged a word about this to anyone, even after landing in Antwerp had made our ruse unnecessary. While the rescue plan would ultimately not be executed, on this critical day it allowed me to focus and gain a perspective that enabled me to cope with the events that were about to unfold. The increased anxiety on board caused the board committee to meet with me already before 10 o'clock. Something must have leaked out about the termination of talks with the "New World." While we held counsel as to what could be done to calm the passengers, the First Officer reported that there was great unrest on board and that passengers were joining forces for a plot. Soon after, a fireman reported that some were already on their way up. The "sabotage committee," I assumed. In their excitement, those desperate young men surely were up to no good. They had to be prevented at all cost from reaching the, by now, fortified bridge.

What I did next, I did instinctively. I asked the First Officer to stay with the board committee and rushed down the main stairs, where the anxious crowd was already coming toward me with great noise. I blocked the stairs and shouted "Stop! What do you want?" which did in fact stop them in their tracks. But that was all my voice could effect. I was surrounded and there was a lot of shouting. I heard things like "We don't want to return to Europe!" "We will force him to turn back!" "We will set fire!" One of those men came to my help by shouting: "Quiet! The captain wants to speak!"[11] That had an impact. I broke the fraught silence with my promise, made in good conscience, that we would somehow manage a landing in England. But I added an urgent plea not to do anything rash that could spoil this chance. But to bring this incident to a close, I called a general assembly in the Great Hall and requested that all passengers be informed of it. The same men who had just acted so excitedly now followed my order with discipline and the hall began to fill up.[12]

The board committee breathed a sigh of relief when I returned and reported the fortunate turn of events. It was decided that one of its members was going to address the crowd. Until then, the committee had understandably not placed much confidence in holding large assemblies, but at this critical point in time it became imperative.

On the way to the hall, we exchanged a few words in confidence and soon thereafter we were facing nine hundred people who were literally homeless. I, too, started to feel a sense of homelessness. I felt as though every single person on the *St. Louis* had been expelled by the world and was now forced to leave this inhospitable planet—because the ship's crew could not expect any appreciation for their pro-Semitic attitude from the government. But it was exactly this feeling that made me so empathetic toward my passengers in their desolate situation and it enabled me to find the right words for my introduction. I then asked the president of the committee, Dr. Joseph, to speak, and he rose to the task as if on a mission.

To this day I regret not having copied down his impromptu speech. It was a masterpiece both in terms of form and content. Dr. Joseph filled all hearts with trust and called for a dignified attitude. "No matter what happens, the whole world is watching us!" he exclaimed. And over the next few days, the effect of his words began to show in the behavior of these heavily tried people.

Of course, I reported the incident to Hamburg in an encrypted telegram. There, too, one became increasingly convinced that crossing the North Sea would be irresponsible and that only a landing in western Europe could still save the emigrants. The Hamburg America Line initiated negotiations to this effect. Three days later, these led to the offer to land in Antwerp, so that the emigrants could be distributed to England, France, Holland, and Belgium. HAPAG sent us an astutely worded telegram that subtly indicated the intended solution and advised the passengers to stay calm and maintain order so as not to jeopardize their prospects of asylum.

Further general assemblies were able to maintain the emigrants' composure. Each morning, we met in the Great Hall. After three days we received final positive news about being allowed to dock in Antwerp. Although the many disappointments had made some passengers distrustful, in due time a sense of calm and contentedness began to spread. Once again, one could see optimistic people and hear music that for the past several weeks would have been considered out of place.

The landing in Antwerp had to be performed quickly because *St. Louis* was put back into the cruise schedule out of New York from which it had already been removed. With the wind blowing from aft at wind force 7–8, we sailed eastward at full steam. I sent off a telegram to Vlissingen and committed to an arrival two days from then at 9 o'clock precisely.

Unfortunately, we did not complete the final stretch without a tragic incident. My best helmsman—his name was Kritsch—had gone missing. He was last seen on the aft deck at the halyard.[13] Following a thorough search of the ship we found him in a small storage room in the forecastle, where he had put an end to his life. God knows why. His death was an irreplaceable loss both for me and for the Hamburg America Line, because there was hardly a more reliable person. Thinking about death's cruel finality depressed me for the third time on this voyage.

The only ones who during all those days never allowed themselves to get worried were the children among the passengers. They rejoiced in spending more time on board. They acknowledged their predicament playfully by inventing a game called "No entry for Jews!" Two boys with a stern, official look on their faces positioned themselves at a barrier made up of two chairs and interrogated their comrades, who requested entry. A little boy from Berlin, whose turn it was, was yelled at: "Are you a Jew?" When he answered "yes" in a subdued tone, they harshly rejected him: "No entry for Jews!" "Just let me pass through," he begged. "I'm only a small child!"[14]

Emigrant Fate

We arrived in Antwerp on time thanks to the favorable weather and the ship functioning reliably, and thanks also to the exemplary attitude of the crew who had mastered a task that demanded not only strength and perseverance, but also much patience and tact. They were frequently aided by the board committee and the spiritual support committee. This fact deserves special recognition.[15] But it would all have been in vain if the passengers had not been so cooperative. Their gratitude toward me at the disembarkation in Antwerp was touching and moved me deeply and unforgettably.[16] Thus, it makes me even sadder that many of those poor souls, who finally believed themselves in safety in France, Holland, and Belgium, because of the insane war would still end up falling into the hands of criminals and perish. It is more than depressing to think that there were people who first were in a concentration camp, then suffered the *St. Louis*'s odyssey, only to be recaptured and taken away to their miserable deaths in a concentration camp. I only know of a few of the *St. Louis* emigrants who made it to shore and are still alive. Among them are:

>Dr. Ernst Vendig and family
>Arthur Maschkowsky
>Adolf Wolff and family
>Leo Haas and wife

I am still in touch with the following gentlemen of the group that went to England, all of whom survived:

>Gustav Weil
>Dr. F. Kassel
>Dr. F. Zellner

I also want to give an account of the refugee experiences of the Wolff and Vendig families. Adolf Wolff and his wife and daughter were in

Northern France and fled to Marseille during the German invasion with throngs of others and under the most difficult conditions. In Marseille they were able to elude being interned. But in 1942, when there was a search for Jews, they had no choice but to flee to Switzerland. They still cannot believe that this adventure turned out well. It was only in 1947 that they were able to go to North America.

Dr. Ernst Vendig, his seventy-year-old mother, and his wife and two children were in Brussels during the German invasion. He was interned and, after having encountered twelve different camps, ended up in the region of Aix-en-Provence. His family's initial attempt to follow him was foiled by the bombing of Dunkirk. But they eventually succeeded despite all difficulties. Beginning in 1942, here too all Jews were being deported to Poland. The whole family was interned in a camp, where for six weeks they witnessed the horrors of deportation. Owing to a miraculous coincidence, they were spared and eventually freed. They, too, fled to Switzerland, where, following long marches on foot through the mountains, they were taken in by relatives. Since May 1946, they have lived in North America, where they, just like the Wolff family, have built a new existence.

Arthur Maschkowsky and Leo Haas, along with others, have asked me who issued the prohibition to land in Havana and how this whole thing had even come to pass. I never found out and have long since given up trying to find clarification. Answering questions about guilt is not something I am comfortable with. And maybe those whom fate had picked to play a decisive role are no longer alive.

This makes me think of one of my old teachers, who always preached tolerance to us pupils. He never uttered a bad word about another person, not even about his opponents. "Do not resent one another," he said, "a really educated person does not do that. Those who do something wrong punish themselves much more than others could." In this sense, I humbly leave the question of guilt unanswered. How much nicer is it to talk about gratitude, gratitude for all the good that others do by us. I have to thank countless people who helped me make life for our *St. Louis* passengers as pleasant as possible. But we shall never forget the warning to all of humanity that lies in the meaning of the tragic fate of the heavily tried passengers of the "emigrant ship," so that cruelty and inhumanity can never again spread anywhere.

Appendix of Documents

Hamburg America Line

The Cuban government is forcing us to leave the harbor. It has permitted us to stay here until day tomorrow and departure has herewith been set for

10 o'clock Friday morning

By no means does the departure mean the abortion of negotiations. The status achieved by the ship's departure is the prerequisite for the intervention of Mr. Berenson and his collaborators.

The ship management remains in contact with all Jewish organizations and all offices and will do everything to enable a landing outside of Germany and, for the moment, we will remain in the vicinity of the coast of America.

Schröder

Captain

∼

Havana remains hopeful. We expect definitive arrangements today.

HAPAG New York—3/6/39

∼

Negotiations continue—please telegraph the last possible moment when your provisions allow you to return to Havana or Santo Domingo.

HAPAG New York—7/6/39

∼

As per wire from New York Warburg and Central Committee make every possible effort to avoid return to Europe.

HAPAG Hamburg—8/6/39

∼

We know your situation—are trying everything with the help of relevant international organizations to find a solution—news about results to follow—

Aid Organization Berlin—8/6/39

∼

Warm Greetings—we are still hard at work—keep up your hopes—

Joint Havana—8/6/39

∼

As the European chair of the American Joint Distribution Committee, I want to assure you of every possible option to find a potentially promising harbor along the way for the St. Louis passengers—we hope to have something more definitive in this regard within the next 36 hours—tell the passengers they should keep up hope

Morris C Troper Paris—12/6/39

∼

Spoke to management today—you can rest assured that everything possible is being tried

Max Warburg New York—12/6/39

∼

Declared port of disembarkation for all passengers is definitively Antwerp from where they will be distributed to the Netherlands, Belgium, France, and England

HAPAG Hamburg—15/6/39

~

Hamburg America Line
16 June 1939
Board
Honored Captain Schröder!

With these lines the Board of the Hamburg America Line wishes to express to you upon arrival in Antwerp its gratitude for having returned the "St. Louis" safely.

The task that presented itself to you and your crew was not an easy one. The purser's report, which has reached us, provides a good illustration of your voyage and has fully met with our approval. The impossibility of landing the passengers in Cuba confronted you with new challenges and your telegrams allowed us to follow with great concern your return to Europe. We congratulate you on your ability to steer the ship, your crew, and your passengers through those critical days and we hope that your crossing to New York will allow you to find new strength in order to complete the New York-based cruises with success.

Kindly requesting that you will convey our gratitude and respect also to your crew, we remain

Hamburg America Line

signed Hoffmann—Holthusen

~

Dr. Ernst Vendig
July 10, 1939
69, rue des Aduatiques
Bruxelles
Honored Captain,

The sudden, rushed disembarkation of the passengers for Belgium on June 17 robbed me of the opportunity to say goodbye to you in person. All I could do was ask Dr. Joseph to express my best wishes to you and my gratitude for all your efforts on behalf of our fates. On behalf of the board committee and thus on behalf of myself, I would also like to present you with a photo that memorializes our notable departure from Havana.

Now that the days of outer and inner turmoil are for the most part behind us and all of us—the 200 members of the Belgium St. Louis group—are back on firm ground (in both a real and symbolic sense) thanks to the empathy of our new home country I feel the need to write you a few lines. I hope that these will reach you as soon as you have a stopover in New York.

Most of all, I would like to express my heartfelt gratitude for your written appreciation, which you, while still on board, had conveyed to me and all gentlemen of the board committee for the efforts we were of course happy to provide on behalf of everyone.

Your letter will remain a valuable memory to me of those days, which, despite their heaviness, became easier to endure and master as they aptly restored our faith in the indestructible idea of the humanitarian spirit, a faith which had almost been lost due to the experiences that are behind us.

In this sense, I owe you, dear Captain, my deepest gratitude. The attitude you assumed in those days and weeks toward us and our special fate, an attitude which spread over the whole ship, became an important source of strength for us. Not only did you have a deep understanding of our situation, but you also knew how to treat all the issues that mattered to us with such tact that it became clear to us that you had made our concerns in those days into yours.

Expressing all this to you again today is the intention of this letter, and I hope that it reaches you as you have regained your fresh form after having been relieved in Antwerp of all the work and concerns regarding us all.

With the deepest respect,
Your devoted
Ernst Vendig

Figure A.3. Front page of captain's log, part 1, for Voyage 98. © HAPAG. *Source:* Hapag-Lloyd AG. Used with permission.

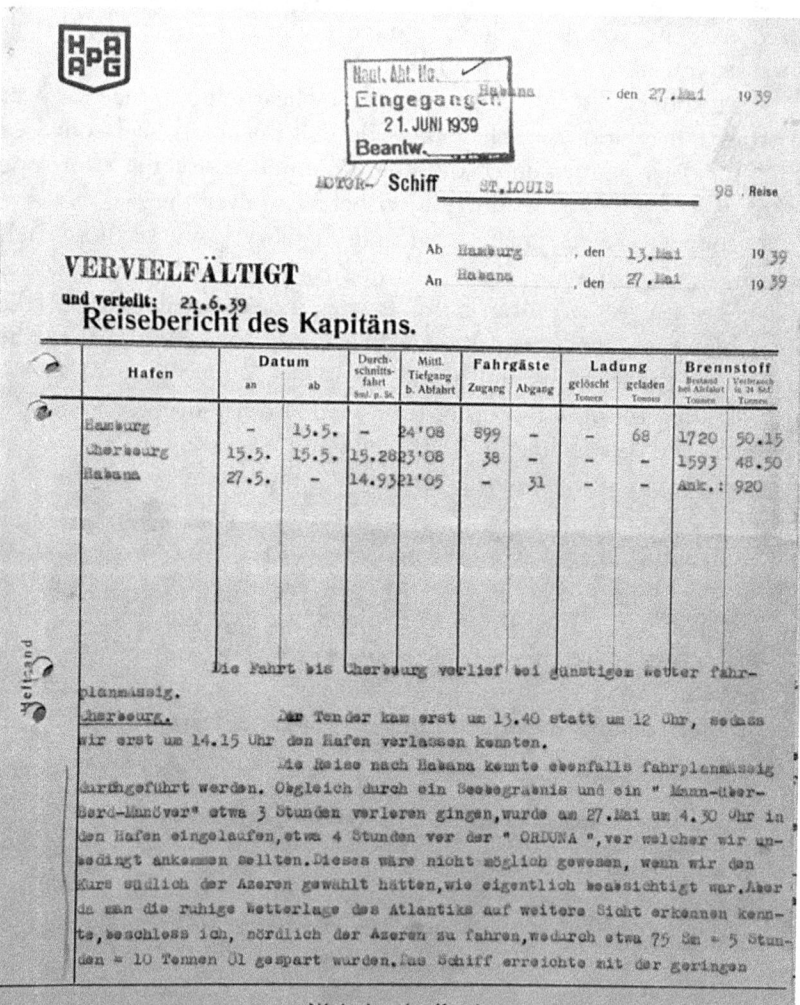

Appendix 3

Captain's Log, Voyage 98, Part 1,
translated by Roy Grundmann

Captain's Log by Gustav Schröder for the Trip to Havana, May 27, 1939

The trip to Cherbourg unfolded as planned and in good weather.[1]

CHERBOURG

The tender arrived only at 1:40 p.m. instead of at noon, so that we could not leave port until 2:15 p.m.

The trip to Havana was also accomplished on schedule. Although we lost three hours due to a sea burial and a "man-overboard maneuver," we arrived in port on May 27 at 4:30 a.m., approximately four hours before "*Orduna*," which we had strict orders to beat. This would not have been possible if we had chosen the course south of the Azores, as had been intended. But as we were able to foresee calm weather on the Atlantic, I decided to go north of the Azores, which saved us about 75 nautical miles (equaling five hours or ten tons of oil). With the low average rpm of 99.5 the ship reached an average speed of 14.9 knots, a very good result, considering that an average of 0.3 knots countercurrent had to be factored in for the whole trip. The low rpm was due to the repeated suspension of a part of the engines because of repairs. That the ship nonetheless ran so smoothly is because of the trim (6 feet at the stern) that we achieved. The experiences of the last three New York trips gave rise to this, during which the ship in nearly consistent weather achieved 15.1 knots on an even keel, 15.4 knots with 2 feet trim at the stern, and 15.6 knots with 5 feet trim at the stern—each time with slightly more than 101 rpm. But the favorable impact of this trim comes into effect only when carrying a light load, as was the case on these trips.

News of the death of the Jewish passenger Weiler and the suicide of the scullery crew Leonid Berg have already been conveyed through telegrams and special reports.

HAVANA

Disembarkation of the passengers was supposed to be performed while it was still dark outside, so as to pre-empt the expected landing prohibition from the president of the Republic of Cuba. But when we arrived, our local representative was unaware of the fact that the president, the evening before, had already forbidden the immigration office from boarding our ship. Now legal counsel, the Joint Committee, and the German legation were trying everything in the way of arguments, offers, and appeals to have him change his mind, but to no avail. The first suicide attempt happened on May 30 in the afternoon. A lawyer traveling with his wife and children tried to slit his wrists and jumped overboard. The sailor Meier jumped after him and kept him above water until the dinghy came and pulled him in against his protests and resistance. The cuts he had made had not damaged his arteries.

Right after him, another passenger, also a lawyer, tried to poison himself, but he was found out and brought to in time. That night, a woman tried to jump overboard and a number of others openly stated they would do the same if they were forced to leave the harbor again on the ship.

With the arrival of Berenson, an influential personality from New York, hopes were rising again. Everyone decided to wait and see. But then, on Thursday, June 1, the well-known decree was issued according to which the ship had to leave port. I immediately went ashore, notified the German *chargé d'affairs* by telephone, and sent him the wording of the decree. Back on board, I drafted, in coordination with the board committee, a message to be posted that announced our departure, but also that negotiations would continue. Further, I promised to do everything to achieve a landing outside of

Germany and, for the moment, to stay near the coast. Thus, news of our departure was greeted somewhat calmly. But when shortly before departure the president of the Republic of Cuba gave special permission to two further families (Friedmann and Boch) to disembark, dramatic scenes unfolded. The only reason calm could be fairly restored was that two gentlemen of the Joint Committee addressed the passengers, firmly promising them that they would not need to land in Germany. Nonetheless, because I feared further incidents during departure, I asked the harbor police, who had already supported us as much as they could over the past few days, to escort us with their launches. I left the harbor at the slowest speed possible, frequently stopping the engines.

The lawyer who had jumped overboard stayed ashore in a hospital. I did not succeed in landing his wife and children, nor the widow of Herr Weiler, who had died at sea. Her son had come from New York and was the only one who received permission to step onto the ship. All other relatives, who were present by the hundreds, were inconsiderately rejected by the immigration officers as per higher orders.

The place where we moored in Havana Bay was so tight that, when drifting west, we constantly ran risk of colliding with a Norwegian steamer and, when drifting east, with a buoy, so that even by night we had to stand clear.

Schröder
Captain

Figure A.4. Front page of captain's log, Part 2, for Voyage 98. © HAPAG.
Source: Hapag-Lloyd AG. Used with permission.

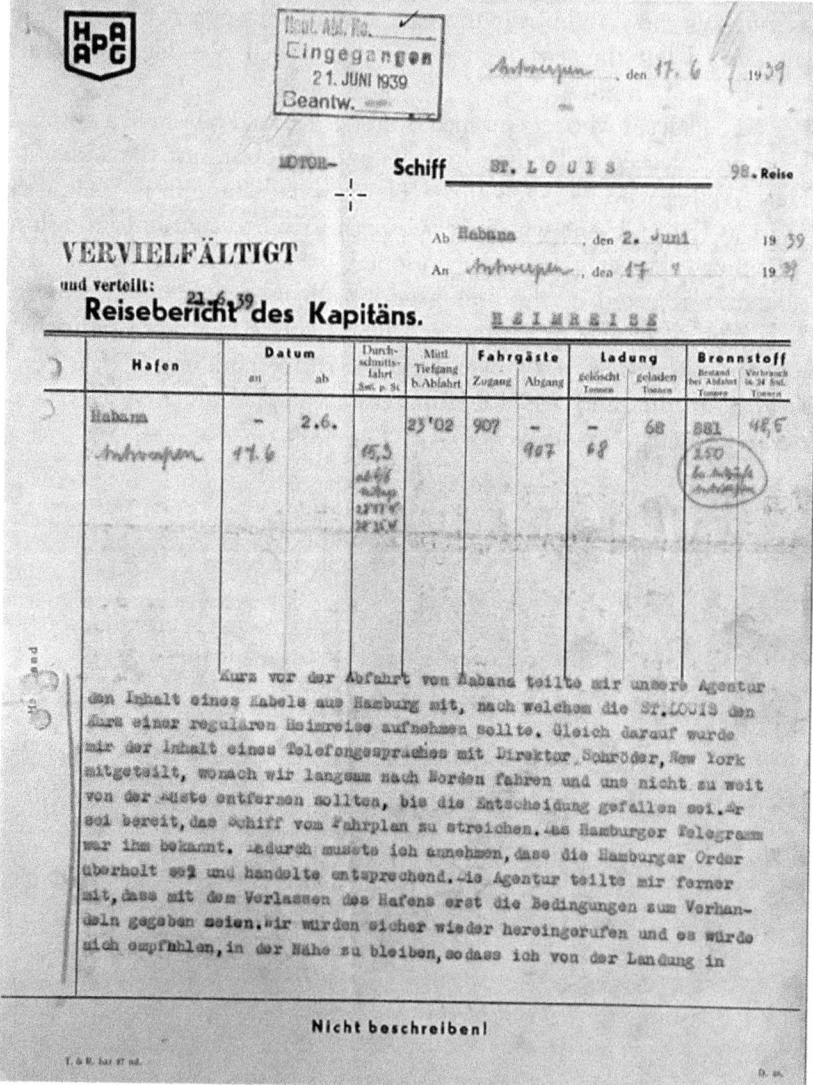

Appendix 4

Captain's Log, Voyage 98, Part 2, translated by Roy Grundmann

Captain's Log by Gustav Schröder for the Return Trip from Havana to Antwerp, June 17, 1939

Shortly before departure from Havana our agency shared the content of a cable with me, according to which *St. Louis* was supposed to take a regular home-bound course.[1] Right after that, the contents of a phone conversation with Director Schröder, New York, were shared with me, which directed us to go slowly north and not move away from the coast too far until a decision would be reached. He was prepared to take the ship out of the regular schedule and was aware of the telegram from Hamburg. This led me to believe that the Hamburg order had been superseded and I acted accordingly. The agency further informed me that our departing the harbor constituted the prerequisite for negotiations. We would surely be called back in and it would be good if we stayed nearby. Thus, I was convinced that we would land in Havana. The next morning, June 3, a cable arrived from New York: "According to current instructions from Hamburg, you are to turn back, as Havana is still hopeful. But if no decision can be reached by noon, the ship must travel to Hamburg." In the evening, another cable arrived from New York. "Following confirmation by phone Dr. Hoffmann, you are authorized to remain put until tomorrow midday 2 p.m., as there is prospect for landing." I used the opportunity to point out Miami to the passengers to distract them. After the period of authorization had passed, I steered north and left the Florida Strait, though the passengers were extremely concerned. The morning of the 5th, another cable arrived from Hamburg: "Proceed at slow speed for the next 24 hours; if you do not hear anything from us or Havana, stop the ship. If necessary, we will instruct you to return to Havana." As we were moving with the strongest current in the gulf stream, I temporarily stopped the engines to save oil. During the day, the passengers received many telegrams from Havana that landing was secured. And that evening I received a telegram from the Centre Israelita (Joint Committee): "Please inform passengers that landing in Pinos has been approved." As I knew the members of the committee to be cautious and reliable, I couldn't imagine that anyone would give the passengers, who had already been disappointed numerous times, yet another unverifiable piece of news. Convinced that I was doing the right thing, I steered the ship onto a southern course, so that the slowed engine would at least keep us in place. But after the time had passed by which the order from Hamburg should have arrived, and because the possibility of an unavoidable return to Hamburg with our current levels of water, oil, and provisions did not allow me to wait any longer, I decided to head for Europe. Not long after, a telegram arrived from Hamburg: "Proceed to Hamburg full speed."

Shortly before arrival in Havana and following a conversation with the first purser, Herr Müller, I had assembled a committee of five reliable gentlemen from among the passengers, who were of excellent service in their efforts to look after the passengers. But a few days later, a counter-committee formed, which was dissatisfied with my own, claiming they were under my sway. One tense day, I invited the counter-committee for a meeting and the next day I succeeded in recruiting two gentlemen of the counter-committee for collaboration, despite the initial protests of my committee. I also asked a group of men who already on the outbound voyage had administered spiritual support to resume their activities. They did excellent work particularly with regard to the frequent nervous breakdowns. When on June 6 we were sailing NE at full steam, a great turmoil started on the ship. We were continually asked where our trip was going. I had no choice but to announce that we were steaming toward a point that was equidistant from Cuba, Haiti, and New York. But there were many who no longer believed anything. Again and again, the purser's office and the ship management received desperate pleas for information. It would have been wrong to turn them away, but it took incredible patience to engage with them.

When on June 9th the hope regarding San Domino [Santo Domingo] began to fade, things became critical. I was about to tell the committee the plain truth that San Domingo [Santo Domingo] was no longer being considered either, as it was doubtful that the necessary funds had been deposited. Somehow, this had been leaked. A few minutes later, it was circulating across the whole ship, creating a panic. Packs of men came up the stairs and rushed toward the bridge. I was in my cabin with the committee when we learned about this. I had no choice but to address the men at the top of the stairs. I tried to give them fresh courage, even though my own faith had waned. I asked them to attend a general assembly in the hall at 5 p.m. and I succeeded in getting them to go there. The committee, which had resisted my previous proposals for such assemblies, was now confronted with a fait accompli. The first speaker was the lawyer Joseph, followed by me. After half an hour, calm had mostly been restored. This bought us time to decide how to maintain calm the following day, on which we then also succeeded in keeping everyone calm. The lawyer Joseph held an excellent speech in which he explained to the men that they had a mission, now that the whole world refused to accept them. This gave the men a little confidence, but the women remained in a desperate mood. Fortunately, the next day brought the first signs of negotiations in Europe, which gave hope and helped most of them to gradually calm down. Once the first positive news about a landing outside of Germany came in, normalcy slowly returned.

The weather on the whole return trip was favorable. From the 47th meridian on, we traveled, as directed, along the A-Track.

On June 14, the helmsman Kritsch committed suicide (cf. special report). His body was embalmed for transportation to Hamburg.

With the exception of some slightly more serious illnesses among the children and the repeatedly occurring nervous breakdowns, the passengers' state of health was satisfactory. There was a serious matter among the crew. The scullery crew member Max Katt was suffering from a dangerous infection of his lower jaw bone, which necessitated surgery. He is now convalescing. At 9:15 a.m. on June 17th, we passed Vlissingen. Here, Captain Mahr, Mr. Vallesen, Mr. Troper of the Joint

Committee, and various other gentlemen came on board to prepare disembarkation in Antwerp.

We reached Antwerp at 2 p.m. and docked at the Scheldekai, Hall 18, at 2:36 p.m. As of now, there are no insurance losses to report.

Gustav Schröder, Captain

Appendix 5

Addendum to the Captain's Log of
Captain Gustav Schröder, MS *St. Louis*,
on the 98th Voyage Home,
translated by Roy Grundmann

6/17/1939[1]
Confidential

When the critical days arrived, the Local Group Leader PG. Zschiedrich warned me about possible acts of sabotage, as he and other members of the crew had overheard conversations in this regard. To take preemptive measures, we appointed a reliable guard, discreetly put the bridge into defense status, and also guarded the entrances to the engine. I placed the suspected passengers under observation. To protect the reputation of the ship and the shipping line, I did not want to use force until it would be absolutely necessary.

The Local Group Leader supports us in every way he can through the deployment of S.A. and volunteers. We agreed on signals in case of alarm and prepared countermeasures in case they would be needed. One of these included talking to the two above-mentioned gentlemen from the counter-committee. After extensive deliberations and conversations with the First Officer and the Local Group Leader, we requested protection for the eventuality that the ship was forced to return the passengers to Hamburg.

             Schröder

             Captain

        Antwerp, June 17, 1939

CC:
Dr. Hoffmann
Mr. Aldag
Mr. Holthusen
Mr. Lütgens
6/21/39
Nautical Department

Notes

Acknowledgments

1. The line is from an essay by Donna Haraway (1988).

Introduction

1. "MS" stands for "motor ship." Though diesel-powered, *St. Louis* is often miscategorized as a steam turbine vessel ("SS" indicates "steamship"). A note on naming and gendering: *St. Louis*'s owner, the Hamburg-Amerikanische Packetfahrt-Actien-Gesellschaft (HAPAG, or Hamburg America Line), named some of its ships after cities in destination countries to appeal to local passengers. Gendering ships female in English, German, and other languages has a long, intricate history that, as scholars have found, is not reducible to patriarchal customs, although it may at times overlap with their effects. See Renisa Mawani, *Across Oceans of Law: The Komagata Maru and Jurisdiction in the Time of Empire* (Duke University Press, 2018), 78–88.

2. NS is short for NSDAP, which stands for Nationalsozialistische Deutsche Arbeiterpartei, the National Socialist German Workers' Party.

3. Colin Bundy, "Migrants, Refugees, History and Precedents," *Forced Migration Review*, no. 51 (January 2016), www.fmreview.org/destination-europe/bundy.

4. Giorgio Agamben, *Homo Sacer—Sovereign Power and Bare Life*, trans. Daniel Heller-Roazen (Stanford University Press, 1998), 10.

5. Agamben, 183.

6. The term was coined by Holocaust survivor David Rousset in his book *L'univers concentrationnaire*. See Griselda Pollock and Max Silverman, "Introduction," *Concentrationary Cinema: Aesthetics as Political Resistance in Alain Resnais's "Night and Fog" (1955)* (Berghahn Books, 2011). See discussion in chapter 5.

7. As chapter 5 explains, the term "shoreless sea" is the coinage of Daniel Heller-Roazen, who translated Agamben's book *Homo Sacer* and, along with it, a German passage by Schmitt that Agamben discusses and that contains Schmitt's metaphor.

8. Michael Rothberg, *Multidirectional Memory: Remembering the Holocaust in the Age of Decolonization* (Stanford University Press, 2009), 70.

9. For an early analysis, see Irwin F. Gellman, "The *St. Louis* Tragedy," *American Jewish Historical Quarterly* 61, no. 2 (December 1971): 144–56. Gellman's findings have been significantly revised. Neither of two prominent 1980s studies, Richard Breitman and Alan M. Kraut, *American Refugee Policy and European Jewry, 1933–1945* (Indiana University Press, 1987) and Irving Abella and Harold Troper, *None Is Too Many: Canada and the Jews of Europe, 1933–1948* (Lester & Orpen Dennys, 1983), treats the *St. Louis* episode in depth. The same holds for Richard Breitman and Allan J. Lichtman, *FDR and the Jews* (The Belknap Press of Harvard University Press, 2013). Robert M. Levine, *Tropical Diaspora: The Jewish Experience in Cuba* (University Press of Florida, 1993), usefully details Jewish life in Cuba, but relies too heavily on Thomas and Morgan-Witts's book *Voyage of the Damned* in its discussion of the *St. Louis* voyage.

10. Two German books from the early 2000s detail the voyage with different emphases. Georg J. E. Mautner Markhof, *Das St. Louis-Drama: Hintergrund und Rätsel einer mysteriösen Aktion des Dritten Reiches* (Leopold Stocker Verlag, 2001), is too speculative regarding NS leadership's role in the voyage. Georg Reinfelder's *MS "St. Louis" Frühjahr 1939—Die Irrfahrt nach Kuba: Kapitän Gustav Schröder Rettet 906 Deutsche Juden vor dem Zugriff der Nazis* (Hentrich & Hentrich, 2005) more successfully sorts fact from speculation. The book includes a full passenger list of Voyage 98 and a first-person survivor narrative, the diary of passenger Erich Dublon. Diane Afoumado's authoritative account, *Exil Impossible: L'errance des Juifs du paquebot 'St.-Louis'* (Editions L'Harmattan, 2005) was the first to link Voyage 98 to HAPAG's economic situation. Three more recent German books focus on different aspects of the *St. Louis* voyage. Stefan Lipsky, Manfred Uhlig, and Jürgen Glaevecke, *Kapitän Schröder und die Irrfahrt der St. Louis* (Mittler, 2019) provides valuable information on Captain Gustav Schröder based on recently unearthed archival materials. Arnd Ziemer and Leon Ziemer, *Aufrecht in Schweren Zeiten: Kapitän Schröder und die Horrorfahrt der St. Louis 1939* (Deutsche Seemannsmission Hamburg-Altona e.V., 2019) provides an impeccably researched summary of the *St. Louis* voyage and detailed biographical information on Schröder. And Eva Schöck-Quinteros, Matthias Loeber, and Simon Rau, eds., *Keine Zuflucht. Nirgends: Die Konferenz von Evian und die Fahrt der St. Louis (1938/39)* (Institut für Geschichtswissenschaft/Milde Buchdruckerei, 2019), is a groundbreaking historical sourcebook with wide-ranging

information on the *St. Louis* voyage and its historical context, including a German translation of the Évian conference proceedings.

11. C. Paul Vincent, "The Voyage of the *St. Louis* Revisited," *Holocaust and Genocide Studies* 25, no. 2 (Fall 2011), 252–89 is the most authoritative account of the JDC's political negotiations with Cuba, the US, and Europe.

12. Alison Lawlor, *"The Saddest Ship Afloat": The Tragedy of the MS St. Louis* (Nimbus Publishing, 2016) usefully details Canada's role in the *St. Louis* affair as a primer aimed at young readers. See also Steve Schwinghamer's valuable article "'The Existing Immigration Regulations Will Not Offer Any Solution': MS St. Louis in Canadian Context," Canadian Museum of Immigration at Pier 21, December 21, 2023, pier21.ca/research/immigration-history/canada-and-ms-st-louis. See further Amanda Grzyb, "From Kristallnacht to the MS *St. Louis* Tragedy: Canadian Press Coverage of Nazi Persecution of the Jews and the Jewish Refugee Crisis, September 1938 to August 1939," in *Nazi Germany, Canadian Responses*, ed. Ruth Klein (McGill-Queen's University Press, 2012), 78–113.

13. Sarah Ogilvie and Scott Miller, *Refuge Denied: The St. Louis Passengers and the Holocaust* (University of Wisconsin Press, 2006), traces the fate of the passengers who failed to escape the Nazis after arriving back in Europe.

14. On the concept of "emplotment," see Hayden White, "Historical Emplotment and the Problem of Truth," in *Probing the Limits of Representation: Nazism and the Final Solution*, ed. Saul Friedlander (Harvard University Press, 1992), 37–53. White has argued that facts and their narration are often not clearly distinguishable. For a critique that White does not go far enough, see Martin Jay, "Of Plots, Witnesses, and Judgments," in Friedlander, *Probing the Limits of Representation*, 97–107, here 98. See also Perry Anderson, "On Emplotment: Two Kinds of Ruin," in Friedlander, *Probing the Limits of Representation*, 54–65.

15. Martin Jay has identified this tendency especially in persons who either initiate or suffer historical events. See Jay, "Of Plots, Witnesses, and Judgments," 98.

16. Jay, 99.

17. James E. Young, *The Texture of Memory: Holocaust Memorials and Meaning* (Yale University Press, 1993), 287–322.

Chapter 1

1. For these laws' impact on Jewish emigration, see Laura Radel, "Ziel der deutschen Judenpolitik: Auswanderung," in *Keine Zuflucht. Nirgends. Die Konferenz von Evian und die Fahrt der St. Louis (1938/39)*, edited by Eva Schöck-Quinteros, Matthias Loeber, and Simon Rau, 13–36 (Institut für Geschichtswissenschaft/Milde Buchdruckerei, 2019).

2. The suspension of the constitution was expected to be temporary. Some antisemitic laws exempted Jewish World War I veterans. See Radel, 14, 24.

3. Mautner Markhof, *Das St. Louis-Drama*, 22, referencing the German Jewish newspaper *Jüdische Rundschau* and figures from the League of Nations.

4. The term arose in the nineteenth century around the question of Jews' political emancipation following their assisting European nations with industrialization and colonial expansion. See *Oxford English Dictionary*, "Jewish question," accessed February 5, 2025, www.oed.com/dictionary/jewish-question_n.

5. Radel, 15.

6. Hindenburg introduced this law in 1931 to stop the draining of capital from Weimar Germany during the economic crisis.

7. Radel, 15.

8. "Die Schmach," *Der Neue Vorwärts*, Nov. 20, 1938, reprinted in Schöck-Quinteros et al., 34–36.

9. Ibid., 34.

10. Jewish expulsion had, however, not gone as planned. In a January 1939 Reich Foreign Office Circular, "Judenreferent" (Specialist for Jewish Affairs) Emil Schumburg lamented that anti-Jewish legislation had failed to coerce Jews to leave Germany. See Emil Schumburg, "The Jewish Question as a Foreign Policy Factor in 1938," in *The Persecution and Murder of the European Jews by Nazi Germany, 1933–1945, Vol. 2, German Reich, 1938–August 1939*, ed. Susanne Heim et al. (De Gruyter Oldenbourg, 2009 [English language edition 2014–2016, coordinating ed. Alex J. Kay]), 824–30. Kindle Edition. At the same time, Schumburg was concerned that the formation of a Jewish state would empower Jews under international law ("würde aber dem Weltjudentum einen Völkerrechtlichen Machtzuwachs bringen"—original German wording of this excerpt reprinted in Radel, 21).

11. Radel, 13.

12. Ibid. For an overview on the Haavara Agreement and its controversial nature both within the Zionist movement (as it placed the aim of moving Jews to Palestine at cross-purposes with the Zionist call for a boycott of German goods) and among Nazi leadership (as it facilitated the exit of Jewish assets from Germany), see "Haavara," *The Jewish Virtual Library*, www.jewishvirtuallibrary.org/haavara, accessed March 23, 2022.

13. Ibid.

14. Michel Foucault, *History of Sexuality, Volume 1: An Introduction*, trans. Robert Hurley (Random House, 1978; orig. *La volonté de savoir* [Gallimard, 1976]), 139–43, as well as Michel Foucault, *"Society Must Be Defended": Lectures at the College de France 1975–1976*, ed. Mauro Bertani and Alessandra Fontana, trans. David Macey (Picador, 2003), ch. 11, "17 March 1976," 239–63, esp.

254–63. While Foucault appears to use the terms "biopower" and "biopolitics" interchangeably, biopolitics is often thought of as the spectrum of concrete modalities by which biopower gets implemented. For a history of both terms, see Sergei Prozorov and Simona Rentea, eds., *The Routledge Handbook of Biopolitics* (Routledge, 2017). See also Louisiana Lightsey, "Biopolitics and Globalization," in *Global South Studies: A Collective Publication with the Global South*, August 17, 2017.

15. Ibid., 243.
16. Foucault, *The History of Sexuality, Vol. 1*, 137.
17. Ibid. See also Foucault, *Society Must Be Defended*, 256, where Foucault reasons that racism was these states' ideological prerequisite for their right to kill.
18. Ibid., 258.
19. As Foucault puts it in *Society Must be Defended* (259–60), "The Nazi State makes the field of the life it manages, protects, guarantees, and cultivates in biological terms absolutely coextensive with the sovereign right to kill anyone, meaning not only other people, but also its own people. . . . We have an absolutely racist State, an absolutely murderous State, and an absolutely suicidal State."
20. Anja Hasler, "Vom Transitland zur Festung: Schweizer Flüchtlingspolitik und Antisemitismus im Jahr der Konferenz von Évian," in Schöck-Quinteros et al., 53 and 57–58. Germany and Switzerland signed the "J" stamp decree on September 29, 1938.
21. Alfred Rosenberg, "Wohin mit den Juden? Gedanken zur Weltkonferenz von Evian," *Völkischer Beobachter*, July 8, 1938, n.p., reprinted in Eva Schöck-Quinteros et al., 155. Hitler himself contemptuously commented on the outcome of the Évian conference in a speech at the Reichstag on January 30, 1939. See Reinfelder, *MS "St. Louis" Frühjahr 1939*, 48–50.
22. Rosenberg. Terms in quotation marks are direct translations by me of Rosenberg's original German text.
23. The "Schacht plan" is named after the proposal the president of the Reichsbank, Hjalmar Schacht, made to England and the US in December 1938, to resettle 400,000 German Jews and other "non-Aryans." The plan died when Hitler fired Schacht. After being cleared by a postwar military tribunal, Schacht argued that, had his plan been implemented, no Jew would have been killed and that the fault lay with the US and Britain.
24. Intergovernmental Committee on Refugees, Proceedings of the Intergovernmental Committee, Evian, July 5 to 16, 1938, 16. Verbatim record of the plenary meetings of the committee; resolutions and reports.
25. Ibid., 19.
26. Ibid., 30.
27. Ibid., 22.

28. Ibid., 15.
29. Ibid., 36.
30. Ibid., 14–15.
31. For evidence of Jewish organizations' genuine interest in emigrating to Africa, see the letter of the Freeland League for Jewish Territorial Colonisation to Myron C. Taylor and the Conference at Evian, June 24, 1938, Myron C. Taylor Papers, Marist Library. The League submitted a detailed proposal for colonizing parts of Africa, for which it lists several prerequisites, including a large thinly populated area so as to avoid "conflict with the native population."
32. Edward Said, *The Question of Palestine* (Vintage Books, 1979), 15–16. I do not mean to peg colonialism entirely to the British. The colonization of Palestine began long before the British intervened in the region, though space does not permit me to assess the phenomenon of Jewish settlement with the nuance it deserves. To stick to the facts, I once more cite Said, who on this particular aspect remains undisputed, namely that Jews who settled in Palestine in the nineteenth century paid scant attention to the non-Jews already living there. Some may claim that this was because Jewish settlers at least initially perceived their own presence to be so diminutive and nonintrusive as to align with a vision of peaceful cohabitation safeguarded by the fact that each group stuck to itself. Said, however, argues otherwise. He states that for Jewish settlers, the status of Palestinians "as sovereign and human inhabitants was systematically denied" (66). Britain was officially confronted with this diagnosis of colonialism in 1922 with the Arab delegation's response to Winston Churchill's formulation of British policy in Palestine (the so called White Paper): "The intention to create the Jewish National Home is to cause the disappearance or subordination of the Arabic population, culture and language" (cited in Said, 83). For a more recent analysis of the subject, see Rashid Khalidi, *The Hundred Years' War on Palestine* (Metropolitan Books, 2020).
33. Said, *The Question of Palestine*, 16.
34. *Report of the Oversea Settlement Board, 1938*, presented by the Secretary of State for Dominion Affairs to Parliament by Command of His Majesty, June 1938, 1–42, here 3–9. Myron C. Taylor Papers, Marist Library.
35. Ibid., 22 and 36.
36. Ibid., 9–10 and 16.
37. Ibid., 36.
38. Intergovernmental Committee on Refugees, 20.
39. Ibid.
40. Ibid.
41. Report of the Oversea Settlement Board, 27.

42. Lawlor, *"The Saddest Ship Afloat,"* 49, referencing Abella and Troper, *None is Too Many*.

43. Ibid.

44. Eduardo Galeano, *Open Veins of Latin America: Five Centuries of the Pillage of a Continent*, trans. Cedric Belfrage (Monthly Review Press, 1973), 12–13.

45. Intergovernmental Committee on Refugees. See especially comments from Colombia (25), Chile and Uruguay (29), Peru (31), and the Dominican Republic (32).

46. Ibid., 35.

47. Ibid.

48. Galeano, 143–44.

49. Intergovernmental Committee on Refugees, 21–22: "Those, however, who intend, whilst living within our territory, to remain permanently bound by the special conditions derived from their country of origin, would do well to abandon their intention while there is time and refrain from going to the Argentine."

50. Ibid., 18.

51. Ibid., 30. He ignores that cattle barons had sold oil concessions to the US and gave the US so much power that it was tasked with drafting Venezuela's petroleum laws. See Galeano, 185.

52. Ibid., 31.

53. Ibid.

54. Ibid.

55. Intergovernmental Committee on Refugees, 32. All subsequent quotations from this statement on same page.

56. Intergovernmental Committee on Refugees, Unpublished Meeting Record of the Technical Sub-Committee, Section 47, Declaration of the Delegate of the Dominican Republic. Myron C. Taylor Papers, Marist Library.

57. On the Dominican Republic's offer, see "Dominikanische Republik," *Geschlossene Grenzen: Die Internationale Flüchtlingskonferenz von Evian 1938*, evian1938.de/dominikanische-republik/, accessed April 8, 2024.

58. Intergovernmental Committee on Refugees, Unpublished Meeting Record of the Technical Sub-Committee, Section 47, Declaration of the Delegate of Cuba. Myron C. Taylor Papers, Marist Library.

59. Ibid.

60. Ibid.

61. Roosevelt instructed Taylor on the Intergovernmental Committee's post-conference path of action: "It is realized that many countries are prepared to admit larger numbers of involuntary emigrants than they are willing publicly to admit. The commitments to be sought at the forthcoming meeting

should accordingly be of two kinds: public and confidential. The public statements, which should be specific, will be of value not only in providing actual opportunities for settlement but also in inducing other countries to make similar commitments. The confidential commitments should concern each Government's contribution over and above what it is prepared publicly to announce." Franklin D. Roosevelt, letter to Myron C. Taylor, November 23, 1938. Myron C. Taylor Papers, Marist Library. Confidential meetings are standard diplomatic practice. The record of Évian's Technical Sub-Committee exists only as a typescript as part of the Myron C. Taylor papers at Marist Library. That said, many confidential statements at Évian are near-identical with their countries' official statements.

62. Intergovernmental Committee on Refugees, 31.

63. Intergovernmental Committee on Refugees, Unpublished Meeting Record of the Technical Sub-Committee, Section 47, Declaration of the Delegate of Colombia. Myron C. Taylor Papers, Marist Library. This statement echoes concerns voiced by Carl Schmitt about the decline of German jurisdiction in the Weimar Republic. See chapter 5.

64. Intergovernmental Committee on Refugees, 41.

65. Letter from Franklin D. Roosevelt to Myron C. Taylor, November 23, 1938, 2, Myron C. Taylor Papers, Marist Library.

66. Ibid.

67. Ibid.

68. Ibid.

69. Letter from F. D. Roosevelt to Myron C. Taylor, Myron C. Taylor Papers.

70. The deportation of Polish Jews from Germany back to Poland constituted one such exception.

71. Bertolt Brecht, "On the Term Emigrants," trans. Minor Kontor, *We Refugees: Digital Archive on Refugeedom*, en.we-refugees-archive.org/archive/bertolt-brecht-on-the-term-emigrants-1937/, accessed June 11, 2022. The poem further states that exiles wait restlessly near the border, awaiting the day they are able to return, not forgetting and not forgiving anything, and hearing the screams from the camps, the rumors of atrocities that travel across the distance that separates their exile from their homeland, all the while remaining resolved to return one day.

72. Ironically, the liner *Campana*, many years later, after having been sold, refurbished, and renamed *Irpinia*, would play the *St. Louis* in the film *Voyage of the Damned*. See chapter 7.

73. Lars Nothdurft, "Die Flüchtlingsschiffe," in Schöck-Quinteros et al., 381, 385.

74. H. R. Knickerbocker, "The Wandering Jews," *L'Oeuvre*, June 30, 1939, trans. Odile Kennal, in Schöck-Quinteros et al., 388–92, here 388.

Lacking access to the original, I have translated relevant passages from German back into English.

75. Ibid., 388.
76. Ibid.
77. Ibid.
78. Ibid.
79. Ibid., 388–89.
80. "Die Totenschiffe Fahren," *Aufbau*, April 1, 1939. Reprinted in Schöck-Quinteros et al., 363–64. Trans. Roy Grundmann.
81. Ibid. Trans. Roy Grundmann.
82. Ibid. The *Königstein* was formerly owned by the Jewish shipping merchant Arnold Bernstein, whose company, the Arnold Bernstein Line, flourished in the 1920s and 1930s, before the Nazis dispossessed and incarcerated Bernstein. Released in the summer 1939, he fled to the US on the eve of World War II. Bernstein was also the founder of the Palestine Shipping Company, which facilitated much of the official Jewish emigration to Palestine in the 1930s. According to *Aufbau*, the *Königstein* carried 780 refugees. The *Globe and Mail* on February 28, 1939, published a front-page story about 185 Jews specifically from Austria trapped on the *Königstein*. On Arnold Bernstein, see Björn Siegel, "Arnold Bernstein," in *Immigrant Entrepreneurship: German-American Business Biographies, 1720 to the Present*, August 22, 2018, www.immigrantentrepreneurship.org/entries/arnold-bernstein/. On the *Königstein*, see Siegel, "Doomed at Sea? Maritime Spaces and the Jewish Refugee Crisis in the 1930s," *Jewish Culture and History* 25, no. 1 (2024): 1–18.
83. Knickerbocker, 390.
84. Ibid. All examples from 390 and 391.
85. These small Greek or Romanian ships were chartered by the clandestine Jewish Immigration Organization Aliyah Bet. See Artur Patek, *Jews on Route to Palestine: Sketches from the History of Aliyah Bet—Clandestine Jewish Immigration*, trans. Guy Russell Tore and Timothy Williams (Jagiellonian University Press, 2012).
86. See Amanda Grzyb, "From Kristallnacht to the MS *St. Louis* Tragedy: Canadian Press Coverage of Nazi Persecution of the Jews and the Jewish Refugee Crisis, September 1938 to August 1939," in *Nazi Germany, Canadian Responses*, ed. Ruth Klein (McGill-Queen's University Press, 2012), 78–113, here 102. Grzyb's findings corroborate many of those reported by Knickerbocker and factually correct some cases listed by *Aufbau*. The *Globe and Mail* on February 27, 1939, lists the *Conte Grande*'s passenger count as 68.
87. *Deutschland-Berichte der Sozialdemokratischen Partei Deutschlands (SOPADE) 1934–1940* 6, no. 7 (July 1939), 938–40, reprinted in Schöck-Quinteros et al., 393–96. The report's account of ships forgotten in no man's land merits summarizing for its archival value: The steamer *Usaramo*

of German East Africa Line for six weeks crisscrossed the Pacific with 500 Jews headed for Shanghai. The 68 refugees aboard the *Orbita*, a Pacific Steamship Company liner and the sister ship of the *Orduña*, were rejected by Ecuador and quarantined in Balboa, Panama Canal Zone, before receiving visas for Panama. The German liner *Cap Norte* of Hamburg-Süd Line left Hamburg on April 28, 1939, with 15 refugees. After Paraguay, Uruguay, and Argentina denied disembarkation, France agreed to receive them. Another Hamburg-Süd ship, the *Monte Olivia*, carried 78 passengers with visas for Paraguay, but Uruguay denied them transit. Eventually, Chile granted them asylum. The *Prosula*, a ship carrying 65 mostly Czech refugees, left the Black Sea port of Sulina on June 25 for Shanghai but only reached Tripoli. Another source identifies the ship as *Frossoula* and lists a May 29 departure date and a higher passenger count of 658. These were eventually transferred to another ship, *Tiger Hill*. See Paul H. Silverstone, "Frossoula," paulsilverstone.com/ship/frossoula/ (accessed May 19, 2022). In *Jews On Route to Palestine* Patek writes that, under contract from Aliyah Bet, *Tiger Hill* had already 750 to 800 refugees on board before adding *Frossoula*'s (90). Another ship referenced by SOPADE is the Greek coal steamer *Dora*, which the report lists as missing. It had left Amsterdam with 500 Jews on June 17, 1939, allegedly for Siam. Another ship, the *Osiris*, was reported idling off Syria, searching for a port for six weeks. The steamer *Thessalia*, carrying 550 refugees, crisscrossed the Mediterranean for weeks after the Syrian coast guard chased it away.

88. See the Captain's account, "22. Juli 1939—Reisebericht des Kapitäns der MS 'Orinoco,'" Hamburger Staatsarchiv StAH 621-1/95 Nr. 4651 HAPAG-Reederei. Schiffsakte MS *Orinoco*, reprinted in Schöck-Quinteros et al., 385–87.

89. *Flandre* and *Orduña* receive brief discussion in chapter 3. For further details on *Orinoco*, *Flandre*, and *Orduña*, see United States Holocaust Memorial Museum, "Seeking Refuge in Cuba," *Holocaust Encyclopedia*, encyclopedia.ushmm.org/content/en/article/seeking-refuge-in-cuba-1939, accessed April 9, 2024.

90. In *Jews on Route to Palestine*, Patek recounts the tragedy of the sailing ship *Struma*. Carrying over 800 refugees, it had come from Constanta with destination Turkey, but was turned back and exploded at sea under mysterious circumstances, causing huge loss of life.

91. For accounts of the ordeal of the *Navemar*, see several articles compiled by Lars Nothdurft in Schöck-Quinteros et al. *Navemar* was an overcrowded freighter chartered by the JDC that left Spain in August 1941 for a five-week journey to New York via Lisbon and Havana.

92. Knickerbocker, 389.

93. Berthold Viertel, "Das Schiff von Cuba," *Aufbau*, June 15, 1939, reprinted in Schöck-Quinteros et al., 365–67. English paraphrase of German text.

94. "Dr. Paul Kl.: Refugees," *Aufbau*, February 2, 1939, in Schöck-Quinteros et al., 361–63. English paraphrase of German text.
95. "Die Totenschiffe Fahren," 363.
96. "Irrend und Hoffnungslos! Einige Trockenen Zahlen aus der Schicksals-Arena des Jüdischen Elends" [Wandering and without hope! Some sobering figures from the fate arena of Jewish misery], *Aufbau*, June 15, 1939, in Schöck-Quinteros et al., 367–68.
97. "Vergässe ich Deiner Je, St. Louis . . ." *Aufbau*, June 15, 1939, in Schöck-Quinteros et al., 369–72, here 370.
98. "Nehmt 900 Nazis!" *Aufbau*, June 15, 1939, in Schöck-Quinteros et al., 368–69.
99. In their June 24, 1938, letter to Myron C. Taylor and the Conference at Evian (see note 31, this chapter), the Freeland League for Jewish Territorial Colonisation signaled Jewish migrants' willingness to become citizens of the African country in question and renounced political organizing. While their proposal is borne from mortal fear of persecution, its envisioning of settlement partakes in a Eurocentric, colonialist imagination.

Chapter 2

1. Adolf Hitler, speech in Königsberg, March 25, 1938. Excerpt cited in translation in the *New York Times* coverage of the speech. See "Hitler is Pleased to Get Rid of Foes," *New York Times*, March 27, 1938.
2. Ibid.
3. *Bremen* and its sister ship *Europa* were built during the Weimar Republic, but capitalizing on the vessels' international reputation for speed, the NS regime made them symbols of Nazi Germany's political ascendancy and aspiration to strength and efficiency.
4. "Reds Rip Flag off Bremen, Throw It into Hudson; 2,000 Battle the Police," *New York Times*, July 27, 1935, 1, 5. Some rioters were believed to have been dock workers, though *The New York Times* does not confirm this. Demonstrators relocated to the West 47th Street police station to support arrested comrades. Next to the front-page story's continued coverage on page 5, a small article, "Demonstrators Condemn 'Religious Persecution,'" reports that demonstrators distributed anti-Nazi leaflets on the *Bremen* that were issued by "The Friends of Catholic Germany" and addressed themselves to Catholics and Jews. The *Bremen* was not the only German ship encountering hostilities from foreign dock workers. When the SS *Cap Arcona* arrived in Buenos Aires in July 1933 with 200 members of the National Socialist paramilitary storm trooper organization SA on board, Argentinian dock workers called a strike to keep the ship from docking. See Philipp Mettauer, "'Die

Schiffsreise war für mich eine Mischung aus Nostalgie, Melancholie, Unsicherheit': Die Überfahrt österreichischer Jüdinnen und Juden nach Südamerika," *Mobile Culture Studies: The Journal* 1 (2015): 167–80.

5. At the time of the incident, the official flag of Nazi Germany was still the imperial tricolor flag that had replaced the black-red-gold banner of Weimar Germany upon Hitler gaining power in 1933. According to *The New York Times*, the swastika had apparently been superimposed on the official German flag flown on the *Bremen*.

6. Peter Longerich, *Politik der Vernichtung: Eine Gesamtdarstellung der Nationalsozialistischen Judenverfolgung* (Piper, 1998), 622.

7. Korrespondenzen über die Konzessionen für die Beförderung von Auswanderern 1938–1940 [Correspondence related to concessions for the transportation of emigrants 1938–1940]. Hamburger Staatsarchiv StAHH 621-1/95_204.

8. Ibid. It is unclear whether the sum at issue was 15 percent of the deposit or of the total price of the ticket.

9. Ibid. ". . . während es dabei im Interesse der Judenpolitik vordringlich auf den Effekt des baldigen und möglichst umfassenden Auszuges der Juden aus Deutschland ankommt." Roy Grundmann trans.

10. Letter by Claus-Gottfried Holthusen for "Patriapost," in Allgemeine Fragen der Passagierschifffahrt [General questions about passenger ship service]. Hamburger Staatsarchiv StAHH 621-1/95_193.

11. Ausarbeitung von C. G. Holthusen: "Gedanken über die Passagierfahrt der Hamburg-Amerika Linie" mit zahlreichen Tabellen und Graphiken, insbesondere zur Fahrpreisentwicklung in den Jahren 1929–1938 in allen Diensten—1940 [Presentation by C.G Holthusen: "Thoughts about the Hamburg America Line's passenger business" with numerous tables and charts, especially regarding the evolution of pricing in the years 1929–1938 in all services—1940], 2. Hamburger Staatsarchiv StAHH 621-1/95_1254. Roy Grundmann trans.

12. Zhava Litvac Glaser, *Refugees and Relief: The American Jewish Joint Distribution Committee and European Jews in Cuba and Shanghai 1938–1943*, PhD diss., City University of New York, 2015, 111.

13. Ships servicing such fixed lines on a regular schedule thus came to be called "line ships" and, with the rise of steam and the increase in ship sizes, were identified by the broader cultural term "ocean liners." Note, however, that the term "line ship" is also used for war ships, specifically those designed to sail in large fleet configurations or lines of ships.

14. Susanne Wiborg and Dr. Klaus Wiborg, *Unser Feld ist die Welt: 150 Jahre Hapag-Lloyd* (Hamburger Abendblatt Axel Springer Verlag, 1997), 20–21. The city of Hamburg in 1858 awarded HAPAG a contract to carry mail to the United States. Starting in 1885 the German Empire also issued

mail route concessions as part of its colonization of Africa and Asia. Though NDL was involved more prominently than HAPAG, both lines were part of Germany's expansionist infrastructure. On the mail steamships of the German Empire, see Christine Reinke-Kunze, *Die Geschichte der Reichs-Post-Dampfer: Verbindungen zwischen den Kontinenten* (Koehlers Verlagsgesellschaft mbH, 1994). On NDL, see Christian Ostersehlte, "Soll und Haben: Ein wirtschaftsgeschichtlicher Blick auf den Norddeutschen Lloyd (1857–1970)," *Bremisches Jahrbuch* 86 (2007), 176–255.

15. Wiborg and Wiborg, *Unser Feld*, 20.

16. Ibid., 27. HAPAG was the first shipping line that gave passengers a certain comfort. By 1870, however, NDL had hegemony in the passage business while HAPAG's cargo transportation figures were higher. HAPAG's passage division competed with NDL in speed and size only intermittently. In 1900, the liner *Deutschland* won the Blue Riband for the fastest transatlantic crossing, and on the eve of World War I, HAPAG launched *Imperator*, then the biggest ship in the world, to be followed by two sister ships, *Bismarck* and *Vaterland*, neither of which, however, would see service due to the outbreak of the war. But these "superliners" were exceptions to HAPAG's fleet of mid-size and moderately paced cargo-passenger combi liners.

17. See Susanne Wiborg, *Albert Ballin* (Eller & Richter Verlag, 2013), 13–31. See also Eberhard Straub, *Albert Ballin: Der Reeder des Kaisers* (Siedler Verlag, 2002), 32–64.

18. Mark A. Russell, *Steamship Nationalism: Ocean Liners and National Identity in Imperial Germany and the Atlantic World* (Routledge, 2020).

19. For the full details of Ballin's rise, see Wiborg, *Albert Ballin*, 16–22.

20. In 1939, HAPAG had 18 sales offices in Germany and 22 in other European countries. In addition, it cooperated with 64 authorized agents in Germany and Europe that were part of larger travel agencies. See Auskunftsmappe der Abteilung Personenverkehr [Folder of Information regarding the Department of Passage], Hamburger Staatsarchiv StAHH 621-1/95_3001, 38–39.

21. Wiborg and Wiborg, 193.

22. Ibid., 152. The village was located on an island in the Elbe River, which provided natural isolation from the town and the harbor.

23. Wiborg and Wiborg, 104.

24. Ibid., 84–88. It was NDL that organized the very first cruise in 1890 up the coast of Norway, but the company billed it strictly as a special, one-off trip.

25. For details, see Wiborg and Wiborg, 214–21.

26. After expanding its South America business, HAPAG in 1907 partnered with the ailing Wöhrmann line, which controlled passenger and cargo traffic to Africa. Both HAPAG and NDL recovered from World War I with

the help of the United States, which did not sign the Versailles Treaty and returned confiscated ships to HAPAG and other lines. In the 1920s HAPAG restored its fleet and reinstated its share agreements with competitors to preempt price wars.

27. Typoskripte und Materialien zu einer Darstellung des Schiffsverkehrs der HAPAG mit Kuba, Mexiko und den westindischen Inseln [Typescripts and materials for a presentation of HAPAG's shipping business with Cuba, Mexico, and the West Indies], Hamburger Staatsarchiv StAHH 621-1/95_3289. According to a HAPAG statistic, Germany in 1929 imported goods worth 27.6 million Reichsmark from Columbia, 81.4 million from Guatemala, 78.8 million from Venezuela, and 45.6 million from El Salvador. Germany received three quarters of all Guatemalan exports and more than half of all exports from El Salvador. In turn, Germany exported goods worth millions of Reichsmark to these countries.

28. Ibid.

29. Wiborg and Wiborg, 113. The La Plata and Brazil service was in cooperation with the Hamburg-South America Steamship Company ("Hamburg Süd"), which dominated service to Argentina, Uruguay, and Brazil from Germany; the Peru and Chile service was in cooperation with the Kosmos Line. Starting in 1930, HAPAG co-serviced the West Coast of South America with NDL and participated in regional shipping on the subcontinent's east coast.

30. Ibid., 222. Wiborg and Wiborg write that by 1923, HAPAG had fully resumed service to Africa, Asia, South America, and the West Indies. *The New York Herald Tribune* called it one of the most astounding restorations in the history of world shipping.

31. Ibid. HAPAG acquired Atlas in 1901. Atlas initially only ran freight service between New York and Latin America, but because Colon was part of the network of routes, HAPAG even participated in the Panama Canal construction business. Passenger service was added a few years later but only lasted until World War I.

32. Claus-Gottfried Holthusen, "Das Passagegeschäft der Hamburg-Amerika Linie im Jahre 1937," in Allgemeine Fragen der Passagierfahrt [General Questions of Passenger Shipping], Hamburger Staatsarchiv StAHH 621-1/95_193.

33. Ibid. Translation by Roy Grundmann. Emphases via quotation marks and underlining are directly adapted from original source.

34. Ibid. Letter from Holthusen to Fachgruppe Reeder, April 12, 1938. We can assume that the majority of second-class passengers, not to speak of the first-class clientele, were not Jewish. Yet, in 1937, before the Nazi dispossession laws had taken effect, some Jewish migrants still had the means to book more expensive passage. Responding to anxious queries that

some Jewish migrants could not be identified as Jews because they had not booked third class, Holthusen responds that the migrant retains his status also when traveling in the more expensive cabin class, a fare category used on several HAPAG combi ships, including the *St. Louis*, that was their most luxurious accommodation.

35. Statistiken über den Mittelamerika-Verkehr: Januar/Dezember 1938 im Vergleich mit Januar/Dezember 1937, Hamburger Staatsarchiv StAHH 621-1/95_3005.

36. Statistik der Passagen von Juden auf allen Linien 1937–1939. Stat. No. 186-39 Unsere Judenbeförderung ab Hamburg. Januar–August 1939 [Statistics of passages of Jews on all lines, 1937–1939; No. 186-39 Our Transportation of Jews from Hamburg, January–August, 1939], Hamburger Staatsarchiv StAHH 621-1/95_3002. According to the statistic, Jews also constituted approximately one third of all passengers to Australia and East Asia, though the total numbers are considerably smaller than for Latin America and the Caribbean (380 for East Asia and 58 for Australia). I have no comparable figures for other lines servicing the same regions.

37. Ibid. Seven passengers were not Jewish.

38. Statistiken über den Mittelamerika-Verkehr: Januar–Dezember 1938 im Vergleich mit Januar–Dezember 1937 [Statistics about the Traffic to Middle America: January–December 1938 in comparison to January–December 1937], Hamburger Staatsarchiv StAHH 621-1/95_3005.

39. Ibid. Second class rose by 35.7%; third class rose only 25.5%. Numbers are for the Caribbean and the Gulf region.

40. On HAPAG's commissioning of films for promoting its sea tourism (Seetouristik) during the 1920s and early '30s, see Michael Töteberg, "Exotik und Tourismus: Die Reisefilme der Hapag," *Sammlungen: Hamburger Flimmern*, Heft 5 (1999), www.filmmuseum-hamburg.de/sammlungen/hamburger-flimmern/heft-05-1999/die-reisefilme-der-hapag.html, accessed March 9, 2025. While often panned by critics, such films as *Mit der HAPAG von Hamburg nach New York* (1924) (With HAPAG from Hamburg to New York), *Eine Mittelmeer- und Orientreise mit der "Peer Gynt"* (1925) (A Mediterranean and Orient voyage with "Peer Gynt"), *Mit dem Kurbelkasten um die Erde* (1924) (Around the World with a hand-cranked camera), *Aus der Tropischen Heimat des Golfstromes* (1927) (From the tropical home of the Gulf Stream), and especially Walter Ruttmann's film *Melodie der Welt* (1929) (Melody of the world) were prime examples of the promotion of cruise tourism through ethnographically inflected travelogues. Töteberg notes that this mediatization of ocean travel after World War I went hand in hand with the practice, begun before World War I, of HAPAG and other lines installing on-board cinemas on ocean liners. (As early as 1935, the HAPAG liner *Caribia* even became part of a five-point television network that broadcast sports and cultural events from Hamburg's

Heiligengeistfeld; see Film- und Fernsehmuseum Hamburg, Fernsehen, "Die Vorgeschichte und erste Phase der Fernsehentwicklung in Deutschland," www.filmmuseum-hamburg.de/fernsehen/geschichte.html, accessed March 9, 2025.) This phenomenon of mediatizing ships and ocean travel supports the view that the ship and the ocean are not merely selected objects of media coverage, but must also be regarded as mediums unto themselves. See "Editorial," *Das Schiff, Archiv für Mediengeschichte*, 2023, edited by Friedrich Balke, Bernhard Siegert, and Joseph Vogl (Verlag Vorwerk 8, 2024). On Nazi entertainment cinema's reflection of Nazi culture's new-found cosmopolitanism, see Eric Rentschler, *The Ministry of Illusion: Nazi Cinema and Its Afterlife* (Harvard University Press, 1996).

41. A HAPAG brochure about land tours in Vera Cruz speaks of the "bunten Leben und Treiben der Bevölkerung" (the colorful lives and hustle and bustle of the native population). All quotes from travel brochures in this chapter are English translations by Roy Grundmann of the original German texts. See Hamburg-Amerika Linie, "14 HAPAG Fahrten nach Westindien," Library of the Deutsches Schifffahrtsmuseum, Bremerhaven.

42. Hamburg-Amerika Linie, "Erholungs-und Studienreisen nach Mittelamerika und Cuba-Mexico" [Pleasure and study tours to Latin America and Cuba-Mexico], Library of the Deutsches Schifffahrtsmuseum, Bremerhaven. This type of rhetoric is also prevalent in some of HAPAG's film travelogues of the previous decade (see footnote 40), but at least in *Melodie der Welt* it occurs in fleeting, scattered, and impressionistic form. The travel brochures of the 1930s discussed here offered a far more systematic and sustained colonialist discourse.

43. "Angebote Prospekte Vergnügunsreisen" [Offers, brochures, cruises]. Roy Grundmann trans. Hamburger Staatsarchiv StAHH 621-1/95_2975. s The term "leader of the Filibuster" echoes NS culture's distrust of western democracies.

44. A telegram, dated July 18, 1936, presumably originating with a HAPAG sales office in Chile, waxes about the "prestige of German passenger shipping" and projects regular bookings of sixty first-class tickets and fifty in tourist class. See "Ermittlung über den Bedarf an Passagierplätzen auf Schiffen in der Südamerika-Westküstenfahrt" [Investigation about needed passenger capacity on ships for the South America–West Indies routes], Hamburger Staatsarchiv StAHH 621-1/95_195.

45. With two brief exceptions—the early 1900s and the mid-1930s, when the Reich temporarily assumed partial ownership—HAPAG had resisted any offers of state subsidy.

46. "Bericht von Dr. W. Hoffmann über seine Reiseeindrücke in Südamerika 1938" [Report by Dr. W. Hoffmann about his travel impressions in South America], Hamburger Staatsarchiv StAHH 621-1/95_3262 UA 25. Excerpts translated by Roy Grundmann.

47. For HAPAG's notes to the NSDAP regarding prominent passengers, see "Meldungen an die NSDAP, Gauleitung Hamburg, über den Transport wichtiger Personen, 1937–1939" [Notices to the NSDAP, District Administration Hamburg, about the transport of important persons, 1937–1939], Hamburger Staatsarchiv StAHH 621-1/95_202.

48. This situation was no different at other shipping lines. For information about the *Cap Arcona*, which on its westbound journeys carried Jewish refugees to Argentina and on its eastbound trips Germans who repatriated to Germany, see Mettauer, 176.

49. See United States Holocaust Memorial Museum, "Refuge in Latin America," encyclopedia.ushmm.org/content/en/article/refuge-in-latin-america, accessed August 29, 2022.

50. Ibid. Bolivia issued visas to German and Austrian Jews through its European consulates. They arrived by ship in the Chilean port of Arica, from where many went on to La Paz, Bolivia, on the so called "Express Judio" (Jewish Express). See *Closed Borders: The International Conference on Refugees in Evian 1939* (Technische Universität), evian1938.de/en/bolivia/, accessed August 29, 2022. The liberal immigration policy Hochschild initiated incurred a backlash and prompted restrictions, which, however, were not fully enforced (this appears to be a typical example of a gray zone generated by inconsistent administrative policy execution). In contrast to the USHMM's Holocaust Encyclopedia article, data on this website claims that only a total of 8,000 Jews made it to Bolivia.

51. Gilberto Bosques Saldivar was Mexico's consul to France in Marseille. Until his arrest by Vichy authorities in 1943, he issued tens of thousands of Mexican visas to Jews, many of whom tried to flee Franco Spain.

52. In addition to the JDC, several Jewish refugee organizations were active. Canada, for instance, had the Canadian Jewish Congress, which helped finance the farm purchases of many Jewish immigrants from Germany, Austria, and Poland, as well as the Jewish Colonization Association. I am grateful to Steven Schwinghamer from the Canadian Museum of Immigration for sharing documentation with me on this. See "CNR—Album—Examples of Settlement of European Refugee Families on Land, 1939," Government of Canada, Library and Archives, January 29, 2025, central.bac-lac.gc.ca/. redirect?app=fonandcol&id=4276610&lang=eng.

53. According to Schwinghamer, another factor were railroad companies. Migrants were part of their business, so they wanted them to pass immigration procedures. An example of the significance of a railroad in Latin America's migrant traffic is the "Express Judio" that operated between Arica in Chile and La Paz.

54. Vincent, "The Voyage of the *St. Louis* Revisited," 256–57. See my detailed discussion on these dynamics in chapter 5.

55. For the higher number, see Vincent, 256–57. For the lower number, see the section on Cuba in *Closed Borders*, evian1938.de/en/cuba/, accessed August 29, 2022.

56. Letter from Claus-Gottfried Holthusen to Victor Neumann, December 12, 1938, file on MS *St. Louis*, Hamburger Staatsarchiv, StAHH 621-1/95_4776 Part 1.

57. Dr. James Bernstein, "Memorandum on SS '*St. Louis*,'—HAPAG," June 27, 1939, JDC Archives, Collection 1933–1944, Folder 386.

58. Ibid. On the infrastructure of Jewish Refugee Organizations, see Glaser, *Refugees and Relief*, 98. As Glaser points out, HICEM was founded in Paris in 1926 to unify the work of three Jewish emigration organizations: HIAS in New York, the Jewish Colonization Association (JCA or ICA) in London, and the United Jewish Emigration Committee (EmigDirect) in Germany. HICEM is an acronym for HIAS, ICA, and EmigDirect.

59. Lord Duncannon to the President, HIAS-ICA Emigration Association, Cable, May 8, 1939, informing HIAS-ICA that the High Commissariat of Refugees at the League of Nations had officially notified HAPAG of the problem. AR1933/44: 378, in Folder SS *St. Louis*, JDC Report on *St. Louis*, 1933–1944 New York Collection.

60. See Vincent, 256–57.

61. "Rundschreiben der HAPAG vom 15.4.1939" [HAPAG Bulletin of April 15, 1939], Online Item "Erinnern für die Zukunft e.V., Bochum," www.bochum.de/C125830C0042AB74/vwContentByKey/W287J9FT046BOLD-DE/$FILE/021_Pander_Max.pdf, accessed August 3, 2022.

62. *St. Louis* was launched on August 2, 1928, after 21 months of construction, and went on her maiden voyage to New York on March 28, 1929.

63. Andrew M. Baxter and Alex Norasteh, "A Brief History of U.S. Immigration Policy from the Colonial Period to the Present Day," CATO Institute, Policy Analysis No. 919, August 3, 2021, www.cato.org/policy-analysis/brief-history-us-immigration-policy-colonial-period-present-day.

64. Victor Neumann, "MS 'St. Louis,'" pp. 1–7, in "Charterung und Fahrtgebiet der MS St. Louis 1938" [Charters and operational territories of MS *St. Louis* 1938], Hamburger Staatsarchiv, StAHH 621-1/95_203.

65. Ibid., 1.

66. *St. Louis* weighed 16,732 GRT and was 574 ft (175 m) long. Her maximum speed was 16 knots. The Hamburg class ships weighed between 21,000 and 22,000 GRT and were between 600 ft (183 m) and 677 ft (206 m) long and were designed to carry around 1600 passengers. But even the ships of the Hamburg class were considerably smaller and slower than the *Bremen* and the *Europa*, the two superliners of HAPAG's competitors NDL. *Hansa*'s original name was *Albert Ballin*, but Ballin's Jewishness required HAPAG to rename the ship in 1935.

67. Neumann, "MS 'St. Louis.'" HAPAG created cabin class because in the 1920s there still existed a segment of relatively prosperous emigrants. But comfort was only one reason for them to book cabin class. Neumann

claims that passengers in that class were not subjected to the same harsh immigration procedures as those in third class.

68. Exact data on the *St. Louis*'s passenger capacity varies. The April 1929 issue of the British nautical publication *The Motor Ship*, vol. X, April 1929–March 1930, n.p., lists *St. Louis*'s passenger capacity as 973; the technical German nautical publication *Werft—Reederei—Hafen* 10, no. 7 (April 1929), p. 13, lists it as 1,100. Passenger data from 1929 shows that for the first six months of transatlantic service *St. Louis* often carried between 700 and 800 passengers, on one trip even as many as 1,036 passengers. This number declined dramatically in the years to come. See "MS St. Louis," Hamburger Staatsarchiv StAHH 621-1/95_4776 Teil 1.

69. Neumann, "MS 'St. Louis,'" 6. Neumann notes the importance of Halifax as a major port of immigration for Canada, though he acknowledges that immigration to Canada had been very slow in the 1930s due to Canada's own restrictions.

70. Neumann, 4–5.

71. "Prospekte Infomaterial Studien u. Erholungsreisen Mittelamerika Kuba" [Brochures and information material for study tours and recreational tours Central America and Cuba], Hamburger Staatsarchiv StAHH 621-1/95_2977.

72. More historical research is needed on how NS culture perceived the relationship between the kind of high-end individual tourism HAPAG offered with its South America study trips and the "Volkstourismus" organized by the German Labor Front and KdF. The two new KdF cruise ships, *Wilhelm Gustloff* and *Robert Ley*, were strictly one-class cruise ships for NSDAP party members, all of whom paid the same fare. In his discussion of films promoting HAPAG's sea tourism, Töteberg discusses the film *Wasser hat Balken* (1933), which translates to something like "Water's Hard Surface," as an example of early Nazi-era media negotiating class difference in the context of sea tourism. He mentions that the film caused a political stir because it was denied the quality seal "educational" by the NS censorship board. Apparently, the board felt that the film's promotion of high-end ocean travel was at variance with NS ideology's promotion of the "Volk," that is, the regular German population among which class distinctions were eliminated or had less and less relevance. Representatives of the city of Hamburg made suggestions for salvaging the film, among which was the inclusion of footage of emigrants traveling in third class and having breakfast on board as proof that ocean travel was not foreclosed to the "Volk" ("Aber auch dem kleinen Mann, dem deutschen Auswanderer, bietet das deutsche Schiff um wenig Geld liebevolle Aufnahme"). It seems that this conflict, by the mid- to late 1930s, had subsided. My discussion of the various NS-directed communities in South America shows that their lauding of HAPAG's liner service to the

region ascribed value to multi-class transatlantic ocean travel (as opposed to cheap one-class KdF-type tourism). Further, HAPAG in its promotional material of the *St. Louis* always featured third-class accommodations, signaling the accessibility of its own brand of ocean travel, not the least for migrants.

73. Neumann, 7: "Wenn nicht alle Anzeichen trügen, muss mit einer überaus starken nichtarischen Auswanderung für die nächsten Jahre gerechnet werden. Mit Rücksicht auf unsere übrige Kundschaft sind wir gehalten, die Zahl der in der Touristen- und 3. Klasse unserer Schiffe der 'Hamburg'-Klasse mitzunehmenden nichtarischen Personen zu beschränken, weil es nicht möglich ist, in diesen Klassen einen grösseren Prozentsatz nichtarischer Personen zu befördern, ohne eine mit der Zeit sich vollziehende Abwanderung des arischen Publikums von unseren Schiffen auf diejenigen der Konkurrenz zu erleiden. Gerade für die Zwecke der Beförderung nichtarischer Personen würde die „St. Louis" sich als geeignet erweisen." HAPAG often received complaints from non-Jewish travelers about the presence of Jews on board. See file "Korrespondenzen von Claus-Gottfried Holthusen über besondere Vorkommnisse im Personenverkehr 1936–1939," Hamburger Staatsarchiv, StAHH 621-1/95_197. The tendency to ghettoize Jewish travelers existed on all passenger ships during the Third Reich. The NDL transatlantic liner *Bremen* had an area in its social rooms that was called the "Judenecke" (the Jew corner).

74. Hamburg-Amerika Linie, "MS St. Louis: Kajüte und Dritte Klasse—Cabin Class and Third Class," Library of the Deutsches Schifffahrtsmuseum, Bremerhaven, Item No. II B 13-620. This brochure gives no conclusive publication date, but it was likely published in 1938. HAPAG collapsed tourist class into third class, using the denomination of third class but upgrading it in the process. The ship's passenger capacity was listed as 925.

Chapter 3

1. See Gustav Schröder, *Heimatlos auf hoher See* (Beckerdruck, 1949). For *Homeless on the High Seas*, English translation by Roy Grundmann, see appendix. See also Gustav Schröder, "Reisebericht des Kapitäns, Motorschiff St. Louis, 98. Reise," in Folder "MS the *St. Louis*," Teil 2 "Kapitänsberichte" [Captain's Log, Motorship *St. Louis*, 98th Voyage, Part 2, Captain's Logs], Hamburger Staatsarchiv StAHH 621-1/95_4776. Roy Grundmann trans., see appendix. For published passenger diaries, see, among others, "Tagebuch von Erich Dublon" [Diary of Erich Dublon] in Reinfelder, *MS "the St. Louis" Frühjahr 1939*, 218–34.

2. On linguistic strategies of distancing in the context of Nazi bureaucracy, see Saul Friedlander, *Reflections of Nazism: An Essay on Kitsch and Death*, trans. Thomas Weyr (Indiana University Press, 1984), 102–3.

3. "Sonder" (meaning "special") was a technical term with a neutral meaning before the Nazis repurposed it for racially othering Jews. See for instance Mautner Markhof, *Das St. Louis-Drama*, 13–14, on the "Sonderbehandlung" ("special treatment"—de facto meaning "execution") of Russian Jews under the German occupation of the USSR. The NS regime also gave German Jews the cynical euphemism "Gastvolk" (guest people).

4. Lipsky, Uhlig, and Glaevecke, *Kapitän Schröder und die Irrfahrt der St. Louis*, 45. In 1934, German Jews had been officially classified as refugees. See Vincent, "The Voyage of the *St. Louis* Revisited," 279n22, on the infrastructure the US State Department and the League of Nations established in the early 1930s to address the problem of Jewish refugees from Nazi Germany.

5. Mautner Markhof, 54.

6. Reinfelder, 26.

7. For passenger accounts of the embarkation procedures, see Reinfelder, 27, and Mautner Markhof, 25 and 45–48.

8. Historians have frequently misidentified Quay 76 as the place of embarkation. Quay 71 was across from HAPAG's main embarkation area in Kaiser-Wilhelm-Höft, the tip of Hamburg's Kaiser-Wilhelm-Hafen, where HAPAG and other large shipping lines loaded passengers. Quay 76 was located further away in the Ellerholzhafen. HAPAG used it only for equipping its ships. See Ziemer and Ziemer, *Aufrecht in schweren Zeiten*, 140.

9. Reinfelder, 27. The song became popularized in English through Elvis Presley's 1960 rendition "Wooden Heart."

10. For passenger accounts, see the website of the United States Holocaust Memorial Museum's *St. Louis* landing page, www.ushmm.org/online/st-louis/, as well as Mautner Markhof, 58–60, and Reinfelder, 30–35 and 15–18.

11. Ogilvie and Miller, *Refuge Denied*, 4 and 27.

12. Reinfelder, 24.

13. Mautner Markhof, 46.

14. Vincent, 255–56.

15. The MS *Iberia* had left Germany before May 5, the day Cuba released Decree 937, and arrived in Havana the week of May 14. As the visas of its Jewish passengers were already invalidated, Benítez personally saw to it that the passengers could disembark, openly defying Laredo Brú. This prompted Laredo Brú to invent the grandfather clause. See Glaser, *Refugees and Relief*, 101, with reference to Lawrence Berenson and Cecilia Rasovsky, *Report on the JDC Efforts in the St. Louis Affair (Highly Confidential)*, June 15, 1939, 1, AR 1933/44:378, AJDC NY Records.

16. See Glaser, 102 and 108, with reference to internal JDC correspondence between Laura Margolis and Cecilia Razovsky, May 22, 1939, AR 1933/44:378, JDC New York, and to Lawrence Berenson and Cecilia Razovsky, *Report on the JDC Efforts in the St. Louis Affair (Highly Confidential)*, 4, 7–9.

17. Glaser, 103, 105, with reference to an exchange between Margolis and Razovsky (see fn13). Margolis further told Razovsky that, following the *Iberia* situation and Benítez's resignation, a new immigration law was being proposed at the House of Representatives and was campaigned for with funds both from local Spanish merchants and Fascists.

18. Vincent, 258.

19. Schröder, "Reisebericht" [Captain's Log], 2. See also Schröder, *Heimatlos*, 9–10.

20. Vincent, 258.

21. Schröder, *Heimatlos*, 11. He was later reunited with his family in England.

22. I base my figures on "Seeking Refuge in Cuba, 1939" in the *Holocaust Encyclopedia*, United States Holocaust Memorial Museum, encyclopedia.ushmm.org/content/en/article/seeking-refuge-in-cuba-1939. *Orduña* carried 120 Austrian, Czech, and German Jews; 48 held landing permits accepted by Cuba, and the others remained on the ship, which left for South America on May 29 without any guarantee that landing would be permitted by any nation. Five passengers were eventually accepted by Chile, the rest by the US, but not until late 1940. The *Flandre* was carrying 104 German, Austrian, and Czech Jewish passengers. Cuba and Mexico declined disembarkation. Eventually, the *Flandre* returned to France, where the passengers were interned by the French government.

23. Vincent, 260.

24. Vincent, 260 and 282n50, citing data from the National Archives and Records Administration (NARA), RG 59, 837.55J/39, "Jewish Refugee Situation in Habana," June 7, 1939, with specific reference to a document titled "Enclosure No. 5 to Dispatch No. 1017," which includes an entry for "June 1, 1939" that, so Vincent believes, was likely authored on that date.

25. See, among others, Reinfelder, 61.

26. Reinfelder, 64; Mautner-Markhof, 69–70.

27. Schröder, *Heimatlos*, 10–11. See also Reinfelder, 63; Lipsky et al., 64. See also Hart Phillips, "Cuba Orders Liner and Refugees to Go—Navy to Escort the *St. Louis* with 917 Aboard Unless She Obeys—Compromise Reported," *New York Times*, June 2, 1939, A1.

28. Vincent, 256–65. See also Afoumado, *Exil impossible*, 55–111; Reinfelder, 35–40, 55–70, and 84–99.

29. See Vincent, 256. Vincent quotes a May 4 *Diario de la Marina* article warning Cubans of the planned *St. Louis* trip. The most detailed analysis of the Cuban press response to the *St. Louis* is furnished by Afoumado, 67–75. See also Lawlor, "The Saddest Ship Afloat," 26, who writes that news about the planned *St. Louis* trip triggered a large antisemitic demonstration in

Havana on May 8, 1939. Domestic labor organizations also opposed the influx of new migrants.

30. Vincent, 256, citing an early historical analysis of the episode by Gellman, "The *St. Louis* Tragedy," 144–56.

31. See Vincent and Glaser for the most comprehensive and authoritative accounts.

32. Vincent, 258 and fn41. Batista was unapproachable all week due to alleged illness.

33. Ibid., 260fn51.

34. Glaser, 108.

35. Glaser, 113, with reference to Laurence Berenson and Cecilia Razovsky, *Report on the JDC Efforts in the St. Louis Affair (Highly Confidential)*, 5. See also Vincent, 261 and 282fn54, with reference to further JDC records.

36. Vincent, 261fn55. In his book *Kein Gelobtes Land: Die Irrfahrt der St. Louis* (Nannen-Verlag, 1961), Hans Herlin writes that Berenson had even toured the Isle of Pines with Batista, who had taken them there by military plane (103). See chapter 5.

37. Vincent, 262.

38. Vincent (263) and Afoumado (97) have expressed astonishment at Berenson's attitude. See also my discussion of Hans Herlin's account of the negotiations in chapter 5. According to Vincent (263n70), Berenson's final offer also involved asylum for the Jews on the *Flandre* and the *Orduña*, but it remains unclear what financial foundation for this inclusion Berenson had in mind.

39. Vincent, 263. On the detailed timeline of the supposedly missed deadline and the JDC's hindsight assessment of it, see Glaser, 120–26, with reference to *Lawrence Berenson and Cecilia Razovsky, Report on the JDC Efforts in the St. Louis Affair (Highly Confidential)*, 13–14. Glaser's research shows that the JDC learned that afternoon that Laredo Brú's office had prepared a news release announcing the unsuccessful end of negotiations as early as 11 a.m. that morning, while keeping the JDC waiting until late afternoon. This made the decision to reject the JDC's offer a foregone conclusion. The JDC's Joseph C. Hyman noted in hindsight that the JDC at all points demonstrated willingness to meet the conditions of the Cuban government, but that the matter was political, not fiscal. See Glaser, 123, with reference to letter from Joseph Hyman to Sam Bober, June 14, 1939, AR 1933/44:378, JDC New York Records.

40. In Vincent's assessment (262–64), Berenson was blinded by having secured the landing of 2000 Jews in Cuba since 1938. Berenson had apparently failed to make clear to the JDC in New York that any prospect of landing the *St. Louis* passengers in Cuba would evaporate at noon on June

6. Vincent summarizes: "Accordingly, the State Department received little intelligence—from either New York or Havana—that might have led it to believe the negotiations were doomed to failure. To be sure, anxious telegrams arrived in abundance from relatives and friends of the passengers—indeed, from the passengers themselves—urging either the State Department or President Roosevelt to inject the power and prestige of the United States into the negotiations. But from the position of the State Department and the White House, the information that counted—that coming from the JDC's 'man on the spot' in Cuba—remained too hopeful to risk accusations of official American meddling" (265).

41. See Arthur D. Morse, *While Six Million Died: A Chronicle of American Apathy* (Random House, 1967); see also Reinfelder, 80, and Mautner Markhof, 107.

42. "Refugee Ship Idles off Florida Coast," *New York Times*, June 5, 1939, 1–2, 4. According to the article, the *St. Louis* was cruising "leisurely through Caribbean waters tonight after twenty-four hours spent idling along the lower Florida East Coast. She had previously anchored twelve miles offshore. . . . The Coast Guard patrol boat CG244, out of Fort Lauderdale, stood by the ship as she moved down the coast, barely making way, to prevent possible attempts by refugees to jump off and swim ashore." The article then inserts a brief Associated Press report that "a large steamship, possibly the St. Louis, dropped anchor off Miami Beach at 1 A.M. today." The article continues: "No overtures were made by Captain Wilhelm [*sic*] Schroeder to dock in this country. . . . The refugees appeared more hopeful than when they left Havana, the Coast Guardsmen said, some even smiling a greeting as the patrol boat passed. A Coast Guard plane that flew over the ship late today on its regular patrol trip reported the St. Louis still was proceeding south-eastward."

43. Schröder, *Heimatlos*, 15. Roy Grundmann trans. For full text, see appendix.

44. United States Coast Guard, "Frequently Asked Questions": "What was the Coast Guard's role in the SS St. Louis affair (otherwise known as the 'Voyage of the Damned')?" www.history.uscg.mil/Frequently-Asked-Questions/, accessed August 25, 2023. The Coast Guard's version of events seems confirmed by other media coverage. See, for instance, "Coast Guard Alert as Refugee Ship Cruises off Florida Coast," *Indiana Evening Gazette*, June 5, 1939, 1: "Coast Guard and Immigration Officials held themselves on the alert today as the German steamship St. Louis cruised in the vicinity of the Florida coast. . . . The big ocean liner was sighted by the Coast Guard yesterday moving slowly past Fort Lauderdale. A patrol boat dropped in behind it and trailed it until sundown. For two hours the ship rode at anchor off the Miami channel light, easily visible from ashore. . . . Two Coast Guard planes were dispatched from Miami to keep the anchored craft under surveillance

and the patrol boat hovered nearby. . . . Immigration Inspector Walter B. Thomas emphasized today that his concern with the German vessel was a routine matter. He had no instructions from Washington, he said, and the attention paid the vessel was only that which would be paid any craft with aliens aboard. It was a routine inquiry by the immigration service that caused the coast guard to locate the ship."

45. United States Coast Guard, "Frequently Asked Questions."

46. Ibid.

47. Ibid.

48. The main reasons for the US's position on the *St. Louis* are reiterated in all major recent accounts, including Reinfelder, 41–54, Afoumado, 111–56, Mautner Markhof, 106–12, and Vincent, 274–76.

49. Vincent, 275.

50. The details are referenced in Robert M. Krakow's film *Complicit* (discussed in chapter 9). See also Lawlor, 51, who asserts that as early as 1938, the islands' governor and legislative assembly had offered refuge to Jewish refugees.

51. Formal response by A. M. Warren of the State Department's Visa Division. See Mautner Markhof, 108–9; see also Lawlor, 51.

52. Lipsky et al., 70.

53. "Refugees Granted Temporary Haven on Cuba's Isle of Pines," *Washington Post*, June 6, 1939, 1.

54. For a discussion of the Canadian petition on behalf of the *St. Louis* and the government's response to it, see Steve Schwinghamer, "'The Existing Immigration Regulations Will Not Offer Any Solution': MS St. Louis in Canadian Context," Canadian Museum of Immigration at Pier 21, December 21, 2023, pier21.ca/research/immigration-history/canada-and-ms-st-louis. See also Lawlor, 41–47.

55. Schwinghamer.

56. Ibid.

57. Mautner Markhof, 100; Reinfelder, 63.

58. Although the financial terms cited by the Dominican Republic were onerous, it remains unclear why Berenson ultimately rejected the offer. See Vincent, 262–66, and Afoumado, 97, for details. Herlin notes that Berenson had learned that Germany was in talks with the Dominican Republic for a resettlement of a much larger number of German Jews and did not want to jeopardize those. Herlin cites no source for this claim. Between June 10 and 12, the JDC also negotiated with Honduras, but the Honduran cabinet was divided over the asylum question, which ended negotiations. For details, see Vincent, 267.

59. Schröder, *Heimatlos*, 26–27. See also Schröder, "Captain's Travelogue," part 2, 2.

60. Schröder, *Heimatlos*, 24–25.
61. Vincent, 266.
62. Ibid., 268.
63. Ibid., with reference to Folder 1933/44: 378, JDC New York Records, Report on SS *St. Louis*.
64. HAPAG's former Director of Passage, Claus-Gottfried Holthusen, told Herlin that he was brought into the meeting by phone from Germany and warned the participants that, if the passengers had to return to Germany, they would meet with an uncertain fate (141). According to Herlin, this was what swayed the British to accept their share of passengers. The Holthusen interview is not available and Herlin's claim is not verifiable.
65. Vincent, 269–71. In Vincent's assessment, Britain's decision to accept some of the refugees had a positive impact on swaying the other host countries (270).
66. Schröder, *Heimatlos*, 41. Schröder writes that HAPAG, too, sent him a telegram indicating that a solution was in sight (29), but this telegram is not included in his collection of documents in his book's appendix.
67. Lipsky et al., 77–78. On June 15, HAPAG sent a telegram to Schröder confirming Antwerp as the destination for the *St. Louis*. See Schröder, *Heimatlos*, appendix, 41.
68. "Refuge Is Assured for All on Liner," *New York Times*, June 14, 1939. At that point, it was apparently not known to the press that one of the passengers of the *St. Louis* was not a refugee.
69. Lipsky et al, 84–86. For a discussion of the fate of the passengers during the war, see especially Ogilvie and Miller.
70. Mautner Markhof, 120.
71. Ibid., 121. Holthusen feared HAPAG would make him into a scapegoat and fire him.
72. Ibid., 122. My translation of Gestapo correspondence, cited by Markhof.
73. Ibid.
74. Ibid., 121. My translation of Markhof's paraphrasing of the German Foreign Office order.
75. Letter from HAPAG to Gustav Schröder, published in *Heimatlos auf hoher See*, appendix.
76. Lipsky et al., 90–95.

Chapter 4

1. Ogilvie and Miller, *Refuge Denied*.
2. Afoumado, *Exil impossible*.

3. Erich Dublon, Diary, in Reinfelder, MS "St. Louis" *Frühjahr 1939*, 218. Excerpts translated by Roy Grundmann.
4. Ibid., 220.
5. Ziemer and Ziemer, *Aufrecht in schweren Zeiten*, 45.
6. Schröder, *Heimatlos auf hoher See*, 7. See appendix.
7. Lipsky, Uhlig, and Glaevecke, *Kapitän Schröder und die Irrfahrt der St. Louis*, 51.
8. Ibid., 51.
9. Ibid., 56.
10. See Erich Dublon, diary, in Reinfelder, 220–23. Dublon writes, "Nothing on board suggests that this ship is special. HAPAG runs this voyage just like any of their regular cruises. I couldn't imagine their service offering anything more. I'm sorry for every day that has passed."
11. Ibid., 222.
12. Schröder, *Heimatlos*, 8. See also Dublon, diary, in Reinfelder, 223. Dublon writes that passengers had collected money for Weiler to be buried in Cuba, but the Cuban government declined. His widow received a sea chart with a mark of the burial place. Dublon also notes that Weiler was buried in a regular coffin.
13. Schröder, *Heimatlos*. See also Ziemer and Ziemer, 79. See also Vincent, "The Voyage of the *St. Louis* Revisited," 258n35.
14. Dublon in Reinfelder, 225.
15. Gisela Feldmann, cited in Lipsky et al., 60. Roy Grundmann trans.
16. Dublon, diary, in Reinfelder, 226. Dublon writes that passengers were aware of the fact that their fate had become a political matter having to do with Cuba's sovereignty.
17. Lipsky, 64. Roy Grundmann trans.
18. Schröder, *Heimatlos*, 20.
19. Lipsky et al., 65. Roy Grundmann trans.
20. Dublon, diary, in Reinfelder, 228.
21. Ibid.
22. Schröder, *Heimatlos*, 20.
23. Dublon, diary, in Reinfelder, 229. The plane sighting seems to confirm the statement the Coast Guard published on its website (see chapter 3) that its planes regularly patrol the area. It cannot have been the plane that the Coast Guard, as per Morgenthau's instruction, sent out specifically to look for the *St. Louis*, because Morgenthau did not place the order until June 6.
24. Dublon, diary, in Reinfelder, 229.
25. On the migrant ship as a space of both dread and delight, see Joachim Schlör, "Die Schiffsreise als Übergangserfahrung in Migrationsprozessen," *Mobile Cultural Studies: The Journal* 1 (2015): 9–22. On Jewish migrants en route to Palestine, who reflect on their position between past and future, see

David Jünger, "An Bord des Lebens: Die Schiffspassage deutscher Juden nach Palästina 1933 bis 1938 als Übergangserfahrung zwischen Raum und Zeit," *Mobile Cultural Studies: The Journal* 1 (2015): 147–63. Migration to Palestine was shaped by the Zionist notion that they represented the future of the Jewish people, but other aspects of refugee life on board mirrored those of the *St. Louis* passengers. Noteworthy is especially passengers' tendency to repress the reality of Nazi terror. See also Arnd Schneider, "An Anthropology of the Sea Voyage: Prolegomena to an Epistemology of Transoceanic Travel," *Mobile Cultural Studies: The Journal* 1 (2015): 31–52.

26. Ibid. 230.
27. Schröder, *Heimatlos*, 27.
28. Ibid.
29. Dublon, diary, in Reinfelder, 231.
30. Lipsky, 77.
31. Ibid., 78.
32. Dublon, diary, in Reinfelder, 233.
33. *New York Times*, June 1, 1939, 16.
34. *Chicago Daily Tribune*, June 2, 1939, 9.
35. *Boston Daily Globe*, June 6, 1939, 1.
36. *Boston Daily Globe*, June 7, 1939, 2.
37. R. Hart Phillips, "Cuba Opens Doors to 907 on the *St. Louis*," *New York Times*, June 6, 1939, A1. The stated figure reflects the eastbound crossing's passenger count.
38. R. Hart Phillips, "Cuba Recloses Door to Refugees; 48-Hour Limit on Offer Expires," *New York Times*, June 7, 1939, A1.
39. My own discussion of media coverage focuses on US newspapers. For a survey of the Canadian press's coverage of the *St. Louis* story, see Grzyb, "From Kristallnacht to the MS *St. Louis* Tragedy." Grzyb's superb study documents Canadian newspapers' strong interest in the plight of Jews after Kristallnacht and, more specifically, with the unfolding *St. Louis* drama. According to Grzyb, most articles were "reactive and event-driven, and most of the reports about pogroms or antisemitic ordinances were descriptive, not overly analytical" (84). Grzyb finds Canada's papers to have been largely sympathetic to the plight of the Jewish refugees and to have urged the government to grant asylum to them (84–85; 101).
40. I am indebted to Linda Williams's groundbreaking scholarship on the conventions of melodrama. See Linda Williams, "Film Bodies: Gender, Genre, and Excess," *Film Quarterly* 44, no. 4 (Summer 1991): 2–13; Williams, "Melodrama Revised," in *Refiguring American Film Genres: History and Theory*, ed. Nick Browne (University of California Press, 1998), 42–88; and Williams, *Playing the Race Card: Melodramas of Black and White from Uncle Tom to*

O. J. Simpson (University of California Press, 2002), chapter 1, "The American Melodramatic Mode," 10–44, esp. 30.

41. R. Hart Phillips, "907 Refugees Quit Cuba on Liner; Ship Reported Hovering off Coast," *New York Times*, June 3, 1939, A1.

42. Williams, "Film Bodies," 11. This figure of carefully timed pathos is, as Williams argues with reference to Italian literary scholar Franco Moretti, a staple of melodrama.

43. Hart Phillips, "Cuba Orders Liner and Refugees to Go—Navy to Escort the *St. Louis* with 917 Aboard Unless She Obeys—Compromise Reported," *New York Times*, June 2, 1939, A1. In *Voyage of the Damned*, Gordon Thomas and Max Morgan-Witts claim that the illumination of the ship had been requested by the *St. Louis*'s passenger committee, whom the ship's captain had tasked with preventing suicide attempts (185). Neither Schröder's nor Dublon's accounts of the voyage confirm this.

44. See, for instance, "Jewish Refugee Liner Ordered to Leave Cuba—Must Sail or Warship Will Take It in Tow," *Chicago Daily Tribune*, June 2, 1939, 9.

45. "Refugee Liner Fails to Obey Cuban Decree," *Boston Daily Globe*, June 2, 1.

46. "Coast Guard Trails Tragic Liner as It Wanders Aimlessly in Florida Waters; Reich Recalls Second Refugee Vessel," *Washington Post*, June 5, 1939, 1.

47. "Wandering Jews at Sea After 900 Are Forbidden to Land in Cuba," *Cumberland Evening Times*, June 5, 1939.

48. "Refugee Ship," *New York Times*, June 8, 1939, 24.

49. "Grim Voyage," *Washington Post*, June 11, 1939, B8.

50. A minority of articles defended Cuba's decision to decline asylum. On June 5, the *Seattle Times* published an article titled "Cuba Did Not Invite Them." On June 2, the *Christian Science Monitor* of Boston opined "Jews Not Able Pioneers Like Other Races." See Reinfelder, 68.

51. On the link between suffering and citizenship, see Linda Williams, *Playing the Race Card*, 24. Citing the work of Lauren Berlant, Williams points out that particularly since the popularization of abolitionist novels in the nineteenth century, the failure of juridical models to grant citizenship to oppressed groups, especially African Americans, had brought about a "sentimental politics" (Berlant's term). As Williams puts it, "a second model of citizenship has emerged around the visible emotions of suffering bodies that, in the very activity of suffering, demonstrate worth as citizens."

52. Hart Phillips, "Cuba Orders Liner and Refugees to Go," *New York Times*, June 2, 1939, A1.

53. "German Liner Leaves Havana with 907 Jews," *Chicago Daily Tribune*, June 3, 1939, 2.

54. "U.S. Is Considering Haven for Jews in Philippine Island," *Chicago Daily Tribune*, June 5, 1939, 5.

55. "907 Jews Reach Belgium; Tell of Suicide Pact—Given Temporary Havens Before Coming to U.S.," *Chicago Daily Tribune*, June 18, 1939, 12.

56. Unspecified American newsreel excerpt, furnished by USHMM: "Jewish Refugees on the SS St. Louis After Denied U.S. Entry," *Matthew Green*, November 25, 2015, video, 1:02, www.youtube.com/watch?v=7Y4WF5g9ZHw.

57. "Refugees Without a Country (1939)," *British Pathé*, April 13, 2014, video, 0:33, www.youtube.com/watch?v=d3ZUb78zuS0.

58. Jay, "Of Plots, Witnesses, and Judgments," 98–99.

59. *Flandre* and *Orduña* received much less attention, as did the *Orinoco*, another HAPAG ship with 200 migrants aboard. After news circulated that Cuba was stalling the disembarkation of the *St. Louis*'s migrants, the *Orinoco* never even left European waters and was recalled to Germany. For details, see the Captain's Log of the *Orinoco* voyage to Antwerp, in Schöck-Quinteros, Loeber, and Rau, *Keine Zuflucht. Nirgends*. See also Reinfelder (76) and Mautner Markhof (82). *The New York Times* did report on the *Flandre* passengers' rescue on June 20, 1939 ("500 Refugees on Way to Temporary Homes"). But most newspapers, with the exception of the German-language Jewish press and the Canadian press, paid scant attention to the fates of other migrant ships. For details on the German Jewish press, see chapter 1; on the Canadian press, see Grzyb, 102.

60. Thomas and Morgan-Witts claim that NS radio broadcasts spun the *St. Louis*'s travails into propaganda (104, 154, 180, 263). While those claims are not implausible, the authors do not mention any specific broadcasts, where those are archived, and how they succeeded in retrieving them. They claim that German radio stations announced "since no one will accept the shabby Jews on the *St. Louis*, we will have to take them back and support them" (263), but they reference no source. See Gordon Thomas and Max Morgan-Witts, *Voyage of the Damned* (Skyhorse Publishing, 2010 [Stein & Day, 1974]).

61. Ibid., 262.

62. Mautner Markhof, Reinfelder, Ogilvie, and Afoumado have expressed reservations about the propaganda thesis.

63. Reinfelder (117–18) quotes correspondence between the German consulate in Havana and the Foreign Office in Berlin, which states that the return of the *St. Louis* to Germany "is not in our interest" (Roy Grundmann trans.), but unfortunately does not include a source. Mautner Markhof claims that on June 8, after the *St. Louis* had started on its trip back to Europe, Goebbels issued a directive to the German press that, until further notice, the *St. Louis* must not receive any news coverage (123). Regrettably, Mautner Markhof does not cite archival sources in support of his claim.

64. I would like to thank Heide Pennigsdorf, whom I asked to survey the daily editions of ten German daily newspapers of my selection for the period between May 13, 1939, and June 21, 1939, with regard to coverage of the *St. Louis* voyage and its immediate aftermath. The newspapers were *Deutsche Allgemeine Zeitung* (both the national edition and the local Berlin edition), *Berliner Allgemeine Zeitung, Hamburger Anzeiger, Hamburger Nachrichten, Deutscher Reichsanzeiger u. Preußischer Staatsanzeiger, Westfälische Landeszeitung/Rote Erde* (formerly *Generalanzeiger für Dortmund*), *Kölnische Zeitung*, and *Frankfurter Zeitung*.

65. "Kuba verhindert Landung jüdischer Emigranten," *Völkischer Beobachter*, June 3, 1939, 5.

66. On the *Wilhelm Gustloff* as a carrier of NS ideology, see Sascha Howind, "Das 'Traumschiff' für die 'Volksgemeinschaft'? Die *Gustloff* und die soziale Propaganda des Dritten Reiches," in *Die Wilhelm Gustloff: Geschichte und Erinnerung eines Untergangs*, ed. Bill Niven (Mitteldeutscher Verlag, 2011), 27–60; and Bill Niven, "Die *Gustloff* in London, die *Sierra Cordoba* in Riga: KdF-Schiffe im Dienst der nationalsozialistischen Politik," in Niven, *Die Wilhelm Gustloff*, 61–92.

67. The return of the Legion Condor on the *Wilhelm Gustloff* was also prominently covered by NS news reels.

68. One gleeful notice in the *Cuxhavener Zeitung* reported on HAPAG having received orders to recall its liner *Orinoco* to Germany. See "Flüchtlingsschiff Orinoco zurückgeschickt," *Cuxhavener Zeitung*, June 5, 1939, quoted in Schöck-Quinteros et al., 138. While the article's tone is indicative of the antisemitism that fueled Germany's expulsion of Jews, there is no evidence of German newspapers systematically instrumentalizing that year's refugee crisis, and the *St. Louis* incident in particular, for this purpose.

69. *Der Stürmer* no. 21, May 1939, facsimile, United States Holocaust Memorial Museum, collections.ushmm.org/search/catalog/pa1092779.

Chapter 5

1. Hannah Arendt, *The Origins of Totalitarianism* (Harcourt Brace Jovanovich, 1973), 299.

2. For a cogent summary, see "Die Dolchstoßlegende," in Lebendiges Museum Online (LEMO), Sept. 1, 2014, www.dhm.de/lemo/kapitel/weimarer-republik/innenpolitik/dolchstosslegende.html. See also A. Dirk Moses, *The Problems of Genocide: Permanent Security and the Language of Transgression* (Cambridge University Press, 2021), 326. Moses notes that the Nazis also accused Jews of having led the Bolshevik revolution in Russia and having caused many deaths there.

3. Agamben, *Homo Sacer*, 131.
4. Agamben, 128–29.
5. See Moses, 18. The intentionalist school of Holocaust studies explores collective beliefs linked to religion, mysticism, and metaphysics as much as questions of individual motivation.
6. On a useful contextualization of "intentionalism" vs. "functionalism," see Dan Stone, "Biopower and Modern Genocide," in *Empire, Colony, Genocide: Conquest, Occupation, and Subaltern Resistance in World History*, ed. A. Dirk Moses (Berghahn, 2008), 240–65.
7. Zygmunt Bauman, *Modernity and the Holocaust* (Cornell University Press, 1989), 8.
8. Ibid., 249.
9. See Carl Schmitt, *Staat, Bewegung, Volk: Die Dreigliederung der politischen Einheit* (Hanseatische Verlagsanstalt, 1933). English translation *State, Movement, People: The Triadic Structure of Political Unity*, trans. and ed. Simona Draghici (Plutarch Press, 2001). My discussion is based on the English translation.
10. Moses, *The Problems of Genocide*, 313.
11. Schmitt, *State, Movement, People*, 49.
12. Ibid.
13. Ibid.
14. Ibid., 50.
15. Ibid. Emphasis mine. The passage in the German original is worded as follows: "So steht die gesamte Gesetzesanwendung zwischen Scylla und Charybdis. Der Weg vorwärts scheint ins Uferlose zu führen und sich immer weiter vom festen Boden der Rechtssicherheit und der Gesetzesgebundenheit, der doch gleichzeitig auch der Boden der richterlichen Unabhängigkeit ist, zu entfernen; der Weg zurück in einen als sinnlos erkannten, geschichtlich längst überwundenen, formalistischen Gesetzesaberglauben kommt ebensowenig in Betracht" (44).
16. Agamben, *Homo Sacer*, 172. As the English edition of Schmitt's book, *State, Movement, People*, was published after *Homo Sacer*, Agamben references the book's German edition in his bibliography, but the English translator of *Homo Sacer*, Daniel Heller-Roazen, notes that while the German edition was consulted, quoted passages have been newly translated (189).
17. At the time of Schmitt's writing, Freisler was state secretary in the Prussian Ministry of Justice. In 1934, he would be promoted to state secretary in the Reich Ministry of Justice.
18. Schmitt, *State, Movement, People*, 48, emphasis in the original.
19. Ibid.
20. Schmitt's perspective reflected that of an increasing part of Germany's population, which, as A. Dirk Moses argues, saw National Socialism as

liberating the country of "Jewish social democracy" and replacing the "modern political imaginary of the social contract and of liberalism represented by 'the Jew' with a pre-modern one of hierarchy and order embodied by National Socialism—though, of course, with ultramodern techniques." See Moses, *The Problem of Genocide*, 302.

21. Carl Schmitt, *Land und Meer: Eine weltgeschichtliche Betrachtung* (Klett-Cotta, 1942 [1981]). My own references are from Carl Schmitt, *Land and Sea: A World-Historical Meditation*, trans. Samuel Garrett Zeitlin, ed. Samuel Garrett Yeitlin and Russell Berman (Telos Press Publishing, 2015).

22. Ibid., 39. Schmitt's juxtaposition between sea people and land people possesses what has been described as a fable-like suggestiveness, but is suffused with commonplaces. Schmitt charges that England, over centuries of naval warfare, had terrorized civilian populations by laying siege to ports and starving inhabitants of coastal areas, whereas land powers such as Germany and Russia had traditionally solved their conflicts more "nobly," that is, on military battlefields removed from towns and villages. Yet Hitler's eastern campaign went hand in hand with the mass extermination of the civilian populations of the conquered territories by the paramilitary death squads of the SS and with the support of parts of the Wehrmacht.

23. John P. McCormick and David Bates, two of the historians who endorse the English-language edition of the book on its back cover, use the term "fable" in their description of Schmitt's argument.

24. Ibid., 93. For another discussion of Schmitt in relation to the ocean as a juridical entity and the fate of a refugee ship, see Mawani, *Across Oceans of Law*. Mawani discusses Schmitt's binary understanding of land and water, but does not comment on it in relation to fascism and the State of Exception.

25. See Moses, *The Problem of Genocide*, 320–23.

26. Griselda Pollock and Max Silverman, "Introduction," in *Concentrationary Cinema*, ed. Pollock and Silverman (Berghahn Books, 2011).

27. Ibid., 10. Pollock and Silverman cite data furnished by Wolfgang Sofsky, *The Order of Terror: The Concentration Camp*, trans. William Templer (Princeton University Press, 1999).

28. Ibid., 18.

29. Ibid., 13.

30. Agamben, 10.

31. See Foucault, *History of Sexuality, Volume 1*, 139–43, as well as Foucault, "Society Must Be Defended," ch. 11, "17 March 1976," 239–63, esp. 254–63. See also my discussion in chapter 1.

32. Agamben, 114 and 168–69.

33. To underscore the abolitionist (as opposed to reformist) nature of Schmitt's thinking, Agamben (172) cites Schmitt's disenchantment with Liberalism, which Schmitt illustrates with the metaphor of the shoreless sea.

34. Agamben believes that the absence of any biopolitical perspective marks the limit of Arendt's study of totalitarianism (120).

35. Ibid.

36. Ibid., 121, citing Karl Löwith, *Der okkasionelle Dezionismus von Carl Schmitt*, in Löwith, *Sämtliche Schriften*, ed. Klaus Stichweh and Marc B. de Launay, vol. 8 (Metzler, 1984), 33.

37. Gordon Thomas and Max Morgan-Witts, *Voyage of the Damned*, 53. See also Dan Diner, *Beyond the Conceivable: Studies on Germany, Nazism, and the Holocaust* (University of California Press, 2000), 81–82. Diner has found that until the November 9, 1938, pogrom, Jewish relief organizations had a relatively productive working relationship with the Reich bureau of emigration (Reichswanderungsamt) in implementing the logistics of migration. With Kristallnacht, however, this changed because the SD—the security service of the SS—gained control of Jewish emigration and accelerated expulsion in ways that made it more precarious for Jews.

38. Agamben, 183. Bare life or *homo sacer* describes "life that cannot be sacrificed and yet may be killed" (82). Agamben has chosen the root word "sacer" for his coinage of *homo sacer*, because for him it transcends the binary distinction between the sacrificeable and unsacrificeable, while not rescinding its relation to sacredness as a concept. This relation, however, has become purely negative—sacredness is understood as that from which bare life is now excluded: "Life is sacred only insofar as it is taken into the sovereign exception" (85).

39. For a case study, see Sarah Sander, "Precarious Passages: On Migrant Maritime Mobilities, ca. 1907," in *Maritime Mobilities in Anglophone Literature and Culture*, ed. Alexandra Ganser and Charne Lavery (Palgrave Macmillan, 2023), 145–70.

40. Edward Ross Dickinson, "Biopolitics, Fascism, Democracy: Some Reflections on our Discourse about 'Modernity,'" *Central European History* 37, no. 1 (2004): 7–45, here 19. See also Stone, "Biopolitics," 251.

41. Dickinson, 25.

42. Hannah Arendt, "We Refugees," in Arendt, *The Jewish Writings*. Jerome Kohn and Ron H. Feldman eds. (Schocken Books, 2007), 265. Arendt elaborates on this crux in her discussion of the dilemma of the stateless in *The Origins of Totalitarianism*, 282.

43. *Los Angeles Times*, "Cuban Concentration Camp Offered to Liner Refugees," June 6, 1939, 1.

44. *Washington Post*, June 6, 1939, 1. See also *New York Times*, "Cuba Opens Doors to 907 on *St. Louis*," June 6, 1939, A1.

45. *New York Times*, June 8, 1939, 24. Press reports that the *St. Louis* passengers threatened mass suicide to avoid being sent to camps suggested

to readers that the function of the concentration camp may be evolving in sinister ways.

46. Dara Lind, "How America's Rejection of Jews Fleeing Nazi Germany Haunts Our Refugee Policy Today," *Vox*, Jan. 27, 2017, www.vox.com/policy-and-politics/2017/1/27/14412082/refugees-history-holocaust.

47. Oliver Marchart, *Die politische Differenz* (Suhrkamp, 2010), 222. While large parts of this book were first published in book form in English as *Post-Foundational Political Thought: Political Difference in Nancy, Lefourt, Badiou, and Laclau* (Edinburgh University Press, 2007), the chapter on Agamben was included only in the German edition. I paraphrase Marchart's critique of Agamben without verbatim translations, but with page references to the German original. For a summary of objections to Agamben's model by further theorists, see Pollock and Silverman's introduction to *Concentrationary Cinema*.

48. Marchart, 223.
49. Ibid., 229.
50. Ibid., 224.
51. Ibid., 232.
52. Pollock and Silverman, 14. Emphasis mine.
53. JDC policy statement, June 21, 1939, quoted in Vincent, 276.
54. Ibid.
55. Ibid.

56. In addition to Gustav Schröder's valiant efforts to delay a return to Germany, JDC officials Cecilia Razovsky and Morris Troper exemplify the importance of individual agency. But not all cases are clear-cut. For an assessment of Lawrence Berenson's mixed legacy, see chapter 3. The role of the HAPAG director of passage, Claus-Gottfried Holthusen, is discussed at the end of the present chapter.

57. An aspect of Marchart's critique that cannot be discussed at length here is his implicit gendering of politics into two associative clusters: Democracy is associated with analysis, action, and pragmatism—in other words, with masculine-coded qualities—whereas Agamben's critique of democracy and his methodological focus on means rather than ends is associated with emotion, passivity, fatalism and, implicitly, with femininity. Marchart at least inadvertently reproduces this division by associating Agamben with the Jewish myth of Messianism. The latter's overarching feature of passive endurance is culturally associated with femininity, whereas Exodus, the Jewish myth of self-preservation through action, is associated with masculinity. Marchart does not make this association explicit in his discussion of Judaic myth (239–41), but it is culturally and historically deeply engrained.

58. Agamben, 172.

59. The Holocaust's uniqueness was vigorously debated in the 1986 Historikerstreit or German historians' debate. The stakes were that establishing the Holocaust's comparability to other genocides would entitle Germany to political rehabilitation and would initiate the process of bringing about historical closure. Upholding the Holocaust's uniqueness would task Germany with the potentially endless and decidedly left-wing project of working through the past by critically interrogating concepts of nationhood and nationalism. For a useful introduction to the subject, see Dominick LaCapra, "Representing the Holocaust: Reflections on the Historians' Debate," in *Probing the Limits of Representation: Nazism and the "Final Solution,"* ed. Saul Friedlander (Harvard University Press, 1992), 108–27.

60. I take the expression "colonial turn" from Rothberg, *Multidirectional Memory*, 70.

61. Hannah Arendt, "Social Science Techniques and the Study of Concentration Camps," *Jewish Social Studies* 12 (January 1950): 49–64.

62. Arendt, "Social Science Techniques," 53.

63. Rothberg, 49.

64. Rothberg, 50. Rothberg cites Chickasaw scholar Jodi Byrd's critique of Arendt's influential reasoning: "What happens to American Indians in such a competition for the 'true' genocide is that we become, yet again, the 'logical,' if tragic victims of modernization who stand in the way of progress." See Jodi Byrd, "'Living My Native Life Deadly': Red Lake, Ward Churchill, and the Discourses of Competing Genocides," *American Indian Quarterly* 31, no. 2 (2007): 310–32, here 329, cited in Rothberg, 49–50.

65. Arendt, *The Origins of Totalitarianism*, 186, 194–97.

66. Ibid., 52–53.

67. As Rothberg points out, Arendt relies less on historical analysis than on a review of English literature, specifically Joseph Conrad, whose novel *Heart of Darkness*, while constituting a critique of colonialism, shares certain limitations of the colonial era that produced it. For Arendt, Conrad's self-reflexive probing of the psyche of the white colonizer, who becomes overwhelmed by the racial and geographical "otherness" of the territory he penetrates, offers a paradigmatic description of the traumatizing effect of racial alterity.

68. Césaire's book was originally published in 1950 under the title *Discours sur le colonialisme*, and then reissued in revised form in 1955. It was translated into English in 1972. My discussion of Césaire's book owes to Rothberg's commentary on it. See Rothberg, 73–87.

69. Aimee Césaire, *Discourse on Colonialism*, trans. Joan Pinkham (Monthly Review Press, 1972), 14.

70. Ibid., 20. Henri Deterding was a director of Royal Dutch oil company, which in 1907 had merged with the Shell Transport and Trading Company of England. Deterding was a Nazi sympathizer all through the

1930s. After being ousted from his directorship, he resettled in Germany and died there. His funeral was hosted by the NS State. In 1940, when Nazi Germany invaded Holland, the headquarters of Royal Dutch were relocated to Curaçao.

71. Ibid., 59.

72. Ibid., 60. Césaire's argument was continued by Eduardo Galeano, *Open Veins of Latin America*, published in English translation by Césaire's US publisher, Monthly Review Press.

73. Latin America played a minor role in Arendt's thinking. Her 1940 essay "We Refugees" treats the Latin American sites of the Jewish diaspora as particles of the Eurocentric self-sameness that fueled what Rothberg terms Arendt's "expectation of homogenous universality" (62). In the few places the essay mentions Latin America, Arendt reduces the subcontinent's nations and cities to mirror images of Europe. Brazil gains relevance as one more spot on earth where Jews are being forced to divest from their assets (267–70). Montevideo and Buenos Aires are copies of Paris, Bucharest, New York, and Los Angeles in that they are simply places where Jews commit suicide. Without belittling Arendt's insight about one of the diaspora's bleaker aspects, we note that she failed to investigate the role of the Latin American metropolis as a place from where European colonialism and US-led neocolonialism have proceeded. This leaves Arendt blind to how colonialism and neocolonialism shaped Latin American nations' negative attitude towards giving Jews asylum.

74. In exchange for supporting Cuba's independence, the US obliged Cuba to political and economic cooperation via the 1901 Platt Amendment. US power over Cuba crystallized in the early 1920s after a dramatic drop in sugar prices on the US market plunged Cuba into a debt crisis and the US extended a 50-million-dollar loan to the country. As Eduardo Galeano writes in *Open Veins of Latin America: Five Centuries of the Pillage of a Continent* (Monthly Review Press, 1973): "On the heels of the credit came General Enoch Crowder who, under the pretext of controlling the use of the funds, became Cuba's de facto governor" (82).

75. Césaire, 22.

76. Galeano, 81.

77. Rothberg, 80–81.

78. Paul Gilroy, *The Black Atlantic* (Harvard University Press, 1993), 213.

79. Ibid.

80. Ibid.

81. Ibid., 205.

82. Ibid., 213–14. Gilroy especially laments Zygmunt Bauman's neglect to consider the ways in which Eurocentric conceptions of modernity have hampered understandings of the relationship between anti-Black racism and antisemitism.

83. Ibid., 214.

Chapter 6

1. See the introduction, note 13.
2. The publisher was a printing business that seems to have let Schröder self-publish the book without editorial supervision. See Ziemer and Ziemer, *Aufrecht in schweren Zeiten*.
3. Stateside copies are at the United States Holocaust Memorial Museum, the Leo Beck Institute, New York, and the New York Public Library.
4. Morse, *While Six Million Died*.
5. Thomas and Morgan-Witts, *Voyage of the Damned*. The hardcover edition does not hyphenate the name Morgan-Witts, but subsequent paperback editions do.
6. On details of Schröder's retirement, see Lipsky, Uhlig, and Glaevecke, *Kapitän Schröder und die Irrfahrt der St. Louis*, 108–27.
7. For a facsimile reproduction of the article's first page in *Revue* (n.d.), a long-defunct illustrated magazine, see Lipsky et al., 109.
8. Ibid., 128–29.
9. In Paris the play ran for 200 performances. See Lipsky et al., 117. For its New York run, see Brooks Atkinson, "Broadway Voyage: John Garfield and 'Skipper Next to God' Move to Playhouse," *New York Times*, February 1, 1948, Section 2, 1. The play became a French film titled *Maître après Dieu*, starring Pierre Brasseur. See Bosley Crowther, "Film Version of de Hartog's Play 'Skipper Next to God' at the 55th Street Playhouse," *New York Times*, January 13, 1953, 24. Crowther calls the film "hackneyed and out of date" and charges that de Hartog's material obscures the captain's motivations, but Crowther does mention the *St. Louis*. On de Hartog's work in the Dutch Resistance and his career as an author whose plays and novels were adapted by Hollywood, see Mel Gussow, "Jan de Hartog, 88, Author of His Own Life," *New York Times*, September 24, 2002, and information by the David S. Wyman Institute of Holocaust Studies, enc.wymaninstitute.org/?p=231, accessed April 18, 2023.
10. See P. Hühnefeld, "Schiff ohne Hafen," Die Zeit, no. 48, September 22, 1949. The review accuses the play of false pathos and vapid humanism that ignores the circumstances of the ship's rejection by other countries. For background information on Italiaander's German adaptation, see Rolf Italiaander, "Ein Hamburger Schiff auf Hamburger Bühnen," unidentified publication, n.d., n.p. Hamburger Staatsarchiv StAHH 731-8_A 769. Italiaander states that, after obtaining the translation rights to de Hartog's play, he visited the *St. Louis* and encountered Schröder, who introduced himself as the ship's former captain and relayed the details of Voyage 98. Italiaander speculates that the play's first run folded quickly because Germans were not ready for the subject. The theater, Haus der Jugend, even received antisemitic threats. By contrast, the 1956 run lasted four weeks and, according to Italiaander,

garnered positive reactions. Italiaander claims that it was he who encouraged Schröder to write up his own account and that Schröder self-published the book after failing to attract publishers. The regional broadcast network Nordwestdeutscher Rundfunk turned the play into a radio play that was aired on October 21, 1949.

11. For background discussion on Schröder obtaining NSDAP membership, see the appendix.

12. Jörn Rüsen, "Holocaust Memory and Identity Building: Metahistorical Considerations in the Case of (West) Germany," in *Disturbing Remains: Memory, History, and Crisis in the Twentieth Century*, ed. Michael S. Roth and Charles G. Galas (The Getty Research Institute, 2001), 263.

13. Rüsen, 262.

14. Ibid., 263. Rüsen argues that many educated Germans who were not expelled and did not leave the country during the Nazi period showed this attitude.

15. Karl Jaspers, *The Question of German Guilt*, trans. E. B. Ashton (Doubleday Broadway Publishing Group, 1948; repr. Fordham University, 2001 [orig. Die Schuldfrage, Lambert Schneider, 1946; repr. 1965 Piper Verlag]), 25–26. Jaspers distinguishes between four basic categories of guilt: criminal guilt (reserved for those who performed crimes by deed, direct command, or explicit decree); political guilt (applying to statesmen and functionaries who created and administered the conditions under which crimes took place); moral guilt (which includes following orders no matter whether a refusal to follow them would have been punitive); and metaphysical guilt (pertaining to anyone who, while merely witnessing a crime passively, failed to do everything they could to prevent the crimes).

16. Jürgen Habermas, "On the Public Use of History," excerpts published in Neil Levi and Michael Rothberg eds., *The Holocaust: Theoretical Readings* (Rutgers University Press, 2003), 63–68, here 66.

17. Saul Friedlander, "Trauma and Transference," in Levi and Rothberg, *The Holocaust*, 208. Friedlander argues that this was due to feelings of shame for having suffered a fate the magnitude and horrors of which were so outlandish as to be difficult to believe.

18. As the copy of the article series does not have any exact publication dates and page numbers, I refer to the book version for citations, but my comments on the cultural impact of Herlin's account are in regard to the article series, which was more visible than the book.

19. Herlin, *Kein gelobtes Land*, republished as "Das Rote J," *Stern*, March 23, 1961. As was customary for *Stern* contributors, Herlin did not receive a byline. All page references in my discussion refer to the book version.

20. See the magazine publisher's website for a summary of its own branding profile: www.ad-alliance.de/cms/portfolio/print/portfolio.html?p=/print/portfolio/stern/. The magazine was founded by Henri Nannen and would

become part of European media conglomerate Gruner & Jahr. It reached a circulation of 9.9 million in 1967 and for decades would remain one of the most widely read magazines in West Germany. In 1983, *Stern* was involved in one of the biggest scandals in the history of German publishing, when it published what it claimed to be Adolf Hitler's diaries, a claim that turned out to be false and lastingly damaged *Stern*'s credibility.

21. Hans Herlin, *Verdammter Atlantik: Schicksale deutscher U-Boot-Fahrer* (Nannen Verlag, 1959). By the time of his death, Herlin's international reputation was significant enough to earn him an obituary in *The New York Times*. See "Hans Herlin, Novelist, 68," *New York Times*, Dec. 24, 1994.

22. On the history and cultural legacy of the sinking of the *Wilhelm Gustloff*, see the superb collection of essays edited by Bill Niven, *Die Wilhelm Gustloff: Geschichte und Erinnerung eines Untergangs* (Mitteldeutscher Verlag, 2011).

23. Herlin died in 1994. I am not aware of any estate or archive that might include audio recordings of his interviews or unpublished research notes.

24. Herlin, 58–59. According to Herlin, the records of Cuba's bureaucratic processing of *St. Louis* are on file in Cuba's Port Authority offices.

25. Ibid., 100–3. While Herlin's claim that Laredo Brú eyed a share of Benitez's illegal profits is ultimately unverifiable, the thesis receives support from Irwin F. Gellman, who in his early article on the *St. Louis* mentions that some Cuban officials demanded a share of Benitez's money and that, when Benitez refused, they shut down his scheme. Gellman bases his claim on correspondence between Curt DuBois, the American Consul General in Havana, and Cordell Hull, June 7, 1939. See Gellman, "The *St. Louis* Tragedy," 147. Another intriguing but unverified claim concerns the failed deal with the Dominican Republic. According to Herlin, Germany wanted to resettle Jews there on a larger scale, and the country's president, Trujillo, did not want to jeopardize this plan by hastily accepting a small contingent of refugees (101). There are other intriguing aspects about Herlin's account. According to Herlin, Berenson and Batista surveyed Jewish resettlement locations on the Isle of Pines. Herlin's book and article include a photo of several men touring the island. While the caption in the book confirms only Berenson's presence among the group, the caption in the *Stern* article also identifies Batista.

26. Ibid., 27–28, 45, 68.

27. Ibid. Passage solicitors asked German emigration offices to share their list of names. Jews with money were urged to advance a deposit for passages that did not yet have departure dates. This account is consistent with Claus-Gottfried Holthusen's statement (see chapter 2) that HAPAG in 1940 was in possession of a large amount of deposits from Jews intending to

emigrate. Herlin's claims about corrupt German and European travel agents are corroborated by JDC archival data. See also Glaser, *Refugees and Relief*.

28. I have found no corroborating evidence of this claim in the HAPAG archive, but archival data may be incomplete. Herlin (*Kein gelobtes Land*, 35–36) claims that HAPAG had already received $45,000 worth from 280 deposits for the ship's return trip.

29. Herlin, 36. According to Herlin, the sum had to be deposited via Clasing and declared as advertising budget.

30. Ibid., 142.

31. Ibid., 87–88. Lüttgens's exchanges with Stella are heavily scripted. While apocryphal, romantic vignettes are a convention of popular historical narratives. In *St. Louis* popular memory, the purpose of such romances is to accentuate the differences between Jews and gentiles through the fateful story of star-crossed lovers. The film adaptation of *Voyage of the Damned* features a romance between the steward Leo Jockl and the daughter of Max Loewe. This vignette does not even appear in Thomas and Morgan-Witts's book.

32. Ibid., 12. Roy Grundmann trans.

33. Two films exemplify this treatment. The first is the 1945 educational short film *The House I Live In*, which was written by soon-to-be-blacklisted Jewish screenwriter Albert Maltz and which garnered an Honorary Academy Award and a Golden Globe Award for Best Film Promoting International Understanding. The second was the Hollywood film *Gentlemen's Agreement*, made in 1947 and directed by Elia Kazan. On *The House I Live In*, see Art Simon, "*The House I Live In*," Library of Congress, www.loc.gov/static/programs/national-film-preservation-board/documents/The-House-I-Live-In_Simon.pdf, accessed May 10, 2023.

34. For a broader overview of Jewishness in American popular culture, see Alan Mintz, *Popular Culture and the Shaping of Holocaust Memory in America* (University of Washington Press, 2001).

35. Ibid., 7–23. While adaptations of the Anne Frank story still sought to downplay Jewishness in favor of a broader human interest angle, *Exodus* appealed to Americans because its representation of heroic Zionism linked Jewishness to strength and victory.

36. Ibid., 22.

37. Ibid.

38. Vincent, "The Voyage of the *St. Louis* Revisited," 277n5. Vincent has found no dispatches that show the State Department warning Wright.

39. For a critique of figurative representations of the Holocaust, see Berel Lang, "The Moral Space of Figurative Discourse," in *The Holocaust*, ed. Levi and Rothberg, 329–34.

40. Vincent, 253.

41. Ibid., 278n9.

42. Thomas and Morgan-Witts, *Voyage of the Damned*, 19. My comments reference the Skyhorse paperback edition. While Hitler's Königsberg speech conveyed the regime's desire to "clean house" and while HAPAG's projections about its migrant business should be read in this context (as this book does), the authors' implanting of the *St. Louis* voyage into this context is purely speculative.

43. Thomas and Morgan-Witts, 40.

44. Ibid., 46.

45. Ibid., 179.

46. Ibid., 129.

47. Ibid., 87.

48. Kurt Vogt et al., "Bemerkungen zum Buch 'Das Schiff der Verdammten,' von Thomas/Morgan-Witts. Verlag Edition Sven Erik Bergh 'Die Irrfahrt der St. Louis!'" n.d. Hamburger Staatsarchiv StAHH 621-1/95_4776 Part 3. The pamphlet is a two-page typed, single-spaced manuscript. In addition to Third Officer Vogt, who composed it, it includes as signatories Third Engineer Alfred Seckerdieck, Third Engineer Brandt, Gardener/Florist Liesel Müller, and Kindergarten teacher Charlotte Faehre. The document appears to have been authored in response to the 1976 German-language version of *Voyage of the Damned*, which was published in Switzerland under the title *Das Schiff der Verdammten*, Helmut Kossodo trans. (Ingse Verlag, Edition Sven Erik Bergh, 1976). It appears that the book also prompted Vogt to write up his own account of Voyage 98, titled "Bericht über die Reise des 'MS St. Louis' der Hamburg-Amerika Linie unter Führung von Kpt. G. Schröder mit jüdischen Auswanderern nach Cuba und zurück! Von Kapitän Kurt Vogt auf dieser Reise 3. Offz., als diensttuender 2.O. auf dem Schiff (Personaloffizier)" [Report on the Voyage of "MS *St. Louis*" of the Hamburg-America Line under the command of Captain G. Schröder with Jewish Emigrants to Cuba and back! By Captain Kurt Vogt, on this trip 3. Officer but serving as 2. Officer (Personnel Officer) on duty].

49. Vogt et al., "Bemerkungen zum Buch 'Das Schiff der Verdammten.'" Vogt is indignant that Thomas and Morgan-Witts changed the person's name from Schiederich (Schröder in his book calls him Zschiedrich) to Schiendick. He criticizes the authors for ascribing too much power to the Gestapo agent: "The public deserves to know what a rascal he was. But I did not take him to be a spy. He was much too stupid for that. But as a Third Officer I had several run-ins with him."

50. Vogt makes the same claims in his own report on Voyage 98. Cf note 48, above.

Chapter 7

1. Judith E. Doneson, *The Holocaust in American Film*, 2nd ed. (Syracuse University Press, 2002), 130.

2. For the ABC reference, see Addison Verrill, "Devalued Pound Brings 'Voyage' In Under Budget," *Variety*, July 28, 1976, 4. See also Doneson, 130. Doneson writes that Allen Rivkin, a screenwriter and member of the Jewish Film Advisory Committee (JFAC), pitched the screenplay to producer Sherril C. Corwin, who questioned its appeal to non-Jewish audiences. To make the film more commercial, its original length was cut from 182 to 150 minutes. Only the film's 1981 VHS release archived the long version, which I have not been able to see.

3. Grade merged his firm, Incorporated Television Company (ITC), with General Cinema Corporation to produce British-American films for the international market under the name Associated General Films. *Voyage* became their first release, although the film still credits ITC as production company.

4. The other writer, Steve Shagan, wrote the 1973 Jack Lemmon vehicle *Save the Tiger*, a New Hollywood–type story about an alienated businessman retreating into his own mental world.

5. Thomas Elsaesser, "American Auteur Cinema: The Last—or First—Picture Show?" in *The Last Great American Picture Show: New Hollywood Cinema in the 1970s*, ed. Thomas Elsaesser, Alexander Horwath, and Noel King (Amsterdam University Press, 2004), 40.

6. William Glover, "Robert Fryer—Clout Plus Taste," *Los Angeles Times*, December 22, 1976, e10. Fryer's directorship of the West Coast Center Theatre Group, which gave film actors the opportunity to do stage work in Los Angeles, directly led to the casting of Faye Dunaway. Fryer knew Dunaway from her 1973 appearance as Blanche DuBois in *A Streetcar Named Desire*. Dunaway's film career has eclipsed both her beginnings in theater and her frequent television work when said film career stalled in the early '70s.

7. Karl and Lili Rosen were names the film gave to passengers Max and Elise Loewe, while Denise and Egon Kreisler stand for Fritz and Babette Spanier. Fritz Spanier's position as a physician made him well known among the passengers. He certified the death of Moritz Weiler (played in the film by Luther Adler), the only Jewish passenger who died at sea.

8. Gilles Deleuze, "On the Movement Image," in *Negotiations 1972–1990*, trans. Martin Youghin (Columbia University Press, 1995), 59, cited in Christian Keathley, "Trapped in the Affection Image: Hollywood's Post-traumatic Cycle (1970–1976)," in Elsaesser et al., *The Last Great American Picture Show*, 293–308, here 294. See also Gilles Deleuze, *Cinema 1: The Movement Image*, trans. Hugh Tomlinson and Barbara Habberjam (The Athlone Press, 1986).

9. Gilles Deleuze, *Cinema 2: The Time Image*, trans. Hugh Tomlinson and Robert Galeta (The Athlone Press, 1989).

10. Christian Keathley, "Trapped in the Affection Image: Hollywood's Post-Traumatic Cycle (1970–1976)," 294–297.

11. Robin Wood, *Hollywood from Vietnam to Reagan* (Columbia University Press, 1986), 31, cited in Keathley, 297.

12. The figure of victims given by the film is 600, which reflects the state of Holocaust research at the time.

13. On the cultural impact of "Vienna, City of My Dreams," see Noah Isenberg, "Vienna Is No More? Film History, Psycho-Geography, and the Great City of Dreams," *Film Quarterly* 67, no. 4 (2014): 67–72.

14. Elsaesser, "American Auteur Cinema," 41.

15. Doneson, 130–32. Doneson's reading of *Voyage* echoes Robin Wood's broader observation, made in *Hollywood from Vietnam to Reagan*, that the New Hollywood dramatized a "breakdown of confidence in American culture and values" (23), which, according to Keathley, generated a cycle of "post-traumatic" films (297). While *Voyage* in some ways is formally more conventional than Keathley's examples, its historical moment of production implicitly extends a reading of America's guilt as "traumatic" from the nation's lack of intervention in the Holocaust to its responsibility for the Vietnam war.

16. Thomas Elsaesser, "The Pathos of Failure: American Films in the 1970s: Notes on the Unmotivated Hero," in Elsaesser et al., *The Last Great American Picture Show*, 279–92.

17. Williams, *Playing the Race Card*, 10–44.

18. Another, even more widely distributed tag line was "The Ship that Shamed the World."

19. Lutz Koepnick, "Reframing the Past: Heritage Cinema and the Holocaust," *New German Critique* 87 (Autumn 2002): 51.

20. An intertextual link between *Cabaret* and *Voyage* is the casting of German actor Helmut Griem.

21. Friedlander, *Reflections on Nazism*, 16–18. See also Susan Sontag, "Fascinating Fascism," *New York Review of Books*, February 6, 1975, www.nybooks.com/articles/1975/02/06/fascinating-fascism.

22. Friedlander, 21. Koepnick, too, charges heritage films about the Nazi period with "turning away from public history and . . . savoring the materiality of the moment—the nostalgic aura of dress, hairstyle, dwelling and song"(49).

23. Miriam Bratu Hansen, "*Schindler's List* Is Not *Shoah*: Second Commandment, Popular Modernism, and Public Memory," *Critical Inquiry* 22, no. 2 (Winter 1996): 292–312. Reprinted in *Spielberg's Holocaust: Critical Perspectives on Schindler's List*, ed. Josefa Loshitzky (Indiana University Press, 1997), 77–103, here 81. Hansen identifies four problem areas for mainstream

Holocaust films: the trivializing techniques of the culture industry; the falsely unifying and ordering principles of neoclassical narrative; the channeling of viewer identification through character subjectivity and star casting; and mass culture giving the illusion of unmediated access to the past and to historical trauma, a practice that violates Judaism's Second Commandment of the prohibition against images (80–83).

24. Cited in Annette Insdorf, *Indelible Shadows: Film and the Holocaust* (Random House, 1983), 4.
25. Insdorf, 4.
26. Insdorf, 15.
27. Ibid., 15.
28. Koepnick, 50.
29. Ibid.
30. Ibid., 50 and 67.
31. Ibid., 68.
32. Ibid.
33. Whether the policy was enforced consistently on all German ships is hard to say, but the *St. Louis* both in reality and in this film had NS personnel on board who would have flagged any use of American music.
34. The German song, performed by Schuricke Terzett (a trio of singers lead by popular German tenor Rudi Schuricke), was not released until 1940. In 1939, Schuricke was drafted for the war. It is unclear whether the song was recorded prior to Schuricke's departure and its release delayed or whether the recording temporarily reunited the trio during the early phase of the war. Nor can we say whether it is serendipity or artistic fiat that accounts for the similarity between both songs' melodies, rhythm, and phrasing. Their lyrics also share a broadly similar romantic theme. Those of "Blue Moon" are "And then there suddenly appeared before me / The only one my arms will ever hold / I heard somebody whisper 'Please adore me' / And when I looked, the moon had turned to gold." The lyrics of the verse of "Ganz leis erklingt Musik" are "Den Dingen, die so wunderbar beginnen / kann man nicht so leicht entgehn / Ja, da gibt es kein Entrinnen / Ja, da gibt es kein Widerstehn" (The things that start in such a wondrous manner / cannot be escaped with ease / taking flight is not an option / resistance is pointless, indeed) (Roy Grundmann trans.). "Blue Moon" makes a second appearance in *Voyage of the Damned* after the *St. Louis* has reached Havana. After gleefully informing NS Deputy Schiendick that the captain has forbidden shore leave for the crew in Havana out of solidarity with the passengers' confinement on the ship, Max plays the song on his record player.
35. Koepnick, 51.
36. Michael Rothberg, *Traumatic Realism: The Demands of Holocaust Representation* (University of Minnesota Press, 2000), 240.

37. Williams, "Melodrama Revised," 48. Citing Peter Brooks, *The Melodramatic Imagination,* Williams points out that melodrama, while related to realism, must be understood as a different epistemological mode. It is structured upon the dual recognition of how things are and how they ought to be. For this, melodrama, even as it is anchored in the realities of bourgeois life, "forces into aesthetic presence desires for identity, value, and fullness of signification beyond the powers of language."

38. Michael Walzer, *Exodus and Revolution* (Basic Books, 1985), 146.

39. Ibid., 138–39.

40. Carol J. Clover, *Men, Women, and Chainsaws: Gender in the Modern Horror Film* (Princeton University Press, 1992), 21–65.

41. Peter Brooks, "The Aesthetics of Astonishment," *Georgia Review* 30, no. 3 (Fall 1976): 615–39. See also Williams, 66.

42. Walzer, 9–10.

43. Williams, 78.

44. Thomas and Morgan-Witts, 272–73.

45. Doneson, *The Holocaust in American Film,* 152. Doneson argues that the film reflects America's collective guilt towards the Jews.

46. It should be noted, though, that *Poseidon*'s and *Voyage*'s respective portrayals of systemic dysfunction have different implications. By identifying its passengers' capacity for teamwork as being key to their rescue, *Poseidon* offsets the chaos it portrays by instilling trust in the importance of smoothly functioning divisions of labor—and arguably becomes an allegory for the tattered film industry's nostalgia for the well-oiled studio system of the 1930s and '40s. By contrast, the systemic dysfunction in *Voyage* runs deeper. We see it in the distrust between some of its characters and the lack of cooperation between various agencies that turns the trip into an odyssey. These aspects, too, can be linked allegorically to the film's mode of production—especially its disorienting medium hybridity and its decentered industry provenance.

47. I disagree with Doneson that the film rhetorically elevates the captain to turn itself into a Christian savior narrative. The film neither falsifies the captain's role (his prevention of the mutiny and his decision not to report the perpetrators are based on fact) nor does it, at least in the 150-minute version, accord him enough screen time to fill this function.

48. On the function of Method acting within the transformation of politics into morals, see Peter Biskind's landmark essay "The Politics of Power in *On the Waterfront*," *Film Quarterly* 29, no. 1 (Autumn 1975): 25–38.

49. On Schindler, see Williams, "Melodrama Revisited," 60 and 76.

50. The legitimacy of this view became vigorously debated around the publication of Cheryl A. Rubenberg's book *Israel and the American National Interest: A Critical Examination* (University of Illinois Press, 1986), which seeks to debunk Israel's status as a threatened outpost of freedom within a

reactionary, undemocratic Arab geopolitical environment as a calculated fabrication on the part of the pro-Israeli lobby in Washington, DC. The numerous reviews of Rubenberg's book form a comprehensive mosaic of the debate.

51. For a comprehensive analysis of cinema and Eurocentrism, see Ella Shohat and Robert Stam, *Unthinking Eurocentrism: Multiculturalism and the Media*, 2nd ed. (Routledge, 2014).

52. Rothberg, *Multidirectional Memory*, 53.

53. Giorgio Agamben, *Remnants of Auschwitz: The Witness and the Archive*, trans. Daniel Heller-Roazen (Zone Books, 1999). In chapter 2, "The Muselmann," 41–87, Agamben explains that while the word "Muselmann" stems from "Muslim," in the camps the only thing the word's Muslim root conveyed was Islam's fatalism, but it applied to any person who signified complete abjection and the loss of will and consciousness (45).

54. *Voyage* is not the only 1970s film that pictures those affected by genocide in this manner. Producer Robert Fryer's film *The Shining* revolves around a protagonist named Jack Torrance (Jack Nicholson), whose transformation, like Rosen's in *Voyage*, takes place in relation to the historical trauma of genocide. The film's setting, the Overlook Hotel, stands on a Native American burial ground, which positions it squarely within the genealogy of genocide. The hotel's spectral ballroom attendees, who present the "other side" to which Jack crosses over or has belonged all along, can be compared to the Jewish attendees of the costume ball in *Voyage*. The spectral impression evoked by the revelers in the ballroom of the *St. Louis* owes to their being earmarked for genocide; the ghosts that populate the ballroom in *The Shining* can be read as the collateral exacted from white civilization in exchange for a genocide it already committed. My thinking converges with that of two scholars who have identified links between interior spaces, biopolitics, and horror. See Marc Olivier, "Carnival of Saints: Mormon Hypernormativity and Herk Harvey's Heterodystopia," and Aviva Briefel, "Ambulatory Gothic: House Tours in the Horror Film"—two papers given at the 2024 Society for Cinema and Media Studies Conference, Boston.

Chapter 8

1. Gordon Thomas and Max Morgan-Witts, *Das Schiff der Verdammten*, trans. Helmut Kossodo (Ingse Verlag, Edition Sven Erik Bergh, 1976).

2. The English title is my translation of the film's German title. Alternative translations can be found on the internet but have not gained official status.

3. Mopo/Focus Online, "Asyl-Streit erinnert an Geschichte der 'St. Louis' vor knapp 80 Jahren," July 2, 2018, www.focus.de/regional/hamburg/

hamburg-hamburg-historisch-er-war-hamburgs-oskar-schindler_id_9187967.html.

4. Gisela Blau, "Ein Ozean aus Tränen," *Journal21.ch*, June 17, 2018, www.journal21.ch/ozean-aus-traenen.

5. Blau, my translation.

6. *Miami Herald*, "Lessons of the Damned," Nov. 20, 2015, www.miamiherald.com/latest-news/article230852284.html.

7. Lily Rothman, "The Long, Sad History of Migrant Ships Being Turned away from Ports," *Time*, June 9, 2015, time.com/3914106/history-migrant-ships-st-louis/.

8. Lind, "How America's Rejection of Jews Fleeing Nazi Germany Haunts Our Refugee Policy Today."

9. Ellen Umansky, "Closing Our Doors," *Slate*, March 8, 2017, slate.com/news-and-politics/2017/03/after-kristallnacht-america-chose-not-to-save-jewish-children-from-the-nazis.html. The article, which features a photo of the ship, cites a 1939 *New York Herald Tribune* article that sharply criticized the US for comparing the Jewish children subject to the Wagner-Rogers bill with an invading parasite. The writer points out that failed refugee policy undermines the mission of US immigration: "Who knows what 20,000 children eligible for entry under the 1939 refugee bill could have accomplished. Or, more pressingly, what would become of a similar number of young Syrian or Sudanese refugees, if we only let them in" (7).

10. Christoph Gunkel, "Irrfahrt eines Schiffs: Wie die Vereinigten Staaten 937 jüdische Flüchtlinge abwiesen," *Spiegel Online*, February 17, 2017, www.spiegel.de/geschichte/irrfahrt-der-st-louis-wie-die-usa-937-juedische-fluechtlinge-abwiesen-a-1134494.html.

11. Merkel, when defending her decision, only referenced the plight of refugees of German origin seeking to flee Soviet Russia and Eastern bloc countries. See Ulrich Herbert and Jakob Schönhagen, "Vor dem 5. September: Die 'Flüchtlingskrise' 2015 im historischen Kontext," *ApuZ: Aus Politik und Zeitgeschichte*, July 17, 2020, www.bpb.de/shop/zeitschriften/apuz/312832/vor-dem-5-september/.

12. This long-standing commitment was codified by Merkel in her 2008 address to the Knesset with the term "Staatsräson," and recently reinforced by German Chancellor Olaf Scholz in the wake of the October 7, 2024, terrorist attacks by Hamas on Israel. Antje Wiener has translated "Staatsräson" as "matter of state" or "reason of state." See Wiener, "Staatsräson: Empty Signifier or Meaningful Norm," Verfassungsblog (On Matters Constitutional), January 12, 2024, verfassungsblog.de/staatsrson-empty-signifier-or-meaningful-norm.

13. Ben Knight, "German Parliament Condemns 'Anti-Semitic' BDS Movement," Deutsche Welle, May 17, 2019, www.dw.com/en/german-parliament-condemns-anti-semitic-bds-movement/a-48779516.

14. Michael Rothberg, "Vergleiche vergleichen: Vom Historikerstreit zur Causa Mbembe," *Geschichte der Gegenwart*, Sept. 23, 2020, https://geschichteder gegenwart.ch/vergleiche-vergleichen-vom-historikerstreit-zur-causa-mbembe/.

15. Masha Gessen, "In the Shadow of the Holocaust: How the Politics of Memory in Europe Obscures What We See in Israel and Gaza Today," *New Yorker*, December 9, 2023, www.newyorker.com/news/the-weekend-essay/in-the-shadow-of-the-holocaust.

16. Ibid.

17. Stefanie Schüler-Springorum, historian and head of the Centre for Research on Anti-Semitism, quoted in Gessen.

18. For detailed information, see "ZDF-Krimi weit vor ARD-Flüchtlingsdrama," *Westfälische Nachrichten*, October 22, 2019, www.wn.de/Welt/Kultur/Fernsehen/4006177-Einschaltquoten-ZDF-Krimi-weit-vor-ARD-Fluechtlingsdrama.

19. Tobias Ebbrecht-Hartmann and Matthias Steinle, "Dokudrama in Deutschland als historisches Ereignisfernsehen—eine Annäherung aus pragmatischer Perspektive (Standpunkte)," *MEDIENwisssenschaft: Rezensionen/Reviews* 25, no. 3 (2008): 250–55, here 251.

20. On the early, more overtly didactic, history of German docudramas, see Christian Hißnauer, "Das Doku-Drama in Deutschland als journalistisches Politikfernsehen—eine Annäherung und Entgegnung aus fernsehgeschichtlicher Perspektive (Standpunkte)," *MEDIENwisssenschaft: Rezensionen/Reviews* 25, no. 3 (2008): 256–65. See also Ebbrecht-Hartman and Steinle, "Dokudrama," 253.

21. On the evolution of the German film and television industry since the 1980s, see Randall Halle, "The New German Television and the Newer German Film: A History of Industry Disruption and Synergy," in *Entertaining German Culture: Contemporary Transnational German Television and Film*, ed. Stephen Ehrig, Benjamin Shaper, and Elizabeth Ward (Berghahn Books, 2023), 39–65. Halle reminds readers that the commercialization of German TV began before its 1990s "eventization" with the emergence of private-sector broadcasters in the mid-1980s (52).

22. Ebbrecht-Hartman and Steinle, 253.

23. Ibid. See also Fredric Jameson's canonized discussion of "pastness" as an imitation of dead styles in Jameson, *Postmodernism, or the Cultural Logic of Late Capitalism* (Duke University Press, 1992). On the role of the "museal gaze" in German films about the Third Reich, see Koepnick, "Reframing the Past."

24. Daniel Dayan and Elihu Katz, *The Live Broadcasting of History* (Harvard University Press, 1992).

25. At issue are two-part or multi-part TV films such as *Die Luftbrücke—Nur der Himmel war frei* (The Airlift) (Dror Zahavi, 2005) and *Dresden*

(Roland Suso Richter, 2006). The term "Erinnerungsboom" (remembrance boom) was coined by Edgar Wolfrum, "Neue Erinnerungskultur: Die Massenmedialisierung des 17. Juni 1953," *Aus Politik und Zeitgeschichte*, Oct. 1, 2003, 33–39, here 33, www.bpb.de/shop/zeitschriften/apuz/27387/die-massenmedialisierung-des-17-juni-1953/.

26. The press notes identify this team as "ARD-Arbeitsgemeinschaft Dokudrama," a team assigned to developing docudramas for all regional networks of the Channel 1 network.

27. The press notes used to be available at docplayer.org/165798935-Die-ungewollten-die-irrfahrt-der-st-louis.html (accessed January 21, 2021; as of August 2024 the link is no longer functional).

28. Marc Brasse (NDR), Silke Schütze (NDR), Esther Schapira (hr), Rolf Bergmann (rbb), and Ulrike Becker (SWR), "*Die Ungewollten—Die Irrfahrt der St. Louis*," in press notes on the film issued by ARD/Das Erste, 3.

29. Volker Herres, "Vorwort," in press notes on the film issued by ARD/Das Erste, 2. Roy Grundmann trans.

30. Commenting on how she played her character, actor Hammelstein is the only one involved with the production who explicitly links the film's subject to the current migrant crisis.

31. Herres, "Vorwort," 2.

32. The NSDAP membership became known only when Schröder's grandnephew in 2018 released a trove of Schröder's personal documents to the public. The complexity of the real Schröder would have been difficult to assimilate to the film's agenda. In his account of the voyage, he neither comments on the totalitarianism of the NS state nor on the circumstances of him joining the NSDAP. Nor does he address HAPAG's complicity with Germany's antisemitic policy of expulsion. See my detailed assessment of Schröder in chapter 6.

33. Gustav Schröder, *Heimatlos auf hoher See*, my translation. Schröder's placing "emigrant ship" in quotation marks carries subtle sarcasm about the world's disavowal of the political duress and despair of Jewish refugees, a sentiment that led to the rejection of the ship's passengers by several countries. By excising Schröder's characterization of the *St. Louis* as an emigrant ship, the article in *Der Spiegel* reshapes his statement into an apolitical, humanist view.

34. Ebbrecht-Hartmann and Steinle, "Dokudrama," 250.

35. Paul Cooke, "Heritage, Heimat, and German Historical 'Event' Television: Nico Hofmann's teamWorx," in *German Television*, ed. Larson Powell and Robert Shandley (Berghahn Books, 2016), 175–92, here 177.

36. The term "ceremonial center" was coined by Dayan and Katz, *Media Events*, cited in Cooke, 178,

37. Cooke, 181.

38. Ebbrecht-Hartmann and Steinle, 251.

39. "MV" stands for "Merchant Vessel." For detailed information on the *Funchal*, see Reuben Goossing's website, ssmaritime.com/funchal-Intro.htm.

40. For an overview of this subject, see Robert G. Moeller, *War Stories: The Search for a Usable Past in the Federal Republic of Germany* (University of California Press, 2001).

41. Elfriede Jelinek, "Die endlose Unschuldigkeit," in *Die Endlose Unschuldigkeit: Prosa—Hörspiel—Essay* (Schwiftinger Galerie-Verlag, 1980), 49–82. In her often overlooked contribution, Jelinek identifies television family shows' paternal contents ("Vaterinhalte") as the main principle of pop culture myths (50).

42. Jelinek, 51–62.

43. A link between 1950s West German U-Boat culture and the *St. Louis* odyssey is constituted by the fact that one of the decade's successful book-length accounts of German World War II U-boat crew was written by Hans Herlin, who also wrote the first in-depth German language book on the *St. Louis*, *Kein gelobtes Land: Die Irrfahrt der St. Louis* (No Promised Land: The *St. Louis* voyage) (Nannen Verlag, 1961).

44. On the role of the *Wilhelm Gustloff* catastrophe in German memory culture and the 2009 film, see Bill Niven, "The Good Captain and the Bad Captain: Joseph Vilsmaier's *Die Gustloff* and the Erosion of Complexity," *German Politics & Society* 26, no. 4 (Winter 2008): 82–98. On Wisbar's film, see Michael Ennis, "Opfer und Täter in den Gustloff Filmen von Frank Wisbar," in *Die Wilhelm Gustloff: Geschichte und Erinnerung eines Untergangs*, ed. Bill Niven (Mitteldeutscher Verlag, 2011), 205–33. See also Ennis's dissertation, *The Wilhelm Gustloff in German Memory Culture: A Case Study on Competing Discourses* (University of Cincinnati, 2013). The other variant of the captain figure, the aging, benignly patriarchal commander of a cruise ship, who must maneuver a rapidly changing peacetime world, is on display in the old-fashioned 1970 comedy *Der Kapitän* (The Captain), a remake of the 1959 British film *The Captain's Table*, in which popular German actor Heinz Rühmann, by then in his late sixties, embodies the virtues of authority put to the test not by war but by screwball comedy–type mishaps.

45. The culturally most enduring portrait of a captain in German culture came with the long-running TV show *Das Traumschiff* (The dream boat), modeled on the US show *The Love Boat*, and featuring several captains over the course of its long run. The most memorable ones were played by Heinz Weiss (1981–99) and Siegfried Rauch (1999–14), widely remembered for their starring roles in two earlier TV shows set during World War II. Weiss played a German POW trying to return home from Russia in *Soweit die Füße tragen* (As far as my feet will carry me), Rauch a bon vivant who, against his will, has to spy for the Germans, the British, and the French in *Es muß nicht immer Kaviar sein* (It can't always be caviar). Both shows position

the German Everyman at a remove from Nazi Germany and as a victim of higher circumstances. *Das Traumschiff* benefited from the formula of the captain as benign authority figure that in 1977 had been popularized by Paul Dahlke as captain of a riverboat freighter on the Rhine in the family show *MS Franziska*. The show's treatment of the aging, oedipally challenged pater familias closely fits Jelinek's ideological and cultural analysis.

46. The seductiveness of the stereotype of the benign patriarch is also reflected in the German press coverage of Schröder. See for example Christoph Gunkel, "Der Papitän," *Spiegel Online*, January 23, 2018, www.spiegel.de/geschichte/juedische-fluechtlinge-kapitaen-gustav-schroeder-und-die-irrfahrt-der-st-louis-a-1188181.html. Note the title of the article, a playful combination of the words "Kapitän" (captain) and "Papi" (Daddy), with which Schröder signed postcards he mailed to his son.

47. See for example Miriam Schaptke, "Warum ein NSDAP-Mitglied 936 Juden rettete," *Die Welt*, Oct. 21, 2019, www.welt.degeschichte/zweiterweltkrieg/article202119188/Irrfahrt-der-St-Louis-Warum-ein-NSDAP-Mitglied-936-Juden-rettete.html. Media coverage invariably lauds Schröder's actions as heroic. See, among others, Thomas Kunze, "Ulrich Noethen als mutiger Kapitän," TV Goldene Kamera, October 18, 2019, www.goldene-kamera.de/tv/article227398215/Ulrich-Noethen-in-Die-Ungewollten.html; Ursula Scheer, "Der nächste Hafen könnte die Rettung sein," *Frankfurter Allgemeine*, Oct. 21, 2019, www.faz.net/aktuell/feuilleton/medien/ard-drama-die-ungewollten-ueber-die-st-louis-16442921.html.

48. Johannnes von Moltke, "Sympathy for the Devil: Cinema, History, and the Politics of Emotion," *New German Critique* 102 (Fall 2007), 35. Von Moltke supports his argument by referencing Christine Noll Brinckmann's important work on empathy. See Christine Noll Brinckmann, "Die Rolle der Empathie oder Furcht und Schrecken im Dokumentarfilm," in *Kinogefühle: Emotionalität und Film*, ed. Matthias Brütsch, Vinzenz Hediger, Ursula von Keitz, et al. (Schüren, 2005). Brinckmann points out that "the preconditions for developing empathy are fundamentally more favorable in the cinema than in reality" (237).

49. Von Moltke. My discussion is indebted to the concepts von Moltke develops for his analysis of the historical period drama *Downfall* (2004). In what feels like a deliberate subversion of the primacy effect, *Voyage of the Damned* begins by showing a handsome young man dressed in business attire exiting the *St. Louis* to attend a meeting. After several brief scenes that show him making his way through town and arriving at his destination, the film identifies him as the NS deputy Schiendick (Helmut Griem).

50. Carl Platinga, "The Scene of Empathy and the Human Face on Film," in *Passionate Views: Film, Cognition, and Emotion*, ed. Carl Platinga and Greg M. Smith (Johns Hopkins University Press, 1999), 239, 249–55.

Platinga points out that polysemic facial close-ups require semantic clarification through additional textual elements.

51. His real name was Zschiedrich, although he is often misidentified as Schiendick, the name he carries in Gordon Thomas and Max Morgan-Witts's *Voyage of the Damned*.

52. Archival information shows that Ostermeyer served as first officer on the *St. Louis* on previous trips, but not on the Cuba voyage. The name of the first officer on that voyage was Frisch.

53. Hendrich's second request comes after he overhears Schröder sharing a plan with Ostermeyer to run the *St. Louis* aground off the coast of England. There is no archival evidence that Schröder shared his plan with his first officer or that Hendrich's real life counterpart caught wind of it.

54. Martha Stern is not listed in the published passenger list for the voyage. Citing Roger Odin's notion of "documentarizing reading" (dokumentarisierende Lektüre), Ebbrecht-Hartmann and Steinle note (252) that historical "event TV" exploits viewers' tendency to integrate nonfiction and fiction materials alike into their historical memory, whereby images *from* the past and images *about* the past blend into each other to give the impression of "history" as actual, authoritative enunciator. See Roger Odin, "Kunst und Ästhetik bei Film und Fernsehen: Elemente zu einem semio-pragmatischen Ansatz," *montage a/v* 11, no. 2 (2002): 42–57.

55. Martha, we learn, paid the second-class fare of 500 Reichsmark. Her quarters, however, look like a first-class cabin. In contrast to *Voyage of the Damned*, the film glosses over actual differences between the *St. Louis* passengers.

56. Von Moltke, "Sympathy for the Devil," 17. Von Moltke traces the German term for the feeling for history, "Geschichtsgefühl," to a speech given by Martin Walser at the anniversary of World War II, "Über ein Geschichtsgefühl," printed in *Frankfurter Allgemeine Zeitung*, May 10, 2002, in which Walser gives his relationship to history the coding of sensation rather than intellectual identification.

57. Thomas Elsaesser, *New German Cinema: A History* (Rutgers University Press, 1989), 256. Elsaesser links the rejection of spectacle and individualized heroism to popular memory's roots in European working class culture. Claude Lanzmann's film *Shoah* is considered one of the prime examples of mourning work as a heterogeneous and unspectacular mode of historical inquiry. For scholarship on Shoah, see especially *Claude Lanzmann's "Shoah": Key Essays*, ed. Stuart Liebman (Oxford University Press, 2007).

58. The film only briefly addresses the difference between those who had experienced a concentration camp and those who had not. Herbert Karliner mentions his father's incarceration after Kristallnacht and Knepel mentions that formerly incarcerated *St. Louis* passengers feared returning to

Germany because it placed them in violation of their agreement to emigrate. In contrast to *Voyage of the Damned*, *Die Ungewollten* avoids depicting the impact of the camps on the bodies and psyches of those exposed to them.

59. See James E. Young's analysis of Peter Weiss's documentary play about the 1965 Auschwitz trial in Frankfurt, *The Investigation*, in James E. Young, *Writing and Rewriting the Holocaust: Narrative and the Consequences of Interpretation* (Indiana University Press, 1988), p. 71.

60. Roland Barthes, *Mythologies* (Hill and Wang, 1970), p. 11, cited by Young (66) as part of his critique of the ideological nature of self-effacing tendencies of documentary theater.

61. I would like to thank Michael Pearson for identifying this ship.

62. The term was coined by Holocaust survivor David Rousset in his book *L'univers concentrationnaire*. See Griselda Pollock and Max Silverman, "Introduction," in *Concentrationary Cinema*, ed. Pollock and Silverman.

63. Jacques Derrida and F. C. T. Moore, "White Mythology," *New Literary History* 6 (1974): 5–74, cited in Young, p. 66.

64. Georges Didi-Huberman, *The Eye of History: When Images Take Positions*, trans. Shane B. Lillis (MIT Press, 2018), xxii.

Chapter 9

1. The organization misidentifies the *St. Louis* as a steam ship ("SS").

2. 111th Congress, 1st Session, S. Res. 111, May 19, 2009. See especially sections stating that the Senate "acknowledges the suffering of those refugees caused by the refusal of the United States, Cuban, and Canadian governments to provide them political asylum" and (4) "recognizes the 70th anniversary of the M.S. *St. Louis* tragedy as an opportunity for public officials and educators to raise awareness about an important historical event, the lessons of which are relevant to current and future generations."

3. Cited in Jennifer Frost, "Challenging the 'Hollywoodization' of the Holocaust: Reconsidering Judgment at Nuremberg (1961)," *Jewish Film & New Media* 1, No. 2 (Fall 2013): 143. Frost credits the authors with coining the term but acknowledges that it has since been used by several other scholars. See for example Hilene Flanzbaum, ed., *The Americanization of the Holocaust* (Johns Hopkins University Press, 1999).

4. Rothberg, *Traumatic Realism*, 250–51.

5. Ibid., 222.

6. Robert G. Moeller, "How to Judge Stanley Kramer's *Judgment at Nuremberg*," in *German History* 31, no. 4 (Winter 2013), 497–522, esp. 506. While West Germany took the film as an opportunity to launch the state's role as official sponsor of memorial culture, in the US it fell to film critics

and op-ed writers to debate the film's political implications, though America's lack of intervention in the Holocaust did not become part of the debate, nor did the US government contribute to public discourse on the film (510).

7. Doneson, *The Holocaust in American Film*, 101. Doneson reads this universalization of guilt as consistent with the film's attempt to universalize the victims. It does not mention Jews and posits the victims of the Holocaust alongside victims of other World War II–related genocides, such as those committed against non-Jewish populations of Eastern European countries.

8. Stanley Kramer interviewed by Alberto Shatowsky in *Nanchete*, Stanley Kramer Collection, Department of Special Collections, University Research Library, UCLA, Box 38, publicity folder. Cited in Doneson, 100.

9. For a detailed discussion of the film and these issues, see Frost, "Challenging the 'Hollywoodization' of the Holocaust," and Moeller, "How to Judge Stanley Kramer's Judgment at Nuremberg." See also Doneson, 101.

10. Young, *Writing and Rewriting the Holocaust*, 11.

11. Young, 69.

12. Burns's reference to Stephen Samuel Wise, a chief architect of American Zionism, is appropriate, given Wise's key role in alerting the US to the threat of Nazi antisemitism. It does, however, constitute yet more evidence of the legacy and overdetermined logic of colonialism that subtends Burns's reasoning. Wise also had a key role in bringing the US to approve the Balfour Declaration by which Britain, Europe's foremost colonial power, spearheaded the founding of a Jewish state in Palestine at the expense of the local Muslim and Christian populations (see chapter 1).

Chapter 10

1. Michael Rothberg, *Multidirectional Memory*, 2.

2. The number of texts and artifacts about the *St. Louis* incident is by now so large that not all can be discussed in these pages. In addition to Padura's novel, there are at least five other novels that touch on *the St. Louis* incident or make it their focus. These include works of historical fiction, such as Julian Barnes's *A History of the World in 10½ Chapters* (Vintage, 1989), Bodie Thoene and Brock Thoene's *Munich Signature (Zion Covenant)* (Tyndale House, 2005), and Armando Lucas Correa's *The German Girl* (Atria Books, 2016). Two books retell the *St. Louis* story in the category of fiction for children/young adults: Kathy Kacer's *To Hope and Back: The Journey of the St. Louis* (Second Story Press, 2011) and Alan Gratz's *Refugee* (Scholastic Press, 2017). The *St. Louis* voyage is also the subject of one opera, *The St. Louis Blues* (1994), by Chiel Meijering, and of three plays, *Sotto Voce* (2014) by Nilo Cruz, *Die Reise der Verlorenen* (2018) by Daniel Kehlmann, and *The*

Good Ship St. Louis (2022) by Philip Boehm. In addition, there are numerous survivors accounts of the journey published in various formats.

3. Rothberg, *Multidirectional Memory*, 11.
4. Ibid., 12.
5. Leonardo Padura, *Heretics*, trans. Anna Kushner (Farrar, Straus and Giroux, 2017; orig. Herejes [Tusquets Editores, 2013]). I would like to thank José Gatti for first bringing this book to my attention.
6. Ibid., 48.
7. Ibid.
8. For the term and concept of "critical fabulation," see Saidiya Hartman, "Venus in Two Acts," *Small Axe* 12, no. 2 (June 2008): 1–14. Hartman's term designates the act of compensating for the silences and gaps of incomplete archives via practices of speculating and hypothesizing. While the theory of critical fabulation is recent, the practice among artists is older.
9. Padura, 48.
10. Ibid.
11. On the transversal nature of the archive, see Rothberg, *Multidirectional Memory*, 18: The transversal archive "cuts across genres, national contexts, periods, and cultural traditions." On the plurality of the archive, see Erika Balsom, "From Singular to Plural," in *Accidental Archivism: Shaping Cinema's Futures with Remnants of the Past*, ed. Vinzenz Hediger and Stefanie Schulte-Strathaus (Meson Press, 2022): "archives—tied as they are to commencement and commandment through the root arkhē—are the domain of absence as much as presence, places of purported origins, policed boundaries, and finite resources." /archivism.meson.press/chapters/new-cinephilias-beyond-the-manspreading-machine/from-singular-to-plural/.
12. Padura, 101–2.
13. Ibid., 51.
14. Ibid., 53.
15. Ibid.
16. Ibid., 11.
17. Ibid., 46.
18. Ibid., 59.
19. Ibid., 105.
20. Ibid., 102.
21. It should be noted that Padura implies that the career of Ricardo, the son of Joseph's mulata lover, as a medical doctor owes not only to his step-uncle's determination to give him an education, but also to some positive changes brought on by communism. And while the book never explicitly criticizes the US for its political boycott of Cuba, its depiction of the day-to-day lives of Conde and his friends foregrounds the devastating consequences of the decades-long political isolation and economic sanctions the US inflicted on Cuba.

22. Art Spiegelman, *The St. Louis Refugee Ship Blues*, *Washington Post*, July 24, 2009, www.washingtonpost.com/wp-srv/special/opinions/outlook/st-louis-refugee-ship-blues/static.html. As I was unable to obtain permission to reproduce the one-page cartoon in this book, I refer readers to the above URL, which links to a webpage displaying the work.

23. Art Spiegelman, *Maus: A Survivor's Tale: My Father Bleeds History (Mid-1930s to Winter 1944)* (Pantheon Books, 1986), and *Maus II: A Survivor's Tale and Here My Troubles Began* (Pantheon Books, 1992). Spiegelman's interviews with his father about surviving the Holocaust were prompted by a short comic strip titled "Maus," which Spiegelman drew in 1972. The interviews became the foundation for the serialized *Maus* comics, on which he started to work in 1978. In 1986 Hollywood filmmaker Steven Spielberg announced the release of his animated film *Feivel: An American Tail*, in which an Eastern European mouse escapes pogroms by fleeing to America. Spiegelman promptly decided to republish the first six chapters of his *Maus* comics (which had been serialized in *Raw*, the magazine he had founded with his wife, Françoise Mouly) in book form ahead of the film's release in order to distinguish his work from Spielberg's. He continued to serialize *Maus* in *Raw* and republished the comics as a second book in 1992, after *Raw* had folded.

24. A further correspondence between *Heretics* and *Maus* emerges in that Elias Ambrosius, the Jewish protagonist of the seventeenth-century section of Padura's novel, is the model for one of Rembrandt's paintings of Christ that depicts Christ from a secular perspective as a real person or rather, in stereoscopic manner, as both a deity and a human. Padura describes Rembrandt's painting as a deeply subversive iconological hybrid, which, at least in the diegesis of *Heretics*, roils the maestro's contemporaries in ways comparable to the disapproval Spiegelman earned initially for depicting the Holocaust through animal characters.

25. For instance, *The New York Times* long listed *Maus* under the rubric of fiction, a category also used by most bookstores to shelve the title.

26. Dominick LaCapra, *History and Memory After Auschwitz* (Cornell University Press, 1998), 143. LaCapra cites critics who have compared Spiegelman to such modernist authors as André Gide, James Joyce, Vladimir Nabokov, and William Faulkner.

27. Art Spiegelman, quoted in Esther B. Fein, "Holocaust as Cartoonist's Way of Getting to Know His Father," *New York Times*, 10 December 1991, C15. See also LaCapra, *History and Memory After Auschwitz*, 145.

28. LaCapra, 141. LaCapra describes Spiegelman as "artist, writer, cartoonist, novelist, historian, biographer, autobiographer, ethnographer, secondary witness, memory-worker, modernist, postmodernist, interviewer, and interviewee" (145), and *Maus* as "documentary art, pictorial literature, novelized comic or cartoon, graphic novel, oral history, biography, autobiography, ethnography, vehicle for testimony, and medium for memory-work" (ibid.).

29. Rothberg, *Traumatic Realism*, 206.

30. In *Traumatic Realism*, Rothberg reads one of Spiegelman's images that shows Artie standing in front of the counterfeit of Disney's Mickey Mouse and holding a realistically drawn mouse in his hand: "This image provides an allegory of the contradictory position of the post-Holocaust artist—an artist who produces formally experimental works about genocide for the smiling, two-dimensional face of the entertainment industry, but everywhere confronts the detritus of the real" (2).

31. LaCapra, 143.

32. See Joshua Brown's book review of both *Maus* volumes (the title of the review is the bibliographical information of the books), *Journal of American History* 79 (1993), 1669, cited in LaCapra, 143.

33. Quoted in Susan Jacobowitz, "'Words and Pictures Together': An Interview with Art Spiegelman," in Jacobowitz, *Writing on the Edge* 6 (1994), 55.

34. LaCapra, 178.

35. Rothberg, *Traumatic Realism*, 206–10.

36. According to composer W. C. Handy, the song was inspired by him meeting a black woman in St. Louis who was alarmed by the disappearance of her husband. See W.C. Handy, *Father of the Blues: An Autobiography*, ed. Arna Bontemps (MacMillan, 1941), 119.

37. Rothberg, *Traumatic Realism*, 204.

38. The Canadian Jewish Congress describes itself as the "democratically elected, national organizational voice of the Jewish community of Canada." See Canadian Jewish Congress Organizational Records, www.cjhn.ca/en/permalink/cjhn2, accessed August 11, 2023.

39. During the 1930s, Halifax was a regular port of call on the transatlantic route of the *St. Louis*. For CJC's reasoning, see Josh Tapper, "Libeskind-Designed Holocaust Monument 'Collecting Dust' in Toronto," *Times of Israel*, December 23, 2014, www.timesofisrael.com/libeskind-designed-holocaust-monument-collecting-dust-in-toronto/amp/.

40. Conversation with Marie Chapman, Director of the Canadian Museum of Immigration at Pier 21, August 11, 2023.

41. Tapper.

42. Studio Libeskind, "The Wheel of Conscience," libeskind.com/work/the-wheel-of-conscience, Accessed July 26, 2023.

43. Alison Atkinson-Phillips, "On Being Moved: Art, Affect and Activation in Pubic Commemorations of Trauma," *Continuum: Journal of Media & Cultural Studies* 32, no. 3 (2018): 381–92. Atkinson-Phillips discusses the affective dimension of memorials that, in the vein of art pieces, ask viewers to engage with a given aesthetic.

44. Atkinson-Phillips, 382. Atkinson-Phillips credits Deborah Britzman with the term "difficult knowledge" and T. Erica Lehrer, Cynthia E. Mil-

ton, and Monica Eileen Patterson with the term "knowledge that does not fit."

45. Cited in CBC News, "Nova Scotia: Libeskind Memorial to Jews Rejected in Halifax Unveiled," Jan. 20, 2011, www.cbc.ca/news/canada/nova-scotia/libeskind-memorial-to-jews-rejected-in-halifax-unveiled-1.1032629.

46. See Schwinghamer, "'The Existing Immigration Regulations Will Not Offer Any Solution': MS St. Louis in Canadian Context," Canadian Museum of Immigration at Pier 21, December 21, 2023, pier21.ca/research/immigration-history/canada-and-ms-st-louis. Schwinghamer points out that Canada's Prime Minister William Lyon Mackenzie King expressed his "fear [that] we would have riots if we agreed to a policy that admitted numbers of Jews." While those numbers remained unspecified, Schwinghamer further states that the Canadian government's stance on Jewish immigrants has often been conflated with the words of a senior official who, when asked how many Jews Canada would admit at the end of World War II, gave the notorious response, "None is too many."

47. Atkinson-Phillips, 382.

48. CBC News, "Nova Scotia: Libeskind Memorial to Jews Rejected in Halifax Unveiled."

49. I have no evidence that the title of the installation was also intended as a play on *Wheel of Fortune* so as to present the fate of the refugee as a gigantic gamble. The comparison does not, however, seem outlandish.

50. Susanne Buckley-Zistel, "Tracing the Politics of Aesthetics: From Imposing, via Counter to Affirmative Memorials to Violence," *Memory Studies* 14, no. 4 (2021): 781–96, here 783.

51. It should be noted here that the Canadian press, as Amanda Grzyb has pointed, out, differed from the US press in that it paid more attention to other refugee ships. See chapter 4.

Epilogue

1. The quotation in the chapter title is from Donna Haraway, "Situated Knowledges: The Science Question in Feminism and the Privilege of Partial Perspective," *Feminist Studies* 14, no. 3 (Autumn 1988), 575–99. A version of this chapter was published under the title "'With Whose Blood Were My Eyes Crafted?' Critical Concepts of Seeing, Knowing, and Remembering in Philip Scheffner and Merle Kröger's *Havarie* (2016)" in *Transit* 14, no. 2 (2014).

2. See examples from the *Miami Herald*, *Time*, *Vox*, and *Slate* referenced in chapter 8.

3. "Asyl-Streit erinnert an Geschichte der 'St. Louis' vor knapp 80 Jahren," Mopo/Focus Online, July 2, 2018, www.focus.de/regional/hamburg/

hamburg-hamburg-historisch-er-war-hamburgs-oskar-schindler_id_9187967.html.

4. Gisela Blau, "Ein Ozean aus Tränen," *Journal21.ch*, June 17, 2018, www.journal21.ch/ozean-aus-traenen. Author's translation.

5. Britta Wagner, "A Shared Space at Eye Level: An Interview with Documentary Filmmaker Philip Scheffner," *Senses of Cinema* 78, March 2016, www.sensesofcinema.com/2016/feature-articles/philip-scheffner-interview. According to Scheffner, after spotting the dinghy with the migrants, the cruise ship captain informed the Maritime Rescue Center in Spain and asked if his ship should take the refugees on board, but the Rescue Unit instructed him to stay near the dinghy to help the rescue helicopter to spot the location of the migrants.

6. For a recent overview of European refugee films and scholarship on them, see Johannes von Moltke, "Ways of Seeing: Ethics of Looking in European Refugee Films," in *The Palgrave Handbook of European Migration in Literature and Culture*, ed. Corinna Stan and Charlotte Sussman, 475–95 (Palgrave, 2024).

7. Johanne Villeneuve and Debbie Blythe, "Adrift: *Havarie*, an Acousmatic Film by Philip Scheffner," *SubStance* 49, no. 2 (2020): 71–92.

8. Alena Strohmaier and Lea Spahn, "Intra-Active Documentary: Philip Scheffner's *Havarie* and New-Materialist Perspectives on Migrant Cinema," *Synoptique: An Online Journal of Film and Moving Image Studies* 7, no. 2 (2018), www.synoptique.ca/_files/ugd/811df8_6311911d8d4d433d941c5f13a78b8e11.pdf.

9. Nilgun Bayraktar, "Beyond the Spectacle of 'Refugee Crisis': Multi-Directional Memories of Migration in Contemporary Essay Film," *Journal of European Studies* 49, no. 3–4 (2019): 354–73, here 359.

10. Anat Tzom Ayalon, "A Tiny Boat Lost at Sea: Trauma and Ethics in *Havarie* [Collision] by Philip Scheffner (Germany, 2016)," *Ekphrasis* 23, no. 3 (2020): 29–49, here 30.

11. Édouard Glissant, *Poetics of Relation*, trans. Betsy Wing (University of Michigan Press, 1997; orig. *Poétique de la relation* [Gallimard, 1990]), 144.

12. Ibid., 169–88.

13. John E. Drabinski, *Glissant and the Middle Passage: Philosophy, Beginning, Abyss* (University of Minnesota Press, 2019), 12.

14. Ibid., 6–8, 69.

15. Ibid., 66, 153–54, 186, 193.

16. Ibid., 169–88. As a result, knowing turns into a continual process of becoming.

17. Édouard Glissant, *Caribbean Discourse: Selected Essays*, trans. J. Michael Dash (University of Virginia Press, 1989), cited in Drabinski, *Glissant and the Middle Passage*, 13 (trans. altered by Drabinski).

18. In *In the Wake: On Blackness and Being* (Duke University Press, 2016), Christina Sharpe speaks of the "black Mediterranean" as a crisis of capital and of representation. "Migrants fleeing lives made unlivable," Sharpe writes, tend to be misrepresented as "refugees fleeing internal economic stress and internal conflicts, but subtending this crisis is the crisis of capital and the wreckage from the continuation of military and other colonial projects of US/European wealth extraction and immiseration" (59).

19. Ayalon, "A Tiny Boat Lost at Sea," 35.

20. Drabinski, 13.

21. *Havarie*'s soundtrack is commensurate with the migrants' visual opacity. While their voices remain unrecorded and form a potentially problematic structuring absence on the soundtrack, Scheffner adds the voices of other migrants who have already arrived on European shores. The soundtrack's compiling of those voices points to a community of the unknown. By describing those who share in the unknown with others whom they have yet to know, for postcolonial theorists such as Glissant "the unknown" harbors future potential.

22. Wagner, "A Shared Space at Eye Level."

23. Rothberg, *Multidirectional Memory*. See discussion in chapter 10. See also Rothberg, "From Gaza to Warsaw: Mapping Multidirectional Memory," *Criticism* 53, no. 4 (2011): 523–48. Though Rothberg's concept figures prominently in Bayraktar's article on migrant cinema, it does not play out prominently in Bayraktar's discussion of *Havarie*.

24. Wagner.

25. Royal Caribbean International is owned by Royal Caribbean Group, a conglomerate that also owns other cruise lines and, along with Carnival, is one of the pioneers of mass-market cruising. *Adventure of the Seas* is comparable to a large middle-class hotel.

26. The geographic, cultural, and ethnic proximity between the Irish and the English and the fact that Ireland's economy and labor force have intersected closely with the British economy makes it difficult to compare Ireland to other British colonies. Yet the war of independence that led to Ireland's decolonization bears similarities to other colonial uprisings. In 1921, the Government of Ireland Act divided Ireland into the Irish Republic and Northern Ireland, with the latter remaining part of the UK. England has tended to endow former colonies with varying states of autonomy, sparking conflicts both within and between those regions. In Northern Ireland, descendants of colonists from Britain retained the demographic majority and clashed with Irish nationalists. In 1969, these differences escalated into the Troubles, a three-decade-long armed conflict in which unionist militias and British police brutally clamped down on the nationalists. The conflict officially ended with the 1998 Good Friday Agreement, which gave Northern Ireland

more autonomy, but the history of domination is engrained in the mentality of the Northern Irish. For a useful introduction to the subject, see Aaron Edwards and Cillian McGrattan, *The Northern Ireland Conflict: A Beginner's Guide* (Oneworld Publications, 2010). I would like to thank Gary Crowdus for his helpful comments on the Northern Ireland conflict.

27. Diamond quoted in Villeneuve and Blythe, 79.
28. Scheffner quoted in Wagner.
29. Glissant, *Poetics of Relation*, 19.
30. Ibid.
31. Haraway, "Situated Knowledges," 589.
32. Ibid., 585.
33. Ibid., 587.
34. Glissant, *Poetics of Relation*, 20.
35. The title not only means "accident" and "shipwreck" in German, but also, if traced to the word's Arab roots, "error" and "damage." See Strohmaier and Spahn for an etymological explanation.
36. Adam Charles Hart, "Extensions of Our Body Moving, Dancing: The American Avant-Garde's Theories of Handheld Subjectivity," *Discourse* 41, no. 1 (Winter 2019): 37–67, here 38.
37. As Scheffner told Wagner, his extending Diamond's video to ninety minutes translated into a total frame count for *Havarie* of 5,400 single frames, which makes one frame last about one second, a way of marking time.
38. See Jordan Schonig, *The Shape in Motion* (Oxford University Press, 2022), 32, and Schonig, "Seeing Aspects of the Moving Camera: On the Twofoldness of the Mobile Frame," *Synoptique* 5, no. 2 (Winter 2017): 57–78, here 59.
39. David Bordwell, "Camera Movement and Cinematic Space," *Ciné Tracts—A Journal of Film, Communications, Culture and Politics* 1, no. 2 (1977): 19–27, here 23, quoted in Schonig, "Seeing Aspects of the Moving Camera," 64.
40. Since spectating is primarily considered a form of knowledge acquisition that tends to privilege content over form, viewers automatically imbue the camera with an agency they actually cannot verify directly, namely that of creating movement. As Schonig puts it: "Automatically attuned to a set of perceptual depth cues, we *see* the onscreen movement of space *as* a movement of the offscreen camera instead of as the movement of space across the surface of the screen" ("Seeing Aspects of the Moving Camera," 64). On the privileging of content over form, which Daniel Morgan has termed cinema's epistemic seduction or the lure of the image, see Morgan, *The Lure of the Image: Epistemic Fantasies of the Moving Camera* (University of California Press, 2021). On the double status of Diamond's pan as both a document and an expression of Diamond's inner need to assure himself of his own location, see Burkhardt Wolf, "Im Blick der Stimmen: Fun Ships und Boatpeople in Krögers und Scheffners *Havarie*," in *Das Schiff: Archive für*

Mediengeschichte 20, ed. Friedrich Balke, Bernhard Siegert, and Joseph Vogl (Verlag Vorwerk 8, 2024), 85–96, here 91.

41. Scheffner quoted in Wagner.

42. Art Simon, *Dangerous Knowledge: The JFK Assassination in Art and Film* (Temple University Press, 1996), 110–18.

43. *Havarie* also begs comparisons to Warhol's early films and to 1960s structural film, particularly for their slowed-down projection speed. Such films as *Eat* (1963), *Sleep* (1964), *Blow Job* (1964), and *Empire* (1964) generate ambivalent feelings in viewers that involve both curiosity and boredom. They invite viewers to peruse the image for its concrete contents and its semi-abstract qualities without, however, delivering concrete epistemological "results." See, among others, Stephen Koch, *Stargazer: The Life, World and Films of Andy Warhol* (Marion Boyars Publishers, 1972), and Roy Grundmann, *Andy Warhol's Blow Job* (Temple University Press, 2003).

44. The literature on the "Fortress Europe" phenomenon is too large to list here. For questions of representation involving anthropological, cultural and media theory discourses, see Yosefa Loshitzky, *Screening Strangers: Migration and Diaspora in Contemporary European Cinema* (Indiana University Press, 2010); T. J. Demos, *The Migrant Image: The Art and Politics of Documentary During Global Crisis* (Duke University Press, 2013); Nilgun Bayraktar, *Mobility and Migration in Film and Moving Image Art: Cinema Beyond Europe* (Routledge, 2016); and Deniz Bayrakdar and Robert Burgoyne, eds., *Refugees and Migrants in Contemporary Art, Film and Media* (Amsterdam University Press, 2022).

45. Thomas Crow, "Saturday Disasters: Trace and Reference in Early Warhol," in Crow, *Modern Art in the Common Culture* (Yale University Press, 1996), 53.

46. Drabinski, 20. At issue is once again Glissant's notion of the quasi ex nihilo reconstitution of Afro-Caribbean identity in the wake of the Middle Passage. Glissant, so Drabinski argues, conceives of loss and failure as "the presencing of roots, even in the experience of absence" (8). To this notion of loss and memory, which is conceived within the longue dureé framework of decolonization, Drabinski juxtaposes Heideggerian notions of loss as traumatic and thus irreversibly ruptured—a thought model that, as Drabinski asserts, "Glissant calls a *penseé continentale*" (8).

47. Rothberg, *Multidirectional Memory*, 12.

48. Ibid.

49. Ibid., 13.

50. Ibid., 11.

51. Walter Benjamin, "Theses on the Philosophy of History," in *Illuminations: Essays and Reflections*, trans. Harry Zohn (Harcourt, Brace & World, 1968), 253–64.

52. Rothberg, *Multidirectional Memory*, 44. Emphasis mine.

53. Benjamin, "Theses," 262.

54. Glissant, *Poetics of Relation*, 20.
55. See Hannah Arendt, *The Origin of Totalitariansim*, 185. See also Rothberg, *Multidirectional Memory*.
56. Drabinski, 10.
57. Marc Tracy, "The Holocaust's Grandchildren are Speaking Now," *New York Times*, October 20, 2024.
58. Amanda Gorman, "In Memory of Those Still in the Water," *New York Times*, July 15, 2023.

Appendix 1

1. Heinz Burmester, "Aus dem Leben des Kapitäns Gustav Schröder," *Deutsches Schifffahrtsarchiv* 13 (1990), 164–200.
2. Lipsky, Uhlig, and Glaevecke, *Kapitän Schröder und die Irrfahrt der St. Louis*, 13–14.

Appendix 2

1. In the unpublished manuscript pages, Schröder notes that HAPAG regarded Voyage 98 as a brief interruption in the ship's regular cruise schedule, which "from New York to the West Indies, Bermuda, and Halifax would not commence until June."
2. "Ship without harbor" is the literal English translation of the play's official German title. The official English title of the play was *Skipper Next to God*, which is a translation of the original Dutch title. (See chapter 6.)
3. The unpublished manuscript explicitly denotes Weiler's colleagues as non-Jewish.
4. In the unpublished version, Schröder adds that the loss of time caused by Weiler's sea burial "was unfortunate because our Havana office urged us to arrive that night. We managed to make it on schedule."
5. In the unpublished version, Schröder writes that he specifically requested that the representative of the American Jewish Joint Distribution Committee (JDC) assure the passengers in his address that everything was being done for them to prevent a return to Germany.
6. The unpublished manuscript specifies that two passengers attempted suicide.
7. The reference to *St. Louis* entering a small port is a puzzling detail in Schröder's published account. The original manuscript mentions the Florida landing attempt only in passing. It is not clear what small port Schröder refers to, but the information is at variance with all known accounts of the incident I am aware of.

8. In the unpublished manuscript, Schröder writes, "The purser and I had constituted a committee consisting of seven lawyers, doctors, and businessmen with whom we closely collaborated, discussing and taking all measures necessary to maintain discipline on board. I am deeply grateful to its president, Dr. Joseph, and to its members, Dr. Vendig, Dr. Zellner, Leo Haas, and Adolf Wolff, for their generous advice. This efficient cooperation was a tremendous source of strength for me during those days." While Schröder makes mention of the fact that the board committee was being expanded by two members, S. Guttman and Dr. Ernst Vendig, he does not mention the circumstances of their addition. But the information he gives in his second captain's log and its confidential addendum lets one infer that it was Guttman and Vendig who had initially been part of the "sabotage committee" and that it was these two passengers whom Schröder successfully talked into defecting from that committee and joining the main board committee instead.

9. In the unpublished manuscript, Schröder adds that he sent daily telegrams to Hamburg that unequivocally reported the despair of the passengers and that he was secretly hoping to get England to allow the passengers to land.

10. The identity of the New York sender of the telegram, which confirms the accuracy of the JDC's response, is not fully clear.

11. The unpublished portion of the manuscript identifies this person as Günter Weil, "who showed up wherever there was trouble."

12. In the unpublished portion of the manuscript, Schröder writes that he never learned what the mutinous passengers intended to do and that perhaps they didn't know either. He adds, "Understanding their excitement prevented me from becoming unjustly angry, and I knew that quelling the panic peacefully was in the interest of the shipping line." He adds that the passengers' willingness to agree to assemble in the Great Hall was something he took as a vote of confidence.

13. The manuscript's unpublished version renders the search for Kritsch in more detail: "Following the rules, I would have had to turn around to search the waters for him for many hours. That would have meant steaming headlong into the stormy sea and possibly losing a whole day. I felt a tingle inside me and almost lost my cool—I had become somewhat nervous after all. But a captain should not show any weakness, so I heard myself say, 'I will make a decision after the ship has been thoroughly searched by the whole crew.' Fifteen minutes later, he was found in a small storage room underneath the foredeck. He had taken his own life."

14. In his unpublished manuscript Schröder adds that he visited the children's room on his daily rounds through the ship and allowed the children to infect him with their optimism and their trust that everything would turn out alright.

15. In the unpublished version, Schröder's commendation for the crew reads as follows: "This applies first of all to the pursers, the doctors, their assistants and nurses as well as the service personnel. The radio station had lots of work, too, and their revenue was at a record high." The reference to the radio station continuing to charge for wires reflects the fact that, despite the extraordinary circumstances of the passengers, some services on board could still only be obtained for a fee. Schröder adds: "But I really don't want to imagine what would have happened if the shipping line had not ensured our landing in Antwerp. Because of HAPAG's sympathetic attitude, the passengers were spared the worst."

16. The unpublished manuscript features the following passage at this point: "All told, I would not want to have missed the whole experience, no matter how much it shook me. It was an assignment that left a greater impact on me than a typhoon in the South Sea. Those who appreciate the desperate situation of my passengers and my concern for them will understand. I had to sacrifice many a night's rest. During the whole critical period, from the denial to land in Havana to the time we received permission to anchor in Antwerp, I spent my days taking care of the passengers and my nights writing coded telegrams in English. But in the end I received recognition. The St. Louis was ordered to sail directly from Antwerp to New York, from where it was scheduled to go on cruises. My family, which had come to visit me in New York, was allowed to stay with me on board during New York port calls." In chapter 6, I discuss the implications of this passage and speculate on why Schröder decided against including it in the published version.

Appendix 3

1. StAH 621-1/95 Nr. 4776. HAPAG. Schiffsakte MS St. Louis. Teil 2 (ship file MS *St. Louis*, part 2).

Appendix 4

1. StAH 621-1/95 Nr. 4776. HAPAG. Schiffsakte MS St. Louis. Teil 2 (ship file MS *St. Louis*, part 2).

Appendix 5

1. StAH 621-1/95 Nr. 4776. HAPAG. Schiffsakte MS St. Louis. Teil 1 (ship file MS *St. Louis*, part 1).

Bibliography

Abella, Irving, and Harold Troper. *None Is Too Many: Canada and the Jews of Europe*. Random House, 1983.

Afoumado, Diane. *Exil impossible: L'errance des Juifs du paquebot 'St.-Louis.'* Editions L'Harmattan, 2005.

Agamben, Giorgio. *Homo Sacer—Sovereign Power and Bare Life*. Translated by Daniel Heller-Roazen. Stanford University Press, 1998.

Agamben, Giorgio. *Remnants of Auschwitz: The Witness and the Archive*. Translated by Daniel Heller-Roazen. Zone Books, 1999.

Allgemeine Fragen der Passagierfahrt. Papers. Hamburg State Archive, Hamburg.

Anderson, Perry. "On Emplotment: Two Kinds of Ruin." In *Probing the Limits of Representation: Nazism and the 'Final Solution,'* edited by Saul Friedlander, 54–65. Harvard University Press, 1992.

Arendt, Hannah. *The Origins of Totalitarianism*. Harcourt Brace Jovanovich, 1973.

Arendt, Hannah. "Social Science Techniques and the Study of Concentration Camps." *Jewish Social Studies* 12 (January 1950): 49–64.

Arendt, Hannah. "We Refugees." In *The Jewish Writings*, edited by Jerome Kohn and Ron H. Feldman, 264–74. Schocken Books, 2007.

Atkinson-Phillips, Alison. "On Being Moved: Art, Affect and Activation in Pubic Commemorations of Trauma." *Continuum: Journal of Media & Cultural Studies* 32, no. 3 (2018): 381–92.

Ayalon, Anat Tzom. "A Tiny Boat Lost at Sea: Trauma and Ethics in Havarie [Collision] by Philip Scheffner (Germany, 2016)." *Ekphrasis* 23, no. 3 (2020): 29–49.

Balke, Friedrich, Bernhard Siegert, and Joseph Vogl. "Editorial." *Das Schiff, Archiv für Mediengeschichte*, 2023, edited by Friedrich Balke, Bernhard Siegert, and Joseph Vogl. Verlag Vorwerk 8, 2024.

Balsom, Erika. "From Singular to Plural." In *Accidental Archivism: Shaping Cinema's Futures with Remnants of the Past*, edited by Stefanie Schulte-Strathaus and Vinzenz Hediger. Meson Press, 2022. archivism.meson.press/chapters/new-cinephilias-beyond-the-manspreading-machine/from-singular-to-plural/.

Barthes, Roland. *Mythologies*. Hill and Wang, 1970.

Bauman, Zygmunt. *Modernity and the Holocaust*. Cornell University Press, 1989.

Baxter, Andrew M., and Alex Norasteh. "A Brief History of U.S. Immigration Policy from the Colonial Period to the Present Day." CATO Institute, Policy Analysis No. 919, August 3, 2021. /www.cato.org/policy-analysis/brief-history-us-immigration-policy-colonial-period-present-day.

Bayrakdar, Deniz, and Robert Burgoyne, eds. *Refugees and Migrants in Contemporary Art, Film and Media*. Amsterdam University Press, 2022.

Bayraktar, Nilgun. "Beyond the Spectacle of 'Refugee Crisis': Multi-Directional Memories of Migration in Contemporary Essay Film." *Journal of European Studies* 49, no. 3–4 (2019): 354–73.

Bayraktar, Nilgun. *Mobility and Migration in Film and Moving Image Art: Cinema Beyond Europe*. Routledge, 2016.

Benjamin, Walter. *Illuminations: Essays and Reflections*. Edited by Hannah Arendt. Translated by Harry Zohn. Harcourt, Brace & World, 1968.

Biskind, Peter. "The Politics of Power in *On the Waterfront*." *Film Quarterly* 29, no. 1 (Autumn 1975): 25–38.

Bordwell, David. "Camera Movement and Cinematic Space." *Ciné Tracts—A Journal of Film, Communications, Culture and Politics* 1, no. 2 (1977): 19–27.

Brecht, Bertolt. "Über die Bezeichnung Emigranten." In *Bertolt Brecht, Die Gedichte*. Suhrkamp Verlag, 2000. Republished on *We Refugees* (Digital Archive). Translated by Minor Kantor. Accessed June 11, 2022. en.we-refugees-archive.org/archive/bertolt-brecht-on-the-term-emigrants-1937/.

Breitman, Richard, and Alan M. Kraut. *American Refugee Policy and European Jewry, 1933–1945*. Indiana University Press, 1987.

Breitman, Richard, and Allan J. Lichtman. *FDR and the Jews*. The Belknap Press of Harvard University Press, 2013.

Brinckmann, Christine Noll. "Die Rolle der Empathie oder Furcht und Schrecken im Dokumentarfilm." In *Kinogefühle: Emotionalität und Film*, edited by Matthias Brütsch, Vinzenz Hediger, and Ursula von Keitz, 333–60. Schüren, 2005.

Brooks, Peter. "The Aesthetics of Astonishment." *Georgia Review* 30, no. 3 (Fall 1976): 615–39.

Buckley-Zistel, Susanne. "Tracing the Politics of Aesthetics: From Imposing, via Counter to Affirmative Memorials to Violence." *Memory Studies* 14, no. 4 (2021): 781–96.

Bundy, Colin. "Migrants, Refugees, History and Precedents." *Forced Migration Review*, no. 51 (January 2016), n.p. www.fmreview.org/destination-europe/bundy.

Burmester, Heinz. "Aus dem Leben des Kapitäns Gustav Schröder." *Deutsches Schiffahrtsarchiv* 13 (1990): 164–200.

Byrd, Jodi. "'Living My Native Life Deadly': Red Lake, Ward Churchill, and the Discourses of Competing Genocides." *American Indian Quarterly* 31, no. 2 (2007): 310–32.

Césaire, Aimé. *Discourse on Colonialism*. Translated by Joan Pinkham. Monthly Review Press, 1972.

Closed Borders: The International Conference on Refugees in Evian 1938. Technische Universität. evian1938.de/en/.

Clover, Carol J. *Men, Women, and Chainsaws: Gender in the Modern Horror Film*. Princeton University Press, 1992.

"CNR—Album—Examples of Settlement of European Refugee Families on Land, 1939." Government of Canada, Library and Archives, Ottawa, January 29, 2025. central.bac-lac.gc.ca/.redirect?app=fonandcol&id=4276610&lang=eng.

Cooke, Paul. "Heritage, Heimat, and German Historical 'Event' Television: Nico Hofmann's teamWorx." In *German Television*, edited by Larson Powell and Robert Shandley, 175–92. Berghahn Books, 2016.

Crow, Thomas. *Modern Art in the Common Culture*. Yale University Press, 1996.

Dayan, Daniel, and Elihu Katz. *The Live Broadcasting of History*. Harvard University Press, 1992.

Deleuze, Gilles. *Cinema 1: The Movement Image*. Translated by Hugh Tomlinson and Barbara Habberjam. The Athlone Press, 1986.

Deleuze, Gilles. *Cinema 2: The Time Image*. Translated by Hugh Tomlinson and Robert Galeta. The Athlone Press, 1989.

Deleuze, Gilles. "On the Movement Image." In *Negotiations 1972–1990*, translated by Martin Youghin. Columbia University Press, 1995.

Demos, T. J. *The Migrant Image: The Art and Politics of Documentary During Global Crisis*. Duke University Press, 2013.

Derrida, Jacques, and F. C. T. Moore. "White Mythology." *New Literary History* 6, no. 1 (Autumn 1974): 5–74.

Dickinson, Edward Ross. "Biopolitics, Fascism, Democracy: Some Reflections on our Discourse about 'Modernity.'" *Central European History* 37, no. 1 (2004): 7–45.

Didi-Huberman, Georges. *The Eye of History: When Images Take Positions*. Translated by Shane B. Lillis. MIT Press, 2018.

Diner, Dan. *Beyond the Conceivable: Studies on Germany, Nazism, and the Holocaust*. University of California Press, 2000.

Doneson, Judith E. *The Holocaust in American Film*. Syracuse University Press, 2002. Originally published in 1987 by The Jewish Publication Society.

Drabinski, John E. *Glissant and the Middle Passage: Philosophy, Beginning, Abyss*. University of Minnesota Press, 2019.

Ebbrecht-Hartmann, Tobias, and Matthias Steinle. "Dokudrama in Deutschland als historisches Ereignisfernsehen—eine Annäherung aus pragmatischer Perspektive (Standpunkte)." *MEDIENwissenschaft: Rezensionen/Reviews* 25, no. 3 (2008): 250–55.

Edwards, Aaron, and Cillian McGrattan. *The Northern Ireland Conflict: A Beginner's Guide*. Oneworld Publications, 2010.

Elsaesser, Thomas. "American Auteur Cinema: The Last—or First—Picture Show?" In *The Last Great American Picture Show: New Hollywood Cinema in the 1970s*, edited by Thomas Elsaesser, Alexander Horwath, and Noel King. Amsterdam University Press, 2004.

Elsaesser, Thomas. *New German Cinema: A History*. Rutgers University Press, 1989.

Elsaesser, Thomas. "The Pathos of Failure: American Films in the 1970s: Notes on the Unmotivated Hero." In *The Last Great American Picture Show: New Hollywood Cinema in the 1970s*, edited by Thomas Elsaesser, Alexander Horwath, and Noel King, 279–92. Amsterdam University Press, 2004.

Ennis, Michael. "Opfer und Täter in den Gustloff Filmen von Frank Wisbar." In *Die Wilhelm Gustloff: Geschichte und Erinnerung eines Untergangs*, edited by Bill Niven, 205–33. Mitteldeutscher Verlag, 2011.

Ennis, Michael. "The Wilhelm Gustloff in German Memory Culture: A Case Study on Competing Discourses." PhD Diss., University of Cincinnati, 2013.

Flanzbaum, Hilene, ed., *The Americanization of the Holocaust*. Johns Hopkins University Press, 1999.

Foucault, Michel. *The History of Sexuality, Vol. 1: An Introduction*. Translated by Robert Hurley. Random House, 1978. Originally published as *La volonté de savoir* (Gallimard, 1976).

Foucault, Michel. *"Society Must Be Defended": Lectures at the College de France 1975–1976*. Edited by Mauro Bertani and Alessandro Fontana. Translated by David Macey. Picador, 2003.

Friedlander, Saul. *Reflections of Nazism: An Essay on Kitsch and Death*. Translated by Thomas Weyr. Indiana University Press, 1984. Originally published as *Reflets du Nazisme* (Editions du Seuil, 1982).

Friedlander, Saul. "Trauma and Transference." In *The Holocaust: Theoretical Readings*, edited by Neil Levi and Michael Rothberg, 206–13. Rutgers University Press, 2003.

Frost, Jennifer. "Challenging the 'Hollywoodization' of the Holocaust: Reconsidering *Judgment at Nuremberg* (1961)." *Jewish Film & New Media* 1, no. 2 (Fall 2013): 139–65.

Galeano, Eduardo. *Open Veins of Latin America: Five Centuries of the Pillage of a Continent*. Translated by Cedric Belfrage. Monthly Review Press, 1973.

Gellman, Irwin F. "The *St. Louis* Tragedy." *American Jewish Historical Quarterly* 61, no. 2 (December 1971): 144–56.

Gessen, Masha. "In the Shadow of the Holocaust: How the Politics of Memory in Europe Obscures What We See in Israel and Gaza Today." *New Yorker*, December 9, 2023, www.newyorker.com/news/the-weekend-essay/in-the-shadow-of-the-holocaust.

Gilroy, Paul. *The Black Atlantic: Modernity and Double-Consciousness*. Harvard University Press, 1993.

Glaser, Zhava Litvac. *Refugees and Relief: The American Jewish Joint Distribution Committee and European Jews in Cuba and Shanghai 1938–1943*. PhD diss., City University of New York, 2015.

Glissant, Édouard. *Caribbean Discourse: Selected Essays*. Translated by J. Michael Dash. University of Virginia Press, 1989.

Glissant, Édouard. *Poetics of Relation*. Translated by Betsy Wing. University of Michigan Press, 1997. Originally published as *Poétique de la relation* (Gallimard, 1990).

Goossens, Reuben. "S.S. Funchal." *ssMaritime* (website). Accessed July 20, 2023. ssmaritime.com/funchal-Intro.htm.

Grundmann, Roy. *Andy Warhol's Blow Job*. Temple University Press, 2003.

Grzyb, Amanda. "From Kristallnacht to the MS *St. Louis* Tragedy: Canadian Press Coverage of Nazi Persecution of the Jews and the Jewish Refugee Crisis, September 1938 to August 1939." In *Nazi Germany, Canadian Responses*, edited by Ruth Klein, 78–113. McGill-Queen's University Press, 2012.

"Haavara." *The Jewish Virtual Library*. Accessed March 23, 2022. www.jewishvirtuallibrary.org/haavara.

Halle, Randall. "The New German Television and the Newer German Film: A History of Industry Disruption and Synergy." In *Entertaining German Culture: Contemporary Transnational German Television and Film*, edited by Stephen Ehrig, Benjamin Shaper, and Elizabeth Ward, 39–65. Berghahn Books, 2023.

Handy, W. C. *Father of the Blues: An Autobiography*. Edited by Arna Bontemp. MacMillan, 1941.

Hansen, Miriam Bratu. "*Schindler's List* Is Not *Shoah*: Second Commandment, Popular Modernism, and Public Memory." *Critical Inquiry* 22, no. 2 (Winter 1996): 292–312.

Haraway, Donna. "Situated Knowledges: The Science Question in Feminism and the Privilege of Partial Perspective." *Feminist Studies* 14, no. 3 (Autumn 1988), 575–99.
Hart, Adam Charles. "Extensions of Our Body Moving, Dancing: The American Avant-Garde's Theories of Handheld Subjectivity." *Discourse* 41, no. 1 (Winter 2019): 37–67.
Hartman, Saidiya. "Venus in Two Acts." *Small Axe* 12, no. 2 (June 2008): 1–14.
Hasler, Anja. "Vom Transitland zur Festung: Schweizer Flüchtlingspolitik und Antisemitismus im Jahr der Konferenz von Évian." In *Keine Zuflucht. Nirgends: Die Konferenz von Evian und die Fahrt der St. Louis (1938/39)*, edited by Eva Schöck-Quinteros, Matthias Loeber, and Simon Rau, 51–72. Institut für Geschichtswissenschaft/Milde Buchdruckerei, 2019.
Herlin, Hans. *Kein Gelobtes Land: Die Irrfahrt der St. Louis.* Nannen, 1961. Republished as "Das Rote J," in *Stern* Magazine (1961).
Herlin, Hans. *Verdammter Atlantik: Schicksale deutscher U-Boot-Fahrer.* Nannen Verlag, 1959.
Hißnauer, Christian. "Das Doku-Drama in Deutschland als journalistisches Politikfernsehen—eine Annäherung und Entgegnung aus fernsehgeschichtlicher Perspektive (Standpunkte)." *MEDIENwisssenschaft: Rezensionen/Reviews* 25, no. 3 (2008): 256–65.
Howind, Sascha. "Das 'Traumschiff' für die 'Volksgemeinschaft'? Die Gustloff und die soziale Propaganda des Dritten Reiches." In *Die Wilhelm Gustloff: Geschichte und Erinnerung eines Untergangs*, edited by Bill Niven, 27–60 Mitteldeutscher Verlag, 2011.
Insdorf, Annette. *Indelible Shadows: Film and the Holocaust.* Random House, 1983.
Isenberg, Noah. "Vienna Is No More? Film History, Psycho-Geography, and the Great City of Dreams." *Film Quarterly.* 67, no. 4 (2014): 67–72.
Jameson, Fredric. *Postmodernism, or the Cultural Logic of Late Capitalism.* Duke University Press, 1992.
Jaspers, Karl. *The Question of German Guilt.* Translated by E. B. Ashton, Doubleday Broadway Publishing Group, 1948; reprint, Fordham University, 2001. Originally published as *Die Schuldfrage* (Lambert Schneider, 1946).
Jay, Martin. "Of Plots, Witnesses, and Judgments." In *Probing the Limits of Representation: Nazism and the "Final Solution,"* edited by Saul Friedlander, 97–107. Harvard University Press, 1992.
JDC Report on SS St. Louis. Archive of the American Jewish Joint Distribution Committee, New York.
Jelinek, Elfriede. "Die endlose Unschuldigkeit." In *Die Endlose Unschuldigkeit: Prosa—Hörspiel—Essay*, 49–82. Schwiftinger Galerie-Verlag, 1980.
"Jewish Refugees on the SS St. Louis After Denied U.S. Entry." *Matthew Green*, November 25, 2015. Video, 1:02. www.youtube.com/watch?v=7Y4WF5g9ZHw.

Jünger, David, "An Bord des Lebens: Die Schiffspassage deutscher Juden nach Palästina 1933 bis 1938 als Übergangserfahrung zwischen Raum und Zeit." *Mobile Cultural Studies: The Journal* 1 (2015): 147–63.

Keathley, Christian. "Trapped in the Affection Image: Hollywood's Post-Traumatic Cycle (1970–1976)." In *The Last Great American Picture Show*, edited by Thomas Elsaesser, Alexander Horwath, and Noel King. Amsterdam University Press, 2004.

Khalidi, Rashid. *The Hundred Years' War on Palestine*. Metropolitan Books, 2020.

Koch, Stephen. *Stargazer: The Life, World and Films of Andy Warhol*. Marion Boyars Publishers, 1972.

Koepnick, Lutz. "Reframing the Past: Heritage Cinema and Holocaust in the 1990s." *New German Critique* 87 (Autumn, 2002): 47–82.

LaCapra, Dominick. *History and Memory After Auschwitz*. Cornell University Press, 1998.

LaCapra, Dominick. "Representing the Holocaust: Reflections on the Historians' Debate." In *Probing the Limits of Representation: Nazism and the "Final Solution,"* edited by Saul Friedlander, 108–27. Harvard University Press, 1992.

Lang, Berel. "The Moral Space of Figurative Discourse." In *The Holocaust: Theoretical Readings*, edited by Neil Levi and Michael Rothberg, 329–34. Rutgers University Press, 2003.

Lawlor, Allison. *"The Saddest Ship Afloat": The Tragedy of the MS St. Louis*. Nimbus Publishing, 2016.

Levi, Neil, and Michael Rothberg, eds. *The Holocaust: Theoretical Readings*. Rutgers University Press, 2003.

Levi, Primo. *The Drowned and the Saved*. Translated by Raymond Rosenthal. New York: Simon & Schuster Paperbacks, 2017. Originally published in 1986.

Levine, Robert M. *Tropical Diaspora: The Jewish Experience in Cuba*. University Press of Florida, 1993.

Liebman, Stuart, ed. *Claude Lanzmann's "Shoah": Key Essays*. Oxford University Press, 2007.

Lightsey, Louisiana. "Biopolitics and Globalization." In *Global South Studies: A Collective Publication with the Global South*, August 17, 2017.

Lind, Dara. "How America's Rejection of Jews Fleeing Nazi Germany Haunts Our Refugee Policy Today." *Vox*, Jan. 27, 2017. www.vox.com/policy-and-politics/2017/1/27/14412082/refugees-history-holocaust.

Lipsky, Stefan, Manfred Uhlig, and Jürgen Glaevecke. *Kapitän Schröder und die Irrfahrt der St. Louis*. Mittler, 2019.

Longerich, Peter. *Politik der Vernichtung: Eine Gesamtdarstellung der Nationalsozialistischen Judenverfolgung*. Piper, 1998.

Loshitzky, Josefa. *Screening Strangers: Migration and Diaspora in Contemporary European Cinema*. Indiana University Press, 2010.

Loshitzky, Josefa, ed. *Spielberg's Holocaust: Critical Perspectives on "Schindler's List."* Indiana University Press, 1997.

Löwith, Karl. *Sämtliche Schriften*, edited by Klaus Stichweh and Marc B. de Launay. Vol. 8. Metzler, 1984.

Marchart, Oliver. *Die politische Differenz*. Suhrkamp, 2010.

Marchart, Oliver. *Post-Foundational Political Thought: Political Difference in Nancy, Lefourt, Badiou, and Laclau*. Edinburgh University Press, 2007.

Mautner Markhof, Georg J. E. *Das St. Louis-Drama: Hintergrund und Rätsel einer mysteriösen Aktion des Dritten Reiches*. Leopold Stocker Verlag, 2001.

Mawani, Renisa. *Across Oceans of Law: The Komagata Maru and Jurisdiction in the Time of Empire*. Duke University Press, 2018.

Mettauer, Philipp. "'Die Schiffsreise war für mich eine Mischung aus Nostalgie, Melancholie, Unsicherheit': Die Überfahrt österreichischer Jüdinnen und Juden nach Südamerika." *Mobile Culture Studies: The Journal* 1 (2015): 167–80.

Mintz, Alan. *Popular Culture and the Shaping of Holocaust Memory in America*. University of Washington Press, 2001.

Moeller, Robert G. "How to Judge Stanley Kramer's *Judgment at Nuremberg*." *German History* 31, no. 4 (Winter 2013): 497–522.

Moeller, Robert G. *War Stories: The Search for a Usable Past in the Federal Republic of Germany*. University of California Press, 2001.

Morgan, Daniel, *The Lure of the Image: Epistemic Fantasies of the Moving Camera*. University of California Press, 2021.

Morse, Arthur D. *While Six Million Died: A Chronicle of American Apathy*. Random House, 1967.

Moses, A. Dirk. *The Problems of Genocide: Permanent Security and the Language of Transgression*. Cambridge University Press, 2021.

Niven, Bill. "The Good Captain and the Bad Captain: Joseph Vilsmaier's *Die Gustloff* and the Erosion of Complexity." *German Politics & Society* 26, no. 4 (Winter 2008): 82–98.

———. "Die Gustloff in London, die Sierra Cordoba in Riga: KdF-Schiffe im Dienst der nationalsozialistischen Politik." In *Die Wilhelm Gustloff: Geschichte und Erinnerung eines Untergangs*, edited by Bill Niven, 61–92. Mitteldeutscher Verlag, 2011.

———, ed. *Die Wilhelm Gustloff: Geschichte und Erinnerung eines Untergangs*. Mitteldeutscher Verlag, 2011.

Nothdurft, Lars. "Die Flüchtlingsschiffe." In *Keine Zuflucht. Nirgends: Die Konferenz von Evian und die Fahrt der St. Louis (1938/39)*, edited by Eva Schöck-Quinteros, Matthias Loeber, and Simon Rau, 381–400. Institut für Geschichtswissenschaft/Milde Buchdruckerei, 2019.

Odin, Roger. "Kunst und Ästhetik bei Film und Fernsehen: Elemente zu einem semio-pragmatischen Ansatz." *montage a/v* 11, no. 2 (2002): 42–57.

Ogilvie, Sarah, and Scott Miller. *Refuge Denied: The St. Louis Passengers and the Holocaust*. University of Wisconsin Press, 2006.

Ostersehlte, Christian. "Soll und Haben: Ein wirtschaftsgeschichtlicher Blick auf den Norddeutschen Lloyd (1857–1970)." *Bremisches Jahrbuch* 86 (2007), 176–255.

Padura, Leonardo. *Heretics*. Translated by Anna Kushner. Farrar, Straus, and Giroux, 2017. Originally published as Herejes by (Tusquets Editores, 2013).

Patek, Artur. *Jews on Route to Palestine: Sketches from the History of Aliyah Bet—Clandestine Jewish Immigration*. Translated by Guy Russell Tore and Timothy Williams. Jagiellonian University Press, 2012.

Platinga, Carl. "The Scene of Empathy and the Human Face on Film." In *Passionate Views: Film, Cognition, and Emotion*, edited by Carl Platinga and Greg M. Smith, 239–56. Johns Hopkins University Press, 1999.

Pollock, Griselda, and Max Silverman, eds. *Concentrationary Cinema: Aesthetics as Political Resistance in Alain Resnais's "Night and Fog" (1955)*. Berghahn Books, 2011.

Prozorov, Sergei, and Simona Rentea, eds. *The Routledge Handbook of Biopolitics*. Routledge, 2017.

Radel, Laura. "Ziel der deutschen Judenpolitik: Auswanderung." In *Keine Zuflucht. Nirgends. Die Konferenz von Evian und die Fahrt der St. Louis (1938/39)*, edited by Eva Schöck-Quinteros, Matthias Loeber, and Simon Rau, 13–36. Institut für Geschichtswissenschaft/Milde Buchdruckerei, 2019.

"Refugees Without a Country (1939)." *British Pathé*, April 13, 2014. Video, 0:33. www.youtube.com/watch?v=d3ZUb78zuS0.

Reinfelder, Georg. *MS "St. Louis" Frühjahr 1939—Die Irrfahrt nach Kuba: Kapitän Gustav Schröder Rettet 906 Deutsche Juden vor dem Zugriff der Nazis*. Hentrich & Hentrich, 2005.

Reinke-Kunze, Christine. *Die Geschichte der Reichs-Post-Dampfer: Verbindungen zwischen den Kontinenten*. Koehlers Verlagsgesellschaft mbH, 1994.

Rentschler, Eric. *The Ministry of Illusion: Nazi Cinema and Its Afterlife*. Harvard University Press, 1996.

Rothberg, Michael. "From Gaza to Warsaw: Mapping Multidirectional Memory." *Criticism* 53, no. 4 (2011): 523–48.

Rothberg, Michael. *Multidirectional Memory: Remembering the Holocaust in the Age of Decolonization*. Stanford University Press, 2009.

Rothberg, Michael. *Traumatic Realism: The Demands of Holocaust Representation*. University of Minnesota Press, 2000.

Rothberg, Michael. "Vergleiche vergleichen: Vom Historikerstreit zur Causa Mbembe." *Geschichte der Gegenwart*, Sept. 23, 2020. geschichtedergegenwart.ch/vergleiche-vergleichen-vom-historikerstreit-zur-causa-mbembe/.

Rubenberg, Cheryl A. *Israel and the American National Interest: A Critical Examination*. University of Illinois Press, 1986.

Rüsen, Jörn. "Holocaust Memory and Identity Building: Metahistorical Considerations in the Case of (West) Germany." In *Disturbing Remains: Memory, History, and Crisis in the Twentieth Century*, edited by Michael S. Roth and Charles G. Salas, 252–70. The Getty Research Institute, 2001.

Russell, Mark A. *Steamship Nationalism: Ocean Liners and National Identity in Imperial Germany and the Atlantic World*. Routledge, 2020.

Said, Edward. *The Question of Palestine*. Vintage Books, 1979.

Sander, Sarah. "Precarious Passages: On Migrant Maritime Mobilities, ca. 1907." In *Maritime Mobilities in Anglophone Literature and Culture*, edited by Alexandra Ganser and Charne Lavery, 145–70. Palgrave Macmillan, 2023.

Schlör, Joachim. "Die Schiffsreise als Übergangserfahrung in Migrationsprozessen." *Mobile Cultural Studies: The Journal* 1 (2015): 9–22.

Schmitt, Carl. *Land and Sea: A World-Historical Meditation*. Edited by Samuel Garrett Zeitlin and Russell Berman. Translated by Samuel Garrett Zeitlin. Telos Press Publishing, 2015. Originally published as *Land und Meer: Eine weltgeschichtliche Betrachtung* (Klett-Cotta, 1942).

Schmitt, Carl. *State, Movement, People: The Triadic Structure of Political Unity*. Translated by Simona Draghici. Plutarch Press, 2001. Originally published as *Staat, Bewegung, Volk: Die Dreigliederung der politischen Einheit* (Hanseatische Verlagsanstalt, 1933).

Schneider, Arnd. "An Anthropology of the Sea Voyage: Prolegomena to an Epistemology of Transoceanic Travel." *Mobile Cultural Studies: The Journal* 1 (2015): 31–52.

Schöck-Quinteros, Eva, Matthias Loeber, and Simon Rau, eds. *Keine Zuflucht. Nirgends: Die Konferenz von Evian und die Fahrt der St. Louis (1938/39)*. Institut für Geschichtswissenschaft/Milde Buchdruckerei, 2019.

Schonig, Jordan. "Seeing Aspects of the Moving Camera: On the Twofoldness of the Mobile Frame." *Synoptique* 5, no. 2 (Winter 2017): 57–78.

Schonig, Jordan. *The Shape in Motion*. Oxford University Press, 2022.

Schröder, Gustav. *Fernweh und Heimweh*. Rütten & Loening, 1943.

Schröder, Gustav. *Heimatlos auf hoher See*. Beckerdruck, 1949.

Schumburg, Emil. "The Jewish Question as a Foreign Policy Factor in 1938." In *The Persecution and Murder of the European Jews by Nazi Germany, 1933–1945, Vol. 2, German Reich, 1938–August 1939*, edited by Susanne Heim, Götz Aly, Ulrich Herbert, et al., 824–830. De Gruyter Oldenbourg, 2009.

Schwinghamer, Steve. "'The Existing Immigration Regulations Will Not Offer Any Solution': MS St. Louis in Canadian Context." Canadian Museum of Immigration at Pier 21. December 21, 2023. pier21.ca/research/immigration-history/canada-and-ms-st-louis.

Scriba, Arnulf. "Die Dolchstoßlegende." Lebendiges Museum Online (LEMO). September 1, 2014. www.dhm.de/lemo/kapitel/weimarer-republik/innenpolitik/dolchstosslegende.html.

Sharpe, Christina. *In the Wake: On Blackness and Being*. Duke University Press, 2016.

Shohat, Ella, and Robert Stam. *Unthinking Eurocentrism: Multiculturalism and the Media*. 2nd ed. Routledge, 2014.

Siegel, Björn. "Arnold Bernstein." *Immigrant Entrepreneurship: German-American Business Biographies, 1720 to the Present*. August 22, 2018. www.immigrantentrepreneurship.org/entries/arnold-bernstein/.

Siegel, Björn. "Doomed at Sea? Maritime Spaces and the Jewish Refugee Crisis in the 1930s." *Jewish Culture and History* 25, no. 1 (2024): 1–18.

Silverstone, Paul H. "Frossula." Paul H. Silverstone Books and Publications. Accessed May 19, 2022 (site no longer available). paulsilverstone.com/ship/frossoula/.

Simon, Art. *Dangerous Knowledge: The JFK Assassination in Art and Film*. Temple University Press, 1996.

Sofsky, Wolfgang. *The Order of Terror: The Concentration Camp*. Translated by William Templer. Princeton University Press, 1999.

Sontag, Susan. "Fascinating Fascism." *New York Review of Books*, February 6, 1975. www.nybooks.com/articles/1975/02/06/fascinating-fascism.

Spiegelman, Art. *Maus: A Survivor's Tale: My Father Bleeds History (Mid-1930s to Winter 1944)*. Pantheon Books, 1986.

Spiegelman, Art. *Maus II: A Survivor's Tale and Here My Troubles Began*. Pantheon Books, 1992.

Spiegelman, Art. *The St. Louis Refugee Ship Blues*. Washington Post, July 24, 2009. www.washingtonpost.com/wp-srv/special/opinions/outlook/st-louis-refugee-ship-blues/static.html.

Stone, Dan. "Biopower and Modern Genocide." In *Empire, Colony, Genocide: Conquest, Occupation, and Subaltern Resistance in World History*, edited by A. Dirk Moses, 240–65. Berghahn, 2008.

Straub, Eberhard. *Albert Ballin: Der Reeder des Kaisers*. Siedler Verlag, 2002.

Strohmaier, Alena, and Lea Spahn. "Intra-Active Documentary: Philip Scheffner's *Havarie* and New-Materialist Perspectives on Migrant Cinema." *Synoptique: An Online Journal of Film and Moving Image Studies* 7, no. 2 (2018). www.synoptique.ca/_files/ugd/811df8_6311911d8d4d433d941c5f13a78b8e11.pdf.

Taylor, Myron C. Papers. FDR Library at Marist College, Poughkeepsie, NY.
Thomas, Gordon, and Max Morgan-Witts. *Das Schiff der Verdammten*. Translated by Helmut Kossodo. Ingse Verlag, Edition Sven Erik Bergh, 1976.
Thomas, Gordon, and Max Morgan-Witts. *Voyage of the Damned: A Shocking True Story of Hope, Betrayal and Nazi Terror*. Skyhorse Publishing, 2010. Originally published 1974 by Stein and Day.
Töteberg, Michael. "Exotik und Tourismus: Die Reisefilme der Hapag." *Sammlungen: Hamburger Flimmern*, Heft 5 (1999). Accessed March 9, 2025. www.filmmuseum-hamburg.de/sammlungen/hamburger-flimmern/heft-05-1999/die-reisefilme-der-hapag.html.
Umansky, Ellen. "Closing Our Doors." *Slate*, March 8, 2017. slate.com/news-and-politics/2017/03/after-kristallnacht-america-chose-not-to-save-jewish-children-from-the-nazis.html.
United States Holocaust Memorial Museum. "Refuge in Latin America." *Holocaust Encyclopedia*. Accessed August 29, 2022. encyclopedia.ushmm.org/content/en/article/refuge-in-latin-america.
United States Holocaust Memorial Museum. "Seeking Refuge in Cuba, 1939." *Holocaust Encyclopedia*. Accessed May 28, 2023. encyclopedia.ushmm.org/content/en/article/seeking-refuge-in-cuba-1939.
United States Holocaust Memorial Museum. "Voyage of the St. Louis." Accessed January 9, 2025. *Holocaust Encyclopedia*. www.ushmm.org/online/st-louis/.
Villeneuve, Johanne, and Debbie Blythe. "Adrift: *Havarie*, an Acousmatic Film by Philip Scheffner." *SubStance* 49, no. 2 (2020): 71–92.
Vincent, C. Paul. "The Voyage of the *St. Louis* Revisited." *Holocaust and Genocide Studies* 25, no. 2 (Fall 2011): 252–89.
Von Moltke, Johannes. "Sympathy for the Devil: Cinema, History, and the Politics of Emotion." *New German Critique* 102 (Fall 2007): 17–43.
Von Moltke, Johannes. "Ways of Seeing: Ethics of Looking in European Refugee Films." In *The Palgrave Handbook of European Migration in Literature and Culture*, edited by Corinna Stan and Charlotte Sussman, 475–95. Palgrave, 2024.
Wagner, Britta. "A Shared Space at Eye Level: An Interview with Documentary Filmmaker Philip Scheffner." *Senses of Cinema* 78, March 2016. www.sensesofcinema.com/2016/feature-articles/philip-scheffner-interview.
Walzer, Michael. *Exodus and Revolution*. Basic Books, 1985.
White, Hayden. "Historical Emplotment and the Problem of Truth." In *Probing the Limits of Representation: Nazism and the Final Solution*, edited by Saul Friedlander, 37–53. Harvard University Press, 1992.
Wiborg, Susanne. *Albert Ballin*. Eller & Richter Verlag, 2013.
Wiborg, Susanne, and Dr. Klaus Wiborg. *Unser Feld ist die Welt: 150 Jahre Hapag-Lloyd*. Hamburger Abendblatt Axel Springer Verlag, 1997.

Williams, Linda. "Film Bodies: Gender, Genre, and Excess." *Film Quarterly* 44, no. 4 (Summer 1991): 2–13.

Williams, Linda. "Melodrama Revised." In *Refiguring American Film Genres: History and Theory*, edited by Nick Browne, 42–88. University of California Press, 1998.

Williams, Linda. *Playing the Race Card: Melodramas of Black and White from Uncle Tom to O. J. Simpson*. University of California Press, 2002.

Wolf, Burkhardt. "Im Blick der Stimmen: Fun Ships und Boatpeople in Krögers und Scheffners Havarie." In *Das Schiff: Archive für Mediengeschichte 20*, ed. Friedrich Balke, Bernhard Siegert, and Joseph Vogl. Verlag Vorwerk 8, 2024.

Wolfrum, Edgar. "Neue Erinnerungskultur: Die Massenmedialisierung des 17. Juni 1953." *APuZ: Aus Politik und Zeitgeschichte*, Oct. 1, 2003, 33–39, www.bpb.de/shop/zeitschriften/apuz/27387/die-massenmedialisierung-des-17-juni-1953/.

Wood, Robin. *Hollywood from Vietnam to Reagan*. Columbia University Press, 1986.

Young, James E. *The Texture of Memory: Holocaust Memorials and Meaning*. Yale University Press, 1993.

Young, James E. *Writing and Rewriting the Holocaust: Narrative and the Consequences of Interpretation*. Indiana University Press, 1988.

Ziemer, Arnd, and Leon Ziemer, *Aufrecht in schweren Zeiten: Kapitän Gustav Schröder und die Horrorfahrt der St. Louis 1939* (Deutsche Seemannsmission Hamburg-Altona, 2019).

Index

Adventure of the Seas (ship), 292, 297, 307, 413n25
aesthetic-discursive historical inquiry, 233
aesthetics of astonishment, 204
AfD. *See* Alternative für Deutschland
Afghanistan, 219, 289
African migrants, 219, 289
African migrants, in *Havarie*. *See* Mediterranean migration crisis
Afro-Caribbeans, 315, 415n46
Agamben, Giorgio, 8, 10, 127, 130
  bare life theory, 133–143
Agios Nicolaos (ship), 43
Aguiler, Francisco, 64
Aid Organization Berlin, 339
Albert (ship), 320
Aldunate, Patricio, 64
Aliyah Bet, 44, *45*, 361n87
Alternative für Deutschland (AfD), 290
Altman, Robert, 185
Anderberg, Carl Gotthard, 64
anti-essentialist identity, 294
Antiga Escobar, Juan, 34
antisemitism, 20, 125–127, 210, 251–252, 254, 264
  Canada and, 284
  colonialism and, 313
  Jews fleeing Germany due to, 284
  propaganda and, 21
  as temporary madness, 214
  US discussions about, 176
  The Wheel of Conscience and, 281, 283
Antwerp, 1–2, 96, 114, 335–336, 350
  docking at, 98, *99*, 100–101, 103
Aquarius (ship), 219, 290
Arab states, 209
archival footage, 222–223, 225, 227, 231–234, *234*, 234–235
Arendt, Hannah, 10, 134, 146, 207, 212, 267, 313
  on concentration camps, 137, 139
  on Conrad, 388n67
  discourse of utility, 143
  on hermeneutics of Holocaust, 144
  on human rights as privilege, 7
  on human rights of refugees, 125–126
  Latin America and, 389n73
  ranking genocides and, 143–144
Argentina, 32, 66
Aristimuño Coll, Carlos, 33
Aryanism, 20

433

Assimi (ship), 43
Astir (ship), 43
asylum, 295–296
    efforts to broker, 8
    JDC negotiations for, 97–98, 112, 140–142, 148–149
Atlas Line, 57, 366n31
Aufbau (newspaper), 42–47
Auschwitz, 2, 9, 127–128, 132
    biopolitical facilities and, 139
    Second Generation and, 315
    trial of 1965 for, 248
Australia
    at Évian conference, 29
    migration to, 29–30
AVCO Embassy, 184

Baerwald, Paul, 97–98
Balfour Declaration, 27–28, 407n12
Balkans, 289
Ballin, Albert, *54*, 54–56, 58, 77, 320
Barak, Michael, *138*
bare life, 133–143
Barthes, Roland, 235
Basic Law (1949), 219
Batista y Zaldívar, Fulgencio, 67–68, 90–91, 122, 146
    plots to overthrow, 270
Bauman, Zygmunt, 127
Bayraktar, Nilgun, 293
BDS (Boycott, Divestment, Sanctions) movement, 220
Belgian Congo, 27
Belgium, 114
    at Évian conference, 27–28
    refugees received by, 100
Bello Codesido, Emilio, 64
Bendowski, Paul, 173
Benítez y González, Manuel, 67–69, 77, 84, 89–91, 147, 211
    demands for share or bribe money from, 392n25
    Herlin on, 173
    Iberia and, 373n15
    Voyage of the Damned on, 180
Benjamin, Walter, 144, 213, 310–312
Berenson, Lawrence, 208, 344, 375n40
    Cuban politics and, 146
    Dominican Republic and, 377n58
    Herlin on, 173–174
    Morse, A., and, 177
    negotiations with Cuba, *89*, 90–92, 95, 207
Berg, Leonid, 344
Bergman, Ingmar, 187
Berliner Allgemeine Zeitung (newspaper), 383n64
Bernstein, Arnold, 361n82
Bertha (ship), 320
Bertolucci, Bernardo, 196
bin Laden, Osama, 277
biomass, 136
biopolitics, 4, 7–8, 134–137, 139, 356n14
    Évian conference and, 47
    Holocaust and, 10
    migration and, 55, 153, 285
    Nazism and, 24, 127
    racism and, 26, 35
    shaping population and, 23, 32–33
biopower, 23, 134, 356n14
Bismarck (ship), 365n16
The Black Atlantic (Gilroy), 151–152, 278
black Mediterranean, 413n18
Blair, Frederick, 30
Block, Herbert Lawrence, "Herblock," 276
"Blue Moon" (song), 199–200, 397n34
Blythe, Debbie, 292

Index

board committee. *See* passenger committee
Boers, 10, 133, 143–144, 314
Bogart, Humphrey, 207
Bolivia, 66, 369n50
Bonnie and Clyde (film), 195–196
boomerang principle, 144, 146
Das Boot (film), 228
Bordwell, David, 305
The Boston Daily Globe (newspaper), 114, 116
Bound for Glory (film), 196
Brandt, Willy, 246
Brazil, 32
Brecht, Bertold, 40–41, 248
Bremen (ship), 50, 54, 123, 363n3, 370n66
Bretagne (ship), 235, *236*
Brideshead Revisited (miniseries), 196
Brooks, Peter, 204
Brown, Joshua, 274
Bukiet, Melvin Jules, 315
bureaucratic subjectivization, 135
Burmester, Heinz, 319
Burns, William, 242, 244, 255–256, *256*, 257–258
Butler, David, 185

Cabaret (film), 196
cabin class, 370n67
California (ship), 238
Campana (ship), 41
Canada, 11, 279
 antisemitism and, 284
 Complicit and, 243–245
 at Évian conference, 29–30
 immigration policies of, 30, 96, 411n46
 St. Louis and, 95–96, 280
 Trudeau apology speech, 243–245, *244*, 257, 285
Canadian Jewish Congress (CJC), 279, 285, 369n52

Canadian Museum of Immigration, 15, 279, 285, 369n52
Canaris, Wilhelm, 179
Cap Arcona (ship), 363n4
Cap Norte (ship), 44, 361n87
capital control taxes, 21
Carballo, Augusto, 64
Cargill, Jesse, 274
Caribia (ship), 57, 64–65, 367n40
Carnival Cruise Line, 297, 413n25
Carter, Jimmy, 14, 243
Casablanca (film), 207
Césaire, Aimé, 144–146, 148–149
CG 244 (Coast Guard cutter), 92
Chandler, Raymond, 263
Chase National Bank Havana, 92, 95
Cherbourg, 343–344
Chicago Daily Tribune (newspaper), 114, 119
Chinatown (film), 195–196, 206
Christianization, 4
Churchill, Winston, 358n32
citizenship, 311
 forfeiting, 83
 German Jews deprived of, 19
 oppressed groups and, 381n51
 protection as privilege of, 7
Civil Rights era, 247
CJC. *See* Canadian Jewish Congress
Clasing, Luis, 84, 119, 173, 180–181, 327
Clinton, Hillary, 15, 242–244
cockfighting, 270
cognitive mapping, 149
Cold War, 209
Colombia, 31–32, 35
colonial genocide, 143, 212–213, 215
colonial turn, 10, 143–154
colonialism, 23, 148, 238, 296
 antisemitism and, 313
 concentration camps as instrument of, 132

colonialism *(continued)*
  Conrad critiquing, 388n67
  as enabling factor for Holocaust, 262
  Évian conference and, 26–28, 35–36
  genocide and, 291, 313–314
  Latin America and, 30–31, 36, 389n73
  migrant crises and, 295
  nativism and, 126
  neocolonialism supplanting, 145
  Palestine and, 358n32
  racism and, 26, 126
  as structuring absence, 234–240
  Voyage of the Damned (film) and, 210–216
combi ships, 55, 57
Communist Party, 247
competitive memory, 310
Complicit (film), 15, 241–244, 261
  agitprop approach of, 258
  America on trial in, 246–255
  convergence of memory cultures and, 255–259
  documentary footage in, 248
  structure of, 245–246
concentration camps, 1–2, 9, 104, 111–112, 337
  Arendt on studying, 143
  experiences of, 405n58
  fluid functions of, 137
  liberation of, 176
  Schröder on, 165
  socially constructed ordering of experience in, 133
  St. Louis as, 136
  system of, 132–133
concentrationary universe, 9, 133
The Conformist (film), 196
conga, 206, 212
Conrad, Joseph, 388n67

consumerism, 269
Conte Grande (ship), 43
Cooke, Paul, 224
Cool Hand Luke (film), 185
Cordillera (ship), 57, 64–65
corruption, 211
Cortés, Claudio, 65
Crow, Thomas, 309
cruise liners, 311–316
cruise tourism, 55–56, 58, 70–71, 77, 321
Cuba, 1, 8, 56–58
  archival footage from, 235
  asylum denied by, 3, 88, 112
  captain's log on, 344–345
  colonization and, 210
  conga banned in, 212
  Decree 937, 69, 84–85, 373n15
  economy of, 145
  fascism and, 147
  German press on, 122
  HAPAG advertising voyage to, 80, *81*
  HAPAG and, 67–69, 119
  Herlin on negotiations with, 173
  immigration policies in, 67–69, 84, 147, 264
  independence of, 389n74
  JDC negotiations with, 88–92, *89*, 113, 115, 119, 375n39–375n40
  Jews in, 263–264
  labor force in, 264
  neocolonialism and, 146–147, 238, 311
  Orinoco and, 41
  racial hybridity and, 268
  Schröder criticism of, 164
  St. Louis and, 41, 69, 77–78, 147–148, 311, *312*, 327–329
  St. Louis passengers disembarking at, 83

tourist visas invalidated by, 86–87
Die Ungewollten and, 235, 238
US political control over, 145–146
Voyage of the Damned and, 180, 210–211
cultural memory, 157
Cumberland Evening Times (newspaper), 117
Cuxhaven, Germany, 2, 112, 330–331

Daily Mirror (newspaper), 118, *118*
Darien Gap, 289
De Sica, Vittorio, 196, 207
death ships, 40–47, 153
decolonization, 262, 295, 298
Decree 937 (Cuba), 69, 84–85, 373n15
defamiliarization, 312
Deleuze, Gilles, 188–189, 294
democracy
    gendering of, 387n57
    Schmitt argument against, 129, 131
    totalitarianism and, 8, 10, 131, 134–135, 139, 141
denationalization, 7, 84
Denmark, 320
    at Évian conference, 27
deportation camps, 137
Derrida, Jacques, 239
detective novels, 262–264
Deterding, Henri, 388n80
Deutsche Allgemeine Zeitung (newspaper), 383n64
Deutscher Reichsanzeiger u. Preußischer Staatsanzeiger (newspaper), 383n64
Deutschland (ship), 53, 70, 320–321, 365n16

Diamond, Terry, 292, 296–299, 305–306, 414n40
The Diary of Anne Frank (film), 176, 184
Dickinson, Edward Ross, 136
Didi-Huberman, Georges, 239
Dietrich, Marlene, 172
von Dirksen, Herbert, 251
disciplinary complex, 136, 139
Discourse on Colonialism (Césaire), 144
Disney, Walt, 276
dispossession, 82
dispossession laws, 366n39
dissolves, in *Voyage of the Damned* (film), 190, *190*
docudrama, 221–224, 233
documentarizing reading, 405n54
Dominican Republic, 33–34, 37, 91–92, 96, 112–113, 377n58, 392n25
Doneson, Judith, 247
Dora (ship), 361n87
Downfall (film), 404n49
Doyle, Jerry, 274
"Dr. Paul Kl.: Refugees" (*Aufbau*), 46
Drabinski, John E., 294–295, 310, 314
The Drowned and the Saved (Levi), 152
du Bois, Coert, 88
Dublon, Erich, 104, *105*, 107, 112–113
Duffy, Edmund, 275
Dunaway, Faye, 187, 195, 206, 395n5
Duncannon (Viscount), 69

East Germany, 185
Ehre, Ida, 161
Eichmann, Adolf, 13, 158, 172, 176–177, 246–247

Eizenstat, Stuart, 256
Ellis Island, 8
Elsaesser, Thomas, 189, 192, 233
emigration
    arguments over recipients of, 26–27
    financial and bureaucratic obstacles to, 52
    to Palestine, 22
    relief organizations and, 386n37
    simultaneous encouragement and restrictions on, 22
    taxes on, 6
emigration laws, 52
Enabling Act, 19
England
    migration to dominions of, 29
    as sea people, 131, 385n22
Enlightenment values, 163, 166, 215–216, 307
    opacity and, 294
entry permits, 41
Eritrea, 289
Errantry (Édouard Glissant), 299, 313
Es muß nicht immer Kaviar sein (television show), 403n45
Esperstedt, Werner, 64
espionage fiction, 178, 180
Estedes, José, 191, 210–211
ethnic homogeneity, fascism and, 134
ethnic identity, 130
eugenics, 126
    racism and, 153
Eurocentrism
    opacity and, 294
    subverting, 292–296
Europa (ship), 54, 363n3–363n4, 370n66
European Union, 307
event television, 221–222, 224

Évian conference (1938), 3–4, 24–25, 37, 97, 125
    causes of failure of, 6–7, 26
    crisis after, 137
    Latin America and, 145
    Latin American countries and, 30–36
    racism and, 36
    repercussions of, 40–47
    rereading, 26–40
    Technical Sub-Committee, 34–35
Évian-les-Bains, 24, 25
exception
    St. Louis and, 141–142
    state of, 10, 128–133
Executive Ordinance on Jewish Atonement, 21
Exodus (film), 176, 393n35
Exodus (Uris), 158, 208
Exodus myth, 201–202, 204–205, 209, 215
    gendering of, 387n57
The Exorcist (film), 187
extermination, 23

Fahrenheit 451 (film), 187
Farber, Bernie, 285
Färber, Elsa, 320
fascism
    Cuba and, 147
    disciplinary complex and, 136
    ethnic homogeneity and, 134
    period dramas and, 196
Feivel: An American Tail (film), 409n23
Fernweh und Heimweh (Wanderlust and homesickness) (Schröder), 168, 322–323
Ferrer, José, 187
figuration, 177–178
Fink, Michael, *138*
Five Easy Pieces (film), 192

Index

Flandre (ship), 44, 85–86, 88, 181, 234, 361n89, 382n59
  JDC and, 97–98
  passengers of, 374n22
Florida, 92–95, 153, 239, 330, 376n42
forced migration, 7
"Fortress Europe" mentality, 231, 290, 307, 315
Foucault, Michel, 23–24, 134–135
  on disciplinary complex, 136
France, 393n35
  colonialism and, 148
  at Évian conference, 26–27
  refugees received by, 100
Frank, Anne, 158
Frankfurt (ship), 321
Frankfurter, Felix, 254
Frankfurter Zeitung (newspaper), 383n64
Freeland League for Jewish Territorial Colonisation, 47, 363n99
Freisler, Roland, 130
Freund, Phil, 107
Friedlander, Saul, 196
Frossoula (ship), 361n87
Fryer, Robert, 184–187, 395n5, 399n54
functionalism, 127–128, 153

Galeano, Eduardo, 31, 146
Gallant, Heinz, *99*
"Ganz leis' erklingt Musik" (song), 200
García Calderón Rey, Francisco, 33
The Garden of the Finsi-Contini (film), 196, 207
gated communities, 139
Gazzara, Ben, 187, 191–192, 208–209
Gellman, Irwin F., 392n25

gendering
  of politics, 387n57
  of ships, 353n1
General Artigas (ship), 44, 321
General St. Martin (ship), 44
genocide, 10, 269. *See also* Holocaust
  colonial, 143, 212–213, 215
  colonialism and, 291, 313–314
  correspondences between instances of, 291
  neocolonialism and, 291
  racial difference and, 144
  ranking, 143–144
  trauma of, 314–315
genre, *Voyage of the Damned* (film) and, 193, 195
Gentlemen's Agreement (film), 393n33
Gera (ship), 321
German Colony Committee (Vorsitzender des deutschen Kolonieausschusses), 63
German East Africa Line, 361n87
German Labor Front, 371n72
German Nautical Observatory, 322
Germany
  elections of 1932 in, 19
  emigration laws, 52
  Guatemala trade with, 366n27
  Holocaust remembrance and, 217, 220–221, 239
  Israel-Palestine conflict and, 220
  Jews' double status in, 135
  as land people, 131, 385n22
  Muslims in, 220
  Peru and, 63
  press coverage in, 121–124
  rise of Nazism in, 20–21
  Schröder criticism of, 164–165
  St. Louis incident impact in, 148–149
  St. Louis refugee crisis and, 100

Gessen, Masha, 221
Gestapo, 2, 100
   migration schemes and, 173
Gilroy, Paul, 151–153, 278, 291
Glaevecke, Jürgen, 319
Glaser, Zhava Litvac, 52
Glissant, Édouard, 294–296, 298, 310, 314–315, 415n46
   on persecution of Jews, 313
Global South, 220, 257
   migrant crisis of, 291
Globe and Mail (newspaper), 44
Goebbels, Joseph, 50, 100, 121–124, 148, 179, 382n63
Good Friday Agreement (1998), 413n26
Good Neighbor Fleet, 238, 259
Good Neighbor Policy, 238
Göring, Hermann, 179
Gorman, Amanda, 316
Government of Ireland Act (1921) (United Kingdom), 413n26
Grade, Lew, 185
von Grafenstein, Ben, 222
Grant, Lee, 187
Great Britain
   at Évian conference, 27
   Ireland and, 413n26
   Oversea Settlement Board, 29
   Palestine and, 26, 358n32, 407n12
   refugees and, 97–98, 100
Great Depression, 70, 94, 96
Greece, 289
Griffith, D. W., 264
Grossherzogin Elisabeth (ship), 320
Grundgesetz (Basic Law) (1949), 219
Guantanamo Prison, 139
Guatemala, 366n27
Guattari, Félix, 294

"guest people" designation, 21
guilt
   types of, 391n15
   universalization of, 407n7
Die Gustloff (film), 228
   colonialism as stucturing absence, 234–240
Guttman, Sally, 85, 109, 331, 417n8

Haas, Leo, 331, 336–337, 417n8
Haavara Agreement, 6, 22–23, 356n12
Habermas, Jürgen, 166
Hackman, Gene, 207
Haie und kleine Fische (Sharks and small fish) (film), 228
Hamas, 400n12
Hamburg (ship), 70, 321
Hamburg, Germany, 1, 2
   bombing of, 161
   St. Louis departure from, 82–83
Hamburg America Line (HAPAG), 3–4, 7–8, 11, 16, 40, 47, 148
   advertising Cuba voyage, 80
   Atlas Line and, 366n31
   cabin class, 370n67
   cruise brochure, 76
   Cuba and, 67–69, 119
   documenting voyages by, 79
   films commissioned by, 367n40
   history of, 53–56, 76–77, 365n16, 365n20, 365n26
   impact of refugee crisis on, 100
   KdF and, 71, 169
   Latin America routes and Jewish migrant traffic, 56–67, *61–62*
   mail service by, 53, 364n14
   migrant business revenue estimates by, 50–52
   negotiations by, 335
   New York office, 330, 338

officials' relationships with, 67
La Plata and Brazil service and, 366n29
processing fee charged by, 51–52
publicity post cards, 72, *72–75*
Schröder career in, 320
Schröder on, 162–163, 166–167
ship naming practices, 353n1
study tours, 59
telegrams from, 338–340
travel brochures, 59–61, *60–61*
Trinidad voyage plans, 80
VIP passenger lists, 65
Voyage of the Damned on, 180
Hamburg class liners, 54, 370n66
Hamburger Anzeiger (newspaper), 121–122
Hamburger Nachrichten (newspaper), 383n64
Hamburg-South America Steamship Company (Hamburg Süd), 44, 361n87
 La Plata and Brazil service and, 366n29
Hammelstein, Britta, 221–222
Hammett, Dashiell, 263
Hansa (ship), 70, 321, 370n66
HAPAG. *See* Hamburg America Line
Haraway, Donna, 296, 298
harraga, 295
Harris, Julie, 187
de Hartog, Jan, 161, 171, 325, 390n10
hatred, 127, 258
 The Wheel of Conscience and, 281, 283
Hausdorff, Arthur, *85*, 109
Havana, Cuba, 1, *110*, 111, *126*
 archival footage from, 235
 captain's log on, 344–345

decaying of, 266
MS *St. Louis* arrival in, *86*, 86–88, *87*, 109–110, *111*, 174–175, 327, 344–345
MS *St. Louis* leaving, 88, 91–92, 237, 311, *312*, 329, 347
St. Louis passengers disembarking at, 83
Havarie (film), 15–16, 279, 291–292, 300–304, 308–309
 aestheticization of pan in, 299–300, 305–311
 dinghy and cruise liner, 311–316
 Eurocentric gaze and, 292–296
 soundtrack, 413n21
Heart of Darkness (Conrad), 388n67
Heimatlos auf hoher See (*Homeless on the High Seas*) (Schröder), 12–13, 79, 104, 158, 319, 322–323, *324*
 appendix of, 166–167
 Coast Guard encounter, 92–93
 St. Louis memory culture and, 159, 161–169, *162*
 writing of, 161
Heller-Roazen, Daniel, 130
Hendrich, Otto, 230
Herblock. *See* Block, Herbert Lawrence, "Herblock"
Heretics (Padura), 15, 262–272, 265–267, 286, 409n24
heritage cinema, 195–200
Herlin, Hans, 13, 93–94, 158, 169, 171–176, 179, 378n64
 bribe demand claims by, 392n25
Herres, Volker, 222–223, 240
Heymann, Arthur, 174
Heymann, Stella, 174
HICEM, 68
The Hindenburg (film), 196
von Hindenburg, Paul, 19

historical constellations, 310–311
historical event television, 222
historical trauma and amnesia, 12, 165–166, 271, 284
Hitler, Adolf, 19–20, 129, 253
  absolute power claims, 127
  Königsberg speech, 49, 123, 394n42
Hochschild, Mauricio (Moritz), 66, 369n50
Hoffman, Robert, 180–181
Hoffmann, Walter, 63–65, 340
Holland, at Évian conference, 27
Holmes, Oliver Wendell, 248, *249*, 251–255
Holocaust, 5, 9
  agendas in studies of, 142
  Americanization of, 246
  biopolitics and, 10
  colonial genocide and, 212–213
  colonial turn in studies of, 143–154
  colonialism and neocolonialism as enabling factors in, 262
  contemporary refugee crises and, 275–276
  convergence of memory cultures, 255–259
  debates about causes of, 127
  debates about uniqueness of, 388n59
  de-singularizing, 221
  disciplinary complex and, 136
  functionalist approach to, 127–128, 153
  hermeneutics of, 144
  interplay between countries and, 128–129
  mass culture and, 196
  museums and archives about, 14
  neocolonialism and, 15, 142
  non-Eurocentric understandings of, 146, 149
  non-utilitarianism of, 143
  problems of films about, 396n23
  remembrance culture, 14
  remembrance of, 12
  St. Louis as bridging phases of, 128
  top-down measures and, 136
  universalization of, 407n7
  US politics and, 176–177
Holocaust (miniseries), 14, 193
Holocaust remembrance, 217, 239
  migration policy and, 220–221
Holthusen, Claus-Gottfried, 100, 340, 378n64
  emigration cruises and, 50–52, 55, 80–81, 148–149
  on HAPAG strategy, 57–58
  Herlin and, 173
Homeless on the High Seas. See *Heimatlos auf hoher See*
homelessness, 104
Homo Sacer (Agamben), 130, 133–134
homosexuals, 132
Honduras, 377n58
Hoover, Herbert, 70
horror fiction, 178
The House I Live In (film), 393n33
Hull, Cordell, 93–95, 251–252, *252*, 253
human rights, 7, 125
  Judgment at Nuremberg and, 247
human trafficking, 152
Hyman, Joseph C., 375n39

Iberia (ship), 84, 373n15
identity
  anti-essentialist, 294
  problematization of, 274

Iller (ship), 88
Immigration Act (1924) (United States), 251
immigration numbers, 40
immigration quotas, 4
immigration visas, 41, 43
Imperator (ship), 365n16
Indelible Shadows (Insdorf), 196
Insdorf, Annette, 196–198
Intergovernmental Committee on Refugees, 359n61
Intergovernmental Conference on Refugees. *See* Évian conference
international law
    Jewish state and, 356n10
    NS antisemitic measures and, 20, 79
    ocean and, 131
    Schmitt on, 131
    statelessness and, 114
internment camps, 9
intertextuality, of star performance, 192
Intolerance (Griffith), 264
The Investigation (play), 248
involuntary migration, 84
Iraq, 219, 289
Ireland, 413n26
Irish Republic, 413n26
Irish Republican Army, 297
Irpinia (ship), 196
Isaza, Antonio, 64
Isle of Pines, 91, 113, 392n25
isolationism, 94
Israel, 209
    Hamas attacks on, 400n12
    Palestinians and, 220
    West Germany support of, 217
Italia Line, 57–58
Italiaander, Rolf, 161, 325, 390n10
Italy, 289

Jacobsen, Edmond, 65
Jaen, Gil Guardia, 64
Jameson, Fredric, 149
Jan van Herckel (ship), 100
Jay, Martin, 11, 120
JDC. *See* Joint Distribution Committee
Jehovah's Witnesses, 132
Jewish Colonization Association, 369n52
Jewish diaspora, 270
    Latin America and, 266–267
    neocolonialism and, 267
Jewish migrant ships, 5, 7, 361n87
Jewish myth, *Voyage of the Damned* (film) and, 201–210
Jewish Relief Committee (JRC), 85
Jewish state, international law and, 356n10
Jews
    attempts to classify, at Évian, 35
    in Cuba, 263–264
    denationalization of, 21–22
    double status of, 135
    economic importance of, 21
    exilic generation of, 270
    Germany depriving of citizenship, 19
    Glissand on persecution of, 313
    "guest people" designation of, 21
    legal discrimination against, 20
    marking of passports of, 24, 39
    NS control of emigration of, 386n37
    Oberrat and, 135
    Palestine and, 358n32
    Poland and Russia invasion and, 132
    from Russia, 53, 55
Jockl, Leo, 173

Joint Distribution Committee
 (JDC), 1, 8, 11, 327–328, 339
 asylum negotiations by, 97–98,
  112, 140–142, 148–149
 Batista and, 68
 Cuban politics and, 146
 Dominican Republic and,
  377n58
 HAPAG Cuba cruise plans and,
  80
 Herlin on, 173
 Honduras and, 377n58
 Latin American efforts, 66
 negotiations with Cuba, 88–92,
  89, 113, 115, 119, 375n39–
  375n40
 "special exceptions" approach, 98
 Trinidad voyage and, 68, 72
 Voyage of the Damned depictions
  of, 207, 209
Joseph, Josef, *85*, 109, 332–334,
 341, 349, 417n8
Joseph, Liesel, *99*
JRC. *See* Jewish Relief Committee
Judengeleit, 22
Judenpolitik, 52, 69
Judgment at Nuremberg (film), 13,
 158, 172, 176, 246–247
Jules and Jim (film), 187

Karliner, Herbert, 112
Karliner, Ruth, *99*
Kazan, Elia, 393n33
KdF. *See* Strength Through Joy
Kein Gelobtes Land (*No Promised
 Land*) (Herlin), 13, 169–171,
 170
Kennedy, Jackie, 306
Kennedy, John F., 248, *250*
Kennedy, Joseph H., 251, 254
Kindertransport, 97
King, Mackenzie, 30, 96, 411n46

Klemmer, Harvey, 251
Knepel, Gisela, 232
Knickerbocker, H. R., 41–44
knowledge acquisition, 414n40
Koch, Friedrich Adolf, 64
Koepnick, Lutz, 195–196, 199–
 200
Kölnische Zeitung (newspaper),
 383n64
Königstein (ship), 43, 361n82
Kordt, Erich, 64
Krakow, M. Robert, 241–245, 247–
 248, 251–253, 255, 258, 261
Kramer, Stanley, 187, 246–247
Krauss, Albrecht, 65
kriah, 202
Kristallnacht, 7, 20, 386n37
 incarcerations after, 83, 405n58
 responses to, 121
Kröger, Merle, 292
Kyphissia (ship), 321

labor camps, 133
LaCapra, Dominick, 273–274, 278
Lancaster, Burt, 247
land people, 131, 385n22
Land und Meer (*Land and Sea*)
 (Schmitt), 131
Langer, Lawrence L., 246
Laredo Brú, Frederico, 67, 69, 110,
 115, 125, 137
 Batista power over, 146
 Berenson and, 90–92, 95
 grandfather clause and, 373n15
 Herlin on, 173
 immigration laws and, 84, 86
 political pressures on, 147–148
 reasons for decision, 88–90
 St. Louis and, 88, 147
 in *Voyage of the Damned* (film),
  187
 Voyage of the Damned on, 180

Latin America
  Arendt and, 389n73
  colonialism and, 30–31, 36, 389n73
  conga and, 212
  Évian conference and, 30–36, 145
  HAPAG routes in, 56–67, *61–62*
  immigration policies in, 264
  Jewish diaspora and, 266–267
  neocolonialism and, 31, 36, 145, 239, 314, 389n73
Law on the Registration of Jewish Assets, 21
Le Breton, Tomas A., 32
leftist historiographic practices, 232
legal theory, 129–133
Legion Condor, 123
Lenneberg, Werner, *108*
Levi, Primo, 152–153
Liberalism, 130–131, 385n33
Libeskind, Daniel, 15, 261, 279–287
Libya, 289
Liechtenstein, Roy, 306
Life (magazine), 306
line ships, 364n13
Llach, José, 64
Lobo, Hélio, 32
Loewe, Max, 83, 87, 180, 202, 213, 328
  suicide attempt, 110–111, 114
Long, Breckenridge, 255
Los Angeles Times (newspaper), 137
The Love Boat (television show), 184, 186, 403n45
Löwith, Karl, 135
Lüttgens, Jan, 172–174, 393n31

MacDonald, Malcolm, 42
mail service, 53
Maître après Dieu (film), 389n74
Maltz, Albert, 393n33

Manasse, Herbert, *85*, 109, 330
Mann, Abby, 247
Marchart, Oliver, 139–142
  gendering of politics by, 387n57
Maritime Rescue Unit, 307
Marmora (ship), 43
Maschkowsky, Arthur, 336–337
M.A.S.H. (film), 185
Mason, James, 187
mass culture, 218
mass murder, 136
mass processing of passengers, 55
Maus (Spiegelman, A.), 273–275, 277–279, 409n23–409n24
McCarthy era, 247
McCormack Lines, 238
media
  depiction of historical events in, 9
  Mediterranean migration crisis and, 290
Mediterranean migration crisis, 14–16, 219, 289–290, 295–296, 413n18
Mein Albatros und andere Tiergeschichten (Schröder), 322
Mein Kampf (Hitler), 20, 129
melodrama, 9, 14, 115–116, 178, 193, 398n37
  Voyage of the Damned (film) and, 201–210
memory, 12
  associative, 261
  competitive, 310
  cultural, 157
  multidirectional, 15, 176, 216, 261–262, 276, 291, 296, 310, 312, 314
  as opaque, 310
memory culture, 12–13, 15, 158
  convergence of, 255–259
  images and, 312

memory culture *(continued)*
   intersection of, 312–313
   postwar West German, 166–167
   Schröder and, 159, 161–169
Merkel, Angela, 219, 240, 289, 400n12
messianism, 201, 387n57
Messinger, Sol, 107, 112
meta-history, 272–279
meta-narration, 272–279
Method acting, 192, 208
Mexican Revolution, 34
Mexico, 34
Middle Passage, 151, 153, 210, 278, 294–296, 314, 316, 415n46
migration
   apparatus for facilitating, 8
   biopolitical dimension of, 55, 153, 285
   conceptual and linguistic gray zone, 6–7
   gray zone between voluntary and involuntary, 5–6, 285, 295
   involuntary, 84
   Mediterranean crisis of, 14–16, 219, 289–290, 295–296, 413n18
   monetization of, 3
   by Muslims, 220
Milwaukee (ship), 70
Ministry of the Interior (Germany), 51–52
Mintz, Alan, 176
miscegenation, 247
modernity, 7
   biopolitics and, 136
   disciplinary complex of, 136
   Holocaust and, 10
von Moltke, Johannes, 229, 404n49
monads, 311–312
Monte Olivia (ship), 44, 361n87
moral conscience, 276
moral occult, 205

Morgan, Henry, 61
Morgan-Witts, Max, 11, 13, 121–123, 158–159, 172, 177–181, 206
   German translation of work, 218
   movie adaptation and, 184, 193
Morgenthau, Henry, Jr., 93–95, 251, 254–255
Morse, Arthur D., 93–94, 158, 177–179
Morse, Robert D., 13
Moses, A. Dirk, 149
MS *St. Louis*, 1–2, *2*, 6–8, 66, *160*, *182*, 325–326
   advertising Cuba voyage of, 80, *81*
   ambiguity of status of ship and passengers, 84
   arrival in Havana, *86*, 86–88, *87*, 109–110, *111*, 174–175, 327, 344–345
   bureaucratic subjectivization and, 135
   cabin-class menu, *106*
   Canada and, 95–96, 280
   captain's log, *342*, 343–345, *346*, 347–352
   classification of, 353n1
   colonial turn and, 143–154
   as concentration camp, 136, 139
   course of voyage, *150*, 150–151
   crew of, 104
   crossing Caribbean, 88–96
   cruise brochure for, *76*
   cruise tourism and, 56, 71, 77
   Cuba and, 41, 69, 77–78
   Cuban politics and, 147–148
   departure from Hamburg, 82–83
   disciplinary complex and, 139
   docking at Antwerp, 98, *99*, 100–101, 103, 114, 335–336, 350
   exception and, 141–142

Florida and, 92–95, 112, 153, 329–330, 376n42
German press coverage of voyage, 121–124
Holocaust and, 10
impact in Germany of incident, 148–149
JDC negotiations and, 88–92, *89*
leaving Cuba, 88, 91–92, *237*, 311, *312*, 329, 347
logic of power and, 140–141
Mediterranean migration crisis and, 290–291
memory culture of, 12–13, 15
misassumptions about voyage, 3–5
museums and archives about, 14
November 1938 voyage plans, 68, 72
NS personnel on board, 164, 351
NS propaganda on, 382n60
outbreak of war and, 101
passenger accounts of voyage, 104–114
passenger capacity, 371n68
phases of Holocaust and, 128
pool, *105*, 107
press coverage of voyage, 9, 137
as prestige object, 50
publicity post cards of, 72, *72–75*
reasons for choice of, for migrant voyage, 70–72, 76–78
refurbishment of, 71–72, 76–77
return to Europe, 96–101
scholarship on, 11
Schröder and memory culture of, 159, 161–169
Schröder career on, 321
seaborne migration and, 44–46
statistics on, 370n66
Trudeau apology speech, 243–245, *244*

Die Ungewollten and archival images of, 222–223, 225, 227, 231–234, *234*
US declining asylum to passengers, 92–96
US press coverage of voyage, 114–120, *117*
after war, 161
in West German mass culture of early 1960s, 169–176
westbound voyage, 83–86
Mühmel, Carl-Heinz, 172
Müller, Erich, 65, 348
multidirectional memory (Rothberg), 15, 216, 276, 291, 310, 312, 314
Heretics and, 15, 262
nature of, 261–262
opacity and Relation and, 296
Murmansk, 101
museal gaze, 196–197
Muselmann, 213–214
MV *Funchal*, 226
Mythologies (Barthes), 235

Nacht fiel über Gotenhafen (Night fell over Gotenhafen) (film), 171, 228
Nannen, Henri, 170, 391n20
National Coordinating Committee of Refugees (NCC), 68, 85
National Socialists (NS)
dispossession laws, 366n39
elections of 1932 and, 19
elites and, 65
ideology of, 126
international shipping and, 59
personnel on *St. Louis* from, 164
propaganda on Jews by, 21
propaganda on *St. Louis* by, 382n60
tourism and, 371n72

nationalism, 388n59
  international shipping and, 59
  Mediterranean migration crisis and, 289
nationhood, 388n59
nativism, 126, 264
Navemar (ship), 361n91
Nazism
  biopolitics and, 24, 127
  racism and, 153
  rise of, 20–21
NCC. *See* National Coordinating Committee of Refugees
NDL. *See* Norddeutscher Lloyd
"Nehmt 900 Nazis!" ("Take 900 Nazis!") *(Aufbau)*, 47
neocolonialism, 4, 7–8, 259, 264, 266, 296
  Cuba and, 146–147, 238, 311
  elites and, 65
  as enabling factor for Holocaust, 262
  genocide and, 291
  HAPAG and, 59–61
  historical stages of, 146
  Holocaust and, 15, 142
  Jewish diaspora and, 267
  Latin America and, 31, 36, 145, 239, 314, 389n73
  migrant crises and, 295
  migration crises and, 291
  tourism and, 57
Network (film), 206
Neumann, Victor, 70–71, 77
New German Cinema, 221, 232
New Hollywood, 185–186, 188, 192–193
New Journalism, 178
New York (ship), 70, 321
New York Actors Studio, 208
New York Herald Tribune (newspaper), 400n9

The New York Times (newspaper), 114, 116, *117*, 117–119, 122, 137, 315
New Yorker (magazine), 277
New Zealand, migration to, 29
Newman, Paul, 185
newsreels, 119–120
Nicholson, Jack, 192
No Promised Land (Herlin), 93
Noethen, Ulrich, 221
non-utilitarianism, 143–144
Norddeutscher Lloyd (North German Lloyd/NDL), 53–54, 365n16, 365n26
North Sea, 332–333, 335
Northern Ireland, 296–297, 413n26
NS. *See* National Socialists
Nuremberg Laws, 19, 134
Nuremberg war crimes trial, 172, 246

Obama, Barack, 244, 277
Obama, Michelle, 277
Oberrat, 135
Obregon, Rafael, 64–65
ocean, international law and, 131
ocean liners, 54, 364n13
  elites and, 65
  prestige of, 49–50
Oceana (ship), 321
Odin, Roger, 405n54
L'Oeuvre (newspaper), 41, 44
Olympic Games (1936), 21
"On the Term Emigrants" (Brecht), 40
opacity (Édouard Glissant), 294, 296, 310
oral history, 274
Orbita (ship), 361n87
Orduña (ship), 85–86, 97–98, 181, 234, 343, 361n87, 361n89
  disembarking passengers, 44, 88

passengers of, 374n22
recall to Germany of, 382n59
The Origins of Totalitarianism (Arendt), 143–144
Orinoco (ship), 41, 44, 57, 64, 77, 123, 149, 382n59
Osiris (ship), 361n87
Oversea Settlement Board, 29–30
overseas territories, 27

Pacific Steam Navigation Company, 57–58
Pacific Steamship Company, 361n87
Packer, Fred, 275
Padura, Leonardo, 15, 261–272, 265–267, 283–286
Palestine, 22, 220, 313
    Balfour Declaration and, 26–27, 407n12
    Britain and, 26, 358n32
    colonialism and, 358n32
    Évian conference and, 26–27
    Jewish settlers and, 358n32
    ships turned away from, 43
Palestine Shipping Company, 361n82
Palestinians, 220
Panagiya Correstrio (ship), 43
Panama Canal, tolls for, 238
Panama Canal zone, 32
Panama Pacific Lines, 238
Papa's Kino, 228
Paper Moon (film), 196
Paraguay, 41
paratext, 193, *194*
Parita (ship), *45*
Parker, Bonnie, 195
Parliamentarism, 131
passenger committee (board committee), 206, 328–329, 331–334, 336, 348, 417n8
    establishment of, 85, *85*, 87, 109
    leaving Cuba and, 112–113
    sabotage committee and, 161
passenger rebellion, 206
passports, marking of, 24, 39
Pathé, 120
pathos, of failure, 192
Patria (ship), 62, 64, 77, 259
patriarchy, 228
Pell, Robert, 97–98
Pennigsdorf, Heide, 383n64
Pennsylvania (ship), 235, *236–237*, 238–239, 259
Pennsylvania/Argentina (ship), 239
performed actuality, 247–248
period dramas, 196
Perón, Juan, 32
Peru, 33, 35
    Germany and, 63
Petersen, Wolfgang, 228
Pinosa, 330
Piscator, Erwin, 248
La Plata and Brazil service, 366n29
Platinga, Carl, 229
Platt Amendment (1901), 389n74
Pluralism, 130
pogroms, 20–21, 53, 386n37
Poland
    death camps in, 132–133
    invasion of, 132
political consciousness, 276
political dissidents, 132
"The Politics of Fear" (*New Yorker* cover), 277
Pollock, Griselda, 133, 140
pop art, 305–306, 309–310
pop culture, 196
populations, shaping of, 23, 32–33
Porter, Katherine Ann, 187
The Poseidon Adventure (film), 184, 193, 195, 207, 398n46, 399n54
postcolonialism, 298
Pozner, Aaron, 179

President's Commission on the Holocaust, 243
press coverage
  "concentration camp" term in, 137
  in Germany, 121–124
  in US, 114–120, *117*
primacy effect, 229
The Prime of Miss Jean Brodie (film), 195
primitivism, 36
prison camps, 133
Proletkult movement, 248
propaganda thesis, 121
Prosula (ship), 361n87
protection, as privilege, 7
public charge statutes, 70

Quebec, 30
Question 7 (film), 185

racial difference, genocide and, 144
racial hybridity, 268
racism, 264
  biopolitics and, 26, 35
  Boers and, 143–144
  colonialism and, 26, 126
  eugenics and, 153
  Évian conference and, 36
  Judgment at Nuremberg and, 247
  Nazism and, 153
  NS ideology and, 126
  state power and, 23
  structural, 153
  US politics and, 176–177
  The Wheel of Conscience and, 281, 283
railroads, 369n53
Rakhotis (ship), 64
Ramos, Juan J., 88
Rassenlehre, 153
Rauch, Siegfried, 403n45

Raw (magazine), 273, 409n23
Razovsky, Cecilia, 177
realist narrative, 271
red decade, 196
"The Red J." *See* "Das Rote J"
Reflections on Nazism (Friedlander), 196
refugee crisis, 3–4, 40–47, 219
  as both new and old phenomenon, 134–135
  Holocaust and contemporary, 275–276
refugee organizations, 369n52
refugee ships, 7, 40–47, *45*, 275–276
Reichsfluchtsteuer, 21
Reichstag Fire Decree, 19
Relation (Édouard Glissant), 294, 296, 298, 313–315
relativization, 129
Rembrandt, 263
remembrance culture, 14, 217, 220–221, 239, 268
reparations program, 217
"Report to the Secretary on the Acquiescence of this Government in the Murder of the Jews" (Morgenthau), 255
resettlement, obstacles to, 6
resettlement organizations, 44, 47
resubjectivization, 212
Revolution of 1848, 53
Revue (magazine), 225
Rey, Fernando, 187
Rhakotis (ship), 100
Rhizome, 294
"Rights of Man" declaration, 125, 141
right-wing political parties, 289–290
Rivero, José Ignacio, 89
Robert Levy (ship), 123, 234, 371n72
Robinson, Edward G., 95

Romani, 132–133
Roosevelt, Eleanor, 253
Roosevelt, Franklin Delano, 3, 148
  Complicit and, 15, 241, 243–245, 250–252, *253*, 254, 259
  concentration camps and, 138
  Cuba and, 92, 95
  domestic politics and, 30, 94
  Évian conference and, 4, 66
  Good Neighbor Policy and, 238
  post-Évian conference actions and, 38–39, 359n61
  refugees and, 94
  Taylor, Myron C., and, 38, 38n65–38n66
  telegrams to, 112
  Troper and, 209
Rosenberg, Alfred, 25–26
Rosenberg, Stuart, 185
Rosenfeld, Alvin, 246
Rosenthal, Hannah, 242, *254*, 256–257
"Das Rote J" (The red J) (Herlin), 170–172, 175–176
Rothberg, Michael
  on Arendt, 143–144
  colonial turn and, 143–144, 148
  on Holocaust as anchor of American modernity, 246
  multidirectional memory and, 15, 216, 261–262, 296, 310, 312, 314
  on *Schindler's List*, 201
  on Spiegelman, 273, 278–279
  transversal and, 268
  on traumatic realism, 273
Rousset, David, 133, 353n6, 406n62
Royal Caribbean, 297, 413n25
Royal Dutch oil company, 145, 388n80
Ruanda-Urundi, 27
Rüsen, Jörn, 165

Russell, Mark A., 55
Russia
  invasion of, 132
  Jews from, 53, 55
  as land people, 131, 385n22

sabotage committee, 332, 351, 417n8
Sandu (ship), 43
Santo Domingo, 331, 349
Schacht, Hjalmar, 357n23
Schacht plan, 6, 26, 357n23
Scheffner, Philip, 292, 297, 299, 306, 310, 413n21
Schell, Maria, 187
Schell, Maximilian, 172, 246
Schiff ohne Hafen (Ship without Harbor) (play), 161, 325
"Das Schiff von Cuba" ("The Cuban ship") (Viertel), 46
Schindler's List (film), 186, 201, 208
Schipper naast God (play), 161, 325
Schmidt-Isserstedt, Hans, 161
Schmitt, Carl, 10, 129–135, 190
Scholz, Olaf, 400n12
Schonig, Jordan, 305, 414n40
Schrader, Paul, 191, 208
Schröder, Gustav, 1–2, 8, 12–13, 16, 79–80, 83, *160*, *318*
  biography of, 319–322
  captain's log by, *342*, 343–345, *346*, 347–352
  on concentration camps, 165
  on course of voyage, 150–151
  on Cuba, 164
  Cuba immigration policy and, 85, 88
  Cuban politics and, 146
  disciplinary chain of command and, 139
  on Germany, 164–165
  grounding plans, 113, 181, 333

Schröder, Gustav *(continued)*
   on HAPAG, 162–163, 166–167
   in Havana, 86–88, 112, 327–329
   Mediterranean migration crisis and, 290
   memory culture and, 158
   message about departing Cuba, 88, *89*
   NSDAP membership, 161, 166, 223, 229–230, 320, 402n32
   passenger committee and, 109, 112, 417n8
   on passengers' status, 103–104
   return to Europe, 96–98, 100–101
   on shipboard service, 104
   St. Louis memory culture and, 159, 161–169
   telegrams from, 338
   in *Die Ungewollten*, 221, 223, 225–227, 229–230
   updates from, 112–113
   US Coast Guard and, 92–94
   in *Voyage of the Damned* (film), 187
   on Weiler, 109
   worldview of, 163
Schumburg, Emil, 23, 356n10
Schuricke Terzett (singing group), 397n34
Schwartz, Michael Ivan, 241
scripted drama, historical characters in, 248
sea people, 131, 385n22
second Boer war, 133
Second Generation (Holocaust survivors), 315
self-denial, 174
self-destruction, 202
self-determination, 295
self-other binary, 297–299

Sharpe, Christina, 413n18
Shell Transport and Trading Company, 145
Shelton, Oscar, 96
The Shining (film), 399n54
Ship of Fools (film), 184, 187, 192
shipping lines, recruitment for expulsion schemes, 40
ships, gendering of, 353n1
shoreless sea, 10, 385n33
silkscreens, 306, 309
Silverman, Max, 133, 140
Simon, Art, 393n33, 415n42
situated knowledges, 296, 298
Six-Day War (1967), 209
slavery, 143
Sobibor, 2, 128
social market economies, 307
"Social Science Techniques and the Study of Concentration Camps" (Arendt), 143
solidarity, discourses of, 307
SOPADE, 44
sovereign power, 139
   over life, 357n19
   state shaped through, 23
Soweit die Füße tragen (television show), 403n45
Spahn, Lea, 292–293
Spain, 289, 295
Spanier, Fritz, 206
Spanish Civil War, 123
spectating, 414n40
Der Spiegel (magazine), 219, 223
Spiegelman, Art, 15, 261, 272–279, 283–285, 315
Spiegelman, Vladek, 273, 278
Spielberg, Steven, 186, 409n23
spiritual comfort committee, 331
SS *St. Louis* Legacy Project, 15, 255

Index

The St. Louis Refugee Ship Blues (Spiegelman, A.), 15, 261, 272–279, 315
Staat, Bewegung, Volk (*State, Movement, People*) (Schmitt), 129
Standard Oil, 145
star performance, intertextuality of, 192
state of exception, 10
    Agamben theory of bare life and, 133–143
    Schmitt critique of Weimar law and, 129–133
    as trope, 128–129
Statue of Liberty, 118, *118*, 253, 275–276
steamship nationalism, 55
Steel, Judith, 255
steerage, HAPAG improving on, 55
Steigerwald (ship), 321
Stern (magazine), 13, 158, 170–171, 175, 391n20
Stern, Martha, 230, 232, 405n54
Storaro, Vittorio, 196
Streicher, Julius, 123, 321
Strength Through Joy (Kraft durch Freude/KdF), 59, 71, 123, 168–169, 234, 323
    Volkstourismus and, 371n72
Strohmaier, Alena, 292
structural racism, 153
study tours, 59
Der Stürmer (pamphlet), 123
subjectivization, 135–136
suicide watches, 87, 112–113, 206
superliners, 50, 54, 365n16
Sweden, at Évian conference, 27
von Sydow, Max, 187
Syria, 219, 289

Taylor, Myron C., 3–4, *37*, 37–39, 359n61
Thessalia (ship), 361n87
Thomas, Gordon, 11, 13, 121–123, 158–159, 172, 177–181, 206
    German translation of work, 218
    movie adaptation and, 184, 193
Thomas, Walter B., 376n44
Three Days of the Condor (film), 187
Tiger Hill (ship), 361n87
time image, 189–190
Titania (ship), 320
totalitarianism, 210, 269, 402n32
    biopolitics and, 134–137, 139
    books as enemy of, 270
    democracy and, 8, 10, 133–135, 139, 141
    resisting, 268
    Schmitt on, 131
"Die Totenschiffe Fahren" ("The death ships are sailing") (*Aufbau*), 42–43, 46
tourism, 58
    cruise, 55–56, 70–71, 77, 321
    neocolonialism and, 57
    NS culture and, 371n72
    study tours, 59
tourist visas, 41, 77, 93
    Cuba invalidating, 86–87
The Towering Inferno (film), 195
transit camps, 9, 133
transit visas, 41
transversal archive, 262–272, 408n11
Trauerarbeit, 233
traumatic realism, 273, 397n36, 410n30
Das Traumschiff (television show), 403n45
Trinidad, 80
Troell, Jan, 187

Troper, Morris, 68, 80, 97–98, *99*, 114, 210–211, 339
  in *Voyage of the Damned* (film), 191–192, 205–209
Trudeau, Justin, 243–245, *244*, 257, 285
Trujillo Molina, Virgilio, 33–34
Truman, Harry, 145
Trump, Donald, 219
Turkey, 289

Ufa Fiction Productions, 222
Die Ungewollten (*The unwanted*) (film), 14, 218–220, 258–259
  archive and work of mourning, 231–234
  captain, ship, and crew in, 224–231, *225–227*
  as docudrama, 221–224, 233
  framing narrative of, 229
  as history lesson, 240
  premiere of, 221
unionization, 307
United Fruit Company, trade routs and, 57
United Kingdom, Ireland and, 413n26
United States
  antisemitism discussion in, 176
  asylum declined by, 92–96
  Cold War and, 209
  Cuba controlled by, 145–146
  Cuba independence and, 389n74
  immigration law in, 136–137, 140, 316
  immigration numbers for, 40
  immigration restrictions in, 70
  Muslim travel ban in, 219
  press coverage in, 114–120, *117*
  tourist visas and, 93
  Zionism and, 407n12
United States Holocaust Memorial Museum (USHMM), 14, 66, 79, 243
L'univers concentrationnaire (Rousset), 133
Unter Segel um die Welt (Schröder), 322
Uris, Leon, 158, 208
Urquiaga, Ibrahim, 64
Uruguay, 32
US Coast Guard, 92–94, 376n42, 376n44
US Maritime Commission, 238
Usaramo (ship), 361n87
USHMM. *See* United States Holocaust Memorial Museum

Vashem, Yad, 229, 322
Vaterland (ship), 365n16
Vendig, Ernst, *85*, 109, 331, 336–337, 340–341, 417n8
Venezuela, 32–33
"Vergässe ich Deiner Je, St. Louis . . ." ("If I ever forget you, *St. Louis*") (*Aufbau*), 46
Versailles Treaty, 8, 129, 321
"Vienna, City of My Dreams" (song), 189, *189*, 206, 212, 216
Viertel, Berthold, 46
Vietnam, 145
view from nowhere, 298
Villa Michel, Primo, 34
Villeneuve, Johanne, 292
Vincent, C. Paul, 92, 94, 98, 178
VIP passenger lists, 65
Virgin Islands, 251–252
Virginia (ship), 238
visas
  immigration, 41, 43
  tourist, 41, 77, 86–87, 93
  transit, 41

vogelfrei, 46
Vogt, Kurt, 181
Völkischer Beobachter (newspaper), 24, 122–123
Volkstourismus, 371n72
Vox (website), 137
Voyage of the Damned (film), 183, 203–204, 205, *214–215*, 393n31, 398n46, 399n54
    casting, narrative, genre, 186–195
    colonialism and, 210–216
    costume ball sequence, *189*, 189–190
    dissolves in, 190, *190*
    genre and, 193, 195
    heritage cinema and, 195–200
    intertext of, 187–188
    Jewish suffering in, 201–202
    melodrama and Jewish myth in, 201–210
    music in, 198–200
    paratexts of, 193, *194*
    production history, 184–186
    Die Ungewollten differences from, 223–224
Voyage of the Damned (Thomas and Morgan-Witts), 11, 13–14, 121, 158–159, 177–181, *178*
    film adaptation of, 184
    German translation of, 218
Voyage of the SS St. Louis (play), 241–242, 245, 248, *249–250*, *252–253*, 259

Wagner-Rogers bill, 94, 400n9
The Waltons (television series), 196
Walzer, Michael, 201
Wanamaker, Sam, 187, 191
"The Wandering Jew" (Duffy), 275
"The Wandering Jews" (Knickerbocker), 41–42

Warburg, Max, 339
Warhol, Andy, 306, 309, 415n43
The Washington Post (newspaper), 116, 118, 137
    The St. Louis Refugee Ship Blues and, 272
Wasser hat Balken (film), 371n72
"We Refugees" (Arendt), 207, 267
    Latin America and, 389n73
Weil, Gustav, 331, 336
Weiler, Moritz, 83, 109, 190, 202, 326–327, 344–345
Weimar Republic, 19–20, 129, 132
Weiss, Heinz, 403n45
Weiss, Max, *85*, 109
Weiss, Peter, 248
Welles, Orson, 191
Werner, Oskar, 187–188, 191–192, 206
West Germany
    Grudgesetz (Basic Law), 219
    historical consciousness in, 171–172
    memory culture of 1960s and 1970s, 233
    postwar memory culture of, 166–167
    reparations program, 217
    St. Louis in early 1960s mass culture of, 169–176
West Indies, 56–57
Westerbork, *138*
Westfälische Landeszeitung/Rote Erde (formerly *Generalanzeiger für Dortmund*) (newspaper), 383n64
"What to do with the Jews?" (Rosenberg), 25
The Wheel of Conscience (Libeskind), 15, 261, 279–287, *280–282*
Wheeler, Burton, 252

While Six Million Died (Morse), 13, 93, 158, 177
White, Hayden, 11, 120
White, T. C., 29
white supremacism, 143–144
Wiesel, Elie, 177, 196–197
Wilhelm Gustloff (ship), 123, 228, 234, 371n72, 403n44
  sinking of, 171
Wilhelm II (Kaiser), 55
Williams, Linda, 119, 201, 205
Winkler, Istvan, 83
Winters, Shelley, 193
Winterton (Lord), 26–28, 98
Wisbar, Frank, 228
Wise, Stephen, 257, 407n12
Woelfert, Fritz, 65
Wolff, Adolf, 336–337, 417n8
Wood, Robin, 188

Wright, J. Butler, 88, 177
Wrong, Hume, 29–30

xenophobia
  Mediterranean migration crisis and, 289
  The Wheel of Conscience and, 281, 283

Yepes, J. M., 31–32
Young, James E., 235
Young German filmmakers, 228
YouTube, 292

Zellner, Max, 85, 109, 332–333, 417n8
Zérega-Fombona, Alberto, 65
Zionism, 14, 174, 207, 407n12

www.ingramcontent.com/pod-product-compliance
Lightning Source LLC
Chambersburg PA
CBHW070746230426
43665CB00017B/2270